WHITMAN COLLEGE LIBRARY

D1006510

OTHER BOOKS BY WALTER ADAMS

THE STRUCTURE OF AMERICAN INDUSTRY

MONOPOLY IN AMERICA: THE GOVERNMENT AS PROMOTER

TRUCKING MERGERS, CONCENTRATION AND SMALL BUSINESS

FROM MAINSTREET TO THE LEFT BANK

IS THE WORLD OUR CAMPUS?

A GUIDE TO STUDY ABROAD

THE BRAIN DRAIN

THE TEST

THE BIGNESS
COMPLEX

WHITMAN COLLEGE LIBRARY

Withdrawn by
Whitman College Library

THE
BIGNESS
COMPLEX

INDUSTRY, LABOR, AND GOVERNMENT IN THE AMERICAN ECONOMY

Walter Adams and
James W. Brock

PANTHEON BOOKS ▪ NEW YORK

HD
2785
.A68
1986

Copyright © 1986 by Walter Adams and James W. Brock

All rights reserved under International and Pan-American Copyright Conventions.
Published in the United States by Pantheon Books, a division of Random House, Inc.,
New York, and simultaneously in Canada by Random House of
Canada Limited, Toronto.

LIBRARY OF CONGRESS CATALOGING-IN-PUBLICATION DATA
Adams, Walter, 1922 Aug 27–
The bigness complex.
1. Big business—United States. 2. Industrial concentration—United States.
3. Industries, Size of—United States.
4. Efficiency, Industrial—United States. 5. Competition—United States.
6. Trade regulation—United States. I. Brock, James W. II. Title.
HD2785.A68 1986 338.6'44'0973 86-42624
ISBN 0-394-54721-7

Manufactured in the United States of America

First Edition

Designed by Ann Gold

PENROSE MEMORIAL LIBRARY
WHITMAN COLLEGE
WALLA WALLA, WASHINGTON 99362

PENROSE MEMORIAL LIBRARY
RECEIVED

DEC 17 1986
87-2062
ACQUISITIONS DEP'T

FOR THE BOYS FROM WASHTENAW—
SWEETWATER, MÁTYÁS, AND TRADEWIND—
AND THEIR DEVOTED LEIBARZT

CONTENTS

TABLES AND CHARTS

PREFACE

I n 1961, Daniel Bell triumphantly proclaimed "the end of ideology." Like the premature report of Mark Twain's death, the announcement was exaggerated. Ideology and dogma, myth and fantasy, experience shows, are made of sterner stuff.

Ideology means taking some idea—often legitimate in its own sphere —to the extreme.[1] One might say that ideology is to philosophy what gluttony is to fine dining. Ideology offers certainty—clear-cut choices between good and evil, truth and falsehood. It pretends to have scientific answers to complex problems and holds out one easy standard to judge all cases. It thus relieves thinkers of the tedium involved in making difficult distinctions. In Procrustean fashion, ideologues cut facts to fit their ideas, rather than ideas to fit the facts. More often than not, their claims to science turn out to be little more than manipulative quackery.

By most objective standards, America's corporate giants have not performed very well over the last fifteen years. They have lost markets to the Japanese and the newly industrializing countries. They have lagged in innovation. The quality of their products has often been inferior and unreliable. And, taken together, America's five hundred largest industrial corporations have failed to generate a single new job since 1970.

Bigness has not delivered the goods, and this fact is no longer a secret. Influential business publications have repeatedly called attention to the malaise of the Bigness Complex. In recent cover stories, for example, *Business Week* has argued that "small is beautiful"; in response to the question "do mergers really work?" its answer was "not very often—which raises questions about merger mania"; and in noting the trend toward "splitting up," it has reported that some large corporations are now "divesting assets, spinning off divisions, even liquidating themselves."[2] *Forbes* has provided case studies to document what would seem an obvious fact; that is, "soap and pastrami don't mix."[3] *The Economist* (London) has featured articles, entitled "Big Won't Work" and "Big Goes Bust."[4] In one of these articles, Norman Macrae predicted "that the world was probably drawing to the end of the era of big business corporations, because it would soon be seen to be nonsense to have hierarchical managements sitting in skyscraping offices trying to arrange how brainworkers (who in the future would be most workers) could best use their imaginations. The main increases in employment would henceforth come either in small firms or in those bigger firms that managed to split themselves into smaller and smaller profit centres which would need to become more and more entrepreneurial."

Yet, paradoxically, America is in the midst of an unprecedented wave of megamergers and acquisitions—fueled by the astronomical promoter fees of Wall Street's M&A shops, the sale of junk bonds, and the benign neglect of Washington's antitrust authorities. If the trend continues, we may soon be approaching the day when (in the words of *Fortune*) "the United States economy might end up completely dominated by conglomerates happily trading with each other in a new kind of cartel system."[5]

The trend is not without its apologists. Bigness, they say, promotes efficiency and technological progress. If a merger did not promise to achieve these objectives, why would a profit-maximizing firm ever want to consummate it? The fact that it does proves that the merger is beneficial—not only to the firms involved but, in the long run, to consumers as well. Hence, there is no need to examine the facts or to amass voluminous evidence. It *must* be so; otherwise it would not happen; it would not be done. Ipse dixit!

Mergers, the apologists claim, have other virtues. Every time a merger takes place, a superior management replaces an inferior management. The market for corporate takeovers protects stockholders against the poor performance of incumbent managers who, in the absence of takeover threats, could continue to suboptimize the investment of their owners. How do we know this? Logic indicates that it must be so. No need to investigate further.

Apologetics, of course, is an ancient and venerable mind-set. Ecclesiastical and profane history are replete with illustrations of the phenomenon. In 1610, for example, when Galileo Galilei, armed with his telescope, scanned the heavens and discovered the Jupiter satellites, a

learned professor at the University of Padua denied the existence of
what Galileo had in fact seen. Articulating the wisdom of his time, the
professor said: "We know that there are seven planets and only seven,
because there are seven openings in the human head to let in the light
and air: two eyes, two ears, two nostrils, and a mouth. And the seven
metals and various other examples also show that there have to be
seven. Besides, the stars are invisible to the naked eye; therefore they
do not influence human events; therefore they are useless; therefore
they do not exist. *Quod erat demonstrandum.*"[6]

In the academic community, the Padua professor is more prototypical
than we would like to admit. As Adam Smith long ago observed: "The
improvements which, in modern times, have been made in several
branches of philosophy, have not, the greater part of them, been made
in universities; though some no doubt have. The greater part of universities have not even been very forward to adopt those improvements, after
they were made; and several of those learned societies have chosen to
remain, for a long time, the sanctuaries in which exploded systems and
obsolete prejudices found shelter and protection, after they had been
hunted out of every other corner of the world."[7]

In this book we shall analyze the anatomy of the Bigness Complex in
its diverse forms, shapes, and manifestations. We shall examine the
quintessential myth of America's corporate culture that industrial giantism is the handmaiden of economic efficiency and consumer welfare. We
shall explore the bigness myth proclaimed by corporate executives, sanctified by scientific soothsayers, propagated by professional storytellers,
and perpetuated by periodic ritual observance. We shall do so by sifting
empirical evidence, by venturing into the world of reality, and by abjur-
ing ideological preconceptions and theoretical abstractions. After all, as
Paul Samuelson tells us, to theorize and yet stay within the constraint
of explaining reality may be a difficult task, "but how much more satisfy-
ing the hunt."

—June 1986

I

THE PROBLEM
OF POWER

CHAPTER 1

POWER AND
PUBLIC POLICY

Power always thinks it has a great Soul, and vast Views, beyond the Comprehension
of the Weak, and that it is doing God's Service, when it is violating all his Laws.
— John Adams

Reports on America's economic health are full of unease and forebodings: a perennial skirmish, first with inflation, then with recession; intractably high unemployment rates; surging imports, escalating trade deficits, and the threat of Japan, Inc.; transformation of the industrial heartland into an obsolescent "rustbelt"; lagging R&D and lethargic innovation; a defunct nuclear power industry drowning in red ink; massive cost overruns in military procurement; government bailouts of industrial giants and bulwarks in banking; overregulation and deregulation. The list seems endless.

Somehow we seem incapable of dealing with problems that are essentially structural in nature. In Washington, politicians react in their accustomed manner. They choose to ignore these problems, devoting their energy instead to passionate debates on abortion or prayer in the schools. Or they treat symptoms of the malaise with makeshift, ad hoc, cosmetic palliatives. On Wall Street, the corporate elite is distracted by merger mania and paper entrepreneurialism. Shuffling corporate assets is the newest game in town, and the best business minds are busy with raiders and white knights; greenmail, shark repellents, and poison pills; leveraged buyouts and golden parachutes. In academia, economists are more concerned with esoteric model building, the latest graffiti of the

3

trade, and the most sophisticated apologia for the status quo than with the real world and its problems. For aficionados of the Theater of the Absurd, the script is all too familiar. It imparts a feeling of depression. In the words of Yogi Berra, it's déjà vu all over again.

There is, to be sure, no dearth of apostles who advocate "new departures" in "new directions" that purport to tackle fundamentals and point to salvation. Attractively packaged to command popular support, and couched in the parlance of liberal chic or conservative platitudes, the shibboleths of our day are little more than ideological cant. On both the Right and the Left of the political spectrum, they are based on assumptions that are incongruent with the structural realities of the American economy. Their fatal weakness, we submit, is that they ignore the political economy of power.

To the Right, especially during the Reagan years, the culprit is Big Government. If we would but reduce the size of government, cut onerous taxes, and eliminate regulation, then (as Congressman Jack Kemp argues) the "entrepreneurial talent, the managerial talent, the creative talent of men and women that is now boxed into mediocrity would be unleashed and would flourish. . . . There's no telling what we can accomplish if only the government would get out of the way and let us load the wagon."[1] Mr. Kemp and his confrères see no danger in a policy of untrammeled laissez-faire because the free market would regulate economic activity, inexorably meting out appropriate rewards and punishments. In this ideal world, corporate size and power could be safely ignored. After all, corporations became big only because they are efficient, only because they are productive, only because they have served consumers better than their rivals, and only because no newcomers were good enough to challenge their dominance. Once an industrial giant becomes lethargic and no longer bestows its productive beneficence on society, it will inevitably wither and eventually die. This is the "natural law" that governs economic life. It demands obedience to its rules. It tolerates no interference by the state.

To students of history, this Weltanschauung is stale wine in old bottles. It is a throwback to the age of social Darwinism and the theories of its high priests—Herbert Spencer in England and William Graham Sumner in the United States. Like latter-day Calvins, they preached the predestination of the social order and the salvation of the industrial elect through the survival of the fittest. Economic life was subject to the laws of natural selection, which preserved the most efficient forms and condemned the less efficient to extinction. Institutions, according to Sumner, were the evolutionary outgrowth of natural forces, "not the artifacts of human purpose or wit." Man, he wrote, had "no more right to life than a rattlesnake; he has no more right to liberty than any wild beast; his right to the pursuit of happiness is nothing but a license to maintain the struggle for existence if he can find within himself the power with which to do it." Such is the system of nature. To try to refashion it by legislation would be "the greatest folly of which a man can be capable." To insist on change in the natural order of things—to tamper with evolution by attempts at social reform—would mean to "take from the better and give to the worse," and to "deflect the penalties of those who have done ill and throw them on those who have done better." Obviously, said Sumner, such a policy would be both unwise and antisocial. (It would be the height of folly, for example, to curb "the captains of industry and the capitalists" who, if successful, amass "great fortunes in a short time." To Sumner, "there are no earnings which are more legitimate or for which greater services are rendered to the whole industrial body.") Far better, therefore, to eschew reform and refrain from meddling. As for the proper role of government, it was twofold: respect for the inviolability of private property rights and an uncompromising adherence to laissez-faire.[2]

On the liberal Left of the political spectrum, there is a similar tendency to search for a bogey man. Here the *bête noire* is the lack of planning—the failure to break down the adversarial relationship between industry, labor, and government. The perceived need is more centralized management and control of the economy, built around tripartite labor-management-government cooperation—a rough imitation of the system that ostensibly succeeded in making Japan a major industrial power in the world. The blueprint is summed up in slogans like "industrial policy" or "industrial strategy." In the neoliberal camp, there are "accelerationists" and "targeters" (Robert Reich, for example) who advocate government promotion of sunrise industries that would enhance exports and serve as engines of economic growth. There are "adjusters" (such as Lane Kirkland of the AFL-CIO) who propose government aid for "mature" industries to help them invest in badly needed renovation and modernization of industrial facilities. There are "Wall Streeters" (such as Felix G. Rohatyn) who envision a federally backed industrial bank that would plan and facilitate the flow of capital in the economy and that would serve as a lever for extracting concessions from management and labor to finance investment in the "reindustrialization" of America.[3] Ironically, even some conservatives endorse the notion of an industrial policy. Kevin P. Phillips, for example, contends that the laissez-faire conception "of the role of government is simply inadequate in today's global economy." Political conservatives, he argues, "must accept a new *probusiness* role for government—from coordination of economic and trade strategies to targeting of export assistance and credits—as a necessity."[4] Such "a neomercantilist appeal," he believes, would strike a responsive chord in the electorate of the 1980s.[5]

Like the proposals of the Right, these prescriptions of the neoliberal Left are not without historical precedents. Ever since 1887—first in railroads, and later in trucking, communications, air transportation, natural gas, and so on—government has been deeply involved in industrial planning. Indeed, the "independent" commissions created to regulate these industries, have, over time, fashioned a prototype of management-labor-government symbiosis—so much so that one observer characterized the regulated industries as "federal protectorates, living in a cozy world of cost-plus, safely protected from the ugly spectres of competition, efficiency, and innovation."[6] Moreover, during the heyday of the New Deal, this system of collaborative planning on an industry-by-industry basis was extended to the whole economy. Under the aegis of the NRA Blue Eagle, management and labor in each industry drafted "codes of fair competition" which, once blessed with the *pro forma* approval of government, became the rules of the trade. Officially exempt from the antitrust laws, the NRA codes were a mechanism for collective control over prices, restriction of output, allocation of markets, and the enforcement of these arrangements by legal sanctions and penalties. The NRA, in short, was an experiment, albeit short-lived, with industry self-government and a blueprint for the complete cartelization of American business. It was an experiment to which today's industrial policy proponents rarely refer.

Alas, neither today's Right, nor its neoliberal counterpart on the Left, has recognized that massive power concentrations have transformed modern economic life. Notwithstanding the ideological cant about "natural selection" and "survival of the fittest," it is a fact that industrial giants have taken the place of market mechanisms in coordinating the activities of the economy and allocating its resources. "In many sectors of the economy," as Alfred D. Chandler, Jr. (a conservative economic historian) points out, "the visible hand of management [has] replaced what Adam Smith referred to as the invisible hand of market forces." The managerial revolution has wrought profound structural changes and, as the large modern enterprise "acquired functions hitherto carried out by the market, it became the most influential group of economic decision makers."[7] In other words, planning is a fact of life, but planning is done not by the state but by private power groups. In this context, a policy of untrammeled laissez-faire means that society is delegating the power to plan, the power to decide, and the power to control to private organizations whose power is not subject to systematic social account-ability. Cynics would characterize it as private socialism.

Similarly, the advocates of more central planning seem blissfully unaware that public policy is not made in a vacuum, that government is not an independent social institution hermetically sealed off from the vested-interest groups that have the power to influence, if not dictate, its decisions. In a world dominated by concentrated industries and pow-erful trade unions, sometimes acting through formal or tacit lobbying alliances, the government is not some Olympian authority decreeing public policies it believes would promote the *summum bonum*. Instead, subjected to a cacophony of diverse pressures, it tends to fall victim to the "soft options" advocated by a consensus of interest groups. Policy-makers, for example, might be persuaded that steel import quotas are damaging to steel consumers, the national economy, and even to the long-run interests of the domestic steel industry, but they are repeatedly bludgeoned by the coalition of steel management and steel labor into compliance with a trade restriction policy contrary to the public interest. Under the circumstances, more planning, more centralization, simply raises the incentives for private power groups to gain control over the governmental decision-making process. It provides few safeguards against the perversion or subversion by those groups of the objectives that planning is designed to achieve. In short, it offers no assurance that the fox won't become master of the henhouse.

We have written this book because we believe, unlike most main-stream economists, that an attempt to analyze power in a political econ-omy context is important and long overdue—for at least three reasons. First, power does exist. It may appear in many guises—economic or political, personal or organizational, private or public. Power, to para-phrase Justice Louis Brandeis, may be exerted upon rivals, upon buyers or upon sellers, upon employers or upon employed. It may be exerted through force or fraud or agreement. It may be exerted through moral or through legal obligations, through fear or through hope. It may exist, although it is not manifested in any overt act, and even though there is no intent to restrain, coerce, or oppress. Power may be exerted through words of advice, seemingly innocent and perhaps benevolent, when ut-tered under circumstances that make advice equivalent to command. For the essence of power is dominance. And dominance may arise simply from disproportionate size.[8] It implies an absence of effective con-straints, a freedom from accountability, and a relative immunity from sanctions.

Such power comprises more than the ability to influence price in a particular market, that is (in the jargon of the economist), to raise the price of mousetraps above the marginal cost of production. The power of concern here is the broad discretion to determine how society's resources shall be used, the rules by which the economic game shall be played, and the kind of society in which we shall live.

For example, the discretion of Mobil to spend $1.5 billion to purchase Montgomery Ward (a mail-order house) rather than investing in oil and gas exploration; the discretion of U.S. Steel to spend $6.3 billion to acquire Marathon Oil rather than investing in badly needed modernization of its outmoded steel plants; or the discretion of ITT to become the champion conglomerator of the 1960s only to be forced to sell in the 1980s the assets it had acquired—such discretion involves a heavy social cost. Whether or not the companies in question are eventually penalized for wrong decisions (by huge write-offs on their profit-and-loss statements) is of secondary importance. More significant is the fact that firms with command over vast social resources are free to make decisions of overarching social consequence with relative immunity from social accountability or social control, and that society is forced to pay the "opportunity costs" of the decisions ostensibly made on its behalf.

Second, economic power is basically rooted in organizational structure, which in turn has a decisive influence on industrial performance. For more than half a century, for example, the American steel industry was organized as a tight oligopoly and manifested the typical performance deficiencies characteristic of such industry structure. Entry was at a minimum, or nonexistent. Innovation was slow, hampered by the bureaucratic dry rot that tends to accompany monopolistic giantism. Price policy was directed at uniformity and inflexibility, except in an upward direction; and, while the leadership role has rotated among the oligopolists, the level of product prices was anything but market determined. Moreover, until 1959, the industry had little to fear from foreign competition, so that the members of its co-fraternal, close-knit group felt it safe to follow concerted, tacitly collusive, and consciously parallel price and product policies. Occasional mavericks might from time to time disturb the industry's quiet life but, like others before them, they eventually became members of the club.

When a rising tide of imports intruded on this well-ordered preserve, where the rules of the game were understood and observed by all parties, the consequences of an entrenched power structure became painfully apparent. A price had to be paid for the years of noncompetitive conduct and lackluster performance. The industry's travails may have been self-inflicted but, once again, society had to pay the piper. The dilemma was a Hobson's choice: to let a basic industry "go down the drain" (not a costless option) or to implement a costly bailout—directly in the form of subsidies or indirectly in the form of import restrictions.

The examples can be multiplied. At this point, suffice it to say that concentrated power in private hands has social consequences and entails social costs.

Third, to the extent that power is a structural phenomenon, and the problems it creates are structural in character, public policy must search for structural solutions. Easy bromides and ideological incantations will not work. Nor will short-run, makeshift measures designed to ameliorate the costs of industrial misfeasance or nonfeasance by private power interests. Indeed, such *ad hoc* measures are counterproductive because they tend to compound and perpetuate the underlying structural problems. Take the auto industry, for example. Like steel, it played the traditional oligopoly game: constant escalation of product prices; indifference to product quality; technological lethargy; and persistent wage and fringe-benefit inflation. Eventually, of course, these policies meant the loss of international competitiveness and the capture of roughly one-fourth of the American market by foreign producers. The impact on the economy was devastating: the layoff of more than 200,000 auto workers; unprecedented deficits for the industry; disarray for states and municipalities dependent on revenues generated by automobile and auto-parts production; human costs associated with large-scale unemployment. The solution? "Voluntary" quotas on Japanese cars. The result? A return to the good old ways, which created the problem in the first place: an escalation of car prices that cost consumers $15.7 billion in four years; generous (indeed, astronomical) bonuses for auto executives; higher wages and fringes for auto workers, putting labor costs some 70 percent above the U.S. (not the Japanese) manufacturing average; attenuation of the pressure to innovate in order to survive. The quotas may have saved 44,000 auto jobs, but at a cost of $357,000 per job, which means that it would have been cheaper to pension off the workers. The policy was a palliative, not a panacea. It provided temporary relief to assuage the costs of incompetence, mismanagement, and greed. It did nothing to cope with the structural infirmities that were at the root of the malaise. It did nothing to confront the power of the automobile oligopoly and the UAW to make society pay the price for their deficient performance.

The moral is clear. Where society tolerates the creation of great power concentrations, it may eventually confront an intractable dilemma: to be a bailout agency of last resort for the malfunctioning of these power aggregates (thereby undermining the essence of market discipline for mismanagement) or to let them pay the price for self-inflicted injury (thereby ignoring the suffering of hundreds of thousands of people adversely affected by private miscalculation or incompetence). In short, society may finesse the power problem, or ignore it altogether, but it cannot avoid the cost of doing so.

For the foregoing reasons, the central focus of this book is on the anatomy of power, its physiology, and its consequences for the health of the economy. What is the distribution of power? Is it concentrated or decentralized? Is its exercise subject to external constraints, either by the invisible hand of the market or the heavy hand of government? Is power responsible and accountable, and if so to whom? What are the safeguards against its abuse or misuses? Are the abuses readily correctible? If so, by what mechanism(s)? In short, we shall ask the perennial questions crucial to understanding any economic system: who makes what decisions, on whose behalf, for whose benefit, and at what cost? The answers are vital, especially in a democracy.

In Part I we comment on the failure of modern, mainstream economics to incorporate power as a significant variable in its grandiose mathematical models. In Part II, we examine the popular mythology about the beneficence of corporate giantism. In Part III, we analyze the competitive market as a social control mechanism, emphasizing the historic goal of antitrust legislation to preserve a decentralized power structure. In Part IV, we explore the role of government as regulator, protector, and promoter of private power concentrations. In Part V, we consider the coalescence (or symbiosis) of power blocs: the labor-management complex and the military-industrial complex. We conclude with a discussion of public-policy alternatives.

The emphasis throughout is on current issues, in their "real world" context, but explored in their historical setting. Our purpose is to make the reader think—to eschew facile generalizations, superficial orthodoxies, and ideological dogmas. Our method is analytical, clinical, and (hopefully) dispassionate. Our heavy reliance on evidence and documentation is based on the belief that, as Bertolt Brecht once observed, "the truth is concrete."

CHAPTER 2

ECONOMISTS AND POWER

Seldom, in modern positive science, has so elaborate a theoretical structure been erected on so narrow and shallow a factual foundation.
— Professor Wassily Leontief, Nobel Laureate and past president of the American Economic Association

I certainly am thankful to God that I am not an economist. I look back when I was a high school drop-out, I had a sort of a flair for mathematics, and I think now that if I had gone on I might have wound up being an economist. And, to me, this is a kind of sad profession, although it is the one profession where you can gain great eminence without ever being right.
— George Meany, former president of the AFL-CIO

The master economist, wrote John Maynard Keynes, "must possess a rare *combination* of gifts. He must be mathematician, historian, statesman, philosopher—in some degree. He must understand symbols and speak in words. He must contemplate the particular in terms of the general, and touch abstract and concrete in the same flight of thought. He must study the present in the light of the past for the purposes of the future. No part of man's nature or his institutions must lie entirely outside his regard. He must be purposeful and disinterested in a simultaneous mood; as aloof and incorruptible as an artist, yet sometimes as near the earth as a politician." The master economist, Keynes hoped, would belong to that small but brave army of men "who prefer to see the truth imperfectly and obscurely rather than to maintain error, reached indeed with clearness and consistency and by easy logic, but [based] on hypotheses inappropri-

11

ate to the facts."[1] Believing as he did that the object of studying economics is to help make a better world, and always anxious to influence public policy toward that end, Keynes advocated the forging of those theoretical tools that were peculiarly useful in the solution of concrete problems.

Judging by some current criticism, there seems to be no oversupply of "master economists"—at least not in the academic world. Like his colleagues in other social sciences, the modern economist, so the critics allege, inhabits "islands of passivity and irrelevance rather than centers of ferment and innovation." He tends his scholarly garden of rare herbs and leafless plants, engaged in "small-scale research backed by large-scale grants."[2] His primary concern seems to be not with the real problems of our time—poverty in the midst of affluence, the degeneration of our inner cities, the growing gap between rich lands and poor lands— but with esoteric model building. A prisoner of self-imposed categories of thought, the academic economist appears to dispense a conventional wisdom and recite an orthodox catechism. He seems to use the most sophisticated techniques to arrive at the most irrelevant conclusions. A professor, some say, teaches what he has been taught, and his students do the same for no better reason than that it was their professor who taught it to them.[3]

It is sobering to note that these criticisms, whatever their validity, are neither novel nor surprising. They always spring up in a time of transition, when the theory developed to explain events of the past no longer seems relevant to the problems of the present. Once a theory is developed and finds public acceptance, it begins to command dogmatic adherence. It becomes progressively more difficult to dislodge; its prestige and authority, its comfortable familiarity, give it an immunity from "internal" reform. Only cataclysmic change, mediated by forces outside the profession, brings about an eventual transformation and reformulation. In the words of Leo Rogin: "As the career of a set of principles is prolonged, adherence to it becomes more uncritical and more precarious —more uncritical, because the original contingence of the theory on a practical issue is lost sight of; more precarious, because the passing of time tends to divest an issue of the rank to which it was originally entitled, or to change the conditions of its practical resolution."[4]

The malaise is neither novel nor unique. At the turn of the century, George J. Stigler reminds us, in the midst of America's most gigantic and unprecedented merger movement, while industrial empires of Brobdingnagian proportions were fashioned by financial magnates and buccaneering promoters, economists (in the academy) were remarkably unruffled and had a ready explanation. Relying on a crude social Darwinism, they parroted the familiar phrases of Herbert Spencer and William Graham Sumner. They could not see the erosive effect of large-scale mergers on the competitive markets that, in theory, they espoused. Says Stigler: "Economists as wise as Taussig, as incisive as Fisher, as fond of competition as Clark and Fetter, insisted upon discussing the movement largely or exclusively in terms of industrial evolution and the economies of scale. They found no difficulty in treating the unregulated corporation as a natural phenomenon, nor were they bothered that the economies of scale should spring forth suddenly and simultaneously in an enormous variety of industries—and yet pass over the minor firms that characteristically persisted and indeed flourished in these industries."[5] Thus, and ironically so, Ida Tarbell, Henry Damarest Lloyd, and the Populist muckrakers did more than the luminaries of the American Economic Association to foster a public understanding of the meaning of competition, and to help forge public policies designed to preserve it.

In 1929, while Herbert Hoover announced (with a naïveté pardonable in a politician) that "We shall soon with the help of God be within sight of the day when poverty shall be banished from this nation," so eminent an economist as Irving Fisher echoed these sentiments. He saw us marching along on a "permanently high plateau"—precisely one week to the day before the stock market tumbled over the brink of that plateau. And, even after the Great Depression was in full swing, academic economists still found it difficult to explain the massive unemployment that had befallen the nation. While the indisputable fact of this unemployment "argued more forcefully than any text that something was wrong with the system, the economists wrung their hands and racked their brains and called upon the spirit of Adam Smith, but he could offer neither diagnosis nor remedy. Unemployment—this kind of unemployment—was simply not listed among the possible ills of the system: it was absurd, impossible, unreasonable, and paradoxical."[6] Again, the phenomenon was too new. No adequate theory had yet appeared to explain it, and no "outsiders" had yet begun to experiment with policies to cure it.

Perhaps this lag is inevitable and inherent in the subject matter. Unlike the natural sciences, economics has no ready-made testing ground for the scientific validation and verification of its theories. "The natural sciences," notes Rogin, "articulate the concept of a constant nature, which finds its empirical reference in the uniformities manifested in the heavens and in the materially isolated setting of the laboratories." Economics, by contrast, deals not with the eternal verities of the physical universe but with the changing character of a dynamic social organism. Its only laboratory is the "marketplace" of reality, and the ultimate test for its theories is their correspondence to that reality. In such a subject matter, "where there is no agreed procedure for knocking out errors," the validity of a theory depends on its usefulness as a cognitive instrument, a working hypothesis, and a guide to action.[7]

In our own day, economic theory is again confronted with the specter of irrelevance to public policy. We can boast of an elaborate, sophisticated, highly mathematical box of analytical tools—replete with Pontryagin Principles, Rubizinski Theorems, Disequilibrium Models, Natural-Rate Hypotheses—but we are embarrassingly incapable of dealing with the nagging problems of the real world. Conventional theory—both neoclassical and Keynesian—is in danger of becoming, as Kenneth Boulding warns, the celestial mechanics for a nonexistent universe.

The difficulty may be, in part, methodological. The overemphasis on the mathematical-econometrics approach has resulted in a formidable misallocation of intellectual resources. Economists have tended to ask themselves questions that can be analyzed with their new techniques, rather than finding techniques to deal with the questions they ought to ask. They play games they find amusing, rather than contemplate issues that are crucial and pressing. They quantify what appears to be quantifiable, even though it may not be important, and pass up what should be analyzed even though it may be decisive. As Boulding points out:

> We have been obsessed with macroeconomics, with piddling refinements in mathematical models, and with the monumentally unsuccessful exercise in welfare economics which has preoccupied a whole generation with a dead end, to the almost total neglect of some of the major problems of our day. . . . The whole economics profession, indeed, is an example of that monumental misallocation of intellectual resources which is one of the most striking phenomena of our times.[8]

Technique, it seems, has taken precedence over substance, and economists have not yet learned that algebra and geometry are a complement to, not a substitute for, thought. No wonder, then, that journalists satirize our profession for having embraced a kind of rigor that resembles rigor mortis.[9]

The difficulty with contemporary economics, however, is conceptual as well as methodological. Unlike the political economists who founded our discipline, we largely ignore the power element in economic statecraft; and, lacking a theory of power, we seek to minimize the use of power in matters affecting the production and distribution of wealth. As Kurt Rothschild put it:

> If we look at the main run of economic theory . . . we find that it is character-ized by a strange lack of power considerations. More or less homogeneous units—firms and households—move in more or less given technological and market conditions and try to improve their economic lot within the constraints of these conditions. This model has been explored in great detail by modern economic science and very important insights into the working of the market mechanism have been gained. But that people use power to alter the mecha-nism itself; that uneven power may greatly influence the outcome of market operations; that people may strive for economic power as much as for eco-nomic wealth; these facts have been largely neglected.[10]

Thus, the typical microtheorist contemplates a "simplified" world, peo-pled by rational entrepreneurs, who are owner-managers of single-plant, single-product firms, operating in single markets, and dutifully maximiz-ing short-run profits by following the "time-tested" rule of equating marginal cost and marginal revenue. It is a world in which competition is the norm in both product and factor markets, and monopoly or oligopoly the exception. It is a world in which power per se is unknown, except with reference to particular firms, particular products, and partic-ular markets. It is a world untroubled by conglomerate giants and undis-turbed by technological upheavals—an *economic* world, separate and distinct from the world of power politics.

In a similar vein, the typical macroeconomist, although no longer exuding the hubris of the 1960s and no longer claiming to master the art of "fine-tuning" the economy, is still incapable of devising contracyclical stabilization policies to cope with the crucial macro-problems of the day. He may have policy prescriptions to deal effectively with inflation *or* recession, but not with inflation in the midst of recession—or with persis-tently high unemployment as the price of controlling inflation. Whether monetarist or Keynesian, he seems imprisoned and immobilized by an intractable dilemma: if he recommends restrictive monetary and fiscal policies, this is likely to aggravate recession; if he counsels expansionary measures, this is likely to exacerbate inflation. And so he takes refuge in the comforts of orthodoxy. Protesting the inescapability from the trade-off between the social goal of price stability and the social goal of full employment, he tells us that we can achieve one or the other, but not both simultaneously. And, depending on his ideological preference, he concludes that—at the margin—it is more important to fight inflation with recession, or recession with inflation. He recommends monetary and fiscal stabilization measures *as if* we could realistically assume that the economy approximated a state of "perfect" competition; *as if* we could assume that market power and/or political power were inconsequential phenomena; and *as if* we could assume that structural impediments in the economy were incapable of distorting or neutralizing macro-stabilization measures.

There is, to be sure, an emerging recognition that there is something amiss in such simplistic theorizing. Some twenty years ago, for example, in an incisive article largely ignored by his mainstream colleagues, Paul Samuelson, a Nobel Laureate and past president of the American Economic Association, observed that aggregate demand analysis is only a partial, not a general, guide to understanding macroeconomic phenomena. He pointed out that "there is a good reason to fear that America may, along with other lands, suffer from an institutional problem of cost-push. I mean by this that at levels below those corresponding to reasonably full employment, our institutions of wage bargaining and price setting may be such as to lead to a price and wage creep, a creep which can be lessened by conventional depressing of demand by monetary and fiscal policy measures but only at the cost of creating greater unemployment and excess capacity."[11] Looking ahead to the decade of the 1960s, he estimated that a 3 percent unemployment rate could be obtained at the cost of a 4.5 percent annual inflation rate[12]—a trade-off that a decade later seemed absurdly cheap and eminently tolerable. In the 1970s, economists were wont to assume an "underlying" or "embedded" inflation rate of roughly 10 percent, accompanied by near double-digit unemployment—a somewhat less-than-spectacular triumph of modern economic policy-making.

In 1975, Gottfried Haberler, an avowed monetarist and another past president of the American Economic Association, confessed that "stagflation, the coexistence of inflation and recession, is an economic disease which, to my knowledge, has never before existed, at least not as long and as severely as in the 1970s."[13] He noted that in most industrialized countries "stagflation could not have become such an intractable problem if our market economy were more competitive than it is, if it were not hamstrung and hobbled by so many restrictions and rigidities, due especially . . . to government intervention designed to keep certain prices and incomes high and by labor unions which have made money wages completely rigid in a downward direction and push them up even in the face of heavy unemployment and slack."[14] Haberler argued that government toleration, protection, and promotion of private monopolies, combined with the restrictionist pressures of organized vested-interest groups in the private sector, created what the Germans call *Anspruchs-Inflation*—a pernicious type of cost-push or "entitlements" inflation. It creates a persistent upward pressure on the general price level, because "the sum of the shares claimed by the various pressure groups exceeds the available social product" and because the government feels constrained to validate these excessive claims by a constant increase in the money supply. Haberler's conclusion is noteworthy:

> I am afraid that our monetarist friends—Karl Brunner, Milton Friedman, Harry Johnson, and Alan Meltzer, to name only a few of the most prominent experts—delude themselves if they believe that things can be straightened out by monetary policy alone. They are of course absolutely right in stressing that inflation cannot be stopped without an appropriate monetary policy. Tight money is undoubtedly a necessary condition, but it is not a sufficient condition for an economically successful and efficient as well as a politically practicable anti-inflation policy. I agree with William Fellner, Friedrich A. von Hayek, and Friedrich Lutz, who are of the opinion that a tight monetary and fiscal policy must be supplemented by measures designed to make the economy more competitive. In the jargon of economics, macroeconomic measures aiming at overall guidance of demand must be accompanied by microeconomic measures designed to promote competition. If we do not succeed in strengthening competition and freeing the market economy at least from its most crippling hobbles, the fight against inflation will generate so much unemployment that it will be terminated prematurely.[15]

Similarly, in 1979, Robert Eisner of Northwestern University—an erstwhile stalwart of orthodox Keynesianism who now labels himself a maverick, post-Keynesian free enterpriser—conceded that a simplistic pursuit of macro-stabilization policies cannot cope with stagflation. He urged that the seemingly endemic inflation of the late 1970s and early 1980s be "perceived as the consequence of a worldwide breakdown in competitive forces that could keep prices in line." This breakdown, he pointed out, was largely the result of government policies promulgated in response to the political blandishments of organized vested interests. Said Eisner:

> The list is much too long to cite in full: price supports for milk as dairy prices skyrocket; trigger prices to "protect" our steel industry from foreign competition as profits of our steel industry soar; licensing arrangements and route restrictions that drastically curtail competition in the trucking industry, laying the ground for repeated increases in prices and wages while trucks suffer from idle capacity and small trucking firms go out of business; sugar quotas and price supports to maintain and raise sugar prices; acreage restrictions

that reduce agricultural supply; import quotas, tariffs, and "orderly marketing agreements" that limit the import of cheaper and frequently better foreign automobiles, television sets, and textiles; and federal, state, and local
restrictions in countless occupations and industries that reduce competition
and raise prices.[16]

In short, here is a recognition of the fact that the inflation bedeviling the
industrialized nations of the West in the 1970s was characteristically of
the cost-push variety, fueled by a seemingly uncontrollable price-wage-
price spiral, and the result of a power grab by highly organized vested
interests for a larger share of a fixed pie or a pie growing more slowly
than the combined appetites of the interests that desire to devour it. And
equally important, there is recognition here that economic power and
political power may be mutually interacting and reinforcing, and that
government is more than a neutral bystander and rule maker in an
essentially self-regulating economy. These insights, however trenchant,
are still isolated and sporadic—*cris de coeur* in the confusing cacophony
of economic policy debates. They have not yet become part of mainstream theorizing, and since it is difficult to assess the quantitative
significance of the "power" element in economic behavior, the model
builders have largely ignored its importance—especially in their macro-
forecasts. This, perhaps, explains—certainly in part—the seemingly endemic inaccuracy of recent predictions.

In 1974, for example, three leading popular magazines—*Business
Week, Fortune,* and *U.S. News and World Report*—assembled a select
group of orthodox economists to predict what the year would bring. With
very few exceptions, they said the stock market would rise; it fell by 300
points. They said the inflation rate would decrease; it rose about 12
percent. They said unemployment would peak at 6 percent; it was above
7 percent at year's end, and rising. Above all, they said there would be
no recession. These soothsayers were so persuasive that President Gerald Ford, as late as the fall of 1974, embarked on his ill-fated WIN
campaign (Whip Inflation Now), urging people to buy less, to retrench
on their consumption of durable goods, to save more, etc.—only to be
forced to reverse himself 180 degrees by year's end and to face up to a
formidable recession.

In 1979, the *Economic Report of the President* stated that "the
increase in consumer prices is expected to fall to an annual rate below
7 percent by late in the year." The actual rate was 13.6 percent for the
fourth quarter and 15.4 percent for December. Private forecasts were
not perceptibly more accurate—perhaps because, as Arthur Burns ruefully observed in his final days as chairman of the Federal Reserve

System, the economy no longer works as it used to work. Despite the sophisticated econometric modeling of the economy—replete with leads and lags and vague references to "supply-side" shocks—the predictive value of economics as a "science" does not inspire confidence. Indeed, a recent poll showed respect for economic forecasters only marginally ahead of stockbrokers and astrologers, and well behind such professions as plumbers and sportscasters.[17]

In this book, we shall attempt to avoid the sterile orthodoxy of conventional models—the simplistic abstractions of neoclassicism and Keynesianism, on the one hand, and the radical chic of the New Left, on the other. We shall analyze the role of the state in a complex, modern, postindustrial economy and assess the effectiveness of public policy in promoting managerial, allocative, and dynamic efficiency in the economic order. Our approach throughout will be guided by what Paul Samuelson considers the first duty of the economist, "to describe what is out there," because "a valid description without a deeper explanation is worth a thousand times more than a clever explanation of nonexistent facts."[18]

This requires, first and foremost, dispensing with the traditional paradigm in which society's resources are allocated in response to "consumer sovereignty"—individuals or households casting dollar votes in the marketplace to determine what goods shall be produced and in what quantities. It requires dispensing with a paradigm in which the individual firm passively responds to exogenous market forces in an eternal quest to maximize short-run profits in producing particular goods in well-defined, "relevant" markets. It requires dispensing with a paradigm in which individual citizens cast their votes in a free political system to determine the policies of the state in a representative democracy.

Put positively, our approach calls for recognizing the dominant role of the giant corporation in the social decision-making process of what John Kenneth Galbraith calls "The New Industrial State." The giant corporation—as Galbraith notes, with somewhat Pickwickian exaggeration—has achieved substantial control over its environment and considerable immunity from the discipline of exogenous control mechanisms, especially the competitive market. Through separation of ownership from management, it has emancipated itself from the control of stockholders. By reinvestment of profits, it has eliminated the influence of the financier and the capital market. By massive advertising, it has insulated itself from consumer sovereignty. By possession of market power, it has come to dominate both suppliers and customers. By judicious identification with and manipulation of the state, it has achieved autonomy. Whatever it cannot do for itself to assure survival and growth, a compliant government does on its behalf—assuring the maintenance of full employment, eliminating the risk of and subsidizing the investment in research and development, and assuring the supply of scientific and technical skills required by the modern techno-structure. In return for this privileged autonomy, the industrial giant performs society's planning function. This model, despite its exaggeration and its lack of elegant precision (which economists value so dearly), does have descriptive value.[19]

Our approach also calls for revising the traditional view of the giant trade union. Whether we examine the role of the United Automobile Workers (UAW), or the United Steel Workers (USW), or the Communications Workers of America (CWA), these unions do not constitute countervailing power with respect to entrenched corporate interests. In bargaining over wages, hours, fringe benefits, and democracy in the workplace, they may assume an adversarial posture toward corporate management; but, in a larger sense, they represent not countervailing but coalescing power in defending the parochial, short-run interests of their industry. In their Washington lobbying, their demands are indistinguishable from those of their corporate counterparts: "the hand is the hand of Esau, but the voice is the voice of Jacob."

Similarly, it is no longer admissible to view government as an outside force regulating the economy in the same manner as a referee regulates the procedural aspects of an athletic event. The government has become an active participant in the economic game, and in some cases has a symbiotic relationship to the interest groups for which it makes the rules of the game. It, too, can no longer be viewed as a countervailing force whose public policies constitute an independent, autonomous, and incorruptible judgment of what is in the public interest. Nor, incidentally, can it be viewed, with naïve simplicity, as "the executive committee of the ruling class." It is far more accurate to view the state as part of a corporate-labor-government complex.

What this means is that we must dispense with paradigms that analyze the economic order in terms of individual actions and individual decisions. We must construct different paradigms that recognize the "organizational revolution" (to use Boulding's term) as a fact of life and try to understand the impact of new structures on economic behavior and ultimately on economic performance. There can no longer be argument over the proposition that, over time, special-interest organizations have gained preeminence in advanced industrial nations and that they now have the power to impede the effective functioning of the economic system—whether they do so through the market or through exercise of their political power to obtain governmental favors and privileges.

In his landmark study, *Capitalism, Socialism and Democracy*, Joseph Schumpeter discounted the significance of the monopoly problem in capitalist society. Monopoly power is dissipated, he believed, not by the static competition adumbrated in economic texts, but by the dynamic competition that comes from "the new commodity, the new technology, the new source of supply, the new type of organization (the large-scale unit of control for instance)—competition which commands a decisive cost or quality advantage and which strikes not at the margins of profits and the outputs of the existing firms but at their foundations and their very lives. This kind of competition is as much more effective than the other as a bombardment is in comparison with forcing a door."[20] This kind of competition, in short, unleashes what Schumpeter called the gales of creative destruction that control monopoly and neutralize the exercise of monopoly power.

Whatever the superficial validity of this theory, it suffers from a fatal defect: those power agglomerations subject to the gales of creative destruction do not willingly submit to their devastating force. They refuse to accept creative destruction as a socially beneficent mechanism for the good and sufficient reason that they themselves are the victims on the altar of the public interest. Not surprisingly, therefore, they try to protect themselves from the Schumpeterian gales by building private storm shelters for themselves where possible and by inducing government to build public storm shelters for them where necessary. They mobilize all the economic and political power at their command to assure survival, growth, and profitability.

That is the essence of the political economy of power. It is the central subject matter of this book.

II

THE APOLOGETICS
OF POWER

Corporate bigness burst suddenly on the American scene at the turn of the century. Between 1895 and 1904, through a lightning succession of unprecedented, large-scale mergers, acquisitions, and consolidations, industry after industry was dramatically restructured. Spurred by lax state incorporation laws, abetted by promoters and financiers who whipped up a frothy fit of financial speculation, and unencumbered by legal restraint, industrial behemoths sprang forth, virtually overnight, like Athena from Zeus's brow. "If the carboniferous age were to return and the earth were to repeople itself with dinosaurs," economist John Bates Clark observed at the time, "the change that would be made in animal life would scarcely seem greater than that which has been made in business life by these monster-like corporations."[1]

Among the corporate giants created during this era were General Electric (a combination of 8 firms controlling an estimated 90 percent of its market); American Tobacco (162 firms controlling 90 percent of the market); Du Pont (64 firms, 65 to 75 percent); International Harvester, now Navistar (4 firms, 70 percent); Nabisco (27 firms, 70 percent); Otis Elevator (6 firms, 65 percent); U.S. Gypsum (29 firms, 80 percent); International Paper (24 firms, 60 percent); American Smelting & Refining Company, now ASARCO (12 firms, 85 percent); Diamond Match (38 firms, 85 percent); and the "combination of combinations," United States Steel Corporation (an amalgam of 180 formerly independent plants controlling 65 percent of the steel industry). Other giant combines created during this period through the marriage of formerly competing rivals included National Lead (now NL Industries), U.S. Rubber (now Uniroyal), Pittsburgh Plate Glass (now PPG Industries), United Fruit (now Nabisco Brands), Allis-Chalmers, United Shoe Machinery, Eastman Kodak, International Salt, Pullman, and Corn Products Refining Company (now CPC International).[2]

Indeed, speculators and financiers struck upon what George J. Stigler later described as "a new and lucrative industry: the production of monopolies."[3] Most notable among these was J. P. Morgan, who "Morganized" industry by creating through consolidation General Electric, American Radiator (then the nation's largest producer of plumbing and heating equipment), International Harvester, American Telephone and Telegraph (AT&T), the Pullman Company, and the United States Steel Corporation (the nation's first billion-dollar corporation, whose capitalized value was at least half "water," and which returned promoter profits of more than $62 million).[4]

All told, more than three thousand companies disappeared through merger during the decade 1895–1904. Three-quarters of these were absorbed in consolidations devouring five or more firms in a single gulp. Nearly half of the disappearing firms (and seven-tenths of the value of merger capitalizations) were involved in mergers that immediately attained market and industry domination. As summarized by one expert, this voracious feeding frenzy "transformed many industries, formerly characterized by many small and medium-sized firms, into those in which one or a few very large enterprises occupied leading positions. It laid the foundation for the industrial structure that has characterized most of American industry in the twentieth century."[5]

This abrupt advent of giantism spawned an animated public policy debate. On the political hustings and in the popular literature of the day, three major policies toward bigness were articulated.

One camp held that great combinations of capital were "natural"; that they thus were inevitable; that it would be a mistake to try to oppose the process by which they were built up; that it would be unwise to try to break them up; and that, therefore, public policy should be directed at regulating monopoly rather than restoring competition. This was the position adopted by the Progressives and their leader, Theodore Roosevelt. "These big organizations are an inevitable development of modern industrialism, and the effort to destroy them would be futile," Roosevelt told Congress in 1902. "The line of demarcation we draw must always be on conduct, not on wealth; our objection to any given corporation must be, not that it is big, but that it behaves badly."[6] The nation, he said, could no more turn back the flood of monopoloid giantism than it could turn back the spring floodwaters of the Mississippi. Government should "regulate and control" the monopoly inundation by constructing levees to protect the public.[7]

A second camp eschewed the notion that regulated monopoly should displace regulated competition. Inspired by the empirical exposés of Justice Louis Brandeis, and led by Woodrow Wilson, this group contended that "the trusts have not grown. They have been artificially created; they have been put together, not by natural processes, but by the will, the deliberate planning will, of men who were more powerful than their neighbors in the business world, and who wished to make their power secure against competition."[8] The Wilsonians believed that "there is a point of bigness—as every businessman in this country knows, though some of them will not admit it—where you pass the limit of efficiency and get into the region of clumsiness and unwieldiness." They contended that this point of maximum economy "has been overstepped many times in the artificial and deliberate formation of trusts."[9] Responding to allegations of the myriad efficiencies of industrial giantism, they asked "how is it that the trusts find competition so troublesome, and consider it 'good business' to resort to the most disagreeable means of driving 'interlopers' out of the field? Such tactics are decidedly 'bad business,' if they are needless; and we can hardly think that the shrewd managers of the trusts would care to arouse public resentment by unnecessarily harsh methods."[10] And, the Wilsonians warned, "once government regulates the monopoly, then monopoly will see to it that it regulates the government."[11]

A third group clung to traditional Darwinism. "The growth of a large business is merely a survival of the fittest," asseverated John D. Rockefeller, the father of the Standard Oil trust. "The American Beauty rose can be produced in the splendor and fragrance which bring cheer to its beholder only by sacrificing the early buds which grow up around it. This is not an evil tendency in business. It is merely the working-out of a law of nature and a law of God."[12] Professor Sidney Sherwood made the point in less florid parlance: "The real function of the Trust is to get rid of the weak *entrepreneur*. It is the natural and spontaneous effort of a progressive industrial organization to get undertaking genius at its head which has produced the Trust. The formation of Trusts," he assured the public, "is a process of natural selection of the very highest order."[13] In this view, gargantuan corporate size posed no problems, either of conduct or industrial structure, and, therefore, should be of no concern for public policy.

In our own day, the quintessential myth of America's corporate culture is the belief that industrial giantism is the handmaiden of economic efficiency. At bottom, modern rationalizations of bigness and the concomitant concentration of power proceed along two major lines of economic theorizing, each of which, if valid, has profound consequences for public policy.

The first—and today the most dominant—brand of apologetics is essentially Darwinian in nature and, with the advent of the Reagan administration, has been enthroned as official government policy. Like some of his intellectual predecessors at the turn of the century, for example, Professor Robert H. Bork (now a judge on the U.S. Court of Appeals for the District of Columbia) sees a striking analogy between a free market system and the Darwinian theory of natural selection and physical evolution. Says Bork: "The familiarity of that parallel, and the overbroad inferences sometimes drawn from it, should not blind us to its important truths. The environment to which the business firm must adapt is defined ultimately by social wants and the social costs of meeting them. The firm that adapts to the environment better than its rivals tends to expand. The less successful firm tends to contract—perhaps, eventually, to become extinct. . . . Since coping successfully with the economic environment also forwards consumer welfare," he contends, "economic and natural selection has normative implications that physical natural selection does not have." He concludes that antitrust "should never attack [concentrated market] structures, since they embody the proper balance of forces for consumer welfare."[14] In like vein, William F. Baxter, President Reagan's first appointee as chief of the Antitrust Division of the Department of Justice, maintains that mergers and takeovers unfold according to a Darwinian dynamic. Merger activity, he recently instructed Congress, "is a very, very important feature of our capital markets by which assets are continuously moved into the hands of those managers who employ them most efficiently and interfering in a general way with that process would, in my judgment, be an error of substantial magnitude."[15] According to these latter-day Darwinists, then, industrial giantism is both inevitable and desirable, and the best public policy toward bigness is *no* policy—that is, laissez-faire. In their view, society should not attempt to interfere with monopoly, oligopoly, mergers, or takeovers; to do so, they argue, would undermine economic efficiency and superior performance.

A second strain of rationalization proceeds by a somewhat different route. Its proponents believe that, in a modern economy, bigness is not merely a reflection of but a prerequisite for economic efficiency and good performance. Schumpeter, the high priest of this belief system, argues that smaller competitive firms are "inferior in internal, especially technological, efficiency." They "waste opportunities." In their endeavor to improve their methods of production, they also waste capital because they are "in a less favorable position to evolve and to judge new possibilities. . . ." What we have to accept, says Schumpeter, is that the large-scale unit of control "is the most powerful engine of progress and in particular of the long-run expansion of total output. . . . In this respect, perfect competition is not only impossible, but inferior, and has no title to being set up as a model of ideal efficiency. It is hence a mistake to base the theory of government regulation of industry on the principle that big business should be made to work as the respective industry would work in perfect competition." In short, Schumpeter and his followers (most prominent among them Galbraith) pose a vexing public policy dilemma: society must sacrifice superior efficiency and performance in return for an unconcentrated power structure, or it must accept industrial giantism as the price of efficiency and progress. While Schumpeter would tolerate the concentration of power (because it is under constant threat of erosion by new competitive technologies), Galbraith would resolve the power dilemma by accepting concentration as inevitable but (like the Progressives of an earlier age) subject it to direct public oversight and control.

Central to the turn-of-the century apologetics, as well as their more recent reincarnation, is the notion that corporate size is indissolubly linked with industrial efficiency. It is a notion that, if supported by scientific evidence, would justify a profound reorientation of government policy. If, however, it is no more than a mythological artifact, this would mean that the Jeffersonian ideal of a democratic society with a decentralized power structure is attainable without a sacrifice of economic welfare.

In assessing the presumed links between size and efficiency, three caveats are in order. First, we must be mindful that the justification of corporate bigness is no more than an assertion. The fact that it is articulated in a drumfire of repetition does not establish it as a scientific truth.

Second, we must guard against oversimplification. Efficiency is a multifaceted concept. There is operating efficiency. Here the question is whether giant corporations are producing mousetraps at the lowest possible cost. Then there is innovation efficiency. Are corporate giants in constant quest for a better mousetrap? Finally, there is social efficiency. Perhaps mousetraps should not be produced at all. Perhaps rodent control should be effectuated through superior pesticides or a greater investment in feline capital.

Third, if efficiency is the goal, it is not enough to say that giant firms will automatically be most productive. The optimum size of firms varies from industry to industry, and optimum size changes over time with the evolution of technology. As Justice Brandeis put it in *The Curse of Bigness,* "there is a point where [the organization] would become too large for efficient and economic management, just as there is a point where it would be too small to be an efficient instrument. The limit of efficient size is exceeded when the disadvantages attendant upon size outweigh the advantages, when the centrifugal force exceeds the centripetal."[16] E. A. G. Robinson has made the point with a military analogy: "A platoon may drill very well as a platoon, but it may not always cover itself with equal glory in battalion drill. A battalion requires officers to coordinate the actions of its companies and platoons over and above the platoon commanders. The battalion has to be fitted into larger organizations, the brigade, the division, and the army. The problem of commanding an army is not simply the sum of the problems of commanding the platoons in it. All sorts of problems of organization and coordination arise because the unit to be controlled is now large instead of small, is out of earshot, takes time, space, and forethought to manage. A mistake made by a platoon commander demands only an instantaneous 'As you were!' A mistake by an army commander may require days of labor to set right. In just the same way the problem of organizing a large firm grows in complication as the firm grows."[17]

Finally, it is significant that the limitations of industrial giantism are now beginning to attract increasing attention in corporate circles. It is rumored, for example, that Roger B. Smith, chairman of the board of General Motors, is seriously considering splitting up the $84 billion auto maker into three separate companies, with the stock spun off to stockholders. Similarly, writing in the *Wall Street Journal,* John C. Sawhill, the federal energy czar under Presidents Nixon and Ford, states: "As recently as 1980, oil-industry critics in Congress offered legislation to force separation of the major companies' exploration and production activities from their refining and marketing operations. At the time, the industry adamantly opposed this proposal. But today things have changed so dramatically that such a rift could be their best option."[18] Equally significant is the spate of voluntary divestitures of conglomerate acquisitions currently taking place.

In the following chapters, we shall examine today's rationalizations of bigness, especially the neo-Darwinist foundation of current government policy, in the light of the available evidence. In chapter 3, we shall ask whether giant firm size is the predicate for operating efficiency. In chapter 4, we shall ask whether giant firm size is the sine qua non for dynamic efficiency, that is, technological progress. In chapter 5, we shall inquire whether giant firm size is conducive to social efficiency, that is, general economic welfare. Throughout, our purpose will be to determine whether society is, *in fact*, confronted by a Hobson's choice between "firms of the most efficient size but operating under conditions where there is inadequate pressure to compel firms to continue to be efficient and pass on to the consumer the benefits of efficiency, and . . . a system in which the firms are numerous enough to be competitive but too small to be efficient."[19]

CHAPTER 3
OPERATING EFFICIENCY

Is it not obvious that a horse falling from a height of three or four feet will break its legs, whereas a dog would not suffer any damage, nor would a cat from a height of eight or nine feet, or a cricket from a tower, or an ant even if it were to fall from the moon? And just as smaller animals are comparatively stronger than larger ones, so small plants too stand up better: an oak tree two hundred feet high cannot sustain its branches in the same proportion as a small oak tree, nor can nature let a horse grow as large as twenty horses or produce a giant ten times the size of man unless it changes all the proportions of the limbs and especially of the bones, which would have to be strengthened far beyond the size demanded by mere proportion.—The common assumption that large and small machines are equally durable is apparently erroneous. — Galileo, *Discorsi*

The big is coming out of manufacturing in this country, because in a lot of businesses we've discovered that small *is* beautiful.
— Gordon E. Forward, president of Chaparral Steel Company, 1984

"While many theoreticians—who may not be too closely in touch with real life—are still engaging in the idolatry of large size," E. F. Schumacher wrote in 1973, "with practical people in the actual world there is a tremendous longing and striving to profit from the convenience, humanity, and manageability of smallness." At the time, Schumacher's comment was derided "as yet another attack on big business in an era when environmentalism and the consumer movement were rampant. It ridiculed the conventional wisdom . . . which held that the bigger a plant—or even a company—the more efficient it was likely to be."[1]

Today, however, the conventional wisdom that "big is better" is increasingly recognized—by business people themselves—to be at odds with reality. In an article of 22 October 1984, for example, *Business Week* reports "a growing number of executives at some of the largest U.S. corporations have now become Schumacher's 'practical people in the actual world.'" The title of the article? "Small is Beautiful Now in Manufacturing."[2] The following spring, the magazine ran a special report: "Small is Beautiful."[3] A 3 June 1985 cover story asked "Do Mergers Really Work?" *Business Week*'s answer? "Not very often."[4] And in July 1985, in a cover story entitled "Splitting Up: The Other Side of Merger Mania," the magazine reported: "More companies are concluding that bigger isn't better . . ."[5]

Nevertheless, idolators of bigness persist in their tautological claim that firms are big because they produce at lowest cost, and that they are least-cost producers because they are big. Yale Brozen, for example, contends, "Concentration occurs and persists where that is the efficient structure for producing and distributing a product and for adapting to changing technical possibilities, shifting demand, and increasing regulatory requirements . . . Concentration," he concludes, "persists only where it brings efficiencies or is the consequence of superior management."[6] In a similar vein, Robert Bork is mystified about why so many "fail to see the obvious point that . . . larger size shows greater efficiency."[7]

To what extent are these assertions the result of dispassionate analysis? To what extent are they supported by empirical evidence? Are they scientific fact or popular mythology?

In examining the empirical evidence, it is important to keep in mind some basic definitional concepts and distinctions. Thus, operating efficiency means manufacturing a given product at the lowest possible cost. It requires that both plants (i.e., production units) and firms (i.e., administrative units) satisfy optimum scale standards.

In mass-production industries, technological imperatives militate toward large *plant* size. Efficiency is achieved by specialization of labor and machinery, the mechanization of production, the uniformity of processes, the interchangeability of parts, and scientific control over the accuracy of results. On this there is general agreement.

The case for large *firm* size is far more controversial. It rests upon alleged efficiencies of management rather than technology. Efficiency, it is said, is enhanced by spreading administrative expenses over multiplant operations; by eliminating duplication of officials, services, and record systems; by providing sophisticated statistical, research, and other staff services that would be ruinously expensive for smaller firms; by hiring more competent executives, more talented legal departments, and more effective lobbyists; by obtaining credit on more advantageous terms; and so forth. Some of these economies, to be sure, reflect advantages of bargaining power; however profitable they may be to the particular firm, they do not benefit the community at large.

Let us now examine the relation between bigness and operating efficiency in three major segments of U.S. manufacturing.

STEEL

The seven largest steel producers in the United States are truly giant corporations. In terms of absolute size, they all rank on *Fortune*'s list of the 500 largest industrials. In terms of relative size, they collectively control nearly 70 percent of raw steel production in the United States, with the two largest (U.S. Steel and LTV) accounting for approximately one-third of the industry total. In addition, these firms are vertically integrated; they operate blast furnaces and steel ovens, rolling mills and finishing facilities, iron ore and limestone mines. Yet, contrary to the claims of the apologists and mythmakers, there is overwhelming evidence that bigness in steel does not make for operating efficiency.

First, the size of today's steel giants does not reflect technological imperatives. It is not the result of internal, programmed, organic growth. It bears the imprint of the investment banker and promoter rather than the industrialist and engineer. It is the end product of mergers and acquisitions, an amalgam of helter-skelter consolidations frequently devoid of economic justification. Historically, virtually every major steel company in America started (and subsequently grew) not by building production facilities but by buying them.[8] Often the individual parts did not add up to an organic efficient whole.

U.S. Steel is prototypical of the industry. Incorporated in 1901, this "combination of combinations" comprised 180 formerly independent plants. These consolidations, the courts later concluded, were "made upon a scale that was huge and in a manner that was wild." Properties were thrown together "with less regard to their importance as integral parts of an integrated whole than to the advantages expected from the elimination of the competition which theretofore existed between them." Successive mergers "were not submissions to business conditions but were designed to control them for illegal purposes, regardless of other consequences."[9] This finding—that, from the very outset, the creation of giant firm size was largely divorced from considerations of operating efficiency—was confirmed by subsequent experience. In the 1930s, for example, Ford, Bacon & Davis, a management-consulting firm retained by U.S. Steel to conduct an internal efficiency study, found that the nation's largest steelmaker was

> a big, sprawling, inert giant, whose production operations were improperly coordinated; suffering from a lack of a long-run planning agency; relying on an antiquated system of cost accounting; with an inadequate knowledge of the costs or the relative profitability of the many thousands of items it sold; with production and cost standards generally below those considered everyday practice in other industries; with inadequate knowledge of its domestic markets and no clear appreciation of its opportunities in foreign markets; with less efficient production facilities than its rivals had. . . .[10]

And today, eight decades after its founding, and after considerable shrinkage in its relative size, U.S. Steel is still (according to *Business Week*) "one of America's most hierarchical, bureaucratic managements . . . an inbred, centralized, autocratic bureaucracy that stifles change."[11] In financial circles, neither the corporation nor most of the other steel giants are perceived as paragons of efficiency.

Second, in an industry such as steel (as in many mass-production industries) operating efficiency is primarily a function of plant size, not firm size. It may be efficient to operate a large integrated plant at Pittsburgh or at Gary, Indiana, or at Birmingham, Alabama; but combining these geographically dispersed production units under the same corporate umbrella yields few, if any, operating economies. Firm size, achieved through multiplant operations, is quite unrelated to efficiency —except, perhaps, negatively. Therefore, the fact that America's major steel companies are giant firms is scarcely probative evidence that they are efficient steel producers. Moreover, the fact that these companies operate many of their plants below the minimum efficient scale casts further doubt on their overall operating efficiency.[12]

Third, the rapid rise of "mini-mills" (which currently account for about 25 percent of domestic steel sales) raises additional questions about the technological imperatives of giant size. Mini-mills are relatively small, nonintegrated companies that convert scrap into finished steel products. They have sprouted up across the country in the past two decades; they are located close to their markets, especially in the Southeast and Southwest; they specialize in making a few products using state-of-the-art technology in ultramodern plants; and they are controlled by genuine entrepreneurs, whose fiery independence keeps them from joining the industry's major trade association. (The American Iron and Steel Institute is the "handmaiden of the big producers," says one. "Who wants to sit around Washington with your competitors? I hate my

competitors."[13]) Most significantly, mini-mills operate far more efficiently than do the industry's giants. The average worker at one mini-
mill, Nucor, produces 700 to 800 tons of steel per year, compared with
Big Steel's rate of 350 tons per year. At Nucor, it takes 30 workers to
produce a cold-finished steel bar; Big Steel needs 130 to do the same job.
According to steel analyst Joseph C. Wyman, "mini-mills often can sell
their products for $300 a ton and make a 10 percent profit, while inte-
grated companies might sell the same product for $450 and make no
money." Nor are mini-mill costs low because of "slave wages"; workers
at Raritan River Steel, a successful mini-mill, are paid an average hourly
wage of $18, compared to average wages of $22 per hour at the big
integrated mills.[14] Indeed, the economies of small size are so great that
even when mini-mill employment costs are higher, these costs are offset
by superior productivity performance.[15] Finally, mini-mill management
operates in a corporate culture dominated by the Puritan work ethic. In
sharp contrast to Big Steel, where executive salaries traditionally "provided for large homes on sprawling acres, raises [that] came regularly,
and there were plenty of assistants to take care of things if a manager
spent an afternoon of golf" at a company-subsidized country club, mini-
mill entrepreneurs disdain fleets of company jets and limousines and chic
executive dining facilities.[16] They occupy Spartan headquarters, close to
the action, and share the rigors (and rewards) of battle with the troops
under their command.

Fourth, specialization in one or a few product lines also makes for
better management and greater operating efficiency. Here, too, the record of mini-mills is significant: "Because they produce relatively narrow
product lines, mini-mills are generally very aware of their cost structure
—an indispensable datum for managerial decision-making. Integrated
firms often have a less thorough grasp of their actual cost structure
(e.g., by product); this failing stems from their oligopolistic past, their
intricate corporate hierarchies, and their extensive vertical integration.
These factors make it difficult for even the best-integrated firms to
identify their cost structures, to target cost-reduction efforts, and to
price according to costs."[17]

Fifth, smaller size enables steel producers to utilize their plant capacity more fully and efficiently. Steel analysts Donald F. Barnett and Louis
Schorsch explain that in the production of a major steel product, cold-
rolled sheets, "a smaller facility would be more adaptable and in closer
contact with its markets, so that it would therefore be less vulnerable
to fluctuations in demand. As a result, operating rates would tend to be
higher in the smaller plant, with salutary consequences for performance."[18]

Sixth, as we shall see in the next chapter, smaller size in steel permits production improvements to be more quickly incorporated into existing operations or, indeed, to replace entire plants. An important reason for this is the greater degree of individual managerial oversight and responsibility in smaller organizations. For example, one mini-mill built a new plant only to find that the technology failed to perform up to expectations; the plant was quickly scrapped and replaced by a more conventional furnace. Referring to this reversal, one steel buyer remarked, "If any of the big companies had done that, there wouldn't be anybody to take the blame, and the damn new thing would sit there until it fell apart from old age."[19]

The ultimate test of efficiency, of course, is comparative performance in the market. If that be the criterion, the record of the steel giants is hardly impressive. To be sure, Big Steel and its propaganda machine have a ready explanation for the endemic losses, massive layoffs, and pervasive plant closings. The culprit, they would have us (and the U.S. government) believe, is the burgeoning volume of imported steel, produced by low-wage labor in countries that subsidize their steel industries unfairly. The culprit, they say, is foreign steel dumped in the United States at prices below actual cost.

These claims, though superficially plausible, are not borne out by the facts. In such steel products as wire rods, bars, and light structurals, for example, U.S. International Trade Commission evidence showed that it was the intense competition of mini-mills, not imports, that was responsible for the catastrophic loss of market share by the steel giants. It is obvious, said Commissioner Paula Stern, "why the integrated producers lost so much of the market to the mini-mills. The latter are modern and efficient mills dedicated to the production of one or two products. The efficiency of their technology, management, and cost-control techniques enable mini-mills to keep their prices low." According to Commissioner Stern's findings, the average delivered price for wire rod charged by mini-mills "was well below the price paid for rod from integrated firms in most regions and in most of the period of investigation. But even more significant is the fact that these efficient U.S. mills were able to sell wire rod at a price that, on average, was below the average price of imported wire rod." Thus, in 1983 in the Detroit market, mini-mills *under*sold imported wire rod by an average of about $50 per ton (15 percent), while the large integrated companies charged an average of $25 (5.7 percent) *above* that of the imported product.[20] Similar pricing patterns prevailed in other product categories where mini-mills were preeminent. No wonder that mini-mills have prevailed in the market, not only against the domestic steel giants but against such "awesome" rivals as Japan Inc.

Clearly, import restraints will not cure Big Steel's lack of competitiveness and relative inefficiency. Nor will a spate of mergers that bloat firm size by proliferating the number of outmoded, anachronistic plants under Big Steel's bureaucratic control. If the goal is greater operating efficiency and enhanced competitiveness, then our strategy must focus on new, state-of-the-art steel plants, not ever larger multiplant steel firms.

AUTOMOBILES

The American automobile industry provides a second case study of the relation between corporate size, industrial concentration, and operating efficiency. The Big Three—General Motors, Ford, and Chrysler—are among the nation's very largest industrial corporations.[21] Moreover, they collectively account for more than 95 percent of domestic automobile production, and 70 percent of new car sales in the United States.[22]

The apostles of bigness assure us that firm size and industry concentration are justified by the large-scale operating efficiencies that characterize the manufacture of automobiles. General Motors, for example, asseverates that its "size has been determined by the product itself, the requirements of efficient manufacture, distribution and service, as well as market demand. Within this context, its present size has been determined by willingness to assume the risks of growth and by the ability to realize the added efficiencies of growth." Similarly, economist John McGee informs the Senate Subcommittee on Antitrust and Monopoly that no automobile firm in the world is big enough to capture all of the apparently unlimited economies of large scale involved in the production of automobiles.[23]

The reality in automobiles, as in steel, is decidedly at odds with these carefully propagated myths.

First, drawing on interviews and inspections of U.S. auto plants, a team of manufacturing engineers recently prepared detailed estimates of production levels at which the gains from successively larger size are exhausted. These estimates (prepared for four different car sizes, and for final assembly as well as for the manufacture of principal parts and components such as engines and transmissions) reveal maximum operating efficiency when producing 200,000 to 400,000 units per year.[24] Though large in an absolute sense, the engineers' estimates may imply that a firm with a 3 to 6 percent share of the U.S. auto production would be big enough to capture all significant economies of scale. In other words, the U.S. industry could support between seventeen and thirty-three efficiently sized producers (at recent aggregate output levels). Another industry expert, Lawrence J. White, concludes that the risks and vagaries of the market might require a viable firm to produce two distinct lines of automobiles, rather than one—thereby implying that the industry could support eight to sixteen efficient firms.[25] These estimates, based on engineering data and analyses, provide no support whatsoever for the conjecture that the observed bigness in autos is dictated by any imperatives of operating efficiency.

Second, in autos, as in steel, the relevant unit of operating efficiency is the plant, not the firm. Yet the Big Three are gigantic not because they operate one or two mammoth plants, but because they run a myriad of plants spread out across the country. General Motors, for example, assembles cars in nineteen different plants from Delaware to California, Ford in ten, and Chrysler in four; they operate an even greater number of different foundry, casting, and parts and accessories plants. By producing cars and components in multiple plants, the Big Three seem to recognize the limits to the economies obtainable from ever larger scale of a single plant. Indeed, an analysis of the size distribution of their assembly plants reveals that the Big Three assemble more than 80 percent of their annual output in plant sizes of 300,000 units or less—a figure entirely in line with the optimum scale estimates just examined.[26] And in this vein, the divergence between plant versus firm size for U.S. producers vis-à-vis their Japanese counterparts is significant. Although GM and Ford are larger than any of the four largest Japanese car companies, the Japanese produce their cars in vastly bigger plants than GM and Ford.[27] That is, the Japanese enjoy greater economies of scale at the plant level, even though they operate with smaller overall firm size. This would seem to indicate that operating efficiency at the plant level does not necessitate firms as large as GM or Ford.

Third, a crushing burden of large-scale bureaucracy stifles operating efficiency in automobiles. In the 1930s, Alfred Sloan, the legendary board chairman of GM, confided:

> In practically all our activities we seem to suffer from the inertia resulting from our great size. It seems to be hard for us to get action when it comes to a matter of putting our ideas across. There are so many people involved and it requires such a tremendous effort to put something new into effect that a new idea is likely to be considered insignificant in comparison with the effort that it takes to put it across. . . . I can't help but feel that General Motors has missed a lot by reason of this inertia. You have no idea how many things come up for consideration in the technical committee and elsewhere that are discussed and agreed upon as to the principle well in advance, but too frequently

we fail to put the ideas into effect until competition forces us to do so. Sometimes I am almost forced to the conclusion that General Motors is so large and its inertia so great that it is impossible for us to be leaders.[28]

More recently, a former vice president of General Motors provided this inside view of Chevrolet, GM's largest operating division: "One of the biggest . . . problems was in the manufacturing staff. It was overburdened with layer upon layer of management. . . . A plant manager reported to a city manager who reported to a regional manager who reported to a manager of plants who reported to me, the general manager. Consequently, the manager of the Chevrolet Gear and Axle plant on Detroit's near east side who was only a few miles from my office, was almost light years away in terms of management reporting channels." In a candid moment, former GM president Elliott M. Estes corroborated this observation: "Chevrolet is such a big monster that you twist its tail and nothing happens at the other end for months and months. It is so gigantic that there isn't any way to really run it. You just sort of try to keep track of it."[29] These assessments hardly comport with the picture of sleek efficiency portrayed by apologists and rationalizers of bigness.

Fourth, recent efforts by the Big Three to pare down the extent to which they manufacture their own parts and components strongly suggests historically excessive vertical size and integration. Domestic auto companies have "wiped out vast networks of parts plants," the *Wall Street Journal* reports, noting as an example that "Chrysler closed a Canadian plant that made seat springs and began buying them from outside suppliers at a saving of as much as 25 percent. . . . Chrysler also hired a supplier to design a new starter motor for its front-drive cars and thus avoided some $50 million in research costs."[30]

Fifth, recent developments undertaken by GM graphically attest to giantism's debilitating impact on production efficiency. For example, GM vice president and chief economist Marina V. N. Whitman has testified that GM's joint production venture with Toyota "will provide a valuable learning experience which will lead to more efficient U.S. small car production."[31] But the very fact that General Motors—long the world's dominant auto producer—would by its own admission be forced to turn to other, smaller firms in an effort to learn how to produce automobiles efficiently is a persuasive indication of the operating infirmities of uncontrolled bigness. So, too, is the firm's recently unveiled Saturn project, a completely new small-car subsidiary to be established, organized, and operated as independently of its parent as possible. An important reason for this, the *Wall Street Journal* observes, is to "free Saturn from the inefficiencies and overstaffing of the current GM bureaucracy."[32] A cynic might ask, as some financial analysts are now doing, how great the efficiency gains would be if each of GM's major divisions (Chevrolet, Oldsmobile, Buick, Pontiac, and Cadillac) were similarly freed from the burden of bigness.[33]

The thought is not as farfetched as the apologists for bigness would suggest. Some years ago in his paean on the organizational virtues of General Motors, Peter Drucker reported:

> The divisional manager . . . is in complete charge of production and sales. He hires, fires and promotes; and it is up to him to decide how many men he needs, with what qualifications and in what salary range—except for top executives whose employment is subject to a central-management veto. The divisional manager decides the factory layout, the technical methods and equipment used. . . . He buys his supplies independently from suppliers of his own choice. He determines the distribution of production within the several plants under his jurisdiction, decides which lines to push and decides on the methods of sale and distribution. . . . In everything pertaining to operations he is as much the real head as if his division were indeed an independent business.[34]

If this be so, what operating efficiencies are gained by subjecting divisional managers to the bureaucratic dictates of the corporation's overlords ensconced in their Detroit headquarters?

Alas, the reality in autos, as in steel, is that firms are neither big because they are efficient, nor efficient because they are big. Indeed, it is noteworthy that it was the recent intensity of foreign competition, not the internal dynamic of giantism, that compelled the Big Three to cut organizational fat, shrink bureaucratic hierarchies, pare excessive vertical integration, increase productivity, lower break-even points, and resist exorbitant wage demands by organized labor. This fact deserves attention because of the public policy implications: contrary to the conventional wisdom, smaller firm size, lower industry concentration, and vigorous foreign competition, may be the most effective prescription for greater efficiency in the manufacture of automobiles.

CONGLOMERATE BIGNESS

The giant conglomerate, as its name implies, is an aggregation of functionally unrelated or incoherent operating subsidiaries that are centrally managed and controlled. For example, the International Telephone and Telegraph Corporation (ITT), one of the nation's very largest industrial concerns, produces a seemingly endless line of wildly dissimilar products and services, including telephone handsets, battlefield radar, bathroom and kitchen fixtures, automotive brakes, lumber and timber, grass and plant seed (O. M. Scott, Burpee), Wonder Bread and Hostess Twinkies (Continental Baking), Sheraton hotels, insurance (The Hartford), fire-extinguishing equipment (Grinnell), air-conditioning apparatus, books, and business and technical training schools. Moreover, as we shall see in chapters 5 and 14, conglomerate giants like ITT, Textron, and others have achieved giant size largely through megamergers and acquisitions, rather than through internal growth reflecting success in the market-place. For example, Gulf & Western, an obscure producer of automobile bumpers, did not rank among the nation's two hundred largest industrial firms in 1960; as a result of nearly seventy acquisitions spread across disparate fields, however, the firm stood as the seventeenth largest concern in the nation just eight years later.[35]

By definition, conglomerate bigness rests on none of the traditional efficiencies of large scale. It does not confer operating economies by virtue of a firm's "horizontal" size—in other words, its ability to mass-produce a given article and thus reduce per-unit costs. Nor does it yield economies because of a firm's "vertical" size, that is, its ability to effectu-ate cost savings by integrating successive, functionally related stages of production and distribution. Clearly, these efficiency rationales do not justify conglomerate bigness, which, by its very nature, cuts across product and industry lines, and hence benefits neither from horizontal nor vertical firm size. Its defense, therefore, would have to rest on other than conventional efficiency criteria.

Apologists soon rose to the challenge of filling this embarrassing intel-lectual void. During the heyday of the conglomerate merger wave of the 1960s, they fabricated novel explanations for this new form of giantism. They rationalized conglomerate bigness by appealing to "synergy," by pointing to what they portrayed as a "revolution in management sci-ence," and by alluding to what they described as a scarce supply of "super-managers" whose wizardry could enhance economy-wide effi-ciency if more and more control were concentrated in their hands. Pro-fessor J. Fred Weston of UCLA told a congressional committee that "synergy translates to lowering cost curves."[36] Professor Neil H. Jacoby, also of UCLA, added that the "conglomerate merger can enable the enterprise to apply over a wider sales base the talents of a skilled general management team in planning, organizing, budgeting, control-ling, and staffing the operations of its several operating divisions"; that the conglomerate can utilize specialists not affordable by "small" ac-quired firms; and that a "real social gain occurs when the assets of a business are transferred via merger into the control of a superior management."[37]

Reality and the weight of the available evidence, however, refute the new rationalizations for corporate giantism.

First, it is a myth that an elite corps of "super-managers" that is blessed with boundless managerial acumen and perspicacity exists. The notion rests on what Professors Robert H. Hayes and William J. Abernathy of the Harvard Business School characterize as "a preoccupation with a false and shallow concept of the professional manager—a 'pseudo-professional' really—an individual having no special expertise in any particular industry or technology who nevertheless can step into an unfamiliar company and run it successfully. . . . Its first doctrine," they caustically add, "is that neither industry experience nor hands-on technological expertise counts for very much."[38] As business consultant Joel Dean points out, the opposite is true. The conglomerate giant's heterogeneous structure exacerbates problems of managerial control, and the "inevitable lack of specialized industry experience makes the High Command unable to master the intricacies and ramifications of the highly diverse competitive situations and technologies of its diverse industries."[39] On the basis of his long experience, Dean concludes that "only in extraordinary individuals—so few as to be practically negligible—do we find the ability to absorb a new game intellectually and then compete successfully with experienced players."[40]

Second, far from streamlining American industry, conglomerate bigness and conglomerate mergers have enmeshed it in a stultifying snare of organization disorder and ill-fitted bureaucracy. "Our major corporations have blossomed into multiproduct, multidivisional, multilocational hydras," *Business Week* reports in a recent issue devoted to an analysis of the problems of the American economy.

> They became far too diverse for any one corporate leader to embrace. So one formerly monolithic company after another decentralized into such things as profit centers, strategic business units, and the like. Every profit center had to have a general manager or a divisional president. Corporate headquarters had to have new staff people to whom the divisional people would report. Layer upon layer of management jobs were added to the structure.[41]

Of course, the result scarcely enhances operating efficiency. The "gap between ultimate authority and on-line responsibility widens, communication channels become more complex and bureaucratized, decision-making is slowed, incentives may be weakened, morale suffers, and worse decisions may result."[42]

Third, the weight of actual experience shatters the apologetics of conglomerate bigness, particularly when attained by merger. For example, officials of three recently divested meat-packing concerns agree that freedom from conglomerate control has been a major factor in their recovery. "I spent a lot of time reporting to people who didn't understand the business or weren't interested in it," one of them recounts, adding that managers of a specialized firm "understand the business and know how to react to the market."[43] Following Carborundum's acquisition by Kennecott, a copper company, *Business Week* reports that "even modest decisions took up an inordinate amount time as Carborundum managers struggled to explain their business to their Kennecott bosses." Not surprisingly, Carborundum's operating efficiency plummeted, inventories ballooned, on-time deliveries dropped, and overhead costs soared.[44] Evaluating the lackluster performance of ITT, the giant conglomerate furiously thrown together by Harold Geneen in the 1960s, one financial analyst concludes: "Geneen was an absolute disaster as an operating manager . . . you have only to look at the record—he could acquire companies but not manage them."[45] These and other cases are neither isolated nor are they unique. After his massive examination of an enormous body of economic and statistical studies, economist Dennis C. Mueller finds "a surprisingly consistent picture. Whatever the stated or unstated goals of managers are, the [conglomerate] mergers they have consummated have on average . . . not resulted in increased economic efficiency."[46]

Fourth, the current spate of divestitures and spin-offs of subsidiaries by large conglomerates belies the myths of operating efficiency newly ascribed to conglomerate bigness. "The thinking used to be that once a conglomerate was put together, the whole was more valuable than its parts. Now the parts seem more valuable than the whole," explains Donald P. Jacobs, dean of the Kellogg School of Management at Northwestern University. "We are likely to see many old-line conglomerates break apart," he concludes.[47] More and more, conglomerates have come to believe that "it's best to divest."

Fifth, striking gains in operating efficiency have been recorded when individual subsidiaries are freed from the burdens of conglomerate bigness. F. M. Scherer reports the following findings in his detailed study of conglomerate subsidiaries that have been sold to their former managers:

Cost-cutting opportunities that had previously gone unexploited were seized. Austere offices were substituted for lavish ones. Staffs were cut back sharply. New and more cost-effective field sales organizations were adopted. Inexpensive computer services were found to substitute for expensive in-house operations. Make vs. buy decisions were reevaluated and lower-cost alternatives were embraced. Efforts were made to improve labor-management relations by removing bureaucratic constraints that had been imposed by the previous conglomerate's headquarters. Tight inventory controls were implemented, cutting holding costs by as much as one-half. Low-volume items were pruned from product lines to trim inventories and reduce production setup costs. Tighter control was exercised over accounts receivable.[48]

Thus, as economic theory and common sense predict, and as the weight of the available evidence confirms, conglomerate bigness seldom enhances, and more typically undermines, efficiency in production. Reality thus refutes the mythology so glowingly described and extensively propagated by bigness and its apostles. Of course, this reality has profound public policy consequences as well. It suggests that problems of lagging productivity and diminishing international competitiveness are to an important degree attributable to the structure of American industry and, in particular, to the economic burden of conglomerate bigness. It also raises the question of whether it is sound national policy to tolerate the efficiency losses of unrestrained conglomerate megamergers, such as U.S. Steel's acquisition of Marathon Oil, and Du Pont's purchase of Conoco.

AMERICAN INDUSTRY: A CROSS SECTION VIEW

Finally, studies of American industry conducted at a broader level confirm the preceding case study findings.

In his classic 1956 study of twenty representative industries, Joe S. Bain found that, in eleven of the twenty cases, the least-cost, most efficient plant would account for less than 2.5 percent of the industry's total national sales; in fifteen, for less than 7.5 percent; and in only one case, for more than 15 percent. Moreover, in estimating economies obtained by a single firm operating several plants, Bain concluded that in six of the twenty industries, the cost advantages of multiplant firms "were either negligible or totally absent"; in another six, the advantages were "perceptible" but "fairly small"; and in the remaining eight industries, no estimates could be obtained.[49]

A more recent study of twelve industries in seven nations carried out by economist F. M. Scherer generally corroborates Bain's earlier findings. After analyzing minimum optimal scale (MOS) plants required for least-cost production, Scherer reports three key findings: (1) With only one exception, "the optimum plant sizes tend to be quite small relative to the national market—too small to warrant high levels of concentration, assuming that each leading firm is large enough to operate only one MOS plant." (2) The loss of production efficiencies in plants vastly smaller than those of optimal scale are surprisingly small; for half of the industries studied, a plant one-third the scale at which unit costs are minimized would suffer cost disadvantages of only 5 percent or less.[50] (3) Even after explicitly allowing for production efficiencies that might be achieved by a single firm operating multiple plants, actual firm sizes and market concentration levels significantly exceed those required by economies of scale: market shares held by the top three producers exceeded scale-dictated shares by a factor of ten in two industries; by four to six times in four industries; and by two to three times in three industries.[51] Thus, Scherer's analysis revealed that "actual concentration in U.S. manufacturing industry appears to be considerably higher than the imperatives of scale economies require"[52] and, further, "that in more than half the industries covered by our research, substantial deconcentration could be effected while forcing at most slight scale economy sacrifices."[53]

Scientific evidence has not been kind to the apostles of bigness and to their mythology. Countless studies and analyses, for specific industries as well as for manufacturing generally, for specialized firms as well as for conglomerates, have demonstrated that giant firm size and extreme industry concentration are *not* technologically determined by the dictates of large-scale economies. As Nobel Laureate George Stigler observed long ago: "One can be opposed to economic bigness and in favor of technological bigness in most basic industries without inconsistency, because our economy is so large that we can have companies large enough to operate efficient plants and numerous enough to be competitive."[54]

In retrospect, Stigler's observation has proved to be prophetic. Today, as *Business Week* notes, "in a rebellion against the conventional wisdom, dozens of manufacturers—including AT&T, FMC, and General Electric—are embracing a new philosophy. Their managers are suddenly talking about 'diseconomies of scale.' They are replacing huge manufacturing complexes with new, smaller plants.... From telecommunications to steel, companies are turning away from bigness to find efficiency."[55]

But production efficiency cannot be captured merely by having giant corporations construct and control a far-flung agglutination of innumerable small plants. For example, Big Steel has to date been singularly unsuccessful in attempting to operate mini-mills of its own.[56] Conversely, we have seen that former subsidiaries of giant conglomerates typically operate far more efficiently when, through divestitures and spin-offs, they are freed from the crush of bureaucratic control. The reason that centralized management of otherwise efficiently sized plants affords no panacea is clear: the disabilities of bigness are rooted in the size of the *unit of control* and not the size of individual plants considered in isolation from the organizations in which they are managerially subsumed. Observes Steven C. Wheelwright, professor at the Stanford University Graduate School of Business: "Companies always thought, 'Our people can manage their way out of the problems size and complexity create.' But the evidence is that they can't."[57] For these reasons, then, a mix of centralized control with decentralized production holds no promise as an elixir of efficiency.

If this be so, a thorough reorientation of public policy is in order. Once it is recognized that corporate giantism is more often a liability than an asset to the efficient organization and operation of American industry; once it is understood that lagging productivity, diminishing international competitiveness, and burgeoning imports may, at least in part, be attributable to the structural infirmities in our economic organization; once it is grasped that corporate size and concentrated power have a decidedly adverse impact on economic performance—then, at last, the government might embrace a radically different approach to the seemingly intransigent economic problems of our day. At the very least, the government would not pursue policies based on assumptions inappropriate to the facts.

CHAPTER 4

INNOVATION EFFICIENCY

Could Hamlet have been written by a committee, or the Mona Lisa painted by a club? Could the New Testament have been composed as a conference report? Creative ideas do not spring from groups. They spring from individuals. The divine spark leaps from the finger of God to the finger of Adam, whether it takes ultimate shape in a law of physics or a law of the land, a poem or a policy, a sonata or a mechanical computer.   —President A. Whitney Griswold to the Yale Class of 1957

Innovation efficiency refers to an economy's technical virtuosity in creating better products and improved manufacturing processes, as well as its facility for introducing and adopting them. The concept is dynamic in nature, encompassing technological betterment over time and improvements in the state of the industrial arts. As such, it stands in contrast with operating efficiency (which as we have just seen, is a static concept concerned with optimum firm size, given a particular technology at a particular point in time).

Perhaps in no other dimension of economic activity does received wisdom vest such unqualified faith in the virtue of bigness as it does in the realm of technological progress. The image—carefully cultivated in advertisements and promotions—is one of corporate armies of highly educated, white-cloaked scientists, housed in ultramodern laboratories, presiding over variegated vessels of brilliantly colored chemicals, scanning printouts spewed from batteries of computers, and monitoring video displays set off against a coal-black background. The image is significant: it legitimizes bigness by imbuing it with an aura of service in the advance of technology while at the same time creating the not-so-subtle impression that technical progress demands large-scale organization where large numbers of researchers work in large-scale facilities and with large-scale budgets.

Academicians also have accepted and indeed helped propagate this image. John Kenneth Galbraith has declared, in his customarily pithy fashion, that a "benign Providence . . . has made the modern industry of a few large firms an excellent instrument for inducing technological change. It is admirably equipped for financing technical development. Its organization provides strong incentives for undertaking development and for putting it into use." There is no more pleasant fiction, he has asserted, "than that technical change is the product of the matchless ingenuity of the small man forced by competition to employ his wits to better his neighbor. Unhappily, it is a fiction. . . . Not only is development now sophisticated and costly but it must be on a sufficient scale so that successes and failures will in some measure average out. Few can afford it if they must expect all projects to pay off."[1]

Joseph Schumpeter declared monopoly to be the essential motive force for technological progress in capitalist society. He argued the rewards of monopoly to be the bait that lures firms on to untried technical trails, while innovation is the primary means by which existing monopolists seek to protect their established positions. This struggle between existing and aspiring monopolists unleashes "gales of creative destruction" as existing monopolies and technologies are displaced by new monopolies erected upon new technologies. As compared with pedestrian price competition, Schumpeter concluded, these technological gales of creative destruction are "so much more important that it becomes a matter of comparative indifference whether competition in the ordinary sense functions more or less promptly; the powerful lever that in the long run expands output and brings down prices is in any case made of other stuff."[2]

But are monopolistic giants really the new Prometheans, bringing us the heavenly gift of technology from their celestial abode and placing it in the service of mankind? Are industrial giantism and monopolistic or oligopolistic markets really the essential prerequisites for technological advance? Are they the price that modern society must pay for progress? Or are these mere myths—elaborate rationalizations of bigness that, though superficially alluring, are bereft of empirical support?

ORGANIZATIONAL SIZE AND
INNOVATION EFFICIENCY

Ostensibly, giant firms might be presumed for a variety of reasons to be superior inventors and innovators: They can afford to hire armies of the best brains and to outfit them in elaborate, extensive, and sophisticated laboratories. Their massive size should permit them to bear the potential losses of risky research into fundamentally new products and production processes. They can further reduce risks by operating a large portfolio of individual projects, so that the success of any one project can compensate for the failures and losses of other projects. They have established channels of distribution that should enable them to quickly bring new products to market. And because giant firms typically are diversified into a number of different industries and markets, they should be better able to capitalize on the unpredictability of research and development by recognizing the potential applicability of research results across diverse fields.

But reality and the available evidence show that despite all of these theoretical advantages, small firms and independent inventors are far more efficient innovators than industrial giants. Specifically, the evidence reveals that independent inventors continue to be an important source of major inventions; that small firms are more prolific inventors than giant companies; that small firms exert significantly greater research and development effort than large ones; that small firms devise and develop inventions at substantially lower cost than large firms; and that giant organizations seem to suffer a number of debilitating and apparently endemic disadvantages as regards invention and innovation.

THE IMPORTANCE OF THE INDEPENDENT INVENTOR

Contrary to popular mythology, the independent inventor is *not* an anachronism, nor has he or she been displaced by the mammoth corporate organization as a superior source of invention. Rather, independent inventors—garage mechanics and backyard tinkerers, toiling on their own with limited funds and simple equipment—are responsible for a surprisingly high share of major modern inventions.

One landmark study selected seventy inventions considered by knowledgeable experts to be among the most important of the twentieth century, traced the origins of these inventions, and determined whether they were due primarily to the efforts of large firms, small firms, or independent inventors.[3] The results were surprising for a society steeped in the belief that invention has become the exclusive preserve of the giant corporation: more than one-half of the seventy inventions resulted primarily from the efforts of independent inventors working on their own. In particular, independent inventors far outstripped large firms as sources of invention. For example, xerography was invented by a physicist working in a patent office who developed the idea in his spare time; air-conditioning resulted from the efforts of a number of independent inventors, some of whose employers refused to support them in their research; Kodachrome amateur color photographic film was primarily developed by two college students majoring in music; while an independent consulting engineer invented power steering for automobiles and other motor vehicles.[4] Other studies have found that independent inventors were primarily responsible for inventing the computer, hot extrusion of steel, natural color television, neomycin, prestressed concrete, and stereophonic sound.[5]

Further, many major inventions have been made with simple equipment and quite modest expenses. For example, the first cyclotron was built with window glass, sealing wax, and wire; similarly crude equipment was employed to develop xerography. "The record of modern invention demonstrates that it is the quality of the researcher, not the elaborateness of his equipment, that determines success," reports one student of the field. "Inventors who place increased reliance on specialized tools and less on thinking power and personal observation may get caught up in the machines and miss solutions lying near the surface of things."[6]

Thus, the continuing important role of the independent inventor, and the modest equipment and expenditures involved in a number of major modern inventions, belie claims that technological inventiveness has become the exclusive domain of the giant corporation. Indeed, the record is replete with established large firms that "frequently missed or overlooked important new departures or remained unconvinced of the merits of an invention which, it might have been thought, would have appealed strongly to them."[7] Examples include telephone, cable, and electrical manufacturing companies that greeted the invention of radio with enthusiastic indifference; aircraft engine producers who accorded a similar reception to the jet engine; chemical companies that resisted penicillin even after its chemotherapeutic virtues had been demonstrated.[8] Likewise, the nation's largest industrial concerns rejected xerography, while Eastman Kodak dismissed the newly invented instant camera as a toy with no commercial appeal.[9]

THE SUPERIORITY OF SMALL SIZE: INNOVATIVE OUTPUT
Further contradicting the folklore of bigness is the fact that small firms are superior to their large counterparts in terms of producing innova-

tions. In the iron and steel, bituminous coal, petroleum, and pharmaceuticals industries, for example, "the biggest few firms did *not* do the most innovating relative to their size" once the full range of firms of various sizes is taken into account.[10] Similarly, for the chemical industry there is *no* evidence "that the biggest chemical firms did any more innovating (or developing) relative to their size, than somewhat smaller firms" in the development and adoption of improved production methods.[11] Indeed, a study of Du Pont, the largest chemical company in the field, found the bulk of the firm's commercially important products to have been invented *outside* the firm.[12]

Additional evidence of the innovative superiority of small firms is provided by the National Science Board of the National Science Foundation. The board examined 310 major technical innovations introduced in the United States over the years 1953 to 1973 and classified them by the size of the firm responsible for their creation and introduction. The results reveal that the very largest firms (those with more than 10,000 employees) accounted for only 34 percent of the total number of innovations studied; in contrast, the three smallest-size classes (firms with fewer than 5,000 employees) accounted for fully 60 percent of the total. When the board examined the rates of innovations produced, it found small firms to have the greater number: "For the whole 1953–73 period, the smallest firms produced about 4 times as many major innovations per R&D dollar as the middle-size firms and 24 times as many as the largest firms."[13]

THE SUPERIORITY OF SMALL SIZE: INNOVATIVE EFFORT

The evidence also reveals that, although large firms may spend large absolute amounts on research and development, smaller firms exert greater inventive "effort" by spending a proportionately larger share of their revenues on research and development activities. This greater effort, in turn, may partially explain why small firms are more prolific inventors as compared with corporate giants.

This phenomenon is portrayed in Table 1, depicting the size and research effort for the nation's ten largest industrial firms and for the ten firms selected by *Business Week* as leaders in research effort. The data show that, while rationalizers of bigness suggest that large companies can afford to spend more on research, in reality it is small firms that spend the largest fraction of their sales for research and development. For example, the nation's largest industrial concern, Exxon, devoted less than 1 percent of revenues to research and development; in contrast, tiny TeleSciences spent nearly one-third of its total revenues for research and

TABLE 1
Research Effort by Small versus Large Industrial Corporations

BIG COMPANIES — SMALL RESEARCH EFFORT			SMALL COMPANIES — BIG RESEARCH EFFORT		
Firm	Total Revenues (Millions)	R&D as a Percent of Revenues	Firm	Total Revenues* (Millions)	R&D as a Percent of Revenues
Exxon	$88,561	0.7	TeleSciences	$52	31.6
General Motors	74,582	3.6	Policy Management Systems	62	26.6
Mobil Oil	54,607	0.3	ADAC Laboratories	59	26.4
Ford Motor	44,455	4.8	Hogan Systems	37	22.9
IBM	40,180	6.0	Fortune Systems	54	22.3
Texaco	40,068	0.3	Management Science America	139	20.8
Du Pont	35,378	2.6	King Radio	87	20.0
Standard Oil (Indiana)	27,635	0.5	Dysan	180	19.4
Standard Oil (California)	27,342	0.6	Modular Computer Systems	75	17.6
General Electric	26,797	2.9	Advanced Micro Devices	582	17.4

*Estimated from data contained in *Business Week.*

SOURCES: *Fortune*, 30 April 1984, p. 276; *Business Week*, 22 March 1985, p. 164.

development—more than thirty times the proportionate effort registered
by Exxon and other leading industrial corporations.

More generally, studies of the statistical relationship between firm
size and proportionate inventive effort—conducted by a variety of researchers, in a variety of ways, and over a variety of time periods—
disclose the proportion of revenues devoted to research and development
to *decline* beyond a relatively modest size of firm. "A little bit of bigness
—up to a sales level of $250–400 million at 1978 price levels—is good for
invention and innovation," economist F. M. Scherer concludes in his
encyclopedic review of the cross-section evidence. "But beyond this
threshold further bigness adds little or nothing, and it carries the danger
of diminishing the effectiveness of inventive and innovative performance."[14]

Nor do giant firms display any appetite for undertaking more fundamental and risky research projects. That is, contrary to the image that
bigness is conducive to risk-taking, there is no statistically significant
tendency for corporate behemoths to conduct a "disproportionately
large share of the relatively risky R&D or of the R&D aimed at entirely
new products and processes. On the contrary, they generally seem to
carry out a *disproportionately small share* of the R&D aimed at entirely new products and processes."[15]

THE SUPERIORITY OF SMALL FIRMS FOR MANAGING
THE COSTS OF INNOVATING

In defiance of conventional belief, smaller firms also conceive and commercialize inventions at lower cost than do corporate giants. That is,
smaller firms are more effective *and* more efficient innovators. For example, economist Jacob Schmookler found the average cost per patent
obtained to uniformly rise with firm size, with the largest firms spending
twice as much per patent when compared to small firms. This result
couldn't be explained by saying the patented inventions of the large
firms were somehow better or more sophisticated. "In brief," Schmookler concluded, "existing comprehensive indexes of output of new technological knowledge suggest that beyond a certain not very large size, the
bigger the firm the less efficient its knowledge-producing activities are
likely to be."[16] Professor Edwin Mansfield arrived at the same conclusion in his analysis of the number of significant inventions made by large
firms in the chemical, petroleum, and steel industries: "contrary to popular belief," he found, "the inventive output per dollar of R&D expendi-
ture in most of these cases seems to be lower in the largest firms than
in large and medium-sized firms."[17]

In a particularly revealing analysis, Professor Arnold Cooper investigated the relationship between organizational size and costs of inventing. He interviewed new-product development managers who had served in small and large firms, managers charged with overseeing rapidly expanding development organizations, and managers noted for their skill in the field. "The evidence collected suggests that large companies tend to spend substantially more to develop particular products than do small firms . . . a magnitude possibly as great as several hundred percent." The consensus among those with direct experience in managing new-product development for both large and small firms was "that a large company typically spends from 3 to 10 times as much as a small one to develop a particular product"—a rather unexpected result in a society trained to envision bigness as a sleek engine of efficient innovation.[18] Indeed, it suggests that large R&D spending by giant firms may reflect considerable *in*efficiency in invention and innovation.

THE CREATIVE BACKWARDNESS OF BIGNESS

Thus we find the reality of bigness is so much at odds with popular belief that, ironically, it is the creative backwardness of giant corporations that calls for explication. We believe this inability to be innovative is attributable to at least five factors.

First, and perhaps most fundamentally, the character traits most serviceable in large organizations are incongruent with those conducive to technical creativity and human inventiveness. In order to function, a giant bureaucracy must command a considerable degree of conformity, adherence to rules and authority, respect for the status quo, and a not insignificant measure of human homogeneity. In contrast, rejection "of accepted routine and convention, rebellion against classical modes of thought, repudiation of the tried and true and of expert authority, insistence on going where 'angels fear to tread'—these are the persistent characteristics of the creative scientist and inventor."[19] In other words, invention is a rebellious act consciously committed by incorrigible nonconformists. As such it defies, and perhaps, therefore, must eventually succumb to, the *raison d'être* of large-scale bureaucratic organization.

Second, human creativity may be further strangled by the snare of red tape—memoranda, authorizations, communication channels, committee meetings, petty politics—ceaselessly spun by giant bureaucracies. The great advantage enjoyed by small firms in this respect, *Business Week* observes, is that they can avoid the lengthy reviews that "often derail innovation in big companies."[20] For example, a number of financial analysts point to bureaucratic "culture shock" in explaining the disastrous performance of small, high-technology firms after they have been acquired by corporate colossi. "The giants' many layers of bureau-cracy often paralyze the freewheeling entrepreneurial style typical in the high-tech world. Recalls one former head of an office-equipment company controlled by Exxon: 'Their MBAs came in and said, "Give us your five-year plan." Our long-range plan was where we'd have lunch tomorrow.' "[21] A former manager at Intel Corporation, one of the na-tion's three hundred largest firms, agrees: "If I wanted to do a new product at Intel," he recounts, "I had to visit all those committees, and that made it extremely awkward to do things."[22]

Third, inventiveness also tends to be stifled by the innate conserva-tism of giant organizations, their attachment to the status quo, and their concomitant resistance to change. Daniel V. DeSimone, the former direc-tor of the Office of Invention and Innovation of the National Bureau of Standards, explains: "Corporations build up expensive production facili-ties, armies of trained service technicians, and large inventories of spare parts and other items all related to the current product. . . . Along comes an inventor who proposed technological revolution—that all of the para-phernalia of stability be modified or discarded in favor of a new and untried product. The natural reaction is to resist such proposals." DeSi-mone further points out that "since the risk is great and the stakes large, a single error of judgment can seriously jeopardize the career of a corporate executive who, in his years of greatest responsibility, is likely to be between 45 and 65 years of age. That is not a time for great mobility. Where does he go after he has taken the great gamble and lost? Is it any wonder, then, that he has a strong tendency to avoid embracing new, untried, disruptive inventions."[23] Further, giant bureaucratic or-ganizations tend over time to clone themselves into centers of resistance to change. They "will naturally place emphasis upon the formal training and academic qualifications of those they employ," John Jewkes, David Sawers, and Richard Stillerman observe. "They will therefore become increasingly staffed by men who have been subject to common molding influences. There is a possibility of in-breeding from which the more eccentric strains of native originality may be excluded." As a result, "originality begins to fight a losing battle with the forces of ossifica-tion."[24]

Fourth, familiarity with a firm's various operations, customers, mar-kets, and needs seems to be an important stimulant to technical creativity and invention—a stimulant that is dissipated in the cavernous halls of giant bureaucracies. "To work most effectively," one student of the field found, "a technical man usually should be sensitive to the needs of the market for which the product is being developed, and he should be familiar with the production facilities and the personnel available to produce it. The difficulties inherent in trying to create this kind of familiarity among the technical people of a large development organization were described to me by one R&D director as 'momentous.' "[25]

Fifth, smaller size tends to reduce invention and innovation costs by promoting greater cost consciousness: "the cost of a single project is usually more important in a small company than in a large one, and the engineers know that. The resources devoted to a particular project usually represent a substantially greater percentage of the small company's resources. Particularly during the early years when no one is quite sure whether the company is going to make it, the knowledge that every dollar is important can cause an engineer to view the cost of a project as more important than he would view it in the opulent research establishments of many larger firms."[26] This helps smaller firms to hold down costs and to make their R&D activities more cost-effective.

INDUSTRIAL CONCENTRATION AND INNOVATION EFFICIENCY

If, as we have just seen, giant size is an organizational impediment to innovation efficiency, may it not still be true that a concentrated industry structure is a predicate to technological progress? May it not be true, as Galbraith contends, that the modern industry dominated by a few large firms is a well-nigh perfect instrument for inducing technical advance? Have we failed to recognize, as Schumpeter argued, the vital, dynamic role of monopoly and oligopoly in unleashing technological "gales of creative destruction"—gales whose consequences more than compensate society for any absence of old-fashioned competition?

To test this hypothesis, we shall examine the record of invention and innovation in three concentrated industries: steel, automobiles, and pain-control drugs. We shall then ask whether these case studies are representative or atypical illustrations of the relation between concentration and innovation efficiency.

INNOVATION LETHARGY: THE CASE OF STEEL

American steel has long been a prototype of a concentrated industry dominated by a few giant producers. As we saw in chapter 3, the largest firm in the field, the United States Steel Corporation, was created through the consolidation of some 180 formerly independent plants. The 4 largest producers collectively account for nearly 50 percent of domestic raw steel production, while the 8 largest hold a combined share of 70 percent of the industry. Rather than presenting a picture of sleek, efficient innovation, however, the record of the American steel industry is most notable for its technological backwardness and lethargic innovation.[27]

On the invention front, it is noteworthy that all major inventions in basic steelmaking have come from abroad. The modern steel industry dates from the invention of the Bessemer process by an Englishman, Henry Bessemer. The open-hearth furnace was developed by William Siemens, a German-born Englishman, and Pierre Émile Martin, a Frenchman. The basic oxygen process was invented by Robert Durrer, a professor of metallurgy in Berlin who conducted experiments at the minuscule Von Roll Werke in his native Switzerland. Continuous casting was devised by Siegfried Junghans, an individual German inventor, who at first conducted private experiments in the family-owned brass works. Vacuum degassing, first suggested by a nineteenth-century inventor, was brought to fruition by the Bochumer Verein, a German steel company rebuilding from the ravages of World War II. None of these major breakthroughs in basic steel making originated in the laboratories of the U.S. steel giants.

The U.S. steel oligopoly also lagged badly in adopting these inventions —both vis-à-vis their smaller domestic rivals and their foreign competitors. This is evident in the case of two key technological breakthroughs in basic steel making in the last thirty years—the oxygen furnace and continuous casting.

The oxygen furnace, a new, fast-melting technique and the most important technological invention in the industry since the turn of the century, was invented and first adopted by a minuscule Austrian steel company in 1950. It was first installed in the United States in 1954 by a small steel company (McLouth) and not adopted by the steel giants until a decade later. As of September 1963, the largest steel companies, operating more than 50 percent of the nation's basic steel capacity, had not installed a single oxygen furnace, whereas smaller companies, operating only 7 percent of domestic capacity, accounted for almost half of the oxygen furnace installations in the United States. Indeed, despite the fact that the new oxygen process entailed operating cost savings of roughly $5 per ton, capital savings of $20 to $25 per ton of installed capacity, and slashed "tap-to-tap" times between pourings, the U.S. oligopoly during the 1950s "bought 40 million tons of the wrong kind of capacity—the open hearth furnace."[28] Attesting to the seriousness of this technical faux pas, *Fortune* pointed out that much of this capacity "was obsolete when it was built," and the industry, by installing it, "prepared itself for dying."[29]

The belated adoption of continuous casting by the domestic steel oligopoly further illustrates its lethargic approach to technical change. This invention, which bypasses the laborious ingot-pouring process as well as the energy-intensive reheating of ingots and primary rolling, was pioneered in the United States by a small firm (Roanoke Electric) in 1962. Other small steel companies followed, so that by 1968, firms with roughly 3 percent of the nation's steel capacity accounted for 90 percent of the continuous-casting production in the United States. The record was embarrassing to the oligopoly. Said William P. Hill, engineering executive of National Steel: "there were eight companies operating continuous-casting machines before 1965 handling small tonnage. The outstanding thing was all of these companies were small, independent companies. They are competing by continuous-casting their entire tonnage. . . . It is a little embarrassing to some of us when we see this."[30]

Thus oligopoly in steel has served as something less than a perfect instrument for inducing technical advance. Rather, as Table 2 shows, a lethargic and technologically somnolent American steel oligopoly fell significantly behind the state of the art in Japan and Europe. And these figures *understate* the extent of the oligopoly's technical backwardness: American mini-mills were continuously casting 51 percent of their steel output by 1978, whereas the integrated oligopoly was producing only 11 percent of its output by this method.[31] To maintain that oligopolistic giantism has nurtured technical progressiveness in steel is, therefore, an exercise in self-delusion that today is belatedly being recognized as such.

TABLE 2
Modernization in the Steel Industry:
Growth in Use of Basic Oxygen Furnace and Continuous Casting,
As Percent of Total Production

	BASIC OXYGEN FURNACE		CONTINUOUS CASTING	
	1960 (Percent)	1981 (Percent)	1971 (Percent)	1984 (Percent)
United States	3.4	60.6	4.8	39.6
Japan	11.9	75.2	11.2	89.1
European Community	1.6	75.1	4.8	65.4

SOURCE: U.S. International Trade Commission, *Carbon and Certain Alloy Steel Products*, Report to the President (Washington, D.C.: July 1984), vol. 1, p. 102; International Iron and Steel Institute, *World Steel in Figures*, 1985.

INNOVATION FORBEARANCE: THE CASE OF THE AUTO INDUSTRY

Automobile production in the United States is, as we also have already seen, one of the most highly concentrated of all major American industries. Since World War II, the Big Three—General Motors, Ford, and Chrysler—have together controlled 90 percent or more of annual domestic auto output. These firms have over their many years of coexistence come to understand that price competition would only undermine their group profitability. Explains the *Wall Street Journal*: "Automakers can maximize profits because in the oligopolistic domestic auto industry the three major producers tend to copy each other's price moves. One auto executive notes that if one company lowered prices, the others would follow immediately. . . . As a result, price cuts wouldn't increase anybody's market share, and 'everybody would be worse off,' he says."[32]

But contrary to Schumpeterian suppositions, suppression of price competition in the automobile industry has *not* served to channel rivalrous instincts into innovation competition thereby sparking the rate of technological advance. Instead, giantism and high concentration have militated toward a parallel forbearance of competition in innovation that, in turn, has obstructed technical progress in the industry.

First, the rate and breadth of product innovation in the domestic industry were greatest in the decades preceding World War II, when the field was populated by a large number of independent producers, and new people with new ideas could put their ideas (the bad along with the good) into practice. The independents were a particularly fertile source of product innovation; owing to what Donald A. Moore has described as "competitive vigor born of necessity," the technological contributions by independents far exceeded their share of the market.[33]

Second, with the demise of the independents and the increase in industry concentration, the pace of product innovation significantly slackened. "I believe that the amount of product innovation successfully introduced into the automobile is smaller today than in previous times and is still falling," a Ford vice president told a gathering of auto engineers in 1964. "The automatic transmission was the last major innovation of the industry," he confessed.[34] Lawrence White confirmed this assessment a decade later: "The major features of today's automobiles—V-8 engines, automatic transmissions, power steering, and power brakes—are all pre-war innovations. These have been considerably improved and refined over the past twenty-five years, but still the industry has been uninterested in pursuing alternatives. The suspension, ignition, carburetion, and exhaust systems are fundamentally the same. Only the pressure of federal legislation on air pollution has effected any changes in these last three systems."[35] This diagnosis remains valid. According to John De-Lorean:

> Today's transverse-engine front-wheel-drive layouts differ little from the British Leyland mini of 25 years ago. . . .
>
> I remember my first visit to the G.M. proving ground in October 1956. I rode in a 1956 Chevrolet with John Dolza, G.M.'s noted engine engineer. In this particular car, he had rigged the V-8 engine to run on all eight cylinders when maximum power was required and to cruise at highway speeds on only four cylinders to save fuel. That was 24 years ago. A Cadillac advertisement recently touted that a V-8 that accelerates on eight cylinders and cruises on four is 1981's hottest feature.[36]

As one U.S. senator observed, "Back garage inventors and operators have done more, far more in the way of innovative research and development than has Detroit."[37]

Third, the Big Three auto companies have relied heavily on their suppliers for technological advances: "The parts suppliers—for example, Bendix, Budd, Kelsey-Hayes, Wagner Electric, Borg-Warner, Dana, Thompson Products (now TRW), Motorola, and Electric Auto-Lite—did much of the pioneering development work on new items like power steering, power brakes, ball joints, alternators, transistorized ignition, and others. . . . Similarly, the materials suppliers—steel, aluminum, glass, plastics, and paint companies—have provided much of the development work on new uses of materials. Effectively, the auto companies have allowed their suppliers to take the risks and absorb the initial costs of developing new technology."[38]

Fourth, contrary to what apologists would have us believe, high concentration and elephantine firm size have nurtured neither appetite nor will for technological risk-taking. The domestic oligopoly's technical timidity contrasts rather sharply with the performance and attitude of foreign auto producers. "I think one element of what foreign auto companies bring to the automotive game is simply a risk-taking front-end posture to try to do some things that we declare to be too risky," James Swain, manager of automotive research programs at Battelle Laboratories, observes. "It is interesting that the only stratified-charge engine in production in a passenger car anywhere in the world today is in the Japanese car—the Honda CVCC. The only Wankel engine in any substantial production anywhere in the world today is the Japanese car—the Mazda. I am not necessarily a proponent of either of those two things from a technological standpoint, but it is evidence of a risk-taking posture."[39]

Fifth, the domestic oligopoly's record in the field of process innovation and adoption of more efficient production methods is equally uninspiring. Here, too, the Japanese have aggressively sought out, experimented with, and adopted new production and management methods. In fact, superior Japanese process innovation rests in important part on the deployment of *American* tools and equipment marketed by *American* equipment manufacturers from the 1950s onward—tools and equipment in which the U.S. oligopoly was uninterested. "This is all a U.S. development," auto productivity expert James Harbour exclaimed while examining Japanese car-manufacturing prowess before a congressional committee. "I am not selling for them, but Danley Press of Chicago developed this system in 1958. The only people they could sell it to were the Japanese, Yugoslavians, and Russians."[40]

Thus, while the U.S. automobile industry is a highly concentrated field traditionally dominated by a triopoly of corporate giants, the actual record of efficiency in innovation in the industry hardly comports with the beatific images purveyed by promoters of bigness. As summarized by one former high-ranking GM official, the domestic industry's record marks "a quarter-century of technical hibernation. In the place of product innovation, the automobile industry went on a two-decade marketing binge which generally offered up the same old product under the guise of something new and useful. There really was nothing essentially new. . . . Each year all we were offering to the customer was a supper warmed over."[41] And instead of any trade-off between price competition and technological advance, bigness in the American automobile industry has offered neither—at least until foreign firms forced the domestic oligopoly to stir from its postwar technical slumber.

INNOVATION SUPPRESSION: THE CASE OF PAIN-CONTROL DRUGS

The market for pain-control drugs sold over the counter is also a concentrated field wherein the four largest producers collectively account for more than half of total sales. Johnson & Johnson is the largest seller in the market; its Tylenol tablets generated sales of $690 million from 1975 through 1979, profits of $134 million, and a pretax profit margin on sales of 19 percent—more than double the margin recorded in the aggregate by all U.S. manufacturing firms in the same period.[42]

The recent record of innovation in the pain-control field reveals that rather than helplessly surrendering themselves to technological progress, powerful firms can rather conveniently vitiate the Schumpeterian gales of creative destruction by gaining control of, and suppressing, potentially competitive technologies.

In 1971, two independent researchers succeeded in designing a solid-state, non-implanted electronic nerve stimulator, or TENS, as a drug-free means for relieving and controlling pain. By utilizing electrical impulses transmitted through pads attached to the patient's skin, TENS blocked the transmission of pain sensations along nerve fibers, thereby ameliorating pain. First constructed by one of the inventors in his basement, the TENS device proved successful in treating headaches, back pain, post-surgical pain, dental pain, arthritic pain, and orthopedic pain. Moreover, unlike over-the-counter drugs, TENS was nonaddictive, non-narcotic, and produced virtually no side effects. The company founded by the inventors to commercialize their device, StimTech, began marketing TENS in 1972. The device was (accurately) promoted as an alternative to ingested drugs which, Judge Miles W. Lord found, "have proven dangerous side effects, especially when used for extended periods of time."

The competition that this new technology potentially posed for over-the-counter pain-control drugs was not lost on Johnson & Johnson, and in 1974, it acquired control of StimTech. That Johnson & Johnson's objective was something other than to unleash technical gales of creative destruction—at the expense of its profitable Tylenol trade—subsequently became clear. Once it had acquired StimTech, Johnson & Johnson delayed the introduction of new products by StimTech; refused to provide StimTech with funds for research and development; imposed an internal pricing system on StimTech products transferred to other Johnson & Johnson divisions that weakened StimTech's cash position; forbade the display of StimTech products at annual meetings; refused to permit StimTech to use the Johnson & Johnson name; imposed a hiring freeze on StimTech; turned down at least $200,000 of orders; prohibited the planning and construction of factories abroad; refused to promote the concept of pain clinics as centers where doctors could refer patients for instruction in the use of TENS devices; and prohibited StimTech from entering international markets. Nor were the consequences of Johnson & Johnson's strategy difficult to discern. "In this case," Judge Lord observed, "Johnson & Johnson's actions resulted in countless individuals having to suffer the debilitating side effects of pain-killing drugs because a product which can afford them the relief they seek without such adverse effects was withheld from competition. . . . The evidence is such that had TENS not been suppressed, it could have benefited millions of people throughout the world." He ruled that Johnson & Johnson had unlawfully restrained innovation.

In this case, then, industry concentration conferred the ability to control invention and to forestall technical advance. It conferred the power to protect an established, lucrative market from competitive encroachment. It produced consequences conspicuously at variance with the "creative destruction" model.

In the foregoing examples, high industry concentration clearly was not an ideal instrument for inducing technological progress. It did not yield the beneficial results touted by the popular propagandists and their academic counterparts. But how typical are these examples? Do they represent more than anecdotal and episodic evidence? After surveying a plethora of statistical cross-section studies, Frederic M. Scherer concludes that "very high concentration has a favorable effect only in rare cases, and more often it is apt to retard progress by restricting the number of independent sources of initiative and by dampening firms' incentive to gain market position through accelerated research and development."[43] Nor is high industry concentration conducive to greater risk-taking in research; cross-industry results "provide little or no indication that very concentrated industries tend to devote a relatively large percentage of R&D to basic research and to long-term, ambitious, and risky projects."[44]

Some business leaders are beginning to recognize as much. In their managerial planning, they are beginning to transcend the bigness mystique that so long dominated their corporate belief system. They are beginning to abjure what they once accepted without question as the conventional wisdom. For example, when he was questioned on 19 March 1985 by the *Detroit Free Press* regarding innovative information-processing systems for the Saturn small-car project, the chairman of General Motors, Roger B. Smith, confided: "Where is all this great stuff coming from? It's not really coming out of IBM . . . it's coming out of little two- and three-man companies, because they're finding out that forty guys can't do something that three people can do. It's just the law of human nature."[45] Other corporate leaders are now launching small, organizationally separate "start-up" subsidiaries that, they anticipate, will be more inventive and entrepreneurial in spirit.[46]

Could it be that some day the Fortune 500 will march into the high-tech future under a banner emblazoned with the revolutionary slogan "Small Is Beautiful"?

CHAPTER 5

SOCIAL EFFICIENCY

As economists we are concerned with how resources may be allocated *efficiently*, and we are prepared to provide the layman and the policymaker with a rigorous definition of efficiency. But "efficient allocation" for whose benefit?
— Robert Aaron Gordon, presidential address, American Economics Association, 1975

Social efficiency is a rough measure of general consumer welfare. This means producing the most desirable combination of goods and services from among those that are technologically possible. It implies questioning whether a different set of permutations and combinations would be socially more desirable or serviceable. Hence, it is a concept much broader in scope than operating efficiency or innovation efficiency. The former is concerned with producing Hula Hoops at the lowest possible cost; the latter involves the search for superior techniques of producing Hula Hoops. Social efficiency deals with the question of whether Hula Hoops should be produced at all—that is, whether society's scarce resources might be more felicitously employed in alternative uses.

That bigness has assumed society's planning function in controlling resource allocation is not seriously questioned. Summarizing American economic development since the Civil War, conservative business historian Alfred D. Chandler, Jr., writes that the "modern business enterprise took the place of market mechanisms in coordinating the activities of the economy and allocating its resources. . . . As modern business enterprise acquired functions hitherto carried out by the market, it became the most powerful institution in the American economy and its managers the most influential group of economic decision makers."[1] Current statistics support Chandler's thesis: The largest 0.1 percent of U.S. manufacturing firms collectively control approximately two-thirds of total domestic assets devoted to manufacturing, while the largest 0.2 percent control three-fourths.[2] Conglomerateur and former ITT chairman Harold Geneen acknowledged the obvious when he asserted: "Increasingly, the larger corporations have become the primary custodians of making our entire system work."[3]

According to the exponents of bigness, this concentration of economy-wide control is as it should be. Bigness, they assure us, is best qualified to perform society's planning function and, therefore, is best able to secure social efficiency. The former chairman of Dow Chemical, Carl Gerstacker, contends that the "problems of our times will require greater, bigger organizations than we have now, rather than smaller ones, for their solution." For this reason he admonishes us to "cast aside our outmoded notions of size and our fear of bigness."[4] Similarly, a former Exxon president informs us that "the large enterprise has the means, capabilities, and experience to perform large-scale economic tasks in a socially responsible manner when given the opportunity and flexibility to do so."[5]

Although bigness has arrogated unto itself the role of "making our entire system work," the core questions of social efficiency remain: Work for whom? For what purpose? To what ends does bigness exercise its planning power in allocating society's resources? Are the ends of bigness necessarily in accord with society's best interests? What social consequences flow from the exercise of this planning power, and for whom? Or, to use a standard suggested long ago by Professor Allyn Young, does bigness represent the kind of economic organization best calculated to give us the kind of society we want?[6]

We shall pose these questions for analysis in three areas—the automobile industry, energy, and corporate conglomerates. We shall see that, contrary to the foregoing rationalizations, bigness can exercise its planning power in ways and toward ends that subvert—not promote—social efficiency and, further, that there is no accountability mechanism to protect the public from antisocial exercise of the planning power.

THE AUTOMOBILE INDUSTRY

As we have seen in earlier chapters, the American automobile industry is a powerful triopoly dominated by General Motors. As one Detroit executive described it: "General Motors is the kind of institution whose like doesn't exist elsewhere in Western civilization. It is America's Japan."[7] At times the nation's largest industrial corporation, at times the second largest, GM can boast of some 750,000 employees in 39 countries; 957,000 stockholders; $83.9 billion in sales and $4.5 billion in profits in 1984; and $52 billion in assets. Its headquarters in Detroit exudes the impression of a stability that outlasts time.

Like its fellow triopolists, Ford and Chrysler, General Motors is integrated horizontally and vertically. Like them, it is integrated internationally, ranking among the largest motor vehicle manufacturers in a myriad of nations around the globe. Like them, it is highly diversified; until recently, for example, General Motors controlled the production of 75 percent of our city and intercity buses, 100 percent of our passenger locomotives, and 80 percent of our freight locomotives.

Such bigness, according to John Kenneth Galbraith, reflects the modern-day exigencies of planning, rather than a lust for monopoly or a quest for efficiency. "The size of General Motors," he writes, "is in the service not of monopoly or the economies of scale but of planning. And for this planning—control of supply, control of demand, provision of capital, minimization of risk—there is no clear upper limit to the desirable size. The corporate form accommodates to this need. Quite clearly it allows the firm to be very, very large."[8]

But what kind of planning does General Motors do? Is the planning sound because the firm is big? Is it calculated to serve the company's self-interest or the national interest? Can we automatically assume (with former Secretary of Defense Charles Wilson) that what is good for General Motors is good for the country, and what is good for the country is good for General Motors? How good has GM's planning been in the past? What has been its impact on urban transportation, smog and air pollution, conservation of energy, auto safety, and so forth? Has it contributed to the solution of these problems or compounded them? In short, to what extent has GM's planning promoted social efficiency? The record is revealing.

URBAN TRANSPORTATION

An important component of social efficiency in urban areas concerns the particular combination of alternative transport modes (mass-transit railways, trolleys, gasoline buses, private passenger cars) best able to move large numbers of people quickly, comfortably, at low cost, and with the least use of scarce land and space. In reality, of course, urban transportation systems are overwhelmingly dominated by the private automobile

—a transport mix that in many respects represents the *least* socially efficient system. As urban expert Wilfred Owen points out, the preeminence of the private car results in

> congestion, pollution, and a growing sense of frustration. Where all-out efforts have been made to accommodate the car, the streets are still congested, commuting is increasingly difficult, urban aesthetics have suffered, and the quality of life has been eroded. In an automotive age, cities have become the negation of communities—a setting for machines instead of people. The automobile has taken over, and motorist and nonmotorist alike are caught up in the congestion, and everyone is a victim of the damaging side effects of the conflict between the car and the community.[9]

Indeed, former Secretary of Transportation Alan Boyd once noted that the description of a city under siege would differ little from that of a contemporary large American city at rush hour.

The actual mix of urban transport modes is neither accidental nor is it due solely to the autonomous play of free market forces innocently responding to the command of consumer preference. Instead, the automobile industry (and General Motors, in particular) has played a decisive role in *planning* an urban transportation system best suited to its own rather than the public interest.

As the nation's dominant producer of buses as well as automobiles, General Motors understood at an early date that if urban railways could be eliminated as a viable competitive option, the sales of its buses could be vastly expanded. And if transit systems using buses could subsequently be made to decline or fail, a huge market would open up for additional sales of private automobiles. Anything that reduced the attractiveness of urban mass transportation—its speed, cleanliness, or reliability—would be perceived as a desirable trend from GM's private perspective, adverse public consequences for urban congestion to the contrary notwithstanding.

According to the findings of a federal court (sustaining a conviction for criminal conspiracy to violate the nation's antitrust laws), General Motors was instrumental in organizing National City Lines, an operating company that proceeded to engineer the demise of forty-six electric mass-transit systems in forty-five cities in sixteen states.[10] Through its National City Lines subsidiary, GM and its coconspirators (a tire producer and an oil company) gained control of urban rail transit systems, literally destroyed them, and replaced them with GM buses.

The impact of GM's planning in one city has been graphically described by Bradford Snell:

> Thirty-five years ago Los Angeles was a beautiful city of lush palm trees, fragrant orange groves and ocean-clean air. It was served then by the world's largest electric railway network. In the late 1930's General Motors and allied highway interests acquired the local transit companies, scrapped their pollution-free electric trains, tore down their power transmission lines, ripped up their tracks, and placed GM buses on already congested Los Angeles streets. The noisy, foul-smelling buses turned earlier patrons of the high-speed rail system away from public transit and, in effect, sold millions of private automobiles. Largely as a result, this city is today an ecological wasteland: the palm trees are dying of petrochemical smog; the orange groves have been paved over by 300 miles of freeways; the air is a septic tank into which 4 million cars, half of them built by General Motors, pump 13,000 tons of pollutants daily.[11]

The former mayor of San Francisco, Joseph L. Alioto, reports that GM's "planning" produced similar results in his city.[12]

In this not insignificant field, then, private planning by bigness can hardly be construed to have been in the service of social efficiency. As transportation expert George Smerk has concluded: "Street railways and trolley bus operations, even if better suited to traffic needs and the public interest, were doomed in favor of the vehicles and material produced by the [National City Lines] conspirators."[13]

AUTOMOTIVE FUEL CONSUMPTION AND THE SMALL CAR

In an ever-industrializing world of fixed, nonrenewable petroleum reserves, the fuel economy designed into automobiles produced by the Big Three not only critically affects their competitive viability but, more broadly, decisively influences the nation's petroleum consumption and its dependence on geopolitically volatile foreign energy sources. Automotive fuel economy thus is crucial to the nation's industrial health and economic security. And, to a not insignificant degree, it determines the urgency, as well as the eventual success, of national energy policy. Given its importance in all of the foregoing respects, fuel economy thus provides a second test of social efficiency and bigness in autos. The Big Three's now familiar (and lackluster) performance in this field paints a less than flattering picture of planning prowess—either with regard to the industry's own private interest or relative to that of the nation.

First, the Big Three traditionally considered neither the fuel efficiency of their products, nor limited petroleum supplies, to be a matter of serious concern. They ignored warnings of impending fuel shortages, even when voiced by responsible officials within the industry itself.[14] When the general manager of GM's Buick division was asked in 1958 what steps his division was taking in the area of fuel efficiency, he flippantly replied: "Oh, we're helping the gas companies, the same as our competitors."[15] Only months before the first OPEC oil embargo in 1973, GM's chairman stressed nuclear power as an important means for resolving the nation's energy "question." One month before the overthrow of the Shah in 1979 and the onset of the nation's second energy crisis in six years, General Motors assured the American public that automotive "fuel economy standards are not necessary and they are not good for America."[16] Likewise, the domestic oligopoly seemed uninterested in engine innovations (including alternative power plants) capable of enhancing fuel economy. A parade of inventors, scientists, and engineers testified to the companies' indifference during congressional hearings conducted in 1973.[17]

As a consequence of the industry's nonchalant attitude, the fuel efficiency of U.S. automobiles steadily worsened from 1958 to 1973. In part, this decline was attributable to the installation of pollution controls (which, as we shall see in the next section, was aggravated by the industry's delinquency on the smog control front), but the principal cause was the increasingly bloated size and weight of the cars the industry elected to produce in its race for styling supremacy. For example, "in 1958 the [Chevrolet] Impala weighed 4,000 pounds and ran at an efficiency of 12.1 mpg; by 1973 the size of the Impala . . . ballooned to 5,500 pounds with an efficiency of only 8.5 mpg."[18] All told, a team of economists estimated styling rivalry to have artificially inflated automobile gasoline consumption by more than 18 billion gallons between 1950 and 1960.[19] Of course, this rendered the industry highly vulnerable to the flood of fuel-efficient imports that eventually swamped the American market in the wake of successive gasoline shortages and skyrocketing fuel prices. Attesting to a less than brilliant display of planning wizardry, *Fortune* later pointed out that had the government not imposed fuel economy standards on the industry, "the auto companies, especially Chrysler, might have been even less prepared than they were for the . . . swing in customer preferences to small cars."[20]

Second, the Big Three's studied refusal to develop the fuel-efficient and inexpensive portion of the car market further exacerbated the nation's petroleum problems, and indeed eventually proved catastrophic for the auto industry and the vast industrial complex dependent on it.

As early as the 1940s, the United Auto Workers urged Detroit to build a small, fuel-efficient car, citing an opinion survey conducted by the

Society of Automotive Engineers that revealed 60 percent of the public favored this type of automobile.[21] Later, a committee of the National Academy of Engineering found that a secular shift in consumer preferences toward small cars "was evident long before OPEC quadrupled the price of crude oil. From 1967 to 1972, for example, the large-car share fell from 71.5 to 57.8 percent, with most of the decline coming from the standard group. At the same time the share of subcompacts more than doubled to reach 22 percent." The academy observed that this long-term evolution in demand toward small cars did *not* occur overnight; instead it "reflected fundamental demographic trends (increased suburbanization, shifts in the age structure, changes in female participation in the labor force) and the growth of multicar families."[22]

Rather than recognizing this evolution in consumer demand, anticipating it, or astutely reacting to it, planning by the Big Three was directed toward ignoring consumer demand and the market, avoiding competition in small cars, and thereby protecting what they perceived as being best for collective, short-run profits.

The Big Three did not seriously undertake to manufacture and market small, fuel-efficient cars until the 1970s, at least in the American market,[23] and only then in the face of energy crises, government-mandated fuel economy standards, and growing foreign competition. Attempts were occasionally made to meet successive import surges, for example, with the appearance of the compact car in the late 1950s, and the subcompacts of the 1960s. But these efforts were, at best, half-hearted and dilatory. In 1962, for example, Ford canceled the planned introduction of its Cardinal, featuring a front-mounted, four cylinder engine and front-wheel drive—a compact car quite similar to the X-cars, Escort, and Omni of the 1980s.[24] The Big Three generally, and General Motors in particular, persisted in their delusion that the small, fuel-efficient car was an aberration. "Of all Detroit auto makers," *Fortune* reported, "GM has been the most scoffingly skeptical of the prospects of the small car in the U.S. market. If GM has said it once, it's said it ten thousand times: 'A good used car is the answer to the American public's need for cheap transportation.' "[25]

This delusion on the part of the Big Three was reinforced by the concentrated structure of the industry and their oligopolistic efforts to protect group profits. According to industry expert Lawrence J. White, General Motors, Ford, and Chrysler each seemed to recognize that vigorous entry into small cars by any one of them would trigger entry into the field by the others. Further, each firm seemed to believe that the demand for small cars was not large enough to permit profits acceptable to the group if all of them should enter this segment of the market.

"Twice, one or two of the Big Three pulled back from plunging ahead with a small car when the market did not look large enough for all three. . . . A sizable niche might well have been carved out at the bottom of the market by a Big Three producer in 1950, or again, with a 'sub compact' in 1962 or 1963. Room-for-all considerations, however, appeared to rule this out."[26] Buttressing this "room-for-all" Weltanschauung was the apparent desire by each of the Big Three to protect their above-average profits in large cars by withholding the small car as an inexpensive substitute: "In this behavior, the Big Three definitely recognized their mutual interdependence, since in the absence of retaliation by rivals a single firm contemplating the production of a small car should have expected to gain more profits from stealing the dissatisfied customers from other firms than he would lose from dissatisfied customers of his own large cars. . . . But the Big Three mutually contemplating a small car could only see lost profits from reduced sales of large cars."[27]

Of course the extent, magnitude, and consequences of the Big Three's misdirected and inept planning in the field of automotive fuel economy and the small car became evident beginning in the 1970s. With the industry and the nation rocked by successive oil shortages, gasoline lines and crises, a torrent of small fuel-efficient cars imported from abroad, record losses and layoffs in automobile plants that reverberated throughout American industry, and the collapse of Chrysler (the nation's tenth largest industrial corporation) in 1978, a dispassionate observer might be forgiven for finding bigness in the auto industry to be in the service of something other than astute planning and social efficiency.

AUTOMOTIVE SMOG AND AIR POLLUTION

By the early 1960s the typical American automobile spewed approximately one ton of pollutants per year into the nation's atmosphere, and motor vehicles accounted for an estimated 60 percent of all air pollution.[28] It first became an acute problem in southern California, but automotive air pollution soon afflicted virtually every major metropolitan area. Here as elsewhere, however, the Big Three's planning performance hardly marks a triumph of social efficiency.

First, they denied that automotive smog was a problem—observation as well as internal company research results to the contrary notwithstanding.[29] "Waste vapors are dissipated in the atmosphere quickly and do not present an air pollution problem," Ford Motor Company lectured Los Angeles county supervisors in the 1950s. "The fine automotive power plants which modern-day engineers design do not 'smoke.' "[30]

Second, as automotive air pollution worsened, and as national concern rose, the Big Three elected to eliminate rivalry between themselves in the research, development, and commercialization of pollution control technology. In an antitrust suit filed in 1969 (which the industry did not contest), the Justice Department found that the auto giants "conspired not to compete in research, development, manufacture, and installation of [pollution] control devices, and did all in their power to delay such research, development, manufacturing, and installation." Specifically, they ignored promising inventions, refused to purchase pollution controls developed by others, delayed installing smog controls already available and known to them, and, at times, disciplined individual members of the cartel whose team "loyalty" flagged temporarily. "Since the industry was fortified from the beginning of the program with the agreement among its members not to take competitive advantage over each other," the Justice Department found, "all auto manufacturers were able through the years to stall, delay, impede and retard research, development, production and installation of motor vehicle air pollution control equipment."[31]

Third, in the 1970s, and under intense public pressure, the Big Three compounded the problem by hastily seizing on the catalytic converter as the preferred pollution-control device—a device that the National Academy of Sciences characterized as "the most disadvantageous with respect to first cost, fuel economy, maintainability, and durability." Said the academy: "It is unfortunate that the automobile industry did not seriously undertake such a [pollution control] program on its own volition until it was subjected to governmental pressure. A relatively modest investment, over the past decade, in developmental programs related to emission control could have precluded the crisis that now prevails in the industry and the nation. The current crash programs of the major manufacturers have turned out to be expensive and, in retrospect, not well planned."[32]

In the light of the evidence, has bigness been a boon to social efficiency in the areas of urban transportation, automotive fuel economy, and automotive air pollution? Hardly. In these fields, planning was either nonexistent or was carried out in a manner that fundamentally conflicted with the public interest.[33] As an official of the Department of Transportation points out, nobody at General Motors can say exactly how the decision was eventually made to "downsize" the company's fleet: "The fact is that GM didn't make the decision by itself. The government helped the company. The government forced GM to take a critical look at its cars—first by setting standards for safety, then by setting standards for cleaner air, and, finally, by setting miles-per-gallon standards for fuel efficiency. Without the miles-per-gallon standards, GM would never have downsized the way it did. But the GM executives fought the standards every step of the way. Even now, they're so tied up in their ideology that they can't admit what the government did for them"—or, more accurately, that their nonfeasance as a social-planning agency compelled the government to perform that role in the interest of social efficiency.[34]

ENERGY

The energy field, while less concentrated than the automobile sector, is dominated by a handful of the nation's—indeed, the world's—very largest corporations. American petroleum companies occupy eleven slots among the twenty largest U.S. industrial firms, and six of them rank among the fifteen largest industrial concerns in the world.[35] The sixteen majors are highly integrated vertically in the production, refining, pipeline transportation, and marketing of crude oil and refined petroleum products; they collectively control an estimated 82 percent of the nation's crude reserves, 75 percent of its refining capacity, 68 percent of retail gasoline sales, and upward of 90 percent of U.S. petroleum pipeline capacity. They are also highly diversified into substitute fuels: in addition to their petroleum holdings, oil and gas companies own at least half of the nation's privately held coal reserves, own nearly half of its proved uranium reserves, and directly or indirectly control 90 percent of solar-energy sales.[36] And they are integrally intertwined with one another through an extensive network of intercorporate relationships, including joint production ventures, joint bidding arrangements, joint ownership and operation of pipelines, exchange agreements, intercorporate stockholdings, and interlocking directorships.[37] In short, energy is administered as a "planning system which operates on an essentially global scale" and commands "extraordinary financial and physical resources greater than those of most industries and many nation states."[38]

But to what ends, and for what purposes, is this intricate planning system administered? With what consequences? With respect to national security, for example, one would suppose that planning in the public interest be directed to two primary objectives: the conservation of domestic crude reserves so as to have them available in periods of national emergency, and the development of alternative energy technologies in order to lessen our dependence on dwindling petroleum supplies. Has the planning by the energy giants promoted these objectives and thus served social efficiency? The evidence suggests that it has not.

PROTECTIONISM AND THE DEPLETION OF
DOMESTIC CRUDE RESERVES

From 1957 to 1973—first on a voluntary, and soon after on a mandatory basis—the U.S. government restricted the importation of foreign crude oil and petroleum products. Originally, these quota restrictions were inaugurated at the behest of, and in concert with, the oil giants. They were not abandoned until OPEC triggered the first energy crisis in 1973. "The primary objective of our government's oil import control program," Exxon's chairman told his stockholders, "has been the maintenance of our national security, or to be more precise, the maintenance of oil reserves at a level adequate to assure our fuel requirements in times of national emergency or international crisis."[39]

Putting aside (for the moment) the symbiotically intimate relationship between Big Oil and OPEC, how rational was the policy of import restrictions, if the goal was national security?[40] Would it not have been preferable to minimize the depletion of *domestic* reserves in peacetime, while maximizing our reliance on *foreign* crude sources—especially those that might be beyond reach in the event of military conflict or instability in politically volatile regions like the Middle East? Viewed from this perspective, Big Oil's success in obtaining import protection may have served its self-interest by artificially inflating oil prices in the United States; it certainly did not improve the country's national security posture.

First, as a result of import restraints, domestic reserves were consumed at an *artificially accelerated* rate, while low-cost, readily available foreign supplies were kept from the American market. As of 1974, Professor Jesse Markham calculated, "we have been drawing down our known domestic reserves by roughly a million barrels a day over the past few years while we were restricting imports. That was during the first period, when foreign oil over much of that period was relatively cheaper than oil in the United States. The presumption, therefore, is that [had] we not been restricting imports, the price mechanism . . . would have used foreign oil rather than drawn down our known reserves."[41]

Second, the United States thus was *less* self-sufficient in petroleum, and became *more* vulnerable to oil embargoes and crises. As Professor Alfred Kahn explained to a congressional committee during the height of the first oil shortage, Big Oil's protectionist planning "accelerated the exhaustion of our cheap and readily available sources of energy, so that now, when the rainy day comes, we are less well off than before."[42]

In this case, then, bigness—aided and abetted by government—compounded the problem of energy *in*security. Private planning did not make for social efficiency. One can only wonder with Kahn "whether we would have clung so long to quotas . . . were it not for the interest of the major oil companies in the protection of the American price that the quotas provided."[43] Milton Friedman provided a blunt answer: "The political power of the oil industry, not national security, is the reason for the present subsidies to the industry. International disturbances simply offer a convenient excuse."[44]

SUPPRESSION OF ALTERNATIVE ENERGY SOURCES
Throughout the 1970s, the American Petroleum Institute was fond of lecturing motorists that "A Country That Runs on Oil Can't Afford to Run Short." This implied not only the conservation of existing oil and gas resources and the search for new supplies, but the aggressive development of alternative energy sources and the technologies to render their use economic. It called for a new look at coal, shale oil, tar sands, uranium, and—above all—the production of "synthetic" fuels by the liquefaction and gasification of our abundant coal reserves.

The institute had no doubt about the best way to proceed. It was prepared to entrust the development of energy alternatives to the same power bloc that already dominated the supply of conventional fuels, i.e., Big Oil. Institute spokesmen assured us that the major oil companies "have proven skills in managing large-capital projects," that their "financial strength can be a great asset in generating the large amounts of capital needed," that they are "interested in maximizing the use of their technical and managerial expertise and experience and their financial resources by entering business activities to which they are especially well suited," and that diversified energy giantism will "make the most of the vast potential of all our nation's energy resources."[45] In this view, energy security and social efficiency would be assured by permitting the major oil companies to transform themselves into multifuel energy conglomerates.

The flaws in this policy posture should be self-evident. When a giant business firm is engaged in multidimensional operations, when it can choose among its various investments, retarding or suppressing some while favoring others, there are no guarantees that its price and product policy will be the same as that of many independent competing firms immune from any conflicts of interest. When investment strategies and price policies are shaped not by vigorous and independent marketplace competition but by committees of top executives of Exxon, Gulf, Texaco, Mobil, Socal, and so on, there is little likelihood that energy scarcities will not be intensified rather than moderated. Can we really expect the petroleum giants to undermine their stake in depletable oil and gas resources —the value and profitability of which are enhanced by their progressive scarcity—by investing the huge sums required to promote the rapid development of economically viable substitutes? Can these firms be realistically expected to unleash those Schumpeterian gales of creative destruction that would signal an end to their market dominance? Can we expect them to be oblivious of the maxim that a person cannot serve two (or more) masters and be equally loyal to each? Or the principle that no firm can reasonably be expected to compete with itself?

Obviously, public policy incurs a major risk in permitting the petroleum giants, with their heavy investments in conventional fuels, to play a significant role in deciding what energy substitutes shall be brought on stream, at what rate, at what cost, and at whose expense. It runs a risk in delegating to a private power complex—neither subject to the discipline of competition or to effective government regulation, nor possessed of a reassuring record of public service—the discretion to plan our industrial future. The point is not academic or conjectural. The risk, as we shall see forthwith, is real.

In the 1920s, the German chemical combine I.G. Farben made a spectacular technological breakthrough that enabled it to produce synthetic gasoline from coal.[46] As the world's largest oil company, Standard Oil of New Jersey (now Exxon) had a direct and immediate interest in this development, which posed a potential threat of monumental proportions. A Standard Oil executive, dispatched to Germany at the time, reported: "Based upon my observations and discussion today, I think that this matter is the most important which has ever faced the company since [its 1911 antitrust] dissolution. . . . [Farben] can make high grade motor fuel from lignite and other low quality coals. . . . This means absolutely the independence of Europe on the matter of gasoline supply." He expressed the fear that, under the circumstances, "straight price competition is all that is left."

In 1929, pursuant to a "marriage" contract between Standard Oil and Farben, Standard obtained worldwide ownership and control (except for Germany) "of I.G.'s hydrogenation processes and any future I.G. processes for making synthetically products having similar uses to those of customary petroleum refinery products, from whatever raw material they might be derived." Not surprisingly, perhaps, Standard's planning aimed at something other than boldly championing synthetic gasoline at the expense of its vast holdings of crude. According to a Twentieth Century Fund study, the manner in which Standard used its rights "shows clearly that its main object in acquiring them was to strengthen its control over the oil industry. . . . Standard and Shell did little to encourage widespread synthetic production of liquid fuels and lubricants from coal. They had acquired these processes primarily to protect their own vast interests in petroleum." A former Standard Oil president conceded as much in an internal company document: "There is little doubt in our minds," he wrote, "but what, if other than oil companies had dominated the situation, the management's conduct of the business would have been along lines better calculated to secure the maximum return on the capital invested."

Recent evidence indicates that the Standard-Farben episode is neither an isolated nor unrepresentative incident of ancient history. Apparently restraint of alternative-fuels development seems to continue to pervade Big Oil's private planning. In the 1970s, for example, in a company document recently uncovered by Canadian antitrust authorities, an official of Humble (an Exxon subsidiary) summarized the firm's planning objectives for alternative-fuels technologies:

> It is therefore desirable for Humble to do research work on shale and coal to know where the processes are headed. . . .
>
> In the meantime, it should not itself initiate commercial production, or take other action or make announcements that would motivate other companies to initiate commercial production or even development.
>
> It is felt that there is a fair amount of mass psychology in the industry and that, while many companies would prefer to go slow because of their domestic crude interests . . . they would feel compelled to start plants if others did and particularly so if a company with the stature of Humble did.[47]

The name of the game, it would seem, was not the development of energy alternatives but their suppression.

Private planning by the energy giants has been something less than a triumph in social efficiency and intelligent resource allocation. Bigness has successfully lobbied for protectionist policies that wastefully depleted dwindling domestic crude reserves; has acted to stifle development of alternative-fuels technologies capable of reducing American dependence on declining petroleum reserves—foreign as well as domestic; and has posed as a champion of competition while dedicating itself to limiting production by private means where possible, and by manipulation of governments where necessary, in order to maintain a "palatable" price structure.[48] Like any quintessential cartel, pervasively protected and generously subsidized by a compliant government, Big Oil has seldom confused its self-interest with the public interest. The promotion of social efficiency was never its strong suit.

CORPORATE CONGLOMERATES

In the last two chapters, we have seen that the conglomerate giant, controlling subsidiaries flung across a dizzying array of functionally unrelated industries and markets, cannot be rationalized either on grounds of superior operating efficiency or efficient innovation. To round out our assessment, we shall now explore the conglomerate's virtues as an instrument of social efficiency. We shall inquire whether conglomerate giantism is conducive to a more intelligent and socially desirable allocation of resources—whether its contribution in this regard is so great as to compensate for its weakness in other areas.

The defenders of bigness contend that capital markets are an imperfect method for optimizing society's investment decisions and its planning for future output patterns of goods and services. Decentralized decision-making by myriads of lenders and borrowers, they contend, is not only based on inadequate information, but involves unnecessary (hence wasteful) transaction costs. The planning of investment expenditures, they argue, is best accomplished through centralized generation, control, and allocation of capital from *within* the giant conglomerate. Such centralized planning, Professor Oliver E. Williamson claims, yields superior results for three reasons: "First, it is an internal rather than external control mechanism with the constitutional authority and expertise to make detailed evaluations of the performance of each of its operating parts. Second, it can make fine-tuning as well as discrete adjustments. This permits it both to intervene early in a selective, preventative way (a capability which the capital market lacks altogether), as well as to perform *ex post* corrective adjustments, in response to evidence of performance failure, with a surgical precision that the capital market lacks. . . . Finally, the costs of intervention by the general office are relatively low." Williamson thus sees the conglomerate "as capitalism's creative response to the evident limits which the capital market experiences in its relations to the firm."[49]

How valid is this claim? Are giant conglomerates, in reality, superior to capital markets in managing and planning the flow of the economy's capital funds? Does conglomerate giantism, in fact, mark an institutional and organizational breakthrough in capital management and planning? Does such centralized control foster a more intelligent and enlightened allocation of investment funds? The evidence suggests not.

First, the recent wave of divestitures by leading conglomerates, selling off previously acquired operating companies, casts considerable doubt on the proposition that conglomerate giants are particularly astute controllers and allocators of capital. "In recent years," as Arthur

Burck, a specialist in corporate mergers and reorganizations, points out, "35 percent of acquisition announcements reflected divestitures, almost all companies that had once been acquired."[50] For example, Gulf & Western was a hyperactive conglomerate, acquiring sixty-seven companies in the short seven-year period 1960–68; now characterized by *Fortune* as "a conceptually messy agglutination," the firm recently disclosed a massive billion-dollar divestiture plan that reportedly includes its operations in zinc, movie theaters, cigars, mattresses and furniture, video games, and Madison Square Garden.[51] ITT, one of the nation's largest conglomerates, acquired forty-seven firms between 1961 and 1968, with assets of $1.5 billion and variously operating in electronics, consumer financing, car rentals, hotels, baking, and lumber; in 1982, however, ITT, too, disclosed a vast divestiture program involving more than 40 subsidiaries—a program described by one Wall Street analyst as "the biggest sell-off of assets in corporate history."[52] And Big Oil is struggling to divest itself of conglomerate acquisitions: Texaco has sold ESPN (the cable-TV sports network); Arco has disposed of its ill-fated investment in the giant Anaconda Copper Company; Mobil is rumored to be seeking a buyer for its spectacularly unsuccessful Montgomery Ward–Container Corporation subsidiary; Exxon has written off Reliance Electric; Amoco has spun off Cyprus Mines (an acquired copper mining company); and Standard Oil of Ohio and Sun Oil have also divested nonoil acquisitions.[53] If conglomerateurs are such astute capital managers, why would they invest so much in so many acquisitions only to later abandon them? Would capital markets have made the same mistakes?

Second, the current "deconglomeration" wave does not mean that the building of conglomerate empires that preceded it was a socially harmless and socially costless experiment. The fact that conglomerate managements are now being punished for their earlier mistakes—that the market is now making them pay the price for delinquent judgment—does not mean that society has escaped unscathed. For society, as for individuals, there is no such thing as a free lunch. Every action taken in its name exacts an "opportunity cost"—that is, the cost of not having done something else. Two decades of managerial energy devoted to the conglomerate quick-growth game are two decades during which management's attention is diverted from investment in new plants, new products, and improved manufacturing techniques. The roughly $84 billion spent (from 1951 to 1977) on exchanging paper claims in conglomerate acquisitions represent an equivalent amount *not* spent on productivity-enhancing equipment or on research and development. The millions of dollars absorbed by legal fees and bankers' commissions in consummating conglomerate mergers are resources *not* plowed back into productive ventures. The funds borrowed by the conglomerateurs are funds *not* available to other firms, especially small businesses. All these are opportunity costs. They are social costs not paid by the giant conglomerates engaged in social planning. Even if a conglomerate is eventually "punished" for bad planning, society still pays a price for its mistakes. And that can hardly be construed as a boon to social efficiency.

Third, conglomerate bigness tends to undermine the capacity of the nation's capital markets to direct investment funds to their best uses. To perform this function, capital markets—investors, savers, lenders, financial analysts—must have access to meaningful economic information. But as the Federal Trade Commission has warned, the "published financial statements of the conglomerates are almost universally presented on a highly consolidated basis. Sales and revenue information is generally reported for such broad and diverse aggregates of activity as to provide little or no information with respect to meaningful product or market categories." As a result, the commission concluded, "the amount of public information available to the economic system is being greatly reduced."[54] It is rather disingenuous for apologists to defend conglomerate bigness as a superior allocator of capital when, in reality, giant conglomeratism itself sabotages capital markets with meaningless, misleading, or distorted financial information.

Finally, it is noteworthy that the social planning by conglomerate giants is embarrassingly similar to the function performed by socialist planning boards. Both exercise centralized control over the generation and disposition of investment funds. Both exercise broad discretion, different in degree but not in kind, over the allocation of society's resources. Both vest power in top managers who cannot possibly have operating experience in all the fields over which they have control. Both exercise power subject to only limited accountability. In a sense, the socialist planning board is the ultimate conglomerate. Its dubious success in promoting social efficiency in countries where socialism has been tried does not inspire confidence that private planning by giant conglomerates can do much better.

THE CENTRAL ISSUE

Social efficiency means exploiting economic resources so that human satisfaction (consumer welfare) is maximized. But how is it to be measured? In their proclivity to rationalize the prevailing power structure, the defenders of bigness, and particularly the high priests of the Chicago

School, equate social efficiency with "aggregate consumer willingness to pay for goods and services." Professor (now Judge) Richard Posner, for example, says that social efficiency is "determined by the willingness to pay, and the only way in which willingness to pay can be determined with certainty is by actually observing a voluntary transaction. Where resources are shifted pursuant to a voluntary transaction, we can be reasonably confident the shift involves a net increase in efficiency. The transaction would not have occurred if both parties had not expected it to make them better off. This implies that the resources transferred are more valuable in their new owner's hands."[55] In short, as long as individuals and corporations are free to do as they please, private interests and public welfare will automatically be harmonized. Society's resources will be used in the best possible way. Obedience to laissez-faire is certain to make this the best of all possible worlds.

Our review of the evidence—and the examples we cite can be proliferated—does not support this apologia. The central issues cannot be finessed by a flight from reality or by abstruse scholasticism. Planning the use of society's resources—determining how resources shall be allocated—is at the core of social efficiency. But planning by whom? By the competitive marketplace or by lethargic oligopolists and swashbuckling conglomerateurs? What kind of planning? Planning that enhances national security and promotes productivity or planning that stifles innovation and change? Planning with what consequences? Planning that promotes investment in new plants and equipment or that diverts resources into unproductive financial razzle-dazzle and paper enterpreneurism? Alas, the Chicago apologists ignore these pivotal questions. Their message—"what is, is right"—provides no answers.

III

THE POLITICAL
ECONOMY OF POWER:
A HISTORICAL
PERSPECTIVE

I n Part II we have examined the mythology of bigness and the apologetics for the concentration of economic power. We have shown that industrial giantism does not ensure economic efficiency, superior performance, or social welfare; and that it wields vast discretionary power that can produce antisocial consequences.

If this be so, the central challenge to a free society is to construct an organizational framework—a governance structure—that simultaneously provides for individual freedom while ensuring that private decision-making will promote economic performance in the public interest.

The problem is not new. In the Age of Enlightenment the world's great political and economic philosophers grappled with this challenge in social engineering. Central to their concern was the proper role of the state in a free society.

In America, the Founding Fathers—colonists living under the absolute power of the British Crown—wanted to draft a political blueprint, a Constitution, providing for a decentralized power structure, complete with checks and balances and overlapping safeguards against potential abuses by an all-powerful state. They understood that the state had to be strong enough to secure the rights of its citizens and to prevent one group from oppressing another. At the same time, they recognized that a government strong enough to protect its citizens might be powerful enough to enslave them. The Founding Fathers knew that the paramount danger of the powerful state (and its enormous capacity for influence) was its susceptibility to capture by special interests (or by coalitions of special interests) intent on perverting government to their private ends. They understood that once the state intervenes on behalf of one special interest group, "the orderly routine of democratic corruption" is set into motion as other organized interests seek counteracting state interference in their private behalf, too. The outcome is what Henry Simons later called "the moral disintegration of representative government in the endless contest of innumerable pressure groups for special political favors."[1]

As the Founding Fathers were pondering these problems, Adam Smith, an ocean away, was writing his economic manifesto, *The Wealth of Nations.* He, too, wrestled with the question of the proper role of the state in a free society. But he framed the problem in an explicit context of political economy. Smith saw in the mercantilist state of his day a perfect example of the "orderly corruption" of (monarchical) government by special interests. In his polemical tract, Smith traced the nature, means, and consequences of the oppression of the public when the state is perverted into a handmaiden for private interest groups—that is, when government is subverted to the end of dispensing private privilege and preferment.

In the following two chapters we shall review the analytical contributions of the Founding Fathers and Adam Smith. We shall see that their insights, in the Constitution and in *The Wealth of Nations,* were strikingly similar—indeed, seem to have been cut from the same cloth. Our purpose is not merely to provide an idle look backward in history. It is, instead, to highlight the problem of power and the proper role of the state. It is a recurrent dilemma in a free society that persists in our own day, and that is exacerbated by bigness in all of its forms and manifestations. It is a problem that we will confront in a variety of guises throughout this book.

CHAPTER 6

THE REVOLUTION OF 1776: AMERICAN GOVERNMENT

Power of all kinds has an irresistible propensity to increase a desire for itself. It gives the passion of ambition a velocity which increases in its progress, and this is a passion which grows in proportion as it is gratified. . . . The root of the evil is deep in human nature. . . . Power will sometime or other be abused unless men are well watched, and checked by something they cannot remove when they please.
— Thomas Burke, 1777

The American Revolution was a demand for government by the consent of the governed—a protest against arbitrary power and special privilege. What the colonists sought was limitation of such power and the disestablishment of such privilege. They believed, as Walter Lippmann said, "in governments which were under the law, in the rights of man rather than the sovereignty of kings and majorities. They held that the improvement of the human lot was to be achieved by releasing thought, invention, enterprise, and labor from exactions and tolls, from the rule of princes, monopolists, great landlords, and established churches."[1]

The arbitrary power to which the colonists objected was personified by the British Crown, which they held responsible for acts of intolerable oppression. In the Declaration of Independence, they cited the specific acts committed by the King (or by Parliament with his approval):

He has refused his assent to laws the most wholesome and necessary for the public good. . . .

He has dissolved representative houses repeatedly for opposing with manly firmness his invasions on the rights of the people. . . .

He has made judges dependent on his will alone for the tenure of their offices and the amount and payment of their salaries. . . .

He has erected a multitude of new offices, and sent hither swarms of officers to harass our people and eat out their substance. . . .

He has kept among us in times of peace standing armies, without the consent of our legislatures . . .

He has affected to render the military independent of and superior to the civil power. . . .

He has plundered our seas, ravaged our coasts, burnt our towns, and destroyed the lives of our people. . . .

The economic consequences of the Crown's arbitrary power were intimately intertwined with its mercantilist policy. The objectives of that policy—promulgated by the Navigation Acts and enforced by British "admirality courts" and colonial governors—were (1) to promote the military and maritime strength of England and its empire; (2) to give English merchants and manufacturers a monopolistic position in colonial markets; (3) to bring into England colonial products, especially raw materials, and to exclude goods that English producers could supply; and (4) to prevent the development of colonial manufacturers that would compete with English industry.

England was "liberal" in permitting the colonies to produce goods in "their raw state" (raw materials) or in "their very first stage of manufacture." However, as one contemporary observer pointed out, "While Great Britain encourages in America the manufactures of pig and bar iron, by exempting them from duties to which the like commodities are subject when imported from any other country, she imposes an absolute prohibition upon the erection of steel furnaces and slitmills in any of her American plantations. She will not suffer her colonists to work in those more refined manufactures even for their own consumption; but insists upon their purchasing of her merchants and manufacturers all goods of this kind which they have occasion for."[2]

These restrictive regulations, designed to stifle the development of colonial industry and trade, were not the result of governmental efforts to promote the public interest. Instead they reflected the influence of British producers and traders, who used their government as a shield against the potential competition from colonial enterprise. In the words of Adam Smith, "Of the greater part of the regulations concerning the colony trade, the merchants who carry it on, it must be observed, have been the principal advisers. We must not wonder, therefore, if, in the greater part of them, their interest has been more considered than either that of the colonies or that of the mother country. In their exclusive privilege of supplying the colonies with all the goods which they wanted from Europe, and of purchasing all such parts of their surplus produce as could not interfere with any of the trades which they themselves carried on at home, the interest of the colonies was sacrificed to the interest of those merchants."[3] It was this system of privilege and discrimination, instituted by the state at the behest of special interests, that the colonists wanted to disestablish.

THE RATIONALE OF DECENTRALIZED POWER

Once the Revolution had succeeded, the Founding Fathers turned to drafting a constitution. As good eighteenth-century republicans, students of Locke and Montesquieu, combining a faith in the Enlightenment with their experience as colonial subjects, they sought to produce a document squarely based on popular sovereignty and opposition to arbitrary rule. Aware of man's shortcomings—his inordinate greed and insatiable lust for power—and believing as they did that it was impossible to reform human nature, they concluded that vice could not be controlled by virtue, but that it was necessary (as Gouverneur Morris claimed) to oppose one vice and interest to another vice and interest. Therefore, they wanted to design a state that would check interest with interest, faction with faction, class with class, and one branch of government with another. Their master plan was to construct a system of checks and balances, a Newtonian mechanism of countervailing powers, operating harmoniously in mutual frustration. Their foremost goal was to prevent the *summum malum:* concentration of power and the abuses that flow from it.

In *The Federalist Papers,* the Founding Fathers articulated their vision of a pluralist society in which special interest groups would be held in check and rendered incapable of subverting the public interest.[4] In *The Federalist No. 51,* James Madison pointed to the importance, not only of guarding society against the oppression of its rulers, but of guarding one part of society against the injustice that may be inflicted by another. The rights of a minority, he wrote, will be insecure when confronted by a majority united by a common interest:

> There are but two methods of providing against this evil: the one by creating a will in the community independent of the majority, that is, of the society itself; the other by comprehending in the society so many separate descriptions of citizens, as will render an unjust combination of a majority of the whole very improbable, if not impracticable. . . . The second method will be

exemplified in the federal republic of the United States. Whilst all authority
in it will be derived from, and dependent of the society, the society itself will
be broken into so many parts, interests, and classes of citizens, that the rights
of individuals, or of the minority, will be in little danger from interested
combinations of the majority. In a free government, the security of civil rights
must be the same as that for religious rights. It consists in the one case in
the multiplicity of interests, and in the other, in the multiplicity of sects. The
degree of security in both cases will depend on the number of interests and
sects.

Madison elaborated on this notion in his discussion of "factions" (i.e.,
special-interest groups), which he defined as "a number of citizens,
whether amounting to a majority or a minority of the whole, who are
united and actuated by some common impulse of passion, or of interest,
adverse to the rights of other citizens, or to the permanent and aggregate interests of the community." The latent causes of faction, Madison
wrote in *The Federalist No. 10*, are sown in the nature of man. There
are many different opinions concerning religion and government. People
are attached to different leaders, ambitiously contending for preeminence and power. They belong to different parties that inflame them with
mutual animosity and render them "more disposed to vex and oppress
each other, . . . than to cooperate for their common good." Most importantly, they are divided by the unequal distribution of property: those
who hold property, and those who are without; those who are creditors,
and those who are debtors; those who have a landed interest as opposed
to those who have a manufacturing, mercantile, or money interest. "The
regulation of these various and interfering interests," Madison felt,
"forms the principal task of modern legislation, and involves the spirit
of party and faction in the necessary and ordinary operation of government." Moreover, it would be vain to believe "that enlightened statesmen will be able to adjust these clashing interests, and render them all
subservient to the public good. Enlightened statesmen will not always
be at the helm: nor, in many cases, can such an adjustment be made at
all, without taking into view indirect and remote considerations, which
will rarely prevail over the immediate interest which one party may find
in disregarding the rights of another, or the good of the whole."

Thus, Madison concluded, the causes of faction cannot be removed, so
relief must be sought in the means of controlling its effects:

> If a faction consists of less than a majority, relief is supplied by the republican
> principle, which enables the majority to defeat its sinister views by regular
> vote. It may clog the administration, it may convulse the society; but it will
> be unable to execute and mask its violence under the forms of the constitu-

tion. When a majority is included in a faction, the form of popular government, on the other hand, enables it to sacrifice to its ruling passion or interest, both the public good and the rights of other citizens. To secure the public good, and private rights, against the danger of such a faction, and at the same time to preserve the spirit and the form of popular government, is then the great object to which our inquiries are directed.

But how is this objective to be accomplished? Primarily, Madison thought, by promoting as large a number and as great a diversity of factions as possible, geographically dispersed over the whole national territory:

> The influence of factious leaders may kindle a flame within their particular states, but will be unable to spread a general conflagration through the other states; a religious sect may degenerate into a political faction in a part of the confederacy; but the variety of sects dispersed over the entire face of it, must secure the national councils against any danger from that source; a rage for paper money, for an abolition of debts, for an equal division of property, or for any other improper or wicked project, will be less apt to pervade the whole body of the union, than a particular member of it; in the same proportion as such a malady is more likely to taint a particular county or district, than an entire state. In the extent and proper structure of the union, therefore, we behold a republican remedy for the diseases most incident to republican government.

Given this fear that a majority faction may become dominant, oppressing minorities and subverting the public interest, it is not surprising, as Walter Lippmann observes, that the Founding Fathers sought to approximate a true representation of the people by providing many different ways of counting heads:

> For the national government, itself a federation of states with complex forms of representation, they provided a House elected for two years from fairly small constituencies of equal size; a Senate in which one third only was elected every two years from the states—that is, from constituencies of varying size; a President, chosen, as they conceived it, by electors from the separate states, and for a term of four years, which did not correspond with that of any one group of the legislators; a judiciary appointed for life after confirmation by the Senate. Thus no two branches of the government were chosen by the same constituency or for the same term of office.[5]

Clearly, the objective was to make it as difficult as possible for a dominant faction to gain control of the government and to exercise arbitrary power over the people.

But the founders were not content with instituting a system of checks and balances in society at large. They wanted additional safeguards against arbitrary power and its abuses by building similar checks and balances into the structure of government. Said Madison in *The Federalist No. 51*:

> It may be a reflection on human nature, that such devices should be necessary to control the abuses of government. But what is government itself, but the greatest of all reflections on human nature? If men were angels, no government would be necessary. If angels were to govern men, neither external nor internal controls on government would be necessary. In framing a government which is to be administered by men over men, the great difficulty lies in this: you must first enable the government to control the governed; and in the next place oblige it to control itself. A dependence on the people is, no doubt, the primary control on the government; but experience has taught mankind the necessity of auxiliary precautions.

Thomas Jefferson made the same point when he objected to the concentration of all governmental powers—legislative, executive, and judicial—in a single legislative body in his native Virginia. To him, concentrating these powers in the same hands was precisely what "despotic government" was all about. The fact that these powers would be exercised by a legislature, popularly elected by majority vote, consisting perhaps of "upright" and decent men, made little difference. "An elective despotism," he said, "was not the government we fought for." The principles of liberty, he believed, required a system "in which the powers of government should be so divided and balanced among several bodies of magistracy, as that no one could transcend their legal limits, without being effectually checked and restrained by the others." In his *Notes on Virginia,* Jefferson urged his colleagues to "look forward to a time, and that not a distant one, when a corruption in this, as in the country from which we derive our origin, will have seized the heads of government, and be spread by them through the body of the people; when they will purchase the voices of the people, and make them pay the price." The structure of the system, he said, was more important than the personal integrity of the individuals who exercised power under it, and the "time to guard against corruption and tyranny, is before they shall have gotten hold of us. It is better to keep the wolf out of the fold, than to trust to drawing his teeth and talons after he shall have entered."[6]

A BLUEPRINT FOR DECENTRALIZED POWER

The separation of powers, so central to the philosophy of the Founding Fathers, became the core of the Constitution. With disarming simplicity, the notion was incorporated into the first three articles:

ARTICLE I: All legislative Powers herein granted shall be vested in a Congress of the United States, which shall consist of a Senate and House of Representatives.

ARTICLE II: The executive Power shall be vested in a President of the United States of America.

ARTICLE III: The judicial Power of the United States shall be vested in one Supreme Court, and in such inferior Courts as the Congress may from time to time ordain and establish.

While it is obviously inaccurate to suppose that these provisions imply a complete separation of powers—that Congress, for example, makes laws and does nothing but make laws, or that the President has no part in the legislative process—it is still true that the Constitution established a tripartite structure for the central government and that it created a federal system in which the central government and the several states exercised different and distinct powers. Indeed, toward the end of his life, John Adams could take satisfaction in noting the extraordinary degree to which the Constitution reflected the balance-of-power principle: (1) states against the central government; (2) the House of Representatives against the Senate; (3) the President against the Congress; (4) the Judiciary against Congress; (5) the Senate against the President in matters of appointments and treaties; and (6) the people against their Representatives. In economic parlance, the purpose of this elaborate system of checks and balances, and of separation of powers, was to prevent (in Richard Posner's words) "the monopolization or cartelization of the coercive power of the state."[7]

The Constitution provided other safeguards against arbitrary government. It included a Bill of Rights; it placed massive obtacles in the way of future amendments; and, above all, it was declared to be the supreme law of the land to which all legislative and executive acts of the government had to conform.

Clearly, this was not a structure for streamlined or efficient government. On the contrary, it was a structure almost deliberately designed *not* to work efficiently. As Justice Louis Brandeis put it, "The doctrine of the separation of powers was adopted by the convention of 1787 not to promote efficiency but to preclude the exercise of arbitrary power."[8] The men who wrote the Constitution were motivated by their fears as much as their hopes. They knew that government could become an instrument of oppression. That is why they wanted to make sure that its powers would be limited. They knew government could become a dispenser of privilege. That is why they wanted to make it as difficult as possible for a dominant group to gain control of the government and to use it to create privilege and promote monopoly. In short, under the Constitution, government was not intended to be the executive committee of powerful private interests.

THE CONTEMPORARY DILEMMA

The Founding Fathers predicated the American political system on the assumption that government—the public power—was the principal enemy of individual freedom and equality. In their view, influenced as it was by the political philosophers of the eighteenth century, government was the most conspicuous and potentially strongest institution for implementing the domination of man by man. If therefore, they reasoned, governmental powers could be reduced to a minimum and constitutional safeguards could be designed (in the form of checks and balances) to guard against the abuses of governmental powers, then American society's commitment to individual freedom and equality would be secure.

The Founders, however, did not foresee that society might generate concentrations of private power that might constitute as potent a threat as government to individual freedom and equality. They did not anticipate the profound economic transformations that would occur after the Civil War and usher in an era of private economic feudalism. They did not face up to the great domestic dilemma of our times: that a government that is too weak to oppress the individual by the abuse of public power is also too weak to protect the individual against the depredations of concentrated private power, or, conversely, as Hans Morgenthau saw, "a government which is strong enough to keep the new feudalism in check in order to protect the freedom of the many is also strong enough to destroy the freedom of all."[9]

Alexander Hamilton hinted at the existence of this dilemma, although he saw it in purely political terms. Writing in *The Continentalist* in 1782, he observed: "In a government framed for durable liberty, not less regard must be paid to giving the magistrate a proper degree of authority to make and execute the laws with rigor, than to guard against encroachments upon the rights of the community. As too much power leads to despotism, too little leads to anarchy, and both, eventually, to the ruin of the people." But, quite understandably, given the economic setting of his time, Hamilton did not see this problem in economic terms. Neither he nor the other Founding Fathers recognized the danger inherent in private concentrations of economic power, and the ultimate danger of a symbiotic alliance between a powerful private economic oligarchy and a politically impotent public authority.

Historically, says Hans Morgenthau, this dilemma has been accentuated by a progressive decomposition of governmental power both from within and from without. From within, government was weakened in its effort to regulate and control—to civilize and tame—great concentrations of power rather than to attack them frontally. Government tried to limit and constrain the conduct of the power concentrations rather than to transform them structurally. It did so by creating an enormous apparatus of quantitative and qualitative complexity. It divided and subdivided the functions of the executive branch, and parcelled them out to a plethora of administrative agencies, often working at cross purposes with one another. These agencies, says Morgenthau, become autonomous centers of power (feudal fiefs), competing with other agencies for determination of policy, defending their bureaucratic turf against other centers of power, and trying to increase their power at the expense of other agencies. This internal competition leads not only to a fragmentation of governmental power but also to a diminution of the sum total of public power. As a result, the "government, instead of speaking with one strong and purposeful voice, speaks in many voices, each trying to outshout the others, but all really weak as well as contradictory."[10]

This decomposition of governmental power from within is accompanied by a weakening of public authority from without—primarily through the influence of powerful vested interests on government. With Big Government exerting an enormous controlling, limiting, and stimulating influence in economic life, private interests—almost inevitably—are drawn into playing the political influence game. In their effort to gain economic advantage, these interests seek political access to the corridors of government in the hope of exerting influence, pressure, and (if possible) control. Mining companies and public utilities seek influence in state legislatures; industries concentrated in a particular area seek control over their congressional representatives; regulated industries want to sway the administrative agencies that are supposed to control them. In the process, as Morgenthau points out:

> legislators and administrators tend to transform themselves into ambassadors of economic forces, defending and promoting the interests of their mandatories in dealing with each other on behalf of them. The result is again a new feudalism which, like that of the Middle Ages, diminishes the authority of the civil government and threatens it with extinction by parcelling out its several functions among economic organizations to be appropriated and used as private property. And just like the feudalism of the Middle Ages, these new concentrations of private power tend to command the primary loyalties of the individual citizens who owe them their livelihood and security. In the end, the constitutionally established government tends to become, in the words of Chief Justice Marshall, a "solemn mockery," glossing over the loss of political vitality with the performance of political rites.[11]

This then, is the basic structural challenge to an advanced industrial society intent on preserving democratic institutions: how to prevent private concentrations of power, organized into powerful political pressure groups, from achieving dominance over the economy and, eventually, over the state; and to do so without creating an omnipotent government, strong enough not only to control private oligarchies but also to become an instrument of oppression beyond public control. To this challenge there are no simple answers.

CHAPTER 7

THE REVOLUTION OF 1776: BRITISH ECONOMIC POLICY

Smith's chief concern was not so much with what man might occasionally achieve
when he was at his best but that he should have as little opportunity as possible to
do harm when he was at his worst. It would scarcely be too much to claim that the
main merit of the individualism which he and his contemporaries advocated is that
it is a system under which bad men can do least harm.
— Friedrich von Hayek, *Individualism and Economic Order*, 1948

Adam Smith's *Wealth of Nations* was more than an analytical disquisition on the virtues of laissez-faire and competition. It was also a polemic—a revolutionary specification of charges—against mercantilism and its system of centralized control over a nation's economic activity. It offered a collection of case studies—admittedly anecdotal and episodic—showing how the institutions of government can be captured by special interests and perverted into instruments of private gain rather than public good. It included classical examples of the coalescence of economic with political power, and it remains to this day a premier study of political economy.

Mercantilism was the name given to governmental policies that prevailed in England and Europe between the Middle Ages and the age of laissez-faire. The central assumption of mercantilist statecraft was that wealth consisted of gold and silver. Its prime objective was to increase not the community's but the state's wealth and power. In an age marked by the emergence of national states and the decline of local feudalism, the state became, almost naturally, both the subject and object of mercantilist endeavors.

In *The Growth of English Industry and Trade,* William Cunningham expounded mercantilism as a system of power: "The politicians of the sixteenth, seventeenth and the greater part of the eighteenth century were agreed in trying to regulate all commerce and industry, so that the power of England relative to other nations might be promoted. . . . On every hand private tastes and personal convenience had to give way to the patriotic duty of strengthening the nation. . . . The mercantile system [was] concerned with man solely as a being who pursues national power."[1] Economic man, serving his private ends and thereby promoting the common weal, had obviously not yet replaced man as the deferential servant of the state.

History offers few parallels to the detailed regulation of industry by the state under mercantilism. Take, for example, the famous system of *règlements* (regulations) whereby Colbert, the finance minister of Louis XIV, sought to codify and generalize the industrial laws of France. As Eli F. Heckscher reports, the *règlements* for the period 1666–1730 were contained in four quarto volumes with 2,200 pages plus three supplementary volumes—for the textile industry alone. The general cloth *règlement* comprised 59 articles, the two dyeing *règlements* 62 and 98 articles respectively, while the largest of all, the general dyeing instruction, contained 317 articles.

An example of the detail of these regulations, complete with local variations, is the special *règlement* for weaving, issued in 1718 and applicable to Burgundy and four neighboring districts:

The fabrics of Dijon and Selongey were to be put in reeds 1¾ ells wide, a warp was to contain 44 × 32 or 1,408 threads including the selvedges, and when it came to the fulling-mill, the cloth was to be exactly 1 ell wide. Semur in Auxois, and Auxerre, Montbard, Avalon and Beaune were to have a warp of 43 × 32 or 1,376 threads, the same width in the reed, and the same width of cloth when it left the fulling-hammer. Saulieu was to have the same width with 42 × 32 or 1,340 (really 1,344) threads, but it seems that the white and the more finely spun cloths were to have 74 × 32 or 2,368 threads. Châtillon on the Seine and five other places were to have 1,216 threads in a width of 1⅝ ells with the same variation for white cloths. The *sardis* fabric, which was produced in Bourg en Bresse and various other towns, was to have only 576 threads with reeds of 1 ell and a width of ½ ell after fulling. . . .[2]

And how did the sovereign know how many threads he should call for in Dijon, Semur, or Châtillon? The answer, Walter Lippmann wryly suggests, is, of course, that he found this out from the established manufacturers, and that his *règlements* were essentially a device for protecting their vested interest against the competition of enterprising innovators. This is the inevitable method of authoritative regulation, for no king and no bureau can hope to imagine a technic of production other than the technic which happens to exist. Occasionally the government may have a bright idea, but its normal procedure must inevitably be to throw the weight of its authority behind the routine of the established interests.[3]

In a sense, what Colbert did under Louis XIV is not unlike what neomercantilist officials do today. Colbert regulated industry and agriculture by fortifying and subsidizing established producers; his contemporary emulators administer the regulated sector of our economy, not by protecting the public from exploitation, but by protecting inefficient and unprogressive insiders from competition.

The punishment for disobeying the *règlements* was, as one might suspect, somewhat harsher than that which would be decreed in a civilized age like ours. In order to suppress the illicit importation of printed calicoes into France, the economic measures taken by the state "cost the lives of some 16,000 people, partly through executions and partly through armed affrays, without reckoning the unknown but certainly much larger number of people who were sent to the galleys, or punished in other ways. On one occasion in Valence, seventy-seven were sentenced to be hanged, fifty-eight were to be broken on the wheel, six hundred thirty-one were sent to the galleys, one was set free and none was pardoned. But even this vigorous action did not help to attain the desired end. Printed calicoes spread more and more widely among all classes of the population, in France and everywhere else."[4]

In addition to the comprehensive regulation of domestic industry and commerce, mercantilism undertook also to control foreign trade. Given its belief that wealth consists of accumulated stocks of gold and silver and that the purpose of economic policy was to aggrandize the wealth and power of the state, it followed, so the mercantilists thought, that the guiding principle in managing international trade—and, for that matter, foreign economic policy—should be the favorable balance of trade doctrine. In his *England's Treasure by Foreign Trade,* first published in 1664, Thomas Mun stated the proposition succinctly: "The ordinary means therefore to encrease our wealth and treasure is by Foreign Trade, wherein we must ever observe this rule: to sell more to strangers yearly than wee consume of theirs in value. . . . That part of our stock which is not returned to us in wares must necessarily be brought home in treasure."[5]

Implementation of this doctrine (which sounds uncomfortably familiar when one listens to current debates in Congress) seemed, quite logically, to call for import restraints on the one hand, and the encouragement of exports on the other. Mercantilist restraints upon imports, Adam Smith reports, were of two kinds: "First, restraints upon the importation of such foreign goods for home consumption as could be produced at home, from whatever country they were imported. Secondly, restraints upon the importation of goods of almost all kinds from those particular countries with which the balance of trade was supposed to be disadvantageous. Those different restraints consisted sometimes in high duties, and sometimes in absolute prohibitions."[6]

The encouragement of exports, as we have previously noted in our discussion of the British Navigation Acts, consisted primarily of tax rebates and subsidies to exporters. In addition, says Smith,

> By advantageous treaties of commerce, particular privileges were procured in some foreign state for the goods and merchants of the country, beyond what were granted to those of other countries.
>
> By the establishment of colonies in distant countries, not only particular privileges, but a monopoly was frequently procured for the goods and merchants of the country which established them.[7]

These policies to encourage exports, combined with the two restraints on imports, were the principal means by which the mercantilist system attempted to assure a favorable balance of trade and, through it, a richer and more powerful nation.

These restraints were not dreamed up by the state, idly speculating on the best ways of promoting the public interest. As we shall see over and over again, protectionist measures are enacted by the state at the behest of the special interests that stand to gain by them—at public expense. Again Smith provides a telling illustration:

> The exportation of the materials of manufacture is sometimes discouraged by absolute prohibitions, and sometimes by high duties.
>
> Our woollen manufacturers have been more successful than any other class of workmen, in persuading the legislature that the prosperity of the nation depended upon the success and extension of their particular business. They have not only obtained a monopoly against the consumers by an absolute prohibition of importing woolen cloths from any foreign country; but they have likewise obtained another monopoly against the sheep farmers and growers of wool, by a similar prohibition of the exportation of live sheep and

wool. The severity of many of the laws which have been enacted for the security of the revenue is very justly complained of, as imposing heavy penalties upon actions which, antecedent to the statutes that declared them to be crimes, had always been understood to be innocent. But the cruellest of our revenue laws, I will venture to affirm, are mild and gentle, in comparison of some of those which the clamour of our merchants and manufacturers has extorted from the legislature, for the support of their own absurd and oppressive monopolies. Like the laws of Draco, these laws may be said to be all written in blood.[8]

The statement that these laws were written in blood was not hyperbole. The punishment for violators was severe:

By the 8th of Elizabeth, chap. 3. the exporter of sheep, lambs or rams, was for the first offence to forfeit all his goods for ever, to suffer a year's imprisonment, and then to have his left hand cut off in a market town upon a market day, to be there nailed up; and for the second offence to be adjudged a felon, and to suffer death accordingly. To prevent the breed of our sheep from being propagated in foreign countries, seems to have been the object of this law. By the 13th and 14th of Charles II. chap. 18. the exportation of wool was made a felony, and the exporter subjected to the same penalties and forfeitures as a felon.[9]

Evidently, it requires something more than gentle admonition to enforce rules that run counter to the incentives of the marketplace.

In attacking the foundations of mercantilism, Adam Smith advocated economic freedom as the soundest principle for organizing society. The pretense, he wrote, that monopoly charters for corporations "are necessary for the better government of the trade, is without foundation. The real and effectual discipline which is exercised over a workman, is not that of his corporation, but that of his customers."[10] Competition, not regulation, is the key to economic welfare.[11] The state, by granting monopoly privileges, prevents resources from flowing into those channels where—in the judgment of consumers—they can contribute most to economic welfare. Governmentally created monopolies, while benefiting the trades, the crafts, and the mysteries, victimize the public by restraining that free competition which results in a reduction of prices and a normalization of profits. Industrial self-government by traders and artificers is oppressive to the public, because it is "the manifest interest of every particular class of them to prevent the market from being overstocked, as they commonly express it, with their own particular species of industry; which is in reality to keep it always understocked."[12] The state, by granting monopoly charters with the attendant rights of

industrial self-government, thus promotes artificial scarcity to the preju-
dice of the consuming public.

If monopoly control over domestic commerce was indefensible, so
were the grants of privilege to the great international trading companies. These companies, wrote Smith, "though they may, perhaps, have
been useful for the first introduction of some branches of commerce, by
making, at their own expense, an experiment which the state might not
think it prudent to make, have in the long run proved, universally, either
burdensome or useless, and have either mismanaged or confined the
trade."[13]

The great trading companies tried to keep their profits as high as
possible by keeping the market, for both their exports and imports,
constantly understocked; by restraining competition; and by discouraging the entry of newcomers into the trade. Without a monopoly grant
from the state, such companies seldom succeeded; frequently they did
not succeed *with* one. "Without an exclusive privilege they have commonly mismanaged the trade. With an exclusive privilege they have both
mismanaged and confined it."[14] Thus the Royal African Company found
itself unable to withstand the unlicensed competition of private adventurers—whom they called interlopers and persecuted as such. Eventually, like its predecessors in the African trade, the company failed,
despite its monopoly charter and its privileges.

Smith opposed governmental grants of monopoly to an individual or
trading company, primarily because "all the other subjects of the state
are taxed very absurdly in two different ways; first, by high price of
goods, which, in the case of free trade, they could buy much cheaper;
and, second, by their total exclusion from a branch of business, which
it might be both convenient and profitable for many of them to carry on."
These burdens on the public, according to Smith, served no useful purpose other than "to enable the company to support the negligence, profu-
sion, and malversation of their own servants, whose disorderly conduct
seldom allows the dividend of the company to exceed the ordinary rate
of profit in trades which are altogether free, and very frequently makes
it fall even a good deal short of that rate. Without monopoly, however,
a joint-stock company, it would appear from experience, cannot long
carry on any branch of foreign trade."[15] It cannot survive whenever
private adventurers are allowed to engage in any sort of open and fair
competition with it.

Smith's policy recommendation was clear: eliminate the mercantilist
restrictions on free enterprise, and stop the government's promotion of
monopoly and privilege. Encourage the kind of competition that protects
the consumer against exploitation and provides opportunity for new

men, new firms, and new ideas. Then, with the state performing its rightful role of umpire, the economic system will tend to assure liberty for the individual and well-being for the masses.

THE CONTEMPORARY DILEMMA

Free enterprise is an ambiguous concept. It might mean, as with the Manchester liberals, a fighting belief in the virtue of competition; or it might mean, as with present-day conservatives, a fighting belief in the vice of government intervention. Both meanings can be traced to the prophet of modern capitalism; both can be found in *The Wealth of Nations*, the bible of laissez-faire.

Unfortunately, Smith's language lent itself not only to an attack on government when it promoted monopoly, but also to an attack on government when it sought to enhance the general welfare. "In the end," says Professor Arthur M. Schlesinger, "business altogether captured the phrases of laissez-faire and used them more or less ruthlessly in defense of monopoly."[16] Big Business, in order to protect itself from competition, opposed any governmental action that would preserve, restore, or promote competition. Instead of fighting for competition, Big Business concentrated its efforts on securing domination over, or subservience by, the government to obtain its monopolistic ends. Ironically enough, therefore, the laissez-faire slogans developed by Adam Smith to destroy monopoly have today become its bulwark.

IV

COMPETITION AND THE CONTROL OF POWER

The core problem of political economy is to design a power structure that provides a workable decision-making mechanism. Who shall make what decisions, on whose behalf, at what cost, and with what consequences? In Part III we examined how the leading intellects of the Enlightenment proposed to meet that challenge. We noted that the Founding Fathers created a political system in which *governmental* powers were decentralized, a system honeycombed with checks and balances, so that the state could not become an instrument for oppressing the individual. We noted that Adam Smith offered an economic blueprint in which power was scattered into many hands, so that the people would be protected against exploitation by the exertion of undue *private* power. Smith's centerpiece was the competitive market, which was to serve both as society's regulatory authority and its planning mechanism.

Contrary to the preachments of modern apologists, the competitive market is not a product of nature, nor is it automatically self-perpetuating. It is a delicate artifact that can be subverted from within by private interests who refuse to submit to the market's control or who arrogate to themselves its planning function. Businessmen, as Adam Smith warned us, "seldom meet together, even for merriment and diversion, but that the conversation inevitably turns into a conspiracy against the public." Some concoct collusive pricing agreements. Others play the merger game, combining their properties to achieve monopoly or oligopoly power, thus to immunize themselves from the dictates of the market. Others forge Brobdingnagian structures that undermine the

107

market's authority by dint of their sheer size and disproportionate influence. When that happens, private decisions are made in furtherance of private ends, but with no assurance that they will be congruent with the public interest. In that event, private power is no longer under social control. It is no longer socially accountable or socially responsible.

A free-enterprise society, therefore, must take positive and deliberate action to protect the competitive market from subversion and erosion. This is the primary task of the antitrust laws. Just as the purpose of the U.S. Constitution was to prevent cartels or monopolies from controlling the coercive power of the state, so the basic objective of antitrust is to prevent them from controlling economic decision-making in a free society.

CHAPTER 8

THE ROLE OF
ANTITRUST

The Sherman Act is a comprehensive charter of economic liberty aimed at preserving free and unfettered competition as the rule of trade. It rests on the premise that the unrestrained interaction of competitive forces will yield the best allocation of our economic resources, the lowest prices, the highest quality and the greatest material progress, while at the same time providing an environment conducive to the preservation of our democratic political and social institutions. But even were that premise open to question, the policy unequivocally laid down by the Act is competition.   — *Northern Pacific Railway Co.* v. *United States,* 1958

I think that the free-enterprise system is absolutely too important to be left to the voluntary action of the marketplace.
                        — Congressman Richard Kelly (R-Fla.), 1979

Every society designing a structure for its economic activity must confront a fundamental policy question: who shall make what decisions on whose behalf at whose cost and for whose benefit? It must face up to the question of how economic power shall be distributed and what safeguards must be erected to prevent its abuse.

In a free-enterprise society, the basic organizing principle is the competitive market. It is at once a mechanism for allocating society's scarce resources—deciding what goods to produce, in what quantities, and by what techniques—and a regulatory mechanism for controlling private power. Like the political framework prescribed by the Constitution, competition rests upon distrust of concentrated power and upon a belief in the maximum possible diffusion of rights and opportunities. Decision-making power over such vital matters as price, production, and investment is to be widely decentralized among many firms, not concentrated in one or a handful. While private enterprisers are free to assume the responsibility and exercise the power of organizing the productive activities on which the life of the community depends, they have to pay a price for that freedom: they have to submit to the discipline of competition. They have to obey the dictates of the market instead of dictating to it. They have to heed the voice of the community (as expressed in the market) rather than serving it only as they deem fit and proper. In short, society grants individuals the privilege of economic freedom only because competition imposes the checks and balances to constrain that freedom in the public interest.

Competition, then, is first and foremost a system of decentralized economic power. It requires, as Corwin D. Edwards observes, "that all persons engaged in business dealings with one another are basically equal in status and are not hopelessly unequal in bargaining power. None is favored by a preferential position at law nor by avoidable special privilege. None is exposed to ganging-up, that is, to coercion or exploitation growing out of concerted action by others. Though single concerns are likely to differ in size, wealth, and power, there must be some limit, even though an ill-defined one, to the bargaining advantages that grow out of such differences."[1] Obviously this calls for some constraints. Economic freedom for the *individual* cannot be allowed to undermine or subvert the freedom of the *system*. Nor can it be treated as an absolute value. Instead, it must be viewed as an instrument for doing the work of a free society.

One further aspect of competition should be noted. As long as the market functions effectively in controlling private power, there is no need for massive government intervention to protect society from economic exploitation. To the extent, therefore, that business accepts the constraints and discipline of competition, it avoids the direct government regulation characteristic of command economies.

THE "CLASSICAL" HERITAGE

Maintaining competition by law is the basic rationale of U.S. antitrust laws. It is an attempt to use the market as the surrogate for direct control. It is an effort to use Adam Smith's "unseen hand" as an alternative to the heavy hand of government. Yet, this social justification for a competitive system is not universally understood. Neoconservatives would agree with Ayn Rand that "the concept of *free* competition *enforced* by law is a grotesque contradiction in terms. . . . The only factor required for the existence of free competition is the unhampered, unobstructed operation of the mechanism of a free market. The only action which a government can take to protect free competition is *Laissez-faire!*"[2]

This view represents a profound misreading of *The Wealth of Nations* and the contribution of the classical economists to the theory of free enterprise. The classicists understood the difference between government intervention to protect competition and government intervention to create privilege and promote monopoly. They regarded the former as a virtue, the latter as a vice. To the classicists, free enterprise was a *social* system whose primary objective was to promote the *general* welfare. It was designed to achieve that objective by utilizing individual freedom as the central motive force in a free economy, and by utilizing competition as the principal safeguard against the abuse of private power.

These points merit elaboration.

Individual freedom, according to the classical economists, was the best method of maximizing social welfare. "The statesman, who should attempt to direct private people in what manner they ought to employ their capitals," wrote Smith, "would not only load himself with a most unnecessary attention, but assume an authority which could safely be trusted to no council and senate whatever, and which would nowhere be so dangerous as in the hands of a man who had folly and presumption enough to fancy himself fit to exercise it."[3] Not the state, but the free play of market forces, should determine the kinds and quantities of goods to be produced, the factors of production to be employed, and the division of distributive shares. Individual economic activity should be coordinated through an autonomous and impartial planning mechanism —free of human control, manipulation, or perversion. The individual appetite for private gain should be harnessed for social ends by an "invisible hand"—the incentives and compulsions of a competitive market.

The central notion here is that individual freedom is conducive to social advantage, that a policy of laissez-faire or *pas trop gouverner* will achieve a harmony between the pursuit of self-interest and the maximization of general welfare. But the classicists were not so naïve as to believe that this harmony was natural, spontaneous, or self-generating. As Lionel Robbins points out: "The invisible hand which guides men to promote ends which were no part of their intention, is not the hand of some god or some natural agency independent of human effort; it is the hand of the lawgiver, the hand which withdraws from the sphere of the pursuit of self-interest those possibilities which do not harmonize with the public good."[4] The invisible hand is the hand of government acting in the role of rulemaker and umpire—creating the framework in which economic freedom can perform its assigned social task.

Individual freedom can be meaningful only within a *pattern* of freedoms, and the crucial question therefore revolves around the distribution of freedoms within an economic power structure. The crucial problem is to "distinguish between [government] interventions that destroy the need for intervention and interventions that tend to perpetuate it." Thus, as Jeremy Bentham points out, it is not enough to shout "Laissez-faire!" and oppose all government action: "To say that a law is contrary to natural liberty, is simply to say that it is a law: for every law is established at the expense of liberty—the liberty of Peter at the expense of the liberty of Paul."[5] If individual rights were absolute and unlimited they would mean license to commit the grossest abuses against society.

The classicists were not content, therefore, with an exclusively negative view of government, summed up in the slogan of laissez-faire. They recognized, with Thomas Hobbes, that a state of nature is fraught with "fear and violent death" and that man's life in nature is "poor, nasty, brutish, and short"; that good order does not arise from a universal perception of a harmony of interests; that government is not a purely voluntary association; that, on the contrary, good order requires an irreducible element of governmental force, coercion, and intervention to maintain the framework in which freedom can flourish. Harmony and mutuality of interests being neither automatic nor inevitable, it becomes the "function of government in the modern world . . . to provide and enforce a framework of rules for securing freedom, and the conditions necessary for effective freedom, in economic life."[6] Laissez-faire was a policy prescription not so much for individual freedom as for a free economic system.

In the classical system, the invisible hand (i.e., the competitive market) had two functions. On the one hand it was to harness the individual to social ends, on the other it was to deprive him of power so great that, if abused, it would harm his fellows. In the words of Adam Smith: "It is not from the benevolence of the butcher, the brewer, or the baker that we expect our dinner, but from their regard to their self-interest. We address ourselves not to their humanity, but to their self love, and never talk to them of our necessities, but of their advantages." Nevertheless, this self-interest is only one side of the coin. It is the motive force that drives men to action. Something else is needed to keep these private appetites within social bounds, and that element is competition. Competition is the coordinator of individual activity, the planner of private choices, the allocator of society's resources. But it is also the device that limits and controls economic power, the safeguard against the abuse of private discretion.

In this view, competition is a regulatory system. Its objectives are the same as any regulatory system's, but its techniques are different. It achieves its social ends, not through direct participation in the economic game, but through a set of prohibitory rules designed to ensure the desired outcome. It relies not on the visible hand of the central planner, but on an autonomous, objective, and impersonal market process. It exercises compulsion, not through direct governmental decision-making, but through rules that guide, limit, and discipline private decision-makers.

In a sense, the regulatory scheme of competition is analogous to the rules of a football game. The team is free to use a running or a passing game, but it may exercise discretion only within prescribed limits. The field is of specified dimensions; rules govern team size, with no mergers allowed; there are prohibitions against off-sides, clipping, ineligible receivers, and similar unfair competitive methods. Most important there is a referee to enforce these rules, and there is an athletic association to change the rules whenever necessary to improve the game.

In the final analysis, that is the role of antitrust in a free economy. It is a regulatory system that functions through prohibitory rules. It sets the limits within which individuals are free to do as they please. But, like any regulatory system, it must protect its own integrity. It must ensure that the freedom it allows to individuals is not used to destroy the freedom of others or to subvert the entire system of freedom.

THE LAWS OF ANTITRUST

As the regulatory framework of a free economy, antitrust is built on a foundation of four basic prohibitions, designed to maintain the prerequisites for an effectively competitive system:

1. A prohibition of *every* contract, combination, or conspiracy in restraint of trade. (Section 1 of the Sherman Act states: "Every contract, combination in the form of trust or otherwise, or conspiracy, in restraint of trade or commerce among the several states, or with foreign nations, is hereby declared to be illegal.")
2. A prohibition of *all* monopolizing or attempts to monopolize. (Section 2 of the Sherman Act states: "Every person who shall monopolize, or attempt to monopolize, or combine or conspire with any other person

or persons to monopolize, any part of the trade or commerce among the several states, or with foreign nations, shall be deemed guilty.")

3. A prohibition of *all* mergers and acquisitions—horizontal, vertical, and conglomerate—that may substantially lessen competition or tend to create a monopoly. (Section 7 of the Clayton Act states: "No corporation engaged in commerce shall acquire, directly or indirectly, the whole or any part of the stock or other share capital and no corporation . . . shall acquire the whole or any part of the assets of another corporation engaged also in commerce, where in any line of commerce in any section of the country, the effect of such acquisition may be substantially to lessen competition, or to tend to create a monopoly.")

4. A prohibition of *all* unfair methods of competition. (Section 5 of the Federal Trade Commission Act of 1914 states: "Unfair methods of competition in commerce, and unfair or deceptive acts or practices in commerce, are hereby declared unlawful." This general prohibition is supplemented by the Clayton Act's prohibitions of specific unfair practices such as price discrimination in Section 2: "It shall be unlawful for any person engaged in commerce . . . either directly or indirectly, to discriminate in price between different purchasers of commodities of like grade and quality . . . where the effect of such discrimination may be substantially to lessen competition or tend to create a monopoly in any line of commerce or to injure, destroy, or prevent competition with any person who either grants or knowingly receives the benefit of such discrimination, or with customers of either of them." Section 3 adds "that it shall be unlawful for any person engaged in commerce . . . to lease or make a sale or contract for sale of goods . . . or other commodities . . . on the condition, agreement or understanding that the lessee or purchaser thereof shall not use or deal in the goods . . . or other commodities of a competitor . . . where the effect of such . . . understanding may be to substantially lessen competition or tend to create a monopoly in any line of commerce.")

The fundamental objective of antitrust is not—as the Chicago School insists and as Professor Robert Bork suggests in his magnum opus—to promote "efficiency" and "consumer welfare."[7] These are only ancillary benefits that are expected to flow from economic freedom. The primary purpose of antitrust is to perpetuate and preserve, in spite of possible cost, a system of governance for a competitive, free-enterprise economy. It is a system of governance in which power is decentralized; in which newcomers have a genuine opportunity to introduce themselves and their ideas; in which the "unseen hand" of competition instead of the heavy hand of the state performs the basic regulatory function on behalf of society. Antitrust, to repeat, is above all a *system of governance*.

Antitrust is deeply rooted in the American tradition. Like the political system prescribed by our Constitution, it calls for a dispersion of power, buttressed by built-in checks and balances, to protect individuals from potential abuse of power and to preserve not only individual freedom but, more importantly, a free system. According to antitrust precepts— to paraphrase Justice William O. Douglas—power that controls the economy should not be in the hands of an industrial oligarchy. Since all power tends to develop into a government in itself, industrial power should be decentralized. It should be scattered into many hands so that the fortunes of the people will not be dependent on the whims, the political prejudices, and the emotional stability of a few self-appointed men. The fact that they are not vicious men but respectable and social-minded is irrelevant. That is the philosophy and the command of the antitrust laws. They are founded on a theory hostile to private individuals amassing a power so great that even a government of the people can be trusted with it only in exceptional circumstances.[8]

THE PROBLEM OF ENDS AND MEANS

The general objectives of antitrust are clear: to promote and preserve competition by legal prohibitions against "restraints of trade," "monopolization," and mergers that "may tend to lessen competition." To implement these objectives, however, antitrust must rely on the legal process—the adjudication of issues in the courts, case by case, in the light of the facts of each particular lawsuit. The process has three major infirmities.

First, antitrust deals with matters that are economic in substance, but it must deal with them through a complex legal process. As Walton Hamilton and Irene Till point out, antitrust policy

> must be fitted out with all the appurtenances of litigation. The symbol must replace the actuality; the real question be commuted into a cause at law; the essential issue be resolved through the observance of the ritual decreed for a genuine case in controversy. . . . The legal issue is whether the conduct of specific officials of particular corporations falls within or without the law. The matter of concern pertains to industrial organization; the process of decision belongs to the rules of litigation. It brings to the settlement of questions of economic order the processes, hazards, confusions, evasions, circumlocutions,

delays of the legal folkways. . . . Every move, every witness, every fact, every document becomes a counter in a legal game. "The record" has come to do vicarious duty for an analysis of the industry in operation; and every item favorable to one side can win admission only against the heavy cross-fire of the other. Every procedural device which may arrest or speed action, flank or snipe the verbal minions of the enemy, color the conduct on parade with innocence or guilt, is called into play.[9]

Second, the effectiveness of antitrust depends on vigorous enforcement. Violators must be apprehended; lawbreakers must be brought to court; cases must be carried through the mazes of protracted litigation. "Then, when the last court has spoken, [the government] must follow up judgments and make sure judicial decrees become an everyday reality."[10] If the enforcement authorities are looking the other way—if, for example, as under the Reagan administration, they choose to regard corporate mergers and takeovers as benign (or beneficial)—it is inevitable that the antimerger statutes will fall victim to desuetude and that the merger mania will continue unabated.

Third, the effectiveness of antitrust also depends on sympathetic interpretation by the courts. Neither the literal text of the law nor the statement of congressional purpose in enacting it necessarily controls its judicial interpretation. The judiciary, as Justice Benjamin N. Cardozo once observed, does not operate in a vacuum; the "great tides and currents which engulf the rest of men, do not turn aside their course and pass the judges by."[11] Or, as Justice Oliver Wendell Holmes put it:

The language of judicial decision is mainly the language of logic. And the logical method and form flatter that longing for certainty and for repose which is in every human mind. But certainty generally is illusion, and repose is not the destiny of man. Behind the logical form lies a judgment as to the relative worth and importance of competing legislative grounds, often an inarticulate and unconscious judgment, it is true, and yet the very root and nerve of the whole proceeding. You can give any conclusion a logical form. You always can imply a condition in a contract. But why do you imply it? It is because of some belief as to the practice of the community or of a class, or because of some opinion as to policy. . . . We do not realize how large a part of our law is open to reconsideration upon a slight change in the habit of the public mind.[12]

The ethos of the times inevitably affects judicial outcomes. "The Constitution may follow the flag," said Mr. Dooley, "but the Supreme Court follows the election returns."

In the next several chapters, we shall examine in greater detail the contours of American antitrust policy with respect to conspiracy, monopoly, and mergers. We shall inquire to what extent antitrust has been a "success" as the basic governance system of a free economy. Has it prevented the concentration of power in the hands of the few? Has it forestalled the usurpation of power by private interests subject neither to public accountability nor public control? Has it preserved a decentralized power structure, replete with checks and balances, that was the dream of the Founding Fathers? In short, has antitrust protected the public not only from oppression by the state, but from the exercise of undue private power?

CHAPTER 9

CONSPIRACY

The best way to get a lower price . . . is to have more bidders; ten is better than
five.   — Robert Costello, executive director of purchasing, General Motors

B etween 16 February and 15 September 1960, a federal grand jury in Philadelphia returned twenty-one indictments against the major electrical-equipment manufacturers in the United States, charging them with criminal conspiracy to fix prices, to rig bids, and to suppress competition in violation of the Sherman Act.[1] The indictments covered a long list of products used in the generation and transmission of electricity—ranging from simple items such as porcelain insulators, lighting arrestors, and meters, to such intricate devices as power-switching gear, power capacitators, and turbine generators. The aggregate annual sales of the products covered by the "great electrical conspiracy" was estimated to be $1.75 billion (in 1960 prices).

The indictment covering "power switchgear assemblies" illustrates how price-fixing and bid-rigging schemes operate.[2] It not only shows the mechanics of conspiratorial behavior among ostensible competitors, but also poses the crucial public-policy question of how to deal with such behavior in a free-enterprise economy.

The indictment named General Electric, Westinghouse, Allis-Chalmers, Federal Pacific, ITE Circuit Breaker, and some of their top executives as defendants. It charged the defendants with having conspired to "fix and maintain prices, terms, and conditions for the sale of power

118

switchgear assemblies"; to "allocate among themselves the business of supplying power switchgear assemblies to Federal, State, and local government agencies"; to "submit noncompetitive, collusive, and rigged bids for supplying power switchgear assemblies to electric utility companies, Federal, State, and local governmental agencies, private industrial corporations and contractors throughout the United States"; to "refrain from selling certain types of power switchgear assemblies or components thereof to other manufacturers of electrical equipment"; and to "raise the prices of certain types of components purchased by nondefendant manufacturers of electrical equipment for use by them in power switchgear assemblies to be sold in competition with defendant manufacturers, so as to eliminate and suppress competition from them."

The indictment described periodic meetings among colluding switchgear producers from 1956 onward and detailed the terms of the agreements arranged at these gatherings (referred to in the trade as "choir practices"). The indictment read:

At these periodic meetings, a scheme or formula for quoting nearly identical prices to electric utility companies, private industrial corporations, and contractors was used by defendant manufacturers, designated by them as a "phase of the moon" or "light of the moon" formula. Through cyclic rotating positioning inherent in the formula, one defendant manufacturer would quote the low price, others would quote intermediate prices, and another would quote the high price; these positions would be periodically rotated among the manufacturers. This formula was so calculated that in submitting prices to these customers, the price spread between defendant manufacturers' quotations would be sufficiently narrow so as to eliminate actual price competition among them, but sufficiently wide so as to give an appearance of competition. This formula permitted each defendant manufacturer to know the exact price it and every other defendant manufacturer would quote on each prospective sale. . . . A cumulative list of sealed bid business secured by all of the defendant manufacturers was also circulated, and the representatives present would compare the relative standing of each company according to its agreed-upon percentage of the total sales pursuant to sealed bids. The representatives present would then discuss particular future bid invitations and designate which manufacturer should submit the lowest bid therefor, the amount of such bid, and the amount of the bid to be submitted by others.

The indictment observed that these arrangements and understandings "necessitated frequent oral and written communications between representatives of defendant manufacturers. In the course of these communications, various procedures were adopted for the purpose of avoiding detection, including the use by each defendant manufacturer of a code number either as the sole identification of the sender or in conjunction with the use of the first name of its representative. . . ."

The effects of this collusion, the grand jury's indictment concluded, included the following: "Price competition in the sale of power switchgear assemblies throughout the United States has been restrained, suppressed, and eliminated"; prices of "power switchgear assemblies throughout the United States have been raised, fixed, and maintained at high and artificial levels"; buyers "have been deprived of the benefits of free competition in the purchase of these products"; and public agencies "engaged in the generation, transmission, or distribution of electricity . . . have been forced to pay high, artificially fixed prices for power switchgear assemblies."

Initially, all the defendants protested their innocence and confidently predicted vindication when the case came to trial. Shortly thereafter, however, in the light of the irrefutable evidence against them, prudence prevailed; they changed their pleas from "innocent" to "guilty" and threw themselves on the mercy of the court.[3] Since the defendants pleaded guilty, no trial was held. The corporations involved were fined a maximum of $80,000, and the individual defendants a total of $21,500. Two of the latter were also sentenced to thirty days in jail, and four others were given suspended jail sentences of thirty days each. The grand total of penalties assessed against the twenty-nine corporate and fifty-nine individual defendants indicted in the "great electrical conspiracy" amounted to fines of $1,924,500, outright jail sentences for seven, and suspended sentences for several others.

THE PUBLIC POLICY OPTIONS

"People of the same trade," said Adam Smith, "seldom meet together, even for merriment and diversion, but the conversation ends in a conspiracy against the public or some contrivance to raise prices." How to counteract this apparently irresistible temptation to engage in conspiracy, and protect the public from its effects, poses a fundamental public-policy problem. Essentially, there are four alternatives:

1. To make any agreements to restrain trade unenforceable at law.
2. To view agreements among competitors as permissible, even though they may restrain competition among the parties, so long as there is adequate competition in the market as a whole.

3. To view agreements among competitors as permissible, so long as the monopolistic market power created by such agreements is not abused.
4. To prohibit all agreements among competitors, irrespective of their effect on the market as a whole, without having to prove that a particular agreement was contrary to the public interest.

The first alternative—permitting restrictive agreements but precluding private suits to enforce their provisions—need not be discussed at length. It is not seriously advocated except by a minority of laissez-faire extremists. Nevertheless, it contains a germ of truth. Cartels (as the recent experience with OPEC illustrates) are congenitally unstable and impermanent. Indeed, they create powerful pressures militating to their demise. Even without legal harassment, a cartel's effort to establish a high price must normally be supplemented by output quotas assigned to all cartel members, lest they increase production in search of increased profits. Elaborate machinery may be needed to implement cartel rules and regulations: exclusive selling agencies, committees to determine the "right" price, to levy penalties for cheating, to arbitrate disputes, to investigate member complaints, to allocate customers or to arrange for geographical market divisions. Setting a noncompetitively high price may not in itself be enough to make a collusive agreement "stick"— especially where the number of participating firms is large, the temptation to cheat strong, the means of detection and punishment inadequate, the elasticity of demand (because of available substitutes) high, and the possibility of entry by newcomers an ever-present threat. This policy alternative is an inadequate protection for the public, but the market forces on which it relies do provide ancillary support for legal prohibitions against conspiracy.

The second alternative would legally prohibit restrictive agreements only where they could be shown to result in unacceptable market performance and thus be deemed prejudicial to the public interest. It would mean applying a rule of reason in judging the legality of cartel-like behavior on a case-by-case basis. Advocates of this position point out that even where agreements to restrain trade are in force, the participants still retain substantial freedom of action.

Almarin Phillips, for example, reasons that even where firms collude to fix prices, they may compete in non-price ways (quality, advertising, new products, systems of distribution, and so forth). The appropriate public policy, he concludes, requires distinguishing "between organizational behavior which is compatible with the larger public interest and that which is not."[4] The logic of this position is to apply a rule of reason, which would require examining particular cases; in the case of price-fixing, for example, we would have to determine:

1. Whether the arrangement is innocuous because it lacks the power to determine market price.
2. Whether the prices fixed and the profits earned are "reasonable" or "exploitative."
3. Whether the industry in question is, in the absence of unrestrained rivalry, peculiarly vulnerable to "ruinous" competition.
4. Whether depressed conditions in the industry make some restraint on price competition imperative.
5. Whether toleration of restraints on price competition is preferable to the merger of independent firms (which can survive only under the price umbrella provided by the agreement).
6. Whether market performance under the agreement can be improved under alternative control mechanisms such as government regulation or ownership.

Implementing such a rule of reason would of course mean embracing a performance standard and would require the kind of economic evidence and prediction that economic science is unable to furnish. It is a standard of legality that, we shall see, is a slender reed on which to rest the public interest.

The third alternative—permitting agreements unless they create monopoly power and can be proven to have abused that power—is really a question of monopolies, not conspiracies. (This approach is the law of the European Economic Community as expressed in Articles 85 and 86 of the Treaty of Rome.)

The fourth alternative—to prohibit collusive agreements *per se*, without examining their intent or effect—is based on the presumption that unfettered competition is the basic organizing principle and regulatory mechanism of a free-enterprise economy; that any restraint of trade interferes with the effectiveness of competition; that the purpose of almost any collusive action is to restrain, moderate, or eliminate competition; and that, therefore, if competition is to be restrained by private action, some other regulatory system, such as governmental supervision over prices and output would be needed. This, indeed, is the rationale for the acceptance of the *per se* rule by the courts in implementing the provisions of the Sherman Act, which, as we have noted, prohibits *every* contract, combination, or conspiracy in restraint of trade. A review of leading court decisions on this point will highlight the public-policy issues at stake.

THE *PER SE* RULE

THE ADDYSTON PIPE CASE

United States v. *Addyston Pipe and Steel Co.* (1898) was one of the early cases decided by William Howard Taft, then an obscure circuit court judge who was later to become president of the United States and an associate justice of the Supreme Court. The facts of the case were as follows:[5] The Southern Associated Pipe Works was an association of the producers of cast-iron soil pipe used for sewers and culverts. It adopted a plan under which sales to specified cities were reserved for designated members of the association. Other sales in the territory covered by the plan (most of the United States outside the Northeast) would be made at prices set by the association. Contracts were awarded to that member of the association who, in a secret association "auction," agreed to pay the highest "bonus" to the association. The bids submitted to cities buying pipe were then rigged accordingly. Members of the association shared in the accumulated bonuses in proportion to their production capacity, and some members found it more profitable to accept their share of the bonus money than to bid a higher bonus for the privilege of making and selling pipe. The United States sued to enjoin the members of the association from engaging in a combination and conspiracy in restraint of trade in violation of the Sherman Act.

The defendants filed affidavits of their managing officers, stating that the object of their association was not to raise prices beyond what was reasonable, but only to prevent ruinous competition—competition that would have carried prices far below a reasonable point; that the bonuses charged were not exorbitant profits and additions to a reasonable price, but deductions from a reasonable price, in the nature of a penalty or burden intended to curb the natural disposition of each member to get all the business possible, and more than his due proportion; that the prices fixed by the association were always reasonable and subject to the very active competition of other pipe manufacturers; that the reason they sold pipe at much cheaper rates in the Northeast than in the "pay territory" was because they were willing to sell at a loss to keep their mills going rather than to stop them; and, finally, that they did not have a monopoly because their aggregate tonnage did not exceed 30 percent of the nation's total capacity.

In considering these facts, Judge Taft rejected the "rule of reason" standard, and refused to set sail on what he characterized as a "sea of doubt" in attempting to determine "how much restraint of competition is in the public interest, and how much is not. . . . The manifest danger in the administration of justice according to so shifting, vague, and indeterminate standard," he observed, "would seem to be a strong reason against adopting it." He ruled that the restraints of trade imposed by the Addyston conspirators were not "ancillary" to an otherwise lawful contract, but had as their main purpose the elimination of competition between the members of the association. He concluded that the association of the defendants, "however reasonable the prices they fixed, however great the competition they had to encounter, and however great the necessity for curbing themselves by joint agreement from committing financial suicide by ill-advised competition" was prohibited under Section 1 of the Sherman Act.

The standard articulated by Judge Taft in *Addyston Pipe* was validated by the Supreme Court in a number of subsequent cases, including *Trans-Missouri Freight Association,*[6] *Joint Traffic Association,*[7] and *Trenton Potteries.*[8]

THE SOCONY VACUUM CASE

The quintessential rationale for the *per se* rule with respect to price-fixing was articulated by the Supreme Court in the landmark *United States* v. *Socony Vacuum Oil Co.* (1940) decision.[9] The case involved a scheme of industry self-regulation under which the major oil companies operating in the Midwest engaged in a concerted program of buying up "distress" (cut-rate) gasoline offered by independents in the spot market. It was a price-support and price-stabilization program designed to prevent the independents from "spoiling" the market by selling their distress gasoline below the prices charged by the majors. The scheme was to work as follows: each of the majors was to select one or more of the independent refiners having distress gasoline as its "dancing partner" and would assume responsibility for purchasing its distress supply. Under the plan, buying power would be systematically apportioned to keep distress gasoline from the open market, thus neutralizing its price-depressing effect. There were to be no formal contracts to buy this distress gasoline, either between the majors or between them and the independents. Rather it was an informal gentleman's agreement whereby each undertook to perform his share of the joint undertaking.

Purchases were to be made at the "fair going market price." In short, this was to be a price stabilization mechanism not unlike the government's agricultural price-support program—with the notable difference that this arrangement lacked legislative approval by the Congress.

Speaking for a majority of the Supreme Court, Justice William O. Douglas stated the rationale of the *per se* rule in the following terms:

> The reasonableness of prices has no constancy due to the dynamic quality of the business facts underlying price structures. Those who fixed reasonable prices today would perpetuate unreasonable prices tomorrow, since those prices would not be subject to continuous administrative supervision and readjustment in light of changed conditions. Those who controlled the prices would control or effectively dominate the market. And those who were in that strategic position would have it in their power to destroy or drastically impair the competitive system.

He emphasized that monopoly power, control of the market, is not a necessary precondition for condemning conspiratorial action. The thrust of the *per se* rule, he said,

> is deeper and reaches more than monopoly power. Any combination which tampers with price structures is engaged in an unlawful activity. Even though the members of the price-fixing group were in no position to control the market, to the extent that they raised, lowered, or stabilized prices they would be directly interfering with the free play of market forces. The Act places all such schemes beyond the pale and protects that vital part of our economy against any degree of interference. Congress has not left with us the determination of whether or not particular price-fixing schemes are wise or unwise, healthy or destructive. It has not permitted the age-old cry of ruinous competition and competitive evils to be a defense to price-fixing conspiracies. It has no more allowed genuine or fancied competitive abuses as a legal justification for such schemes than it has the good intentions of the members of the combination. If such a shift is to be made, it must be done by the Congress. Certainly Congress has not left us with any such choice. Nor has the Act created or authorized the creation of any special exception in favor of the oil industry. Whatever may be its peculiar problems and characteristics, the Sherman Act, so far as price-fixing agreements are concerned, establishes one uniform rule applicable to all industries alike.

In short, Justice Douglas concluded, *all* forms of collective action among competitors are "banned because of their actual or potential threat to the central nervous system of the economy."

According to the *Socony* decision, as well as subsequent cases, the following pricing actions, jointly undertaken by independent enterprises, are covered by the *per se* rule:

1. Price-fixing agreements regardless of both the substantiality of the trade controlled by the parties and conditions of ruinous competition, financial disaster, evils of price cutting and the like.
2. Any combination which tampers with price structures.
3. Agreements to raise or lower prices whatever machinery for price-fixing is used.
4. Agreements setting the range within which purchases or sales will be made.
5. Combinations formed for the purpose and with the effect of raising, depressing, fixing, pegging, or stabilizing the price of a commodity.
6. All or any of the above, even though the alleged conspiracy is not to be found in any formal contract or agreement and hence must be pieced together.

Section 1 of the Sherman Act applies not only to price-fixing agreements, but to other types of collusive action as well. These include agreements to deprive others of access to necessary facilities for doing business (such as credit, materials, labor, or transportation); agreements to restrict production or sales; agreements to limit research; and agreements to allocate territories or customers.[10]

THE "RULE OF REASON" ALTERNATIVE

One exception to the Supreme Court's consistent application of the *per se* rule to pricing conspiracies should be noted. Despite the fact that it has no value as a legal precedent, *Appalachian Coals, Inc.* v. *United States* (1933) illustrates the philosophical and practical differences between a rule of reason and the *per se* interpretation of Section 1 of the Sherman Act.[11]

The facts in the case were as follows: One hundred thirty-seven producers of bituminous coal, controlling 54.21 percent of the total production in the Appalachian territory (or 64 percent if the output of the "captive" mines be deducted) and 11.96 percent of bituminous coal production east of the Mississippi River, combined to organize an exclusive selling agency, Appalachian Coals, Inc. The producers owned all the capital stock in the company (in proportion to their output) and constituted the company as the exclusive agent for the sale of all coal they mined in the Appalachian territory. The company agreed to establish standard classifications, to sell all the coal of all its principals at the best prices obtainable, and, if all could not be sold, to apportion orders among producers upon a stated basis. Selling prices were to be fixed by the officers of the company at its central office rather than by the individual producers. At the time of the Court's decision, the company had not yet begun operations.

The government contended that this scheme violated the law because "it eliminates competition among the defendants themselves and also gives the selling agency power substantially to affect and control the price of bituminous coal in many interstate markets." The Supreme Court, speaking through Chief Justice Charles Evans Hughes, disagreed. It found the motives of defendants in organizing the company to be "good"; it held that "the primary purpose of the formation of the selling agency was to increase the sale, and thus the production, of Appalachian coal through better methods of distribution, intensive advertising and research, to achieve economies in marketing, and to eliminate abnormal, deceptive, and destructive trade practices." Defendants disclaimed, and the Court did not find any intent to restrain or monopolize interstate commerce; it stated that "the evidence in the case clearly shows that [defendants] have been acting fairly and openly, in an attempt to organize the coal industry and to relieve the deplorable conditions resulting from overexpansion, destructive competition, wasteful trade practices, and the inroads of competing industries." The Court held that the "legality of an agreement or regulation cannot be determined by so simple a test, as whether it restrains competition. Every agreement concerning trade, every regulation of trade, restrains." Therefore, said the Court, "the question of the application of the statute is one of intent and effect, and is not to be determined by arbitrary assumptions."

The Court then proceeded to review the "deplorable" economic conditions of the industry. First, bituminous coal suffered from serious overexpansion, due largely to the stimulus of World War I. Second, coal had been losing markets to oil, natural gas, and water power, and had also been losing ground due to greater efficiency in the use of coal. Third, the industry's unfavorable situation was compounded by such "destructive practices" as the sale of "distress" coal and the "pyramiding" of coal sales (multiple offers to sell the same coal, thus depressing its price). Fourth, the industry was disadvantaged by monopsony and oligopsony —concentration of buyers—in the market. Its decentralized competitive structure put it at a bargaining disadvantage in dealing with concentrated power among its major customers such as steel companies, railroads, and public utilities. Finally, the industry suffered from unfavorable freight rates in penetrating highly competitive markets. These considerations, the Court felt, militated in favor of a scheme to promote "orderly marketing" in the industry without sanctioning any limitation on production.

The Court concluded that the exclusive selling agency would "not have monopoly control in any market nor the power to fix monopoly prices," and that, wherever the selling agency operates, "it will find itself confronted by effective competition backed by virtually inexhaustive [sic] sources of supply, and will also be compelled to cope with the organized buying power of large consumers." Thus, the agency could not injure competition "either through possession or abuse of power."

Moreover, in a statement pregnant with policy implications, the Court observed that if a rule-of-reason standard is applied to monopoly under Section 2 of the Sherman Act, and if, as we shall see in the next chapter, the courts seem to condone "good" monopolists while condemning "bad" monopolists, it would be wrongheaded public policy to condemn agreements between competitors *per se.* Put differently, if the Supreme Court could sanction a massive close-knit combination like U.S. Steel (as it did in 1920) or International Harvester (as it did in 1927), would it not be foolish to condemn outright a loose-knit association of independent firms like Appalachian Coals? Would it not be counterproductive to force the bituminous coal producers into a merger of their facilities in order to correct "deplorable" competitive conditions rather than to permit them to join into an agreement aimed at the same objective while permitting them to retain their corporate independence?

The obvious answer to this dilemma is not to inject a rule of reason into Section 1 of the Sherman Act but to abandon the rule of reason as a standard in enforcing Section 2. The law, after all, is perfectly clear in its intent and its language. It forbids "*every* contract, combination, or conspiracy in restraint of trade" *as well as every* act to "monopolize or attempt to monopolize any part of the trade or commerce among the several states or with foreign nations" (emphasis added). It is based on the presumption that competition is the regulatory mechanism in a free economy and that neither collective action among competitors nor monopolization must be allowed to undermine the viability of that regulatory mechanism. If competition is to perform its social role of protecting the community from the actual or potential abuses of private interests, then competitors must compete rather than cooperate; they must strive for an ever larger share of the market without being allowed to dominate it. If, for reasons of public interest, competition is not a suitable instrument for regulating particular markets or protecting the community, Congress must provide an alternative system to accomplish these social goals. The long line of decisions, culminating in *Socony*, make the ratio-nale for this position abundantly clear.

In other words, the courts are not the proper forum for considering such protestations as "ruinous competition," "financial distress," or "the evils of price-cutting" as justifications for price-fixing. The courts are not —nor should they become—regulatory commissions overseeing hun-dreds of separate industries. Their role is to enforce the rules of competi-tion, and not to provide day-to-day regulatory surveillance. Straying from this role would defeat the philosophical thrust of antitrust.

This does not mean, of course, that Sherman Act strictures must be a Procrustean bed imposed on all industries and all market situations. Obviously, public policy must be flexible enough to make exceptions and modifications where that would better serve the public interest. And Congress has been quite sensitive to pleas for exemptions from the Sherman Act. Indeed, some disinterested observers say it has been *too* responsive to political pressure, granting exemptions for agricultural cooperatives (Capper-Volstead Act, 1922), export associations (Webb-Pomerene Act, 1918), transportation industries (Reed-Bulwinkle Act, 1948), insurance companies (McCarran Act, 1945), and defense contrac-tors (Section 708 of the Defense Production Act, 1950), among others.[12] In each of these cases, Congress has ostensibly provided for safeguards of the public interest other than competition, although that point is hotly disputed. Be that as it may, however, the fact remains that under the American system of government, Congress, not the courts, is the proper agency for granting exemptions from the antitrust laws.

THE OLIGOPOLY DILEMMA

Collusion is a difficult game to play when the numbers involved are large. It is hard to keep a thousand firms in line when their cost structures are different, and when some have an incentive to cheat on a price agreement or to violate output restrictions. "What harm can I possibly do to the other firms," a company reasons, "if I shade my prices slightly below the level I agreed to maintain? What harm do I cause to the others if I exceed my assigned output quota? I am much too small a factor in the market for my actions to have an impact on the group. So I'll just pursue my own self-interest, maximize profits as best I can, and let the devil take the hindmost—agreement or no agreement!" As long as only one firm rea-sons this way, of course, the conclusion is correct. But if many of the thousand firms reason that way, the agreement is undermined. That is why, as noted earlier, large cartels tend to be impermanent and to break down—there is always the "danger" that competition will break out and render conspiracy ineffective.

Numbers do make a difference. When numbers are large, conspiracies are difficult to negotiate, difficult to conceal, and difficult to enforce. But, as the great electrical conspiracy shows, industries dominated by a handful of firms sometimes harbor outright collusion—in part, no doubt, because the conspirators underestimate the probability of detection.

Public policy faces a serious challenge in such industries when the leading firms eschew outright collusion and rely instead on a strategy variously characterized as "tacit collusion," "conscious parallel action," or "recognition of mutual interdependence" to achieve the same results as could be obtained under overt conspiracy. Then the problem becomes one of culpability under the Sherman Act—how to convict oligopolists for achieving by tacit collusion what would be unlawful if accomplished by outright collusion, how to get a conviction for conspiracy when there is no "smoking gun."

The mechanics of tacit collusion, as conventional price theory has long recognized, is predicated on rational behavior by participants in the oligopoly game. And as long as each player behaves rationally, tacit collusion will yield the same results as outright conspiracy. In an industry dominated by a duopoly or the "Big Three" or the "Big Four," each firm quite naturally recognizes its interdependence with its rivals. Firm A knows that if it cuts price in order to increase its market share, its aggressive move will immediately be detected by firms B and C, which will make retaliatory price cuts. Market shares would be unaffected, but all firms would now operate at a lower level of prices—and presumably of profits. Firm A therefore cannot expect to increase its market share (or its revenues) at the expense of its rivals. It cannot afford to calculate in terms of maximizing its own profits, but instead must constantly ask itself whether a particular decision on price or output will be not only in its own best interests, but also in the best interests of its rivals. Recognizing interdependence, it must be concerned with group profit and group welfare. In short, under oligopoly, independent, aggressive, competitive behavior is counterproductive—an "irrational" strategy for the individual firm.

The same kind of thinking will characterize a firm's strategy when contemplating price *increases*. Firm A can be almost certain that if it announces a price increase, the other firms will follow (unless A has totally misjudged the market)—for the simple reason that they know that their refusal to follow would inevitably compel firm A to come back down to the original price level. In other words, they understand that a refusal to follow A's increase would not get them additional market share at A's expense. The only practical option open to them is to share the market with A in the accustomed proportions at the higher price announced by A, or at the original (lower) price. And, as even a casual reading of the *Wall Street Journal* indicates, oligopolists more often than not follow price increases as promptly as they match price cuts—and certainly with more joyful alacrity. The reason, as already noted, is obvious: in an oligopoly, the individual firm cannot "go it alone." Each must recognize that its welfare is intertwined with that of its rivals. Rationality requires that this recognition of mutual interdependence be the cornerstone of every oligopolist's strategy. "Group think" therefore has to replace the calculation of individual advantage, and the firm must behave as a "responsible" member of the group, rather than as an undisciplined, self-seeking competitor.

In oligopolies, this recognition of mutual interdependence ordinarily extends to nonprice competition too—as we have seen in the American steel and automobile industries. After all, if oligopolist A refrains from aggressive price competition but seeks to increase market share by an aggressive innovation program, he cannot expect his rivals to sit idly by. He must expect them to increase their research efforts as a simple matter of self-defense, thus nullifying his expected gains. Anticipating such retaliation—which might erode any oligopoly (above-normal) profits earned by the group—firm A quite rationally may refrain from innovation for the same reasons as it would avoid price-cutting. Rationality again commands "responsible," nonaggressive behavior; the most effective profit-maximization rule under oligopoly is to "get ahead by getting along."

Undoubtedly the degree to which oligopolistic interdependence approximates perfect collusion varies from industry to industry and situation to situation. It depends on such factors as whether the oligopoly is tight-knit (small number of firms) or loose-knit (a larger number); whether it is homogeneous (with a standardized product) or heterogeneous (with a differentiated product); whether it is symmetrical (having firms of roughly equal size and market share) or asymmetrical (with one firm disproportionately larger); whether or not the industry is mature (having had time to develop its internal arrangements and institutions to promote cooperation); whether the industry is populated by "reasonable" managers or by mavericks. But there can be no doubt that rational firm behavior under oligopoly militates toward tacit collusion, that the effects of tacit collusion resemble the effects of outright conspiracy, and —perhaps, most important—that oligopolistic rationality and its collusive effects are the inevitable concomitants of oligopoly industry structures.

To the extent that oligopolistic interdependence and the inevitable tacit collusion are inherent in the structure of oligopoly markets, the public-policy dilemma turns on formulating an effective remedy. How can Section 1 of the Sherman Act deal with oligopolistic collusion? Can the government hope to stop the practice by invoking criminal sanctions —while leaving the industry's underlying oligopoly structure intact? Should it seek an injunction that merely prohibits each oligopolist from considering his rivals' probable reactions when determining his own price and output? In short, can the government require oligopolists to behave irrationally—in defiance of the logic dictated by industry structure—in order to comply with the law?

These questions were poignantly raised in *United States* v. *American Tobacco Co.* (1946), where the Supreme Court condemned conscious parallel action by the Big Three (R. J. Reynolds, Liggett & Myers, and American Tobacco) both in the sale of cigarettes and the purchase of leaf tobacco.[13] The Court convicted the defendants for engaging in anticompetitive practices that, in effect, were the natural, normal, and intelligent consequences of an oligopolistic market structure—something that the defendants' lawyers were quick to point out. One, for example, argued that, even if guilty, the defendants were "entirely without guide as to how they may lawfully avoid creation of evidence of future Sherman Act violations against themselves, unless they ceased business altogether." Must Reynolds, for example, refrain from "percentage buying" of leaf tobacco? If it does and its rivals do likewise, "will it not then be accused of manipulating prices, allocating tobaccos, and discriminating against growers through intermittent buying?" Or "Must Reynolds desist from charging for its product the price charged for a competitive product, and must Reynolds, by prosecution or otherwise, attempt to prevent a competitor from selling at Reynolds' price?" Does the Court's decision mean that "if each seller reacts similarly to the stimulus of the same economic conditions, . . . all are guilty of a criminal act?" Or again, "What are the specific policies and practices we must abandon, modify, or adopt in order to conduct our business according to law? . . . Is everything the [defendants] do illegal, or evidence of illegality, if done by more than one of them?"[14]

These questions are legitimate; they go to the very heart of the public-policy dilemma. If collusion is to be treated—and justly so—as a *per se* violation of the Sherman Act, and if tacit collusion produces substantially the same economic effects as outright collusion, and if tacit collusion is the natural consequence of an oligopolistic industry structure— does it make sense to forbid behavior that is inherent in structure? Or should that behavior be tolerated, while outright conspiracy is condemned, even though both produce identical effects? Or should the government, in prosecuting oligopolistic conspiracy, have the burden of showing evidence of overt collusion—even though we know that the economics of tacit collusion is hardly distinguishable from that of overt collusion?

Current policy against conspiracy clearly does not and cannot deal effectively with the conscious parallel action under oligopoly. If oligopolistic behavior is to be deemed contrary to the public interest, public policy will have to devise means of dealing with the oligopoly structure that militates toward oligopolistic behavior and the consequences flowing from it. It must treat oligopolistic collusion as a structural, "shared monopoly" problem. This is the only way to harmonize the legal strictures against conspiracy with the economic realities of oligopoly.

CHAPTER 10

MONOPOLY

Vice is a monster of so frightful mien,
As, to be hated, needs but to be seen;
Yet seen too oft, familiar with her face,
We first endure, then pity, then embrace.
— Alexander Pope

The wave of corporate consolidations at the turn of the century left the American economic landscape with a number of conspicuous monopolies. They concentrated the output of many major industries in the hands of single dominant firms —notably steel, gypsum, tobacco, copper, explosives, matches, tin cans, farm equipment, baked goods, elevators, lead, railroad cars, electrical equipment, rubber products, paper, brick-making, sugar, business machines, leather, chemicals, photographic equipment, and shoe machinery.[1]

Since then, however, outright single-firm dominance of major industries has decreased. In part, this has been due to the subsequent merger wave of the 1920s, during which small "second-tier" companies in formerly monopolistic industries were combined to create industry structures dominated by the "Big Two" or "Big Three."[2] In part, it has been due to successful government prosecution of some major monopoly corporations. Most recently and perhaps more importantly, it has resulted from increased competition from abroad, and from the deregulation of monopoly industries at home. Indeed, economist William G. Shepherd concludes that owing to these latter factors, "the U.S. economy now

134

appears to be far more competitive than at any time during the modern industrial period"—although he stresses that this outcome is attributable to definite public policies and not just a spontaneous occurrence.[3]

But this does not mean that the monopoly problem has vanished. About $80 billion of U.S. income originates in industries monopolized or dominated by a single firm. Particularly prominent are IBM's dominance in computer equipment, and Kodak's in photographic products.[4]

More significantly, while the *shape* of the monopoly problem has changed, the nature of the problem persists. Rather than overwhelming dominance by a single firm, the nature of the problem today has instead become one of "shared" monopoly and high industry concentration, wherein a few large firms collectively dominate major American industries, such as automobiles, steel, energy, and breakfast cereals.

Hence the core challenge of the monopoly problem in a free-enterprise economy remains one of noncompetitive industry structure and concentration of private economic power. Thus an analysis of monopoly policy in America is important, both because it illustrates the problems posed by disproportionately large firm size and structural market power (whether singly or collectively held), and because it provides a foundation for assessing efforts to resolve the problems created by such market configurations.

THE PUBLIC-POLICY OPTIONS

Basically, there are five public-policy alternatives for dealing with the monopoly problem:

1. A policy of laissez-faire, which would rely on the erosion of monopoly power over time, whenever the monopolist failed to perform in the public interest. Joseph Schumpeter, for example, argued that monopoly power is dissipated, not by the classic notion of competition, but by the dynamic competition that comes from "the new commodity, the new technology, the new source of supply, the new type of organization (the large-scale unit of control for instance)—competition which commands a decisive cost or quality advantage and which strikes not at the margins of profits and the outputs of the existing firms but at their foundations and their very lives."[5] This kind of competition unleashes Schumpeter's "gales of creative destruction" to control monopoly and neutralize the exercise of monopoly power. More recently George Gilder assures us that monopoly positions "are not at all unlimited, because they are always held—unless government in-

tercedes to enforce them—under the threat of potential competitors and substitutes at home or abroad. To the question of how many companies an industry needs in order to be competitive, economist Arthur Laffer answers: one. It will compete against the threat of future rivals. Its monopoly can be maintained only as long as the price is kept low enough to exclude others. In this sense, monopolies are good. The more dynamic and inventive an economy, the more monopolies it will engender."[6] Under this policy, then, government would tolerate both the existence and creation of monopoly.

2. A policy of prohibiting monopoly only where it is created as a result of predatory action against competitors. This policy would tolerate monopoly where it is the result of "normal" business activity. It would distinguish between "good" monopolies and "bad."

3. A policy of prohibiting monopoly only where it has abused its power or where its performance is deficient. Under this policy, intervention would be permitted where the monopolist has charged unreasonable prices, earned exorbitant profits, produced shoddy goods, or failed to demonstrate technological progressiveness.

4. A policy of prohibiting monopoly per se. Under this policy, monopoly would be banned merely because of its structural characteristics—based on the belief that a noncompetitive market structure breeds noncompetitive market conduct, and eventually noncompetitive market performance. Under this policy, monopoly would not be tolerated because, like conspiracy among putative competitors, it is incompatible with the operation of the competitive market as the regulator of a free-enterprise economy.

5. A policy of tolerating private monopoly, but subjecting it to direct surveillance by a specialized government regulatory commission so as to obviate any deleterious effect on the public interest. A variation of this model would be public ownership of monopolized industries, replacing private monopoly with public monopoly.

Congress rejected both the "regulatory" and "laissez-faire" options as a general policy for dealing with monopoly. In Section 2 of the Sherman Act it declared: "Every person who shall monopolize or attempt to monopolize, or combine or conspire with any other person or persons to monopolize any part of the trade or commerce among the several States, or with foreign nations, shall be deemed guilty . . . and . . . punished." Noteworthy in this section is that Congress prohibited monopolizing, not monopoly; it banned mere attempts to monopolize; it forbade single firms as well as groups of firms acting jointly from gaining a stranglehold on the market; it proscribed monopolization of both regional and national markets. In short, just as Section 1 deprived businesses of the freedom to collude and conspire, so Section 2 deprived them of the freedom to monopolize.

The goal of these antimonopoly strictures is clear and unequivocal.[7] But how is this goal to be implemented? How are the courts to determine whether and to what extent monopoly power has subverted impersonal and independent competition "as the mechanism for allocating resources, stimulating and determining the rate of innovation, establishing price, and establishing the terms and conditions for entry and exit from markets?"

In resolving these questions the courts can, as in the case of collusion and price-fixing, follow one of two general policy paths and still remain within the proscriptions of the Sherman Act: (1) they can adopt a structural approach, and declare monopoly to be illegal in and of itself; or (2) they can declare monopoly to be illegal only if it has been achieved (or preserved) by predatory conduct. The first constitutes a *per se* approach, whereby "monopoly" and "monopolization" are held to be synonymous. The second option represents a "rule of reason" approach, whereby the fact of monopoly is not necessarily tantamount to "monopolization." Unlike the Supreme Court's consistency in interpreting Section 1 (collusion), its decisions in monopoly cases have vacillated between these two standards.

THE RULE OF REASON

THE STANDARD OIL CASE

In 1911, the Supreme Court handed down a decision against one of the largest industrial concerns in the country—the Standard Oil Company of New Jersey.[8] In this decision, the Court relied on the rule of reason —or, as it is sometimes called, the "abuse theory of mergers"—which became the ruling precedent in antimonopoly cases for the next forty-five years.

The facts were indisputable. The "trust" controlled nearly 90 percent of petroleum refining in the United States. It achieved this control pursuant to a deliberate plan to obtain a monopoly and to exclude competition from the industry. It implemented that plan by a panoply of predatory practices that filled fifty-seven pages of the lower court's record. Most notable among these "unfair" practices were the following:

1. Standard obtained preferential rebates from the railroads, at times amounting to fully 50 percent of the transportation costs, not only on its own shipments but also on those of its competitors.
2. Standard obtained a near-monopoly of pipelines, primarily by systematic absorption of competitors, and then used its control to discriminate against rival shippers. Its dominance of shipments both by rail and over pipelines was, according to independent observers, perhaps the most significant factor in monopolizing the petroleum industry.
3. Standard systematically lowered prices to an extent ruinous to others in competitive markets, while maintaining them at extortionate levels in other areas. According to the Bureau of Corporations, "in some cases net prices in one locality in a single state, after deducting freight, have been almost double the net prices in another locality in that state."[9] In this way Standard forced competitors out of business, or "persuaded" them to sell out, whenever they had the temerity to try to gain a market share at the expense of the trust.
4. Standard maintained an organized system of espionage and bribery of railroad employees and of its competitors in order to keep informed on every aspect of the business of the few independents that succeeded in retaining a precarious foothold in the industry. (This the lower court and the public considered particularly reprehensible on moral grounds.)
5. Standard allocated exclusive sales areas to its constituent companies so as to eliminate competition among them.

In deciding the Standard Oil case, the Supreme Court promulgated the rule of reason that emphasized not the size of the consolidation in question, nor the number of acquisitions and mergers, nor the resulting degree of market control, but rather the defendant's *intent* to monopolize the industry and the exclusionary practices employed to achieve and maintain dominance. In the light of the facts, the Court concluded that "no disinterested mind can survey the period in question without being irresistibly driven to the conclusion that the very genius for commercial development and organization which it would seem was manifested from the beginning soon begot an intent and purpose to exclude others, which was frequently manifested by acts and dealings wholly inconsistent with the theory that they were made with the single conception of advancing the development of business power by usual methods, but which, on the contrary, necessarily involved the intent to drive others from the field and to exclude them from the right to trade, and thus accomplish the mastery which was the end in view." The evidence of such wrongful purpose and intent, the Court felt, was "so certain as practically to cause the subject not to be within the domain of reasonable contention."

Section 2 of the Sherman Act, according to the Court, did not prohibit monopoly per se, because Congress understood that "the freedom of the individual right to contract, when not unduly or improperly exercised, was the most efficient means for the prevention of monopoly, since the operation of the centrifugal and centripetal forces resulting from the right to freely contract was the means by which monopoly would be inevitably prevented if no extraneous or sovereign power imposed it and no right to make unlawful contracts having a monopolistic tendency were permitted." Put simply, under the rule of reason, monopoly is to be prevented by preserving the freedom to compete (what the Court called "the right to freely contract") and by curbing the predatory practices which destroy that freedom. It is the responsibility of the Court, case by case, to determine whether market control was achieved by "normal" business methods or as a result of "exclusionary" tactics. It must distinguish between "good" trusts and "bad" trusts, and draw the distinction between them on the basis of the defendant's conduct. If, as in *Standard Oil* (and its companion case, *American Tobacco*) the defendants were guilty of "wrongful" intent and "unfair" or "predatory" acts, they must be found guilty and their monopoly dissolved. If, on the other hand, a defendant's conduct was devoid of these baneful characteristics, its market power, however substantial, must be adjudged to be benign and allowed to remain intact.

THE UNITED STATES STEEL CASE

In the U.S. Steel case of 1920, this interpretation of the Sherman Act's monopoly strictures was applied with devastating consequences. The corporation was a holding company organized in 1901, controlling 80 to 90 percent of the nation's steel trade. The announced motives behind the formation of the corporation were to form a completely integrated steel company, to secure the advantages of the most advanced technical organization, and to develop an extensive export trade. Most disinterested observers, however, contend that the primary motives were a desire to "prevent utter demoralization of business and destructive competition" as well as to yield handsome promoter profits to the J. P. Morgan interests.

Shortly after its formation, U.S. Steel embarked on a systematic program of acquiring coking coal and iron-ore resources—far in excess of its likely needs. This led the Bureau of Corporations to conclude that the only "reasonable explanation" for these acquisitions was "to prevent [these resources] from falling into the hands of competitors of the Corporation" and thus to assure its monopoly control over the steel industry.[10]

After the panic of 1907, however, U.S. Steel apparently abandoned these long-range plans for preempting entry and turned to the short-run problem of curbing incipient price competition. It did so by organizing the famous "Gary Dinners," at which Judge Gary, the president of U.S. Steel, exhorted his guests like a Methodist minister at a camp meeting to follow the price leadership of the corporation. These dinners, attended by men representing fully 90 percent of the industry, seemed to accomplish their purpose. They were unceremoniously abandoned in 1911, when the government filed its antitrust suit seeking the dissolution of U.S. Steel.[11]

Applying the rule of reason, the Supreme Court found U.S. Steel not guilty, because the corporation had not "abused" its power. "The Corporation," said the Court,

> did not at any time abuse the power or ascendency it possessed. It resorted to none of the brutalities or tyrannies that the cases illustrate of other combinations. It did not secure freight rebates; it did not increase its profits by reducing the wages of its employees—whatever it did was not at the expense of labor; it did not increase its profits by lowering the quality of its products, nor create an artificial scarcity of them; it did not oppress or coerce its competitors—its competition, though vigorous, was fair; it did not undersell its competitors in some localities by reducing its prices there below those maintained elsewhere, or require its customers to enter into contracts limiting their purchases or restricting them in resale prices; it did not obtain customers by secret rebates or departures from its published prices; there was no evidence that it attempted to crush its competitors or drive them out of the market, nor did it take customers from its competitors by unfair means, and in its competition it seemed to make no difference between large and small competitors.[12]

The Court was not impressed by the contention that U.S. Steel possessed monopoly power over price. It noted that the corporation's market share had declined from near 90 percent in 1901 to roughly 50 percent in 1911. It reasoned that monopoly had not been attained because the firm's ostensible competitors "had to be persuaded by pools, associations, trade meetings, and through the social form of dinners" to stay in line and follow Big Steel's lead. The Court looked upon the Gary Dinners and similar price-fixing activities as evidence of U.S. Steel's "good" conduct; instead of driving competitors out of business like Standard Oil, U.S. Steel had colluded with them in a spirit of live-and-let-live. And this, the Court concluded, was evidence that U.S. Steel had not monopolized the steel industry. In other words, the Court regarded price-fixing to be a foolproof defense against a charge of monopolizing.

The Court was also reassured by the fact that the "company's officers, and, as well, its competitors and customers, testified that its competition was genuine, direct, and vigorous" and that "no *practical* witness was produced by the government in opposition" (emphasis added). The Court therefore rejected the government's argument that competitors followed the corporation's prices because they made money by the imitation; that such imitation was evidence of the corporation's power; and that "universal imitation" was evidence of U.S. Steel's monopoly power.

Finally, in the climax of the decision, the Court stated: "The Corporation is undoubtedly of impressive size, and it takes an effort of resolution not to be affected by it or to exaggerate its influence. But . . . the law does not make mere size an offense, or the existence of unexerted power an offense. It, we repeat, requires overt acts, and trusts to its prohibition of them and its power to repress or punish them. It does not compel competition, nor require all that is possible." In sum, the Court held, not monopoly control of the market, but exclusionary acts, are the essence of a Section 2 violation.

The decision became the controlling precedent in monopoly cases for the next twenty-five years. It vindicated Judge Gary's policy of "friendly competition," which he pursued in spite of some opposition on his board of directors. As *Fortune* observed, Gary's "directors, worthy men but of a cruder age, were honestly puzzled. It was bewildering to hear their Chairman preach the community of interests of all steelmakers, to see him consistently refusing to use the Corporation's size as a club over the rest of the industry. Destructive competition, they pointed out, had made hundreds of millions for Rockefeller's oil trust. But the day came when Gary could point out that the oil trust was busted and that the steel trust had survived, and that its survival was largely due to his policy of 'friendly competition.' "[13]

CRITIQUE OF THE RULE OF REASON

The rule of reason, as we have seen, was concerned not so much with the existence of monopoly power, but the manner in which it was acquired and used. Its distinction between "good" trusts and "bad" trusts virtually converted Section 2 from a law against monopoly to a law against predatory competition.

Professor Milton Handler has emphasized—from a legal point of view —the undesirability of applying an "intent" standard in monopoly cases:

The proponents of any combination always profess the most exalted motives. Since their hearts and minds cannot be searched by the Courts, the Government, in the absence of admissions, must rely on the objective facts for contradiction. To infer intent from extrinsic circumstances is to add another link to the chain of proof and to open the door to metaphysical distinctions, evasions, and further uncertainty. It is the existence of monopoly, and not the reasons which prompted those responsible for its creation, which calls for corrective action. . . . The distinction between good and bad trusts belongs to that outmoded era when the antitrust laws were regarded as a moral pronouncement rather than a charter of economic freedom.[14]

From an economic policy point of view, the "rule of reason" or "abuse" theory of mergers is subject to equally serious criticisms—primarily because it is economically unrealistic and practically unenforceable. Experience indicates that a mere attack on monopolistic practices rarely succeeds in curbing monopoly and fostering competition—especially in industries that show basic structural deviations from the competitive norm. Numerous illustrations could be cited to support this claim, but let us examine only one—the case of the United Shoe Machinery Company. In 1922 the courts perpetually enjoined the company's use of the tying contract, thinking that the primary means for lessening competition and creating monopoly in the industry had thus been eliminated.[15] But the company merely substituted other provisions in its leasing contracts to achieve the same unlawful ends. Moreover, it used its overwhelming financial power to crush independent competitors whenever they appeared, and it infringed on the patents of numerous small competitors and then distributed machines covered by those patents at disastrously low prices, so as to drive their rightful owners out of the industry. The net result was that twenty-five years after the 1922 decree, the Department of Justice was impelled to file a dissolution suit against United Shoe Machinery Corporation as the only way of restoring competition in the industry.[16]

The United Shoe Machinery case and, more recently, the Kodak case, tend to show that drastic surgery, though painful, is often the only means of restoring competition.[17] There are few industries in which monopolistic power can be neutralized by eradicating a single "critical" restraint, for if all the possible highways of restraint are blocked, the monopolist will simply travel cross-country. Moreover, a decree that attempts to block every single highway of restraint—assuming the Antitrust Division had the omniscience to fashion such a decree—would require constant and careful surveillance, the kind of policing job the Antitrust Division is not prepared to undertake. The competitive system is designed to minimize, as much as possible, the administrative regulation and supervision of private industry by the government. Hence the ideal type of decree is one that is basically self-enforcing. A dissolution, divorcement, or divestiture judgment has the great virtue of meeting that requirement, for it creates the type of structural arrangement in an industry that makes direct interference and control unnecessary.

The abuse theory is also unrealistic (from an economic point of view), because once a firm has attained a dominant position in the marketplace, it no longer has to engage in predatory practices to achieve its monopolistic ends. Its mere existence will be sufficient warning to smaller competitors that noncooperation is tantamount to suicide. As Justice Brandeis so brilliantly expressed it:

> Restraint of trade may be exerted upon rivals; upon buyers or upon sellers; upon employers or upon employed. Restraint may be exerted through force or fraud or agreement. It may be exerted through moral or through legal obligations; through fear or through hope. It may exist, although it is not manifested in any overt act, and even though there is no intent to restrain. Words of advice, seemingly innocent and perhaps benevolent, may restrain, when uttered under circumstances that make advice equivalent to command. For the essence of restraint is power; and power may arise merely out of position. Whenever a dominant position has been attained, restraint necessarily arises.[18]

It would appear impossible to attain the objectives of the Sherman Act if only predatory behavior is prohibited while monopoly as such goes unchallenged. The reason is obvious. Section 1 of the act forbids conspiracy in restraint of trade; Section 2 enjoins monopoly and attempts to monopolize. If Section 2 were repealed or allowed to die for lack of enforcement, corporations could achieve by combinations, mergers, and holding companies a more complete control over price and output than they could ever hope to realize under the most elaborate forms of conspiracy. So if we believe that group control over prices, effectuated through concerted action, is economically undesirable, logic and realism require us to oppose similar control achieved through the combination of independent firms into corporate aggregations of Gargantuan proportions.

Finally we must bear in mind that the abuse theory of size is based on the rather dubious assumption that bigness is the guarantor of efficiency in a mass-production economy. In the U.S. Steel case, for example, there is repeated reference to the importance of preserving U.S. Steel as a going concern, and the "risk of injury to the public interest" if that great organization were broken up, including the danger of "a material disturbance of, and, it may be serious detriment to, the foreign trade" —a supreme irony in the light of the industry's subsequent travails with foreign competition. This fear, as we earlier have seen, more often than not is devoid of factual support.

ALCOA AND THE REHABILITATION OF STRUCTURE

In 1945, after the long hiatus of the 1920s and 1930s, during which Section 2 of the Sherman Act had, for all practical purposes, become inert and moribund, the rule of reason was finally reversed in Judge Learned Hand's celebrated *Alcoa* decision.[19] In this decision, which injected renewed force and vigor into antimonopoly prosecutions, Judge Hand, in unmistakable terms,

> interred and reversed the old dictum that size is not an offense under the Sherman Act. Size, he concluded, was not only evidence of violation, or a potential offense, . . . it was the essence of the offense. Size, meaning market control, was what competition and monopoly were about. All other aspects of the case were subordinated to the central and decisive fact that the Aluminum Company of America, many years after its patents had expired, made and then fabricated or sold over 90 percent of the virgin aluminum used in the United States. Its arrangements with foreign companies for dividing the world markets were further evidence of monopolizing. That it had engaged in deplorable tactics to prevent other companies from entering the field helped compound the offense. But the case was proved, in Judge Hand's view, by showing the company's market power. It made over 90 percent of virgin aluminum and therefore had monopoly power.[20]

The reasoning of the opinion took clear aim at the precedent set in *U.S. Steel.* After defining the relevant market and noting that Alcoa controlled 90 percent of it, Judge Hand set forth the underlying purposes of the Sherman Act. Concentrated economic power, he said, was undesirable even if not used extortionately. "Many people believe that possession of unchallenged economic power deadens initiative, discourages thrift and depresses energy; that immunity from competition is a narcotic, and rivalry is a stimulant, to industrial progress; that the spur of constant stress is necessary to counteract an inevitable disposition to let well enough alone. Such people believe that competitors, versed in the craft as no consumer can be, will be quick to detect opportunities for saving and new shifts in production, and be eager to profit by them." In any event, he continued, the mere fact that a producer, having command of the domestic market, has not been able to make more than a "fair" profit, is no evidence that a "fair" profit could not have been made at lower prices. . . . True, it might have been thought adequate to condemn only those monopolies which could not show that they had exercised the highest possible ingenuity, had adopted every possible economy, had anticipated every conceivable improvement, stimulated every possible demand. No doubt, that would be one way of dealing with the matter, although it would imply constant scrutiny and constant supervision, such as courts are unable to provide. Be that as it may, that was not the way that Congress chose; it did not condone "good trusts" and condemn "bad" ones; it forbade all.

Judge Hand suggested that the Sherman Act's proscriptions against monopolization were "not necessarily actuated by economic motives alone. It is possible, because of its indirect social or moral effect, to prefer a system of small producers, each dependent for his success upon his own skill and character, to one in which the great mass of those engaged must accept the direction of a few. . . . Throughout the history of these [antitrust] statutes it has been constantly assumed that one of their purposes was to perpetuate and preserve, for its own sake and in spite of possible cost, an organization of industry in small units which can effectively compete with each other."

The act's prohibition against conspiracy among independent competitors (Section 1) and its prohibition against monopolizing (Section 2), Judge Hand said, must, in order to make sense as economic policy, be interpreted as part of a unified, overall legislative pronouncement:

Starting, however, with the authoritative premise that all contracts fixing prices are unconditionally prohibited, the only possible difference between them and a monopoly is that while a monopoly necessarily involves an equal, or even greater, power to fix prices, its mere existence might be thought not to constitute an exercise of that power. That distinction is nevertheless purely formal; it would be valid only so long as the monopoly remained wholly inert; it would disappear as soon as the monopoly began to operate; for, when it did —that is, as soon as it began to sell at all—it must sell at some price and the only price at which it could sell is a price which it itself fixed. Thereafter the power and its exercise must needs coalesce. Indeed it would be absurd to condemn such contracts unconditionally, and not to extend the condemnation to monopolies; for the contracts are only steps toward that entire control which monopoly confers; they are really partial monopolies.

There can be no doubt, Judge Hand concluded, "that the vice of restrictive contracts and of monopoly is really one; it is the denial to commerce of the supposed protection of competition."

The rule of reason's emphasis on intent, according to Judge Hand, is as irrelevant in monopoly cases as its preoccupation with competitive practices: "No monopolist monopolizes unconscious of what he is doing. So here, 'Alcoa' meant to keep, and did keep, that complete and exclusive hold upon the ingot market with which it started. That was to 'monopolize' that market, however innocently it otherwise proceeded."

Finally, Judge Hand faced up to the perennial problem of distinguishing, as a matter of policy, between the monopoly that has come into being "naturally"—as a result of superior skill, foresight, and efficiency —and a monopoly that does not represent "natural" superiority in the marketplace. In other words, he tried to distinguish between "monopoly" (on which the law is silent) and "monopolizing" (which the law prohibits). He was cognizant that because monopoly might be "thrust upon" the monopolist,

> from the very outset courts have at least kept in reserve the possibility that the origin of a monopoly may be critical in determining its illegality. . . . This notion has usually been expressed by saying that size does not determine guilt; that there must be some "exclusion" of competitors; that the growth must be something else than "natural" or "normal"; that there must be a "wrongful intent," or some other specific intent; or that some "unduly" coercive means must be used. . . . What engendered these compunctions is reasonably plain; persons may unwittingly find themselves in possession of a monopoly, automatically so to say: that is, without having intended either to put an end to existing competition, or to prevent competition from arising when none had existed; they may become monopolists by force of accident.

Or, he allowed, a "single producer may be the survivor out of a group of active competitors, merely by virtue of his *superior skill, foresight and industry*" (emphasis added). The successful competitor, Hand concluded, "having been urged to compete, must not be turned upon when he wins. . . ." Superior skill, foresight, and industry, then, was the famous "thrust upon" exception that Judge Hand recognized as a valid defense to a charge of monopolization. If the defendant was the "passive beneficiary" of market power, he may have a monopoly but he has not illegally monopolized.

The doctrine of the *Alcoa* case was given the approval of the Supreme Court in the *American Tobacco* decision of 1946.[21] There the court found it to be unnecessary that unequivocal expressions of the intent to monopolize be shown or a premeditated and calculated plan to obtain a monopoly be demonstrated. Said the court: "It is not the form of the combination or the particular means used but the result to be obtained that the statute condemns. . . . The . . . material consideration in determining whether a monopoly exists is not that prices are raised and that competition actually is excluded but that power exists to raise prices or to exclude competition when it is desired to do so." With this decision the highest court of the land accepted the proposition that grave injury to competition can result from size and power, standing by themselves, and that monopoly means predominant size within an industry, regardless of the methods by which such size was achieved.

POST-*ALCOA* ISSUES

Two main issues remained to be resolved in the wake of *Alcoa:* How to define the "relevant market" within which the presence, or absence, of monopoly can be determined; and if monopoly is found to be present, how can unlawful monopolization be differentiated from monopoly meritoriously "thrust upon" the firm solely by virtue of "superior skill, foresight, and industry"?

THE "RELEVANT-MARKET" RULE

The Court's definitive treatment of the relevant-market issue came in the *Du Pont Cellophane* opinion of 1956.[22] Du Pont had long dominated the production of cellophane, traditionally accounting for 75 percent or more of American cellophane sales. For many years it also controlled sales by its only other U.S. rival, Sylvania, through various licensing arrangements. The government charged Du Pont with monopolizing, attempting to monopolize, and conspiring to monopolize interstate commerce in cellophane. Du Pont countered by contending that cellophane was merely one among many competing "flexible packaging materials" (foil, glassine, wax paper, grease-proof paper, etc.); that the relevant market thus encompassed all of these materials and their producers; that Du Pont's share of this market was less than 20 percent; and, therefore, that the firm did not have a monopoly (or monopoly power) in any economically meaningful sense.

Proper definition of the relevant market became a critical point of contention in the case. To decide the issue, the Court turned to the economist's concept of "cross-price elasticity of demand"—that is, the willingness of buyers to substitute one good (cellophane) for another (foil) in response to price changes. "Every manufacturer is the sole producer of the particular commodity it makes," the Court held, "but its control in the [monopoly] sense of the relevant market depends on the availability of alternative commodities for buyers: i.e., whether there is a cross-elasticity of demand between cellophane and other wrappings. . . . If a slight decrease in the price of cellophane causes a considerable number of customers of other flexible wrappings to switch to cellophane, it would be an indication that a high cross-elasticity of demand exists between them; that the products compete in the same market. . . ." The relevant market for purposes of ascertaining market share, the Court ruled, "is composed of products that have reasonable interchangeability for the purposes for which they are produced—price, use and qualities considered."

The Court thus ruled that determination of the relevant market was an essential first step in Section 2 cases. And a majority of the Court held that the relevant market in the instant case comprised all flexible wrapping materials, pointing out "there are various flexible wrapping materials that are bought by manufacturers for packaging their goods in their own plants or are sold to converters who shape and print them for use in the packaging of commodities to be wrapped." The majority agreed with Du Pont that, because the firm's share of this market was less than 20 percent, Du Pont had no monopoly. The firm thus was exonerated of monopolization charges.

In his dissenting opinion, however, Chief Justice Earl Warren argued that the concept of cross-elasticity of demand, while correct in principle, had been misapplied in the light of the facts before the Court. He rejected the notion that physical interchangeability was proof of high cross-elasticity. He contended that the true measure of cross-elasticity was economic interchangeability, not physical interchangeability, and that the weight of the available evidence strongly suggested that cellophane was sufficiently distinct on economic grounds as to constitute a relevant market unto itself. For example, cellophane sales grew substantially and continuously for decades, despite the fact that it was two to seven times more expensive than other flexible packaging materials; producers of these other materials consistently ignored both the level of, and changes in, Du Pont cellophane prices; the only firm to respond to Du Pont prices was Sylvania, a producer of cellophane; and where desired, Du Pont had demonstrated the capacity to raise the price—and the profit rate—of cellophane at will. Therefore, Justice Warren concluded, "cellophane is the relevant market. Since Du Pont has the lion's share of that market, it must have monopoly power."

THE "THRUST UPON" RULE

Resolution of the second key issue in the post-*Alcoa* era—distinguishing monopoly "thrust upon" a firm by virtue of "superior skill, foresight, and industry" from unlawful anticompetitive monopolization—can perhaps best be analyzed in the context of the *Kodak* case. The facts of the case also reveal the limitations of the relevant-market concept as a tool for evaluating market power when a monopolist is integrated across interdependent stages of an industry.

In this case, Berkey Photo charged that Kodak illegally monopolized a number of amateur photographic products, including inexpensive amateur snapshot cameras.[23] That Kodak wielded monopoly power was not seriously questioned. "There is little doubt that the evidence supports the jury's implicit finding that Kodak had monopoly power in [inexpensive snapshot] cameras," Judge Irving R. Kaufman wrote on appeal, and it is "clear that Kodak possessed a monopoly in the film and color paper markets during the period relevant to this suit."[24]

The critical question in the case, then, concerned the reasons for Kodak's monopoly. Did Kodak's monopoly result from good performance, or was it the result of anticompetitive market control?

As Judge Kaufman viewed the record, Kodak's snapshot-camera monopoly seemed to be attributable to superior innovativeness.

In 1963 Kodak first marketed the 126 Instamatic instant-loading camera, and in 1972 it came out with the much smaller 110 Pocket Instamatic. Not only are these cameras small and light, but they employ film packaged in cartridges that can simply be dropped in the back of the camera, thus obviating the need to load and position a roll manually. Their introduction triggered successive revolutions in the industry. Annual amateur still camera sales in the United States averaged 3.9 million units between 1954 and 1963, with little annual variation. In the first full year after Kodak's introduction of the 126, industry sales leaped 22 percent, and they took an even larger quantum jump when the 110 came to market.

He found Kodak's integration across the industry's various fields, as well as the firm's practice of marketing its products as photographic systems, to be unobjectionable:

The first firm, even a monopolist, to design a new camera format has a right to the lead time that follows from its success. The mere fact that Kodak manufactured film in the new format as well, so that its customers would not be offered worthless cameras, could not deprive it of that reward. Nor is this conclusion altered because Kodak not only participated in but dominated the film market. Kodak's ability to pioneer formats does not depend on its possessing a film monopoly. Had the firm possessed a much smaller share of the film market, it would nevertheless have been able to manufacture sufficient quantities of 110-size film . . . to bring the new camera to market. It is apparent, therefore, that the ability to introduce the new format without predisclosure was solely a benefit of integration and not, without more, a use of Kodak's power in the film market to gain a competitive advantage in cameras. . . .

Finally, Judge Kaufman held Kodak's success in the market and consumer acceptance of its products to be proof of good performance: "No one can determine with any reasonable assurance whether one product is superior to another. Preference is a matter of individual taste. The only question that can be answered is whether there is sufficient demand for a particular product to make its production worthwhile, and the response, so long as the free choice of consumers is preserved, can only be inferred from the reaction of the market."

Judge Kaufman therefore reversed the jury's verdict that Kodak had illegally monopolized snapshot cameras: "Because . . . a monopolist is permitted, and indeed encouraged, by [Section] 2 to compete aggressively on the merits, any success that it may achieve through 'the process of invention and innovation' is clearly tolerated by the antitrust laws. . . ." In other words, Kodak's monopoly position in the camera market was not to be equated with monopolization; its position, he felt, was the result of "superior skill, foresight, and industry" and hence not unlawful.

Yet Judge Kaufman's opinion is troublesome on at least two counts, both of which ultimately stem from Kodak's integrated monopoly. First, while they seem plausible on the surface, consumer acceptance and market success may be defective gauges of good performance and technological progressiveness in an industry such as amateur photography, which comprises functionally interdependent products and markets, and which is dominated by an integrated monopolist able to transfer power between markets. For example, Kodak for decades prevented other camera producers from introducing innovative, compact, cartridge-loading cameras merely by refusing to make its films—and, given its film monopoly, virtually all films—available in the needed format. In fact, Judge Kaufman touched on this in his opinion: "Kodak has never supplied film to fit the Minox, a small camera that uses a cartridge similar to that of the Instamatics, and that has been on the market since the 1930s, or similar cameras by Minolta and Mamiya that were also introduced before the Kodak 126. Merchants of these cameras, including Berkey, made numerous requests that Kodak sell film packaged in their formats, with or without the Kodak name. As an alternative, they asked Kodak to sell bulk film rolls large enough to permit the camera manufacturers economically to cut the film down to the appropriate size and spool it. Kodak denied all such appeals. Some of the miniature cameras did survive but, as even Kodak's own economic expert testified, its policy drastically reduced the ability of rival manufacturers to compete by introducing new camera formats." Thus, consumer acceptance and commercial success may reflect either superior innovativeness or, instead, illegal monopolization of trade by preventing others from innovating. A review of performance alone and in isolation, in other words, cannot distinguish "good" monopoly from unlawful monopolization. Instead, performance can only be meaningfully analyzed when viewed in conjunction with industry structure.[25]

  Second, it follows then that industry structure, as opposed to the structure of any particular market, must be the relevant point of departure in evaluating the existence, nature, and magnitude of monopoly power in an industry encompassing functionally interdependent products and markets. Kodak's control of the camera field ultimately rests in its *film* monopoly and its power to control or block camera innovation by choosing (or refusing) to make its films available in the formats required by other camera producers. The relevant-market concept, however, focuses attention on the precise boundaries of a particular narrowly defined market, the firm's share of that particular market, trends over time in the firm's share of that particular market, and so forth. Relevant market analysis alone is incapable of identifying monopoly power that flows from the structure of the industry in which a particular market is subsumed—power that arises in one market but can be exercised in other, related markets. In these cases, the facts in *Kodak* show that an economically meaningful appraisal of monopoly power must begin with an analysis of the structure of the industry, rather than with an analysis of any individual market viewed in isolation.[26]

In closing our examination of monopoly policy, certain propositions can be asserted with some assurance: Prolonged contention over the accurate definition of the "relevant market," especially in cases involving control over several interdependent adjacent markets, is likely to be crucial in any monopoly litigation. The same applies to inevitable disputes over the exact meaning of the concepts of "thrust upon" and "superior skill, foresight, and industry." Finally, in cases where the courts find that Section 2 has been violated, the persistent problem of fashioning an appropriate remedy will continue to bedevil the antitrust enforcement authorities. Indeed, we shall see in chapter 15 that these nagging problems have to an important extent impeded antimonopoly policy in practice, and we will discuss some options that have been proposed to ameliorate them.

CHAPTER 11

THE MERGER PROBLEM

Matchmaker, matchmaker,
Make me a match,
Find me a find,
Catch me a catch.

Matchmaker, matchmaker,
Make me a match,
Look through your book,
And make me a perfect match!

— *Fiddler on the Roof*

"If big businesses are not more efficient," economist George J. Stigler once asked, "how did they get so big? The answer is that most giant firms arose out of mergers."[1]

Corporate consolidations at the turn of the century marked America's first wave of merger mania. A second wave of merger-induced giantism occurred in the period from World War I to the beginning of the Great Depression. A third wave began in the 1960s, peaked in 1969, temporarily diminished during the 1970s, but reached unprecedented hundred-billion-dollar proportions by the early 1980s. In 1984, a record-breaking $122 billion was spent on corporate mergers and acquisitions. In 1985, yet another record, of $179 billion, was set.

THE 1914 MERGER LEGISLATION

Shortly after the turn of the century, the government became mired in monopolization proceedings against Standard Oil, American Tobacco, Du Pont, and other combines assembled during the first merger movement. At the time, the perception arose that if potentially anticompetitive acts and practices, including mergers, could be arrested in their incipiency, the difficulties, costs, and complications of Sherman Act correctives—including divestiture and reorganization—could be avoided. That is, the recognition grew that prevention was better than correction —that the best way to curb monopoly would be to halt merger-based trends toward concentration and market control early, before they necessitated complex structural reorganization proceedings. In other words, it would be easier to maintain competitive market structures than to reestablish them once they had been destroyed through acquisition and consolidation.

The Clayton Act of 1914, heralded as a cornerstone of Woodrow Wilson's New Freedom, contained an antimerger plank among its various provisions. As originally enacted, Section 7 of the act provided that "no corporation engaged in commerce shall acquire, directly or indirectly, the whole or any part of the stock or other share capital of another corporation . . . where the effect of such acquisition may be to substantially lessen competition between the corporation whose stock is so acquired and the corporation making the acquisition, or to restrain such commerce in any section or community, or tend to create a monopoly of any line of commerce."[2] Ostensibly this section was preventive. It sought not to prohibit all mergers, but to bar only those that threatened to substantially lessen competition and those that might *tend* to create a monopoly.

Yet as subsequent events demonstrated, this section contained at least two fatal loopholes—defects further exacerbated by the courts' interpretations. First, it barred only those anticompetitive mergers effectuated through acquisitions of *stock*, but not those involving the direct acquisition of *assets* (including, according to Supreme Court interpretation, instances where stock purchases were liquidated following acquisition in order to create asset ownership). Second, the "acquiring-acquired" language of Section 7 seemed to cover only horizontal combinations, leaving vertical and conglomerate mergers unaffected. Moreover, in interpreting and applying the 1914 merger provision, the courts eventually adopted Sherman Act monopolization standards for determining illegality: mergers had to comprise market shares of monopolistic proportions before they would be struck down as threatening to substantially lessen competition—an interpretation that destroyed the preventive purpose of the policy.

Hence, by the 1930s the Federal Trade Commission reported Section 7 to have been "completely emasculated."[3] Only fifteen mergers were ordered dissolved as a result of all antitrust action between 1914 and 1950—and only five from Clayton Act proceedings.[4]

THE 1950 MERGER AMENDMENTS

Not until 1950 were the loopholes in Section 7 closed and its preventive purpose legislatively asserted. The Celler-Kefauver Amendment substituted new language for Section 7: "No corporation engaged in commerce shall acquire, directly or indirectly, the whole or any part of the stock of other share capital and no corporation . . . shall acquire the whole or any part of the assets of another corporation engaged also in commerce, where in any line of commerce in any section of the country, the effect of such acquisition may be substantially to lessen competition, or to tend to create a monopoly."

The effects of the Cellar-Kefauver Amendment were three: First, it explicitly brought asset acquisitions within the reach of the law. Second, it eliminated the "acquiring-acquired" language, which meant that the new Section 7 would apply to *all* types of mergers, including the following (as defined by the Federal Trade Commission):

1. Horizontal mergers: those in which the merging companies produce one or more closely related products in the same geographic market —for example, two fluid milk companies in the city of Washington, D.C.
2. Vertical mergers: those in which the merging companies have a buyer-seller relationship before merger—for example, an aluminum-ingot manufacturer and an aluminum-product fabricator.
3. Conglomerate mergers:
   a. Geographic-market-extension mergers: those in which the acquired and acquiring companies manufacture the same products, but sell them in different geographic markets—for example, a bakery in Washington, D.C., and a bakery in Chicago. Because such mergers frequently closely resemble horizontal mergers, they are sometimes called "chain" horizontals.
   b. Product-extension mergers: those in which the acquired and acquiring companies are functionally related in production or distribution

but sell products not in direct competition with each other—for example, a merger between soap and bleach manufacturers.
c. Other conglometrate mergers: those involving the union of two companies having neither a buyer-seller relationship nor a functional relationship in manufacturing or distribution, such as a shipbuilder and an ice-cream manufacturer.

Third, it stressed the preventive purpose of merger policy. Said the House Committee on the Judiciary in its report recommending passage of the amendment: "Acquisitions of stock or assets have a cumulative effect, and control of the market sufficient to constitute a violation of the Sherman Act may be achieved not in a single acquisition but as the result of a series of acquisitions. The bill is intended to permit intervention in such a cumulative process when the effect of an acquisition may be a significant reduction in the vigor of competition, even though this effect may not be so far-reaching as to amount to a combination in restraint of trade, create a monopoly, or constitute an attempt to monopolize."[5]

THE POLICY POSTURE OF THE WARREN COURT

The Supreme Court first interpreted the meaning of the new Section 7 in the celebrated *Brown Shoe* case.[6] Speaking for a unanimous Court, Chief Justice Earl Warren stated:

First, there is no doubt that Congress did wish to "plug the loophole" and to include within the coverage of the Act the acquisition of assets no less than the acquisition of stock.

Second, by the deletion of the "acquiring-acquired" language in the original text, it hoped to make plain that Section 7 applied not only to mergers between actual competitors, but also to vertical and conglomerate mergers whose effect may tend to lessen competition in any line of commerce in any section of the country.

Third, it is apparent that a keystone in the erection of a barrier to what Congress saw was the rising tide of economic concentration, was its provision of authority for arresting mergers at a time when the trend to a lessening of competition in a line of commerce was still in its incipiency. Congress saw the process of concentration in American business as a dynamic force; it sought to assure the Federal Trade Commission and the courts the power to brake this force at its outset and before it gathered momentum.

Fourth, and closely related to the third, Congress rejected, as inappropriate to the problem it sought to remedy, the application to Section 7 cases of the standards for judging the legality of business combinations adopted by the courts in dealing with cases arising under the Sherman Act, and which may have been applied to some early cases arising under original Section 7.

Fifth, at the same time that it sought to create an effective tool for preventing all mergers having demonstrable anticompetitive effects, Congress recognized the stimulation to competition that might flow from particular mergers. When concern as to the Act's breadth was expressed, supporters of the amendments indicated that it would not impede, for example, a merger between two small companies to enable the combination to compete more effectively with larger corporations dominating the relevant market, nor a merger between a corporation which is financially healthy and a failing one which no longer can be a vital competitive factor in the market. The deletion of the word "community" in the original Act's description of the relevant geographic market is another illustration of Congress's desire to indicate that its concern was with the adverse effects of a given merger on competition, only in an economically significant "section" of the country. Taken as a whole, the legislative history illuminates congressional concern with the protection of competition, not competitors, and its desire to restrain mergers only to the extent that such combinations may tend to lessen competition.

Sixth, Congress neither adopted nor rejected specifically any particular tests for measuring the relevant markets, either as defined in terms of product or in terms of geographic locus of competition, within which the anticompetitive effects of a merger were to be judged. Nor did it adopt a definition of the word "substantially," whether in quantitative terms of sales or assets or market shares or in designated qualitative terms, by which a merger's effects on competition were to be measured.

Seventh, while providing no definite quantitative or qualitative tests by which enforcement agencies could gauge the effects of a given merger to determine whether it may "substantially" lessen competition or tend toward monopoly, Congress indicated plainly that a merger had to be functionally viewed, in the context of its particular industry. That is, whether the consolidation was to take place in an industry that was fragmented rather than concentrated, that had seen a recent trend toward domination by a few leaders or had remained fairly consistent in its distribution of market shares among the participating companies, that had experienced easy access to markets by suppliers and easy access to suppliers by buyers or had witnessed foreclosure of business, that had witnessed the ready entry of new competition or the erection of barriers to prospective entrants, all were aspects, varying in importance with the merger under consideration, which would properly be taken into account.

Eighth, Congress used the words "*may* tend substantially to lessen competition" [emphasis supplied], to indicate that its concern was with probabilities, not certainties. Statutes existed for dealing with clear-cut menaces to competition; no statute was sought for dealing with ephemeral possibilities.

Mergers with a probable anticompetitive effect were to be proscribed by this
Act.

These considerations, the Supreme Court ruled, must guide the judicial
interpretations of the new Section 7.

The antimerger policy embodied in the Celler-Kefauver Act and its
sympathetic interpretation by the Warren Court represent one public-
policy alternative. It rests on a specific presumption against growth by
combination, and in favor of growth by internal expansion. This presumption, in turn, is based on four major postulates.

According to the first postulate, firms should grow by methods that
create competition rather than lessen it—by building rather than buying. Internal growth, manifest in new plants or new products, can
scarcely avoid intensifying competition, whereas combination, which
eliminates an independent unit from the market, tends to lessen competition.

A second postulate holds that internal growth reflects success in the
market, whereas combination implies the artificial elimination of a going
concern. Funds for internal growth can come either from profits, reflecting consumer acceptance of the firm's products, or sale of securities,
reflecting investor approval of the firm's financial performance. In either
case, the firm's growth has presumably been justified by objective market standards—in contrast to the merger process, which implies an artificial short-circuit of market judgment. This does not mean that a
monopoly might not grow by internal means alone and still yield undesirable social consequences. It means only that growth by merger, if permissible without restraint, would hasten the structural transformations
in industry that the antitrust laws are designed to prevent.

The third postulate states that economies of scale can be realized
through internal growth as well as through acquisition and merger. To
forbid size achieved through merger does not condemn a firm, an industry, or society to a loss of economic efficiency. A firm that must be big
in order to be efficient may achieve the necessary size through internal
growth—without destroying a competitor. It may be argued, of course,
that a strict antimerger statute will stifle the creation of optimum-size
firms, because some markets are too small to accommodate two firms
operating at maximum efficiency. Whether this reservation is relevant
in many industries—or, indeed, any—has not yet been demonstrated,
except in such public utilities as electric light and power, local tele-
phones, and gas distribution. (In these "natural monopoly" industries,
the market is clearly too narrow for duplicate firms of optimum size—
but these industries are not in the free-enterprise segment of the econ-

omy, nor are they expected to operate in accordance with the structural model presupposed by the antitrust laws. Their performance in the public interest is not compelled by competition, but controlled by public regulation or public ownership.)

The fourth postulate states that collective action in restraint of trade —whether among competitors or between suppliers and customers—is incompatible with a competitive free-enterprise system. Thus, any agreement to fix prices is a *per se* violation of the law. Given this unconditional prohibition of price control by agreement, how can the law permit price control by merger? Obviously, if contracts, agreements, and conspiracies in restraint of trade strike at the central nervous system of a competitive economy, mergers and combinations have the same effect. Both represent a "denial to commerce of the supposed protection of competition."[7] Both are inimical to a system that operates through the compulsions that exogenous, untrammeled market forces bring to bear on numerous and independent centers of initiative—a system that cannot tolerate in any form collective action that seeks to immunize firms from the pressure of the marketplace.

THE CURRENT CRITIQUE OF THE WARREN COURT

Today, both the Clayton Act and its interpretation by the Warren Court have come under increasing criticism, and alternative policies are being propounded to deal with the merger problem. Three of these alternatives merit particular attention.

First is the policy approach advocated by Robert Bork, Richard Posner, and other adherents of the Chicago School. (This approach is embodied in the 1984 Justice Department merger guidelines, and in the Reagan Administration's proposals for "liberalizing" Section 7.) In an apparent return to pre-1950 policy, they would permit *all* mergers— horizontal, vertical, and conglomerate. The only exception to the rule would be horizontal mergers that reach monopolistic proportions. The rationale is twofold: first, so the argument runs, mergers are designed to achieve efficiency and economies of scale, and rarely have any anticompetitive consequences. In this context, says Bork, the notion of "incipiency" is nonsense:

> The difficulty with stopping a trend toward a more concentrated condition at a very early stage is that the existence of the trend is prima facie evidence that greater concentration is socially desirable. The trend indicates that there are emerging efficiencies or economies of scale—whether due to engineering

and production developments or to new control and management techniques —which make larger size more efficient. This increased efficiency is valuable to the society at large, for it means that fewer of our available resources are being used to accomplish the same amount of production and distribution. By striking at such trends in their very earliest stages the concept of incipiency prevents the realization of those very efficiencies that competition is supposed to encourage.[8]

Accordingly, Bork contends that horizontal mergers affecting up to 60 or 70 percent of any market should automatically be permitted.[9] Second, public policy should, according to Bork, be wholly unconcerned with vertical and conglomerate mergers since, by definition, they do not involve direct competitors and thus, he reasons, they can pose no competitive threat.[10] Vertical and conglomerate power, in other words, are optical illusions.

A second policy approach builds on the foregoing and views mergers (especially takeovers) as a valuable instrument for forcing corporate managements to perform in the best interest of the stockholders. According to the President Reagan's Council of Economic Advisers, for example, the separation of management from ownership in the modern corporation, and the delegation of authority by stockholders to management, "creates a possibility that management will operate the corporation in management's best interests, and not in the best interests of the corporation's stockholders." The adverse consequences of this are serious, the council warns, "because, if unchecked, it can deter socially beneficial mergers, keep assets from being allocated to higher valued uses, impede adoption of more profitable capitalization plans, and otherwise prevent publicly traded corporations from making the largest possible contribution to aggregate economic performance." Takeovers and the generalized "market for corporate control," according to this view, prevent a divergence of interests by forcing incumbent management to "demonstrate that its performance is competitive with the performance of other potential managers. . . . In this fashion, the external market for corporate control disciplines managers who believe they have maximized the value of the corporation's shares when, in fact, they have not." Superimposed upon this (undocumented) belief that mergers improve efficiency and transfer resources to higher valued uses, the Council warns that restraints on takeover activity would only protect inefficient managers from the discipline of the merger market for corporate control.[11]

Yet a third policy alternative would explicitly take into account the alleged efficiencies involved in particular mergers and would permit anticompetitive mergers where efficiency gains could be shown to out-weigh losses in competition. Professor Joe Bain was an early advocate of this approach. Said Bain, "a standard of reasonableness, or definition of the grounds on which otherwise offending mergers could be found legal, is clearly needed and should be set forth in Section 7. The one simple rule that is obviously needed is that a merger which may substantially lessen competition should be allowed if the merging firms can demonstrate that the merger would substantially increase real efficiency in production and distribution. . . . This sort of amendment would strengthen a very significant piece of legislation, and tend to assure that its enforcement would be in accord with accepted principles of economic rationality."[12]

One variant of this policy has been proposed by Professor Oliver Williamson.[13] Another is found in the Revised Merger Guidelines of June 14, 1984, in which the Department of Justice propounds an "efficiency/anticompetitiveness" trade-off approach. These twice-revised guidelines specify: "Some mergers that the Department might challenge may be reasonably necessary to achieve significant net efficiencies. If the parties to the merger establish by clear and convincing evidence that a merger will achieve such efficiencies, the Department will consider those efficiencies in deciding whether to challenge the merger. . . . The parties must establish a greater level of expected net efficiencies the more significant are the competitive risks identified in [these guidelines]."[14] It is important to note that the Revised Merger Guidelines—by administrative interpretation—change the legislative content of Section 7 and represent a fundamental shift in enforcement policy.

THE RIGHT POLICY TOWARD MERGERS?

The foregoing summarizes the history of merger policy and current merger-policy debates. In the next three chapters we shall examine how merger policy evolved after the Celler-Kefauver Amendment of 1950—specifically, policy toward horizontal mergers, vertical mergers, and conglomerate mergers. We shall explore the anticompetitive problems posed by each, the decisions of the courts, and the economic aftereffects of merger-policy enforcement (or lack of it). Finally, we shall inquire whether current criticisms of post-1950 policy (and their theoretical underpinnings) have any basis in fact—whether, as some critics contend, American merger policy is desperately in need of major repair.

CHAPTER 12

HORIZONTAL MERGERS AND JOINT VENTURES

In any collaboration, whether by an agreed merger or a subsidiary joint venture, it is likely that at least one partner will be fleeing the full force of competition (otherwise, why not stay separate?). — *Economist*, June 1986

As we have seen, Judge William Howard Taft in 1898 struck down a bid-rigging scheme involving the Addyston Pipe & Steel Company and five other firms. But the government's victory in the case was easily nullified by a merger between the erstwhile conspirators: "Three months after Judge Taft's decree enjoining the pool, the four Tennessee and Alabama companies consolidated to form the American Pipe and Foundry Company. Nine months later, in March 1899, the merger was extended, under the name United States Cast Iron Pipe and Foundry, to take in the two remaining defendants and five firms in the northeastern states, thus including 75 per cent of the entire industry." As Simon Whitney observed, the "consolidated company could now do even better than achieve the goal of the pool, for it included some of the pool's competitors."[1]

The Addyston episode is instructive. It shows how horizontal mergers —mergers between rivals—can be used to dampen competition and restructure markets, a ready alternative to collusion as an instrument of market control. The episode highlights the critical role that merger policy plays in a well-orchestrated, balanced antitrust program. Obviously it is fruitless to outlaw collusion and conspiracy under a *per se* rule if the conspirators can achieve the same objective—more effectively—by consolidation of control via merger.

161

The Clayton Act's prohibition of mergers that tend to substantially lessen competition is designed to close that potential loophole in antitrust policy. It seeks to prevent horizontal mergers that would increase concentration in already concentrated industries and to prevent such concentration from developing in relatively *un*concentrated industries and markets.

But how large must the combined market share of merging competitors be before a combination between them threatens to substantially lessen competition? Clearly, a horizontal consolidation of all competitors in a market would create a monopoly—but this presumably would trigger the monopolization proscriptions of the Sherman Act. On the other hand, a merger between rivals collectively accounting for 1 percent of a market would be of trivial proportions, and by itself would portend no competitive threat. But what of mergers between these two extremes? At what level might horizontal mergers threaten to substantially lessen competition? In a related vein, what of joint ventures, like that between General Motors and Toyota, where rivals *partially* combine *some* of their operations, but not all?

HORIZONTAL MERGERS

The use of Section 7 of the Clayton Act (with the Celler-Kefauver Amendment) is best illustrated by two landmark horizontal-merger cases—one in an already concentrated industry, and one not.

THE BETHLEHEM STEEL CASE

In *United States* v. *Bethlehem Steel* (1958), the Southern District Court of New York upheld the government's challenge to Bethlehem Steel's attempted acquisition of one of its major rivals, Youngstown Sheet and Tube.[2]

At the time, Bethlehem was the country's second largest steel producer and ninth largest industrial firm. Youngstown was the fifth largest steel company and fifty-third largest industrial concern. Each was fully integrated, from mining through smelting to making ingots and finished steel products. And they were clearly competitors: 75 percent of their combined production capacity was devoted to the production of the same steel products; each firm maintained sales offices throughout the nation, including at least twenty-four of the same large cities; and each shipped between 86 and 94 percent of its output to the midcontinent market.

The government filed suit against the merger on the grounds that it threatened to substantially lessen competition. In their defense, the firms urged that any lessening of competition between them would be more than offset by "the benefits which would accrue from Bethlehem's plan to expand the Youngstown plants, thus creating new steel capacity . . . and enhancing the power of the merged company to give United States Steel more effective and vigorous competition than Bethlehem and Youngstown" could separately provide. Indeed, Bethlehem pleaded that only by acquiring Youngstown could it undertake to produce steel in the Chicago area; construction of an entirely new, fully integrated mill, according to Bethlehem, was simply out of the question.

In deciding the case, the court placed the merger in structural context. It observed the steel industry to be a concentrated field wherein the twelve largest integrated firms collectively held almost 83 percent of total ingot capacity, the six largest had almost 68 percent, and the two largest (United States Steel and Bethlehem) had 45 percent. The court found mergers to be responsible to an important degree for the industry's concentrated structure. For example, "Bethlehem was incorporated in 1904 as a consolidation of ten companies. Since its formation, it has acquired the properties of more than thirty independent companies. Its initial entry into each new steel-producing location in various parts of the country has been achieved through the acquisition of other companies. Indeed, *Bethlehem has never built a new steel plant in a new location*" (emphasis added). Likewise, a substantial portion of Youngstown's size was attributable to mergers and acquisitions.[3] The court further found that the industry was effectively insulated from new competition and that its concentrated structure was correspondingly entrenched. Finally, the court observed price competition in the industry to be essentially nonexistent: "The record establishes that United States Steel initiates the price changes for steel products and that its lead is followed by all other steel producers. With few exceptions, the mill price for each steel product does not vary significantly from company to company."

In the light of the industry's structure and conduct, the court ruled that the Bethlehem-Youngstown combination unlawfully threatened to substantially lessen competition in at least three important ways.

First, if permitted, the merger "would add substantially to concentration in an already highly concentrated industry and reduce unduly the already limited number of integrated steel companies." Indeed, the court found that it would result in "the greatest increase in concentration in the iron and steel industry from 1901 to 1958 . . . with the exception of the decade 1920 to 1930 when Bethlehem and other large companies were engaged in a series of important mergers and acquisitions."

Second, the merger would not only eliminate Youngstown as an independent entity, it would also "make even more remote than at present the possibility of any real competition from the smaller members of the industry who follow the leadership of United States Steel."

Third, to permit the Bethlehem-Youngstown consolidation on the grounds that the merged firm would be better able to compete with U.S. Steel, the largest producer in the industry, would likely touch off a chain reaction of further mergers. This, in turn, would further exacerbate concentration in steel:

> If there is logic to the defendants' contention that their joinder is justified to enable them, in their own language, to offer challenging competition to United States Steel . . . which exercises dominant influence over competitive conditions in the steel industry . . . then the remaining large producers in the "Big 12" could with equal logic urge that they, too, be permitted to join forces and to concentrate their economic resources in order to give more effective competition to the enhanced "Big 2"; and so we reach a point of more intense concentration in an industry already highly concentrated—indeed we head in the direction of triopoly.

Given these anticompetitive threats, and in the light of the industry's structure and conduct, the court struck down Bethlehem's attempted takeover of Youngstown.

The economic consequence of the court's decision in the case is particularly significant. Once the avenue of expansion through merger was blocked, Bethlehem proceeded to do exactly what it had earlier pleaded was impossible—it built an entirely new plant at Burns Harbor, Indiana, "the only integrated green-field blast furnace oxygen converter–rolling mill complex built during the 1960s and 1970s to provide a U.S. counterpart to the modern steel-making capacity growing by leaps and bounds abroad"—in order to better compete in the midcontinent market.[4] Thus, contrary to the dire warnings incessantly sounded by laissez-faire ideologues, antitrust enforcement in this case did not spell economic catastrophe. Instead, it resulted in the building of a new, state-of-the-art facility, which enhanced operating efficiency in a technologically backward industry. At the same time it afforded steel buyers one more—rather than one less—source of supply.

THE VON'S GROCERY CASE

An equally important task of merger policy is to prevent concentration and horizontal power from arising as a result of mergers and acquisitions between competing rivals. *United States* v. *Von's Grocery* (1966) is important because in this and a number of companion suits the government sought to stem a rising tide of merger-induced concentration in grocery retailing, a traditionally unconcentrated field.[5] Subsequent events are highly significant here, for they again demonstrate how enforcement—or nonenforcement—of the merger statute can shape the evolution of industry structure.

In this case the government challenged a merger between two Los Angeles grocery retail chains, Von's and Shopping Bag. Here, as in steel, the structural context was critical. Over the fifteen-year period preceding the suit, grocery chains acquired 621 other chains, comprising 4,581 individual stores, with aggregate sales of $4.5 billion. Moreover the bulk of this consolidation was being carried out by the twenty largest grocery chains in the nation; they accounted for 67 percent of the stores acquired and 70 percent of total acquired grocery sales. Finally, nearly 60 percent of these mergers involved retailers whose stores were located wholly or partially in the same counties. This consolidation movement in turn had a substantial concentrating impact on the structure of regional retail food markets.[6]

In this milieu, then, the government moved on a systematic basis to challenge mergers involving leading national food chains, as well as those involving local or regional chains, such as Von's and Shopping Bag.

In deciding the case, the Court observed that Von's and Shopping Bag were leading, rapidly expanding, and highly successful regional chains. The Court found the Los Angeles market to mirror developments in the industry nationwide, marked by a decline in independent groceries and their absorption by chains. Finally, the Court observed that neither firm was failing, nor did the two need to merge in order to save themselves from destruction by more powerful competitors.

Viewing the merger in this context, the Court found it to be a development in precisely the kind of anticompetitive trend that Congress sought to arrest by enacting the Celler-Kefauver Amendment:

> The facts of this case present exactly the threatening trend toward concentration which Congress wanted to halt. The number of small grocery companies in the Los Angeles retail market had been declining rapidly before the merger and continued to decline rapidly afterwards. This rapid decline . . . moved hand in hand with a larger number of significant absorptions of the small companies by the larger ones. In the midst of this steadfast trend toward concentration, Von's and Shopping Bag, two of the most successful and largest companies in the area . . . merged to become the second largest chain in Los Angeles.

The Court concluded that the Von's–Shopping Bag consolidation constituted a "case of two already powerful companies merging in a way which makes them even more powerful than before." Adhering to Congress's fear "that a market marked at the same time by both a continuous decline in the number of small businesses and a large number of mergers would slowly but inevitably gravitate from a market of many small competitors to one dominated by one or a few giants, and competition would thereby be destroyed," the Court struck down the merger.

Developments following this and other government suits to bar large grocery mergers are highly instructive. First, the share of acquisitions involving the twenty largest grocery chains plummeted, from 70 percent over the period 1949–64, to 9 percent in 1965–74. Second, contrary to criticisms voiced by some, the government was *not* nostalgically attempting to resurrect the Mom-and-Pop corner grocery of yesteryear. Rather, the government's enforcement program aimed to rechannel the urge to merge away from the very largest chains while permitting retailers other than the top twenty to combine. Third, for reasons best known to itself, however, the government abandoned its antimerger efforts in the industry beginning in the mid-1970s. The results of this dereliction of duty have been predictable: the share of grocery acquisitions by the top twenty chains leaped from 9 percent back up to 66 percent by the end of the 1970s—a development that, given the direct relationship between increased market concentration and higher food prices, is something less than a boon for the nation's grocery buyers.[7]

JOINT VENTURES

Thus far we have examined instances where ownership of all of an acquired firm's operations are completely transferred to the acquiring company. But what are the problems posed by partial combinations—joint ventures between competitors? How should they be treated as a matter of public policy? What of the situation where General Motors and Toyota combine to produce small cars in the United States, even though they heretofore competed in this segment of the market? A joint venture between rivals does not involve a complete consolidation of their operations. But because competition is eliminated between the venturers in the fields in which they elect to cooperate rather than compete, the anticompetitive threats posed by joint ventures can be the same as those posed by horizontal merger.

THE PENN-OLIN CASE

In the landmark *United States* v. *Penn-Olin Chemical Co.* decision (1964), the Supreme Court held joint ventures to fall within the reach of the proscriptions of Section 7 of the Clayton Act.[8] Writing for the majority, Justice Tom C. Clark stated: "The joint venture, like the 'merger' . . . often creates anticompetitive dangers. It is the chosen instrument of two or more corporations previously acting independently and usually competitively with one another. The result is 'a triumvirate of associated corporations.' " The same considerations apply to joint ventures as to mergers, he reasoned, "for in each instance we are but expounding a national policy enunciated by the Congress to preserve and promote a free competitive economy." The Court enunciated the following criteria for evaluating the potential anticompetitiveness of joint ventures:

> The number and power of the competitors in the relevant market; the background of their growth; the power of the joint venturers; the relationship of their lines of commerce; the competition existing between them and the power of each in dealing with the competitors of the other; the setting in which the joint venture was created; the reasons and necessities for its existence; the joint venture's line of commerce and the relationship thereof to that of its parents; the adaptability of its line of commerce to noncompetitive practices; the potential power of the joint venture in the relevant market; an appraisal of what the competition in the relevant market would have been if one of the joint venturers had entered it alone . . . and such other factors as might indicate potential risk to competition in the relevant market.[9]

In short, the majority ruled that joint ventures, like mergers, must be evaluated within their structural context.[10]

THE GM–TOYOTA JOINT VENTURE

Assessed in the light of *Penn-Olin,* the following structural considerations would be relevant in evaluating the joint venture between General Motors and Toyota for cooperative production of a small car at GM's plant in Fremont, California:

1. It represents a partial combination between the first and third largest auto companies in the world. These two firms together sell one out of every four cars sold on the planet. Moreover, they are major competitors in the U.S. subcompact auto field.
2. The automobile industry generally, and the subcompact segment in particular, are extremely concentrated: at the time of the joint venture, the four largest sellers collectively accounted for nearly 70

percent of U.S. subcompact sales, with the largest eight firms dominating over 90 percent of the field.[11]

3. Small, fuel-efficient cars have become a key segment of the industry,
accounting for nearly 60 percent of the cars sold in the United States
in recent years.

4. Foreign producers of subcompacts have been a key source of competition in price, product, and innovation in the otherwise lethargic, un-
imaginative, and noncompetitive U.S. automobile oligopoly. The role
of providing vigorous competition "has been left to the Japanese, and
perhaps most especially to Toyota," economist John Kwoka observes.
"With high-quality, low-cost cars, indeed, [Toyota] could be seen effectively as the key firm, despite its smaller size than GM. Nissan because of its size and Honda because of it[s] independent streak have
both been pro-competitive forces as well." Kwoka further points out
that an important part of the competitive stimulus provided by Japanese producers stems from the fact that, in contrast to domestic
oligopolists, they refuse to hew to monotonously predictable patterns
of products, costs, pricing, and marketing.[12]

5. However, there is some danger in overestimating the impact of foreign competition on the U.S. market. One must remember that "voluntary" import restraints (i.e., quotas), ostensibly temporary, have
repeatedly been extended, both formally and, more recently, infor-
mally. This raises the question whether foreign competition is a permanent or merely transitory disciplining force in the American auto
market, and whether it can be curtailed whenever the industry's labor-management coalition can persuade government to immunize it
from this competitive discipline.

Viewed against this background, the GM-Toyota joint venture raises
a number of public-policy issues, both in its possible anticompetitive
impact and in its broader economic ramifications.

The central issue to be resolved is whether the joint venture might
substantially lessen competition. This it would seem to do:

1. By eliminating direct competition between GM and Toyota, as well as
the innovations that GM would have been forced to make in order to
compete.

2. By preventing the more vigorous competition that would have taken
place if, instead, Toyota on its own had constructed a new manufacturing facility (as Honda and Nissan have done) in the large, lucrative
U.S. market.

3. By facilitating an intimate familiarity between the firms through the

sharing of information regarding pricing and plans, thereby reducing the measure of uncertainty that has made Toyota a potent competitor of the domestic oligopoly.

4. By serving to sanction additional joint ventures involving other leading producers, thereby encouraging further concentration in an already overconcentrated field.

Despite these anticompetitive aspects, a majority of the Federal Trade Commission voted to permit GM and Toyota to carry out their joint venture, with only minor modifications. Observing that "American auto makers have steadily lost ground to imported small cars," and that the "principal reason for this loss is that Japanese auto manufacturers produce small cars less expensively than do U.S. producers," the commission's majority reasoned that the joint venture would enable GM to observe and absorb superior Japanese manufacturing technology and, therefore, to become a far stronger competitor. The majority concluded that the venture "creates a substantial likelihood of producing significant procompetitive benefits to the American public" and that these benefits outweighed any anticompetitive risks.[13]

But the commission's "technology-transfer" rationale raises a host of troubling questions.

Does the joint venture *in its actual organization* permit GM to derive any real, significant insight into Japanese manufacturing wizardry? In his dissent, Commissioner Michael Pertschuk argued that it does not, pointing out that the bulk of manufacturing for the joint venture (parts, components, engines) will be carried out in Japan and, further, that GM had already begun to incorporate Japanese production methods in its American operations.[14]

Was this particular joint venture, involving the first and third largest auto firms in the world, the *only* way for GM to learn efficient production methods? Or were less anticompetitive alternatives available? Why couldn't GM join with a smaller foreign producer, or exploit its substantial ownership of two smaller Japanese auto manufacturers (Isuzu and Suzuki) to learn how to produce subcompact automobiles efficiently? Might not these "toe-hold joint ventures" enhance—rather than threaten to substantially lessen—competition?

Does the commission's "technology-transfer" argument threaten to emasculate the anticombination proscriptions of the Clayton Act? As Commissioner Patricia P. Bailey put it in her dissent, "if Ford had a 30 percent cost advantage over GM, attributable solely to some Ford management mystique, would the antitrust laws permit GM to learn Ford's special production techniques by jointly producing a Lincoln/Cadillac-type car?"[15]

Sanctioning cooperation between GM and Toyota could be expected to trigger a predictable "domino effect" by encouraging other U.S. and Japanese rivals to arrange joint ventures. In fact, since the government blessed GM-Toyota, Chrysler and Mitsubishi have also arranged joint production of small cars in the United States. So have Ford and Mazda. But does this not inevitably lead to a substantial lessening of competition between U.S. carmakers and their primary—often only—rivals? Does it not portend an intricate community of interests in which cooperation, not competition, is the rule? Does it not contain the seeds for a cartelization of the automobile industry?

In all of these respects, then, the Federal Trade Commission's approval of the GM-Toyota venture is hardly cause for jubilation by consumers—in autos and perhaps in other markets as well.

THE BASIC POLICY ISSUES

Three points seem relevant: (1) horizontal mergers and joint ventures directly and immediately affect the competitive structure of markets; (2) antitrust enforcement—at least until recently—has played a significant role in blocking horizontal mergers and joint ventures that tended to stifle competition or increase concentration; and (3) the principal benefit of a stringent enforcement policy is to channel entrepreneurial energies into growth by "building" rather than by "buying." Thus, only after Bethlehem was prevented from acquiring Youngstown did it construct the only modern, fully integrated steel complex built in the United States during the 1960s and 1970s. One can only speculate how the American steel industry would have performed if horizontal mergers had been halted at the turn of the century. Would steel imports today be so devastating if American steel companies had been forced to grow through competitive success in the marketplace rather than through anticompetitive mergers? Would timely action against horizontal mergers have spared the nation its current dilemma of having to choose between import restraints, which inflate steel prices and undercut the competitiveness of our steel-using industries on world markets, and free international competition, which is decimating steel-producing communities across the country?

In some quarters it is fashionable to advocate relaxing antitrust action against mergers and acquisitions. A more permissive stance, it is said, would let firms grow to world scale; larger size would make them more efficient; greater efficiency would enable them to compete better internationally and this, in turn, would redound to the national interest. Such claims, as we have seen earlier, are seldom supported by empirical evidence; they are little more than wishful thinking. Can anyone seriously contend, for example, that an efficient, integrated steel company can be created by merging LTV and Republic, when the constituents are a potpourri of obsolete and anachronistic plants? Are such mergers any substitute for the new, world-class facilities that are needed if American steel companies are to compete with their technologically advanced rivals abroad? Mergers like LTV-Republic, which are currently sanctioned by a compliant Justice Department, may be psychologically therapeutic for indolent or incompetent managements. They clearly increase concentration in a concentrated industry. But they do not address the fundamental problems crying out for solution.

Similarly, it is doubtful whether the Justice Department's current permissiveness toward horizontal consolidation of Big Oil has any socially redeeming virtues. Recent multi-billion-dollar megamergers among the twenty largest oil companies—Chevron-Gulf (acquisition price, $13.4 billion), Texaco-Getty ($10.1 billion), Mobil-Superior ($5.7 billion), and Occidental-Cities Service ($4 billion)—clearly pose anticompetitive problems and point to further concentration.[16] But beyond that, what are the social benefits of these mammoth mergers? Do they add one more drop to the nation's dwindling stock of proven crude-oil reserves? Do they lessen American dependence on foreign oil? Do they augur a more secure energy future? Or do they divert managerial efforts from exploration and development into paper entrepreneurialism—buying existing oil on the floor of the New York Stock Exchange instead of searching for new oil? An observation by *Petroleum Intelligence Weekly* is not reassuring: "The overriding implication of escalating United States oil industry takeover battles seems to be reduced investment in exploration and, in the long run, a likely increase of U.S. dependence on foreign supplies."[17]

Finally, there are no indications that joint ventures have a beneficial effect either on market competition or the competitiveness of the participating firms. Certainly the recent agreements between the U.S. auto giants and their foreign competitors have not, so far at least, lived up to their claims. The FTC's approval of the GM-Toyota venture had the predictable domino effect, triggering many new joint ventures—some ostensibly "defensive"—so that several of the world's largest auto producers are now linked. In addition to GM-Toyota, we have GM-Isuzu, GM-Suzuki, GM-Daewoo, Chrysler-Mitsubishi, Chrysler-Samsung, Ford-Mazda, and (reportedly) Ford Europe–Fiat. Other linkages no doubt are

being planned. All this is supremely ironic. For years the domestic industry had campaigned for import protection and regulatory dispensations
so as to get the "breathing space" it said it needed to cut costs, increase
productivity, compete better, and, in the process, save American jobs.
The industry (supported by the UAW) got "voluntary" quotas and
regulatory relief. But what was the denouement? Instead of using this
respite to gird for battle against its foreign competitors, it preferred to
combine with them in a series of joint ventures. This, as Commissioner
Pertschuk pointed out in his GM-Toyota dissent, was tantamount to
running up the white flag. It signaled the surrender of American jobs
and the U.S. small-car market to Japan, Korea, and the newly industrializing nations.[18]

In short, public policy toward horizontal mergers and joint ventures
is of capital importance. It can have a decisive impact not only on the
structure of particular industries and markets, but on economic performance generally. The objectives of the law seem clear. Whether or not
these objectives are realized, however, depends on how assiduously the
law is enforced—for good or, eventually, for ill.

CHAPTER 13

VERTICAL MERGERS

Man, as I have hinted before, naturally loves to imitate what he sees others do, which is the reason that savage people all do the same thing: this hinders them from meliorating their condition, though they are always wishing for it: but if one will wholly apply himself to the making of bows and arrows, whilst another provides food, a third builds huts, a fourth makes garments, and a fifth utensils, they not only become useful to one another, but the callings and employments themselves will, in the same number of years, receive much greater improvements, than if all had been promiscuously followed by every one of the five.

— Mandeville, *Fable of the Bees*, 1729

In 1981, the Mobil Oil Corporation sought to acquire the Marathon Oil Company. Mobil is the nation's second largest petroleum company, and is fully integrated through successive stages—crude oil, refineries, pipelines, and retailing. At the time, Marathon ranked as the seventeenth largest domestic oil company and it, too, operated at each of the industry's major stages.

Since the firms competed in a number of markets, the attempted acquisition would have eliminated some "horizontal" competition. But it was anticompetitive in another important respect. Unlike Mobil and other petroleum majors, Marathon was a substantial supplier of refined gasoline to independent, "unbranded" retailers—outlets that are a key source of price competition for the integrated majors (like Mobil). As Judge Manos found, about "60 percent of all gasoline sold by Marathon is eventually resold at retail prices that are generally several cents per gallon below that sold in Mobil branded outlets." The absorption of Marathon by Mobil thus threatened to remove Marathon as a "supplier

173

of price conscious independents," and thereby to undercut the ability of the independents to compete with the giants.[1]

This illustrates a central problem raised by vertical mergers generally. So long as a firm is symmetrically integrated—self-contained through its successive operations—vertical integration does not accord it any special power beyond that which springs from its market share or its aggregate size. But, as Corwin Edwards points out, once the firm becomes "disproportionately integrated, so that at one or more stages of production or distribution it acts as supplier or customer for enterprises with which it is in competition at other stages," vertical integration is no longer benign. It endows the firm with special power to discipline its nonintegrated competitors and dependent rivals. Such power can be variously deployed. As a supplier of raw materials, the integrated firm may squeeze the operating margins of its customer-competitors by charging artificially high prices for materials and low prices for finished products; it may restrict supplies to its nonintegrated rivals or cut them off altogether. As a purchaser of materials, it may do the reverse, holding down the price of raw materials, which it both makes and buys, thus enhancing the operating margins it enjoys in subsequent stages of the production process. In other words, the integrated firm can juggle its profits up and down the chain between production stages in which it is relatively strong and stages in which it is relatively weak. Given enough market power it can not only manipulate profit margins in its own operations, but impose them on nonintegrated rivals. This enables the integrated firm to limit access to markets ("downstream" integration) or access to materials ("upstream" integration). In short, it enables the integrated firm to foreclose competition.[2]

Where integration is pervasive, vertical mergers tend to reduce competition. They constrict (or "thin") markets because they eliminate the arm's-length transactions that previously occurred between independent buyers and sellers. In that sense, vertical mergers preempt and short-circuit the functions of the marketplace. This preemptive effect is particularly injurious because vertical mergers, once begun, become cumulative and self-reinforcing: "one vertical integration is likely to lead to another. The nonintegrated concerns vie with each other to assure themselves adequate sources and outlets before they are preempted by their rivals. Their efforts, of course, make the market still thinner and create problems for their smaller rivals."[3] This succession of vertical mergers, in turn, has structural consequences. It raises barriers to new competition by making vertical integration through two or more stages a virtual prerequisite to entry. As Willard Mueller put it, "when entry into two separate stages of production is already difficult because of

large capital requirements or for other reasons, combining successive
stages will further raise entry barriers, because new entrants must
enter two stages rather than one."[4] Finally, where vertical power is
entrenched and insulated, it may have adverse effects on economic performance—obstructing price competition, slowing technological advance, or making markets vulnerable to import competition.[5]

Public policy should guard against these antisocial consequences. But
how is this to be done within the constraints of the antimerger law? How
much foreclosure must occur before a vertical merger can be deemed to
"substantially lessen competition"? To what degree must it raise entry
barriers before such a merger can be said to "tend to create a monopoly"? In what "relevant" market(s)? Obviously, these issues can be
resolved only by placing a particular merger in a structural context and
assessing its impact in the light of industry trends, as in the two cases
we now shall examine.

THE BROWN SHOE CASE

The definitive treatment of vertical mergers under amended Section 7 of
the Clayton Act was provided in *Brown Shoe* v. *United States* (1962),
a case in which the government challenged Brown Shoe's acquisition of
G. R. Kinney Company.[6] At the time of the merger, Brown Shoe ranked
as the nation's fourth largest shoe manufacturer; Kinney was primarily
engaged in operating the nation's largest chain of family shoe stores—
a chain of over 400 stores in more than 270 cities. Thus, the merger
represented a vertical combination between a shoe manufacturer and a
shoe retailer.[7] Viewed in isolation, the amount of commerce involved
appeared modest: nationwide, Brown Shoe accounted for 4 percent of
footwear production, Kinney for 1 to 2 percent of shoe sales.

But, as the Court held, in such cases, "in which the foreclosure is
neither of monopoly nor *de minimus* proportions, the percentage of the
market foreclosed by the vertical arrangement cannot itself be decisive.
In such cases, it becomes necessary to undertake an examination of
various economic and historical factors in order to determine whether
the arrangement under review is of the type Congress sought to pro-
scribe." The anticompetitive significance of the Brown-Kinney consolidation must be evaluated in the light of structural trends in the industry:

1. A wave of vertical mergers between manufacturers and retailers had
   engulfed the industry: "International Shoe Company had no retail
   outlets in 1945, but by 1956 had acquired 130; General Shoe Company

had only 80 retail outlets in 1945 but had 526 by 1956; Shoe Corporation of America, in the same period, increased its retail holdings from 301 to 842; Melville Shoe Company from 536 to 947; and Endicott-Johnson from 488 to 540." Moreover, the large firms had absorbed nine independent shoe store chains, operating 1,114 stores.

2. This trend marked a substantial constriction of the market as parent shoe manufacturers moved "to supply an ever-increasing percentage of the retail outlets' needs, thereby foreclosing other manufacturers from effectively competing for the retail accounts."

3. The Brown Shoe Company had been a leading factor in this wave of vertical consolidation. Operating no retail outlets of its own prior to 1951, Brown had acquired fully 845 outlets by 1956. Acquisition of Kinney would give Brown a total of nearly 1,600 outlets and make it the second largest shoe retailer in the nation.

4. Also in line with the industry trend, Brown Shoe steadily foreclosed access to its acquired outlets by other manufacturers by supplying an increasing proportion of the shoes handled by its acquired retailing subsidiaries. "Thus although prior to Brown's acquisition of Wohl in 1951, Wohl bought from Brown only 12.8 percent of its total purchases of shoes, it subsequently increased its purchases to 21.4 percent in 1952 and to 32.6 percent in 1955. Wetherby-Kayser's purchases from Brown increased from 10.4 percent before acquisition to over 50 percent after." And, although Brown had sold no shoes to Kinney at the time of its acquisition, within two years Brown had become the leading outside supplier of shoes to Kinney.

Given the leading positions held by Brown and Kinney, Brown's policy of forcing its shoes upon its retail subsidiaries, the rapid pace and large scale of vertical consolidation in the industry generally, and the additional impetus to further combination likely to result from defensive acquisitions by other manufacturers trying to maintain access to retail outlets, the Court concluded that "in this industry, no merger between a manufacturer and an independent retailer could involve a larger potential market foreclosure." Therefore, the Court struck down the merger as a violation of amended Section 7 of the Clayton Act.

In reviewing this case it is important to point out that, in ruling against Brown's acquisition of Kinney, the Court did *not* deny the possibility that integrated operation of the manufacture and retailing of shoes might be more efficient, nor did it prohibit Brown from retailing its own shoes. Brown was perfectly free to integrate vertically by *internal* expansion. All the Court did was to prohibit Brown from integrating by merger. In effect, it told Brown: You may integrate vertically by building your own stores rather than by buying Kinney's. This will enhance rather than foreclose competition. It will preserve for other shoe manufacturers a free, equal, and nondiscriminatory access to retail outlets.

THE CEMENT CASES

The cement industry provides a second study of the anticompetitive consequences of vertical mergers, and the importance of vertical-merger policy.

In 1965 the government filed suit to block United States Steel Corporation's acquisition of Certified Industries.[8] U.S. Steel's Universal Atlas Cement division was then one of the four largest cement producers in the nation, and the second largest in the New York City area. Certified Industries bought cement, then mixed it with water and mineral aggregate, and sold the ready-mixed concrete. Certified was one of the four largest ready-mix concrete companies in the New York City area, and one of the ten largest purchasers of cement in the Northeast. This combination between a producer and a buyer of cement was part of a wave of vertical consolidations in the industry across the country.

The Federal Trade Commission found that although the cement industry in 1960 was virtually free of vertical integration, by the end of 1965 no fewer than forty ready-mix concrete companies around the country had been acquired by leading cement producers. In fact, *all* of the vertical integration by cement producers forward into ready-mix concrete between 1959 and 1964 had been effected through merger and acquisition—and the acquired ready-mix companies, almost without exception, ranked among the leading buyers of cement in their markets. A major stimulus to this movement, the commission found, was a desire on the part of cement producers to avoid competition by obtaining captive outlets for their cement: "Through purchase, permanent access to product outlets is assured without resorting to price or nonprice competition. Through forward vertical foreclosure the impact of rivals' aggressive price and nonprice strategies can be neutralized and rendered ineffective, at least for the foreclosed portion of the market."[9] The constricting impact on commerce was substantial; whereas prior to merger the acquiring companies supplied about 35 percent of the cement consumed by acquired firms, this proportion jumped to 65 percent following acquisition. Vertical consolidation thus diminished competition among cement producers while shrinking the "open market" available to new entrants at both stages of the industry.[10]

Within this milieu, the Federal Trade Commission moved to challenge a number of vertical mergers and acquisitions, including U.S. Steel's acquisition of Certified.[11] The commission found that it threatened to substantially lessen competition, and hence ordered it dissolved. U.S. Steel appealed the commission's order.

Writing for the court, Judge Anthony J. Celebrezze observed that the New York market was a concentrated field in which the four and eight largest cement producers accounted for 53 and 70 percent of sales, respectively. He found the market marked by rapid, large-scale vertical integration, primarily via merger and acquisition. The court further found that following the U.S. Steel–Certified merger, U.S. Steel had effectively removed Certified from the market as an outlet for cement produced by others.

The court agreed with the commission that, in context, U.S. Steel's vertical acquisition of Certified unlawfully threatened to substantially lessen competition in at least six important respects:

1. Other cement producers were immediately foreclosed from a large portion of the ready-mix market.
2. Capture of this prized outlet greatly advantaged U.S. Steel's Universal Atlas cement division, with its position having advanced "from sixth to second largest producer of Portland cement in the [New York metropolitan area] because of its vertical relationship with Certified."
3. "The acquired company would not be free to choose for itself who shall supply its needs solely on the basis of price, service, and quality of goods because the acquiring company has the power to substitute its own suppliers, and the intention of doing so."
4. The merger "had immediate and significant effects on several of the cement and concrete competitors in the [New York area]. Alpha Portland Cement Company, which manufactured cement in the Hudson River valley and opened a terminal on Long Island, was forced to close its local terminal because of its loss of Certified as a customer for its cement. Triangle Cement, which acted as a distributor for Atlantic Cement, closed its terminal in Brooklyn at the end of their distributorship contract. Triangle was Certified's third largest supplier in 1963, but sold it no cement in 1964."
5. The elimination of Certified from the market as a key buyer was certain to trigger further vertical consolidation by nonintegrated cement producers who would be forced to merge in an attempt to protect their access to the market.
6. In the light of industry trends, the U.S. Steel–Certified merger threatened to raise barriers to entry at both stages of the industry. That is,

outlets for a new cement company were systematically being constricted; so were sources of supply for new ready-mix firms. As a result, economically viable entry into the industry was increasingly coming to hinge on entry at both stages of the field, rather than one.

In sum, the court concurred with the commission that U.S. Steel's acquisition of Certified was unlawful because of its adverse effect on competition.

The consequences of the government's challenge of U.S. Steel–Certified and other vertical acquisitions in the cement industry are significant from a public-policy perspective. The rate of vertical consolidation and foreclosure in the industry declined significantly: while more than twenty vertical mergers occurred in each of the years 1965 and 1966, the rate of vertical consolidation averaged fewer than five per year over the next nine years.[12] The government not only halted further vertical consolidation, it accomplished substantial vertical *dis*integration of the industry. In the New York area, for example, it obtained divestiture of the second, fourth, fifth, and sixth largest ready-mix companies from the cement producers that had acquired them.[13] Finally by halting and in important respects by reversing the trend toward vertical consolidation, and by thus unclogging channels of trade, the government's attack on vertical mergers may well have played an important role in the decline of concentration in cement since 1967.[14] In short, the government successfully protected the competitive market from subversion via vertical integration.

THE BASIC POLICY ISSUES

As might be predicted, the writers of the Chicago School do not consider these court decisions to be good public policy. Robert Bork puts the matter bluntly: "in the absence of a most unlikely proved predatory power and purpose, antitrust should never object to the verticality of any merger; much less should it adopt the stance of virtual *per se* illegality reflected in *Brown Shoe* and other cases. Properly drawn horizontal rules are all we need." Why? Because vertical mergers promote efficiency! A vertical merger, says Bork, "is merely an instance of replacing a market transaction with administrative direction because the latter is believed to be a more efficient method of coordination." He surmises (on purely theoretical grounds) that vertical mergers "may cut sales and distribution costs, facilitate the flow of information between levels of the industry (for example, marketing possibilities may be transmitted more effectively from the retail to the manufacturing level, new product possibilities may be transmitted in the other direction, better inventory control may be attained, and better planning of production runs may be achieved), create economies of scale in management, and so on." Antitrust's concern with vertical mergers, he asserts (without troubling himself to offer supporting evidence), is misguided because such mergers "are means of creating efficiency, not of injuring competition. . . . The vertical mergers the law currently outlaws," Bork concludes boldly, "have no effect other than the creation of efficiency." Today's law, therefore, "is clearly destroying a valuable source of efficiency for no reason."[15]

Doubtless vertical integration makes economic sense in some situations. Doubtless there are instances where unified operation and management of tightly linked, technologically intertwined, and intimately interdependent activities can yield economic gains. But this does not mean that the mere existence of vertical integration is in itself proof that it is rooted in economic efficiency, nor that vertical mergers are ipso facto motivated by a desire to increase efficiency rather than to lessen competition. If efficiency is the goal, a steel company does not have to *own* coal companies in order to produce at lowest cost. United Airlines does not have to *acquire* Boeing in order to procure superior planes for its passenger fleet. Consolidated Edison does not have to merge with General Electric to assure itself of an adequate, economical supply of generators and transformers. General Motors does not have to *own* its dealerships to provide an efficient conduit for its automobiles to its customers. It is well to remember that there is a miraculous institution that is designed to intermediate between buyers and sellers, an institution that has the specific function of coordinating successive stages of production and distribution. It is the competitive market—so often heralded, worshipped, and beatified in the litany of corporate apologetics, yet less often defended and protected in practice.

What, then, can we conclude with respect to vertical mergers and vertical power?

In the cases we have examined, there was no persuasive evidence that the mergers were primarily (or even largely) driven by economic efficiency. With respect to *Brown Shoe*, F. M. Scherer reports that, *at best*, only slight efficiencies could have been realized if Brown had been allowed to acquire Kinney.[16] Likewise, no overwhelming efficiencies were discernible in the rush by cement producers to integrate vertically; obtaining captive outlets, eliminating competition, or preserving access to markets were the major motives at work.[17] More recently, few social gains could have been anticipated from the proposed merger between the nation's largest for-profit hospital chain and the largest equipment supplier when, as a number of financial analysts point out, the hospital chain is already large enough to have "achieved major economies of scale in purchasing supplies."[18]

As we have pointed out, a strict policy against potentially anticompetitive vertical mergers and acquisitions does not rule out integration by internal expansion. If vertical efficiencies can, in fact, be obtained, firms are perfectly free to enjoy them by building their own facilities—an option that not only preserves competition in important markets, but can enhance it.

As we saw in chapters 3 to 5, the alleged efficiencies of vertical bigness are, more often than not, both ephemeral and mythical. In steel, vertical giantism has wrought no miracles of operating efficiency; today, the lowest-cost American steel producers are the vertically nonintegrated, specialized minimills. In autos, under the press of foreign competition, the Big Three have sought to improve their operating efficiency in part through vertical disintegration. Moreover, as Hayes and Abernathy of the Harvard Business School report, vertical integration has been of dubious benefit to the oligopoly's innovation efficiency.[19] Nor, if Big Oil can be believed, is vertical giantism a boon to efficiency in petroleum. Exxon has convincingly and repeatedly *denied* before state tax commissions that its production, refining, marketing, and pipelining operations "are integral parts of a unitary business composed of all functions combined"; the firm has insisted that each of its vertical functions "is independent and not unitary to, or an integral part of any other function."[20]

Whatever its hypothetical benefits, vertical integration entails both private and social costs. A steel company that has captive coal or iron-ore mines feels constrained to patronize its in-house suppliers instead of "playing the market." It thus forsakes the opportunity of buying its raw materials at a lower price from unaffiliated sources. An integrated oil company is tempted to use its own crude for refinery operations even when it may be advantageous to enter the world spot market for crude. In short, as long as markets are reasonably competitive, the ownership of natural resources (or retail outlets, at the other end of the vertical chain) may be a private albatross without socially redeeming virtues.

Alas, vertical acquisitions by industrial giants cannot be rationalized as a quest for the holy grail of efficiency. Vast vertical control over chains of adjacent functions is not a better blueprint for economic organization than the competitive market. Large-scale, authoritarian, bureaucratic control is not a better allocator of society's resources than a network of competitive markets that coordinates successive stages of production and distribution. It is quite proper, therefore, that public policy protect markets from subversion by vertical mergers that "tend to substantially lessen competition or tend to create a monopoly."

CHAPTER 14
CONGLOMERATE MERGERS

Radical changes occurred in the science of enterprise management after World War II. . . . The concurrent phenomenal development of electronic computers has promoted and facilitated the expansion of management science . . . This fundamental development has created opportunities for profits through mergers that remove assets from the inefficient control of old-fashioned managers and place them under men schooled in the new management science. Managers are able to control effectively a larger set of activities. Being of general applicability to business operations, management science makes possible reductions in financial and managerial costs and risks through acquisitions of firms in *diverse* industries. These gains differ markedly from the familiar economies of scale in production, purchasing, or marketing that normally accrue from mergers of firms with *related* products. Thus the new management science is the primary force behind conglomeration.
— Professor Neil Jacoby, University of California at Los Angeles, 1969

There are various reasons for diversification and most of them are invalid.
— Robert Boni, president and chief operating officer, Armco Steel

I n 1960, the Gulf & Western Corporation was an obscure car bumper company that did not rank among the nation's 200 largest industrial concerns. Just eight years later, however, Gulf & Western (satirized in a Mel Brooks movie as "Engulf & Devour") was a colossus—the thirty-fourth largest industrial firm in the country, the seventeenth largest in terms of consolidated assets.

The company's meteoric rise was not the fruit of patiently planned long-term investment or irresistible product innovations. Instead, it was bought through mergers and acquisitions. During the 1960s, Gulf &

Western's acquisitions included thirty-three wholesalers of automotive parts; manufacturers of automobile pistons and parking-brake levers; a full-line integrated producer of zinc; a manufacturer of fittings and flanges used in atomic power plants and missile launch pads; the nation's largest producer of horse saddlery and harnesses; Paramount Pictures, a producer, financer, and distributor of motion pictures; Desilu Productions, a producer and distributor of television programs; a horse-racing track; the South Puerto Rico Sugar Company; Consolidated Cigar Company, maker of Dutch Master, El Producto, and Muriel cigars; a manufacturer of firefighting equipment; an artillery shell and air-conditioning concern; Brown Paper, a producer of tissue and writing paper with extensive timber holdings; and two large financial institutions, Providence Washington Insurance and the Associates. (The firm also tried to acquire Armour Meat, Allis-Chalmers, and Sinclair Oil, but failed.)

In all, Gulf & Western came to control nearly seventy firms by 1968. Its corporate purchases accounted for 84 percent of the firm's rise to the heights of the *Fortune* 500. Moreover, the bulk of the firm's acquisitions were *conglomerate* in nature—that is, the acquired firms were neither direct competitors of Gulf & Western's existing operations, nor were they vertically related to them.[1]

In both its scale and character, Gulf & Western's acquisition program is typical of the nation's recent, and most massive, merger movement. Fully 74 percent of the total assets acquired from 1948 to 1978 involved conglomerate mergers. Moreover, a majority of these acquisitions were made by the largest firms in the nation; the top two hundred industrial corporations accounted for 53 percent of the total assets taken over between 1948 and 1978.[2] The result of this merger mania was a significant increase in aggregate concentration, or the share of all U.S. manufacturing assets controlled by the top two hundred. Their share rose from 54.3 percent in 1960 to 61.4 percent by 1976; detailed analysis reveals that "without mergers these 200 corporations' share would have declined between 1960 and 1976, from 54.3 percent to 47.4 percent."[3]

What are the implications of this massive restructuring of economic organization? Does it constitute a threat to a competitive-market society? Should giant conglomerate mergers and conglomerate bigness be a concern of public policy and the antimerger provisions of Section 7 of the Clayton Act?

Chicago School ideologues, their fuglemen, and their converts, who specialize in rationalizing corporate bigness, assure us that large conglomerate mergers pose no particular competitive problems. After all, the apologists reason, "the conglomerate merger does not put together rivals, and so does not create or increase the ability to restrict output through an increase in market share."[4] The logic is simple: if Exxon were to acquire a yogurt company, this would create no competitive threat since Exxon was not even remotely involved in the production of yogurt prior to the merger; the yogurt company's market share would be the same the day after the merger as the day before; therefore, its influence on the yogurt market presumably would be unaffected by the merger. Devotees of scholastic abstractionism also dismiss, as irrelevant, concerns about aggregate concentration of control in the economy at large. As former antitrust chief William Baxter put it: "There is nothing written in the sky that says that the world would not be a perfectly satisfactory place if there were only 100 companies, provided each one had 1 percent of every product and service market. In that case, there would be extremely high aggregate concentration and, at the same time, perfect competition."[5] Hence the recommendation that "antitrust should never interfere with any conglomerate merger."[6]

This Panglossian unconcern may be relevant in the utopian world inhabited by Chicago theorists, but it is quite incongruent with realities in the business world. An even rudimentary understanding of the anatomy and physiology of conglomerate bigness indicates that the exercise of conglomerate power has a variety of anticompetitive consequences. Conglomerate power is quite different from horizontal (monopoly) control of a particular market, or vertical control over a chain of adjacent markets. It derives from diversified operations in many different fields, so that the fortunes of the firm do not depend upon profit or loss in a particular transaction, location, or activity. As Corwin Edwards explains, the large conglomerate wields "power in a particular market not only by virtue of its place in the organization of that market but also by virtue of the scope and character of its activities elsewhere. It may be able to exploit, extend, or defend its power by tactics other than those traditionally associated with the ideas of monopoly."[7] Conglomerate power, in other words, primarily flows from the structure of the large firm, rather than from the structure of any single market in which the firm operates; according to the Federal Trade Commission, it is "inherent in the firm's anatomy."[8]

In this chapter we shall examine some landmark court decisions dealing with conglomerate mergers. We shall focus on the primary weapons employed by conglomerate giants—cross-subsidization, reciprocal dealing, and competitive forbearance—and assess their impact on competition. Finally, we shall explore the government's effectiveness in enforcing Section 7 of the Clayton Act against mergers and acquisitions that may substantially lessen competition and increase aggregate concentration.

THE PROBLEM OF CROSS-SUBSIDIZATION

Because the operations of giant diversified firms span a diversity of markets, they are able to cross-subsidize operations in one field with resources drawn from other fields—an option not available to the firm's nonconglomerate, specialized rivals. The conglomerate's power to do this derives from "the fact that it can spend money in large amounts. If such a concern finds itself matching expenditures or losses, dollar for dollar, with a substantially smaller firm, the length of its purse assures it of victory. . . . Moment by moment the big company can outbid, outspend, or outlose the small one; and from a series of such momentary advantages it derives an advantage in attaining its large aggregate results."[9] The instruments for achieving these ends, the Federal Trade Commission has found, "include, in addition to price cutting, new or more intensive advertising, promotion, and other marketing activities, with the outcome based on the diversified resources of the conglomerate firm."[10] Thus the large conglomerate's power and its market "success" may be due to its "deep pocket" rather than to its innately superior competitive skill, foresight, or industry.

The government's challenge to Procter & Gamble's attempted acquisition of Clorox illustrates the cross-subsidization threat. Procter & Gamble acquired Clorox, a bleach producer, in 1957. The Federal Trade Commission challenged the acquisition on the grounds that it might substantially lessen competition or tend to create a monopoly in violation of amended Section 7 of the Clayton Act.[11]

At the time, Clorox was the nation's leading manufacturer of liquid household bleach. The market was highly concentrated: Clorox alone accounted for 49 percent of the market and Purex for 16 percent; the six largest producers collectively accounted for 80 percent; the remaining 20 percent was divided among more than two hundred small firms. Because all bleach is chemically identical, these market shares reflect the relative ability of the competing firms to underwrite substantial sales, promotion, and advertising expenditures.

Procter & Gamble was one of the nation's largest diversified manufacturers of household products, including soaps, detergents, and cleansers. It ranked as the largest advertiser in the country, with an advertising budget in 1957 of $80 million—equivalent to the total annual *sales* of bleach nationwide. In addition, owing to its enormous advertising budget, Procter & Gamble received substantial discounts from the media in which it advertised. Before acquiring Clorox, Procter & Gamble had produced no household liquid bleach.

On appeal, the Supreme Court agreed with the Federal Trade Commission that this conglomerate acquisition unlawfully threatened to substantially lessen competition in household liquid bleach. The Court found the acquisition to be anticompetitive on three main grounds, two of which squarely involved Procter & Gamble's conglomerate power to cross-subsidize its Clorox subsidiary.

First, the interjection of Procter & Gamble's massive size and promotion power in support of Clorox, the dominant firm in a concentrated market where advertising was critical to success, threatened to concentrate the market even further, thereby lessening competition: "The liquid bleach industry was already oligopolistic before the acquisition, and price competition was certainly not as vigorous as it would have been if the industry were competitive. Clorox enjoyed a dominant position nationally, and its position approached monopoly in certain areas. . . . The interjection of Procter into the market considerably changed the situation. There is every reason to assume that the smaller firms would become more cautious in competing due to their fear of retaliation by Procter. It is probable that Procter would become the price leader and that oligopoly would become more rigid."

Second, the Court found that this same ability of Procter & Gamble to cross-subsidize Clorox also threatened to raise entry barriers in the bleach market, and thereby to diminish the likelihood of new competition: "The major competitive weapon in the successful marketing of bleach is advertising. Clorox was limited in this area by its relatively small budget and its inability to obtain substantial discounts. By contrast, Procter's budget was much larger; and, although it would not devote its entire budget to advertising Clorox, it could divert a large portion to meet the short-term threat of a new entrant. Procter would be able to use its volume discounts to advantage in advertising Clorox. Thus, a new entrant would be much more reluctant to face the giant Procter than it would have been to face the smaller Clorox."

Third, the Court observed that owing to the nature of Procter & Gamble's product line, the company's expertise, and its record of diversification into the production of household cleaning products generally, the firm was a likely *potential* entrant into the bleach market. Thus, acquisition of Clorox eliminated the competition that would have occurred had Procter & Gamble entered the market on its own. Indeed competition would have been enhanced, and new production capacity and employment opportunities created, had the latter avenue been followed.

For these reasons, the Court vetoed Procter & Gamble's conglomerate acquisition of Clorox. Procter & Gamble was perfectly free to enter the bleach market on its own, if it so desired, or to make a small, "toe-hold" acquisition; in either event, this would have enhanced competition in liquid bleach. The Clorox acquisition, by contrast, was tainted because it had precisely the opposite effect. That is why it ran afoul of the law.

THE PROBLEM OF RECIPROCAL DEALING

Reciprocal dealing is a second component of conglomerate power. As between two firms, the essence of reciprocal dealing "is the willingness of each company to buy from the other, conditioned upon the expectation that the other company will make reciprocal purchases. The goods bought are typically dissimilar in kind, and in the usual case could be obtained from other sources on terms which, aside from the reciprocal purchases, would be no less advantageous."[12] In other words, reciprocal dealing is a case of "we'll scratch your back if you scratch ours"—or, in its more coercive form, "we'll *stop* scratching your back if you don't start scratching ours." It is a special aspect of conglomerate power because the large conglomerate, unlike the specialized single-line producer, can use its voluminous purchases in many fields as levers for inducing suppliers to buy the conglomerate's products and services in other, unrelated markets.

In the hands of giant conglomerates, reciprocal dealing is a powerful anticompetitive weapon. It dampens rivalry based on price, quality, and service; it can compound and further rigidify administered prices in oligopolistic markets; it raises barriers to the entry of new competition by "tying up" market sales; it intensifies concentration by enabling the large conglomerate's divisions to grow at the expense of specialized rivals unable to exert such power; and it encourages further conglomerate mergers and acquisitions, as the victims of reciprocity seek large conglomerate parents capable of exercising such power. "The ultimate result," the Federal Trade Commission has warned, "is an inflexible economic system composed of an industrial elite knit together by the exchange of reciprocal favors"—a system "wholly alien to the tenets of a free market economy."[13]

The anticompetitive dangers are illustrated by General Dynamics' acquisition of Liquid Carbonic in 1957.[14] General Dynamics was one of the nation's twenty largest industrial firms at the time of the merger, with 75 to 85 percent of its sales made to the government, including the Pentagon, the Atomic Energy Commission, and NASA. Its purchases from 80,000 suppliers amounted to $500 million annually. Liquid Carbonic, on the other hand, was the nation's largest producer of gaseous, liquid, and solid carbon dioxide, accounting for 35 to 40 percent of the market. The Justice Department challenged the merger as unlawfully tending to substantially lessen competition in carbon dioxide, primarily because of systematic reciprocal dealing by General Dynamics and Liquid Carbonic following their consolidation.

Writing for the court, Judge John M. Cannella found reciprocal dealing to be pervasive and a prime motive for the acquisition. In particular, the merger provided General Dynamics with an important lever to activate the latent power of its vast purchases in many markets: "While the defendant's 1957 purchases from its vendors totalled approximately one-half billion dollars, it was not in a position to convert this huge purchasing power into market power, for the bulk of the corporation's products were sold to the government. In making Liquid Carbonic a division, this situation was altered in that General Dynamics then marketed a product which many of its suppliers used." Indeed, as evaluated by the president of Liquid Carbonic, acquisition by General Dynamics would mean that "Liquid's management would have at its disposal the entire purchasing power of General Dynamics' other divisions for reciprocal buying purposes. . . ." Consequently, "Liquid Carbonic considered the opportunities for reciprocity as its most significant advantage to be derived from the merger."

A "Special Sales Program" put into place following the acquisition represented a systematic plan for exploiting reciprocal dealing opportunities. "The purpose of the program," the court found, "was succinctly stated by Senior Vice-President C. R. MacBride to be 'to aid the Liquid Carbonic sales picture via General Dynamics' reciprocity leverage.' It was felt that profits could be 'greatly increase[d]' by 'capitalizing on the tremendous value of our purchasing power—by soliciting reciprocal trade.' " Through this program, General Dynamics confronted suppliers with records of its purchases from them as a means for inducing reciprocal business for its Liquid Carbonic subsidiary. According to the court: "In those few instances where the implied threat of a curtailment in the account's sales to General Dynamics was apparently not grasped, or where it was understood but rejected, this information was forwarded to headquarters in Chicago so that appropriate action could be taken. The prospective account would be told of this so that he could appreciate the cost of his reluctance" to reciprocate by patronizing General Dynamics' newly acquired carbon dioxide division.

The court concluded that the reciprocity program significantly boosted Liquid Carbonic's sales and, therefore, substantially lessened competition in carbon dioxide in violation of amended Section 7 of the Clayton Act. In an important passage, Judge Cannella noted Liquid Carbonic's history of antitrust violations in attempting to control its market; he observed that reciprocal dealing via conglomerate merger constituted an alternative route to the firm's goal of market control. Perhaps most significantly, the court recognized that reciprocity might be inseparably attached to large conglomerate size, and competition almost inevitably undermined, *quite apart from any overt, formal program of reciprocal dealing:* "even without the overt utilization of leverage, its mere presence may operate to artificially produce sales. A major vendor of General Dynamics . . . may be well advised from a business standpoint, to purchase these products from Liquid Carbonic. Indeed, a potential vendor of General Dynamics might pursue the same course of conduct as part of a program of improving its sales presentation to General Dynamics." Finding the mere presence of this power sufficient to subvert competition, the court ordered General Dynamics to divest itself of Liquid Carbonic.

The case illustrates how reciprocal dealing can be used by a conglomerate to undermine competition. In particular, it shows how the systematic leveraging of purchasing power in some markets can be employed to enhance sales in other, unrelated markets—sales ultimately derived from conglomerate size, not competitive merit. But is this surprising? Is reciprocal dealing an anomalous aspect of conglomeration? Is it not a matter of rational self-interest for suppliers to curry favor with giant conglomerates by purchasing their products in preference to those of smaller, less diversified sellers? Is not free, equal, nondiscriminatory access to markets subtly, but effectively, undermined as a result? In other words, does not conglomeration, by its very existence, almost inevitably have a chilling effect on competition? In *Ingersoll-Rand,* Judge Louis Rosenberg cut to the heart of the issue of conglomerate bigness and reciprocal dealing: "the mere existence of this purchasing power might make its conscious employment toward this end unnecessary; the possession of the power is frequently sufficient, as sophisticated businessmen are quick to see the advantages in securing the goodwill of the possessor. . . . In this situation, it is the relative size and conglomeration of business rivals, rather than their competitive ability, that may determine success."[15]

THE PROBLEM OF
CONGLOMERATE INTERDEPENDENCE
AND COMPETITIVE FORBEARANCE

A third element of conglomerate power is what can best be described as conglomerate interdependence and competitive forbearance.

As conglomerate megamergers such as Du Pont–Conoco, U.S. Steel–Marathon, and Allied-Bendix proceed apace, as aggregate concentration rises, and as control over more diverse economic activity thus becomes concentrated in the hands of fewer and larger conglomerates, these firms necessarily come into contact with each other as buyers, sellers, rivals, or potential competitors at more points throughout the economy. As a result, competitive vigor is corroded because conglomerate giants come to recognize their mutual interdependence and community of interests *across* diverse markets and industries:

> A large concern usually must show a regard for the strength of other large concerns by circumspection in its dealings with them, whereas such caution is usually unnecessary in dealing with small enterprises. The interests of great enterprises are likely to touch at many points, and it would be possible for each to mobilize at any one of these points a considerable aggregate of resources. The anticipated gain to such a concern from unmitigated competitive attack upon another large enterprise at one point of contact is likely to be slight as compared with the possible loss from retaliatory action by that enterprise at many other points of contact. There is an awareness that if competition against the large rival goes so far as to be seriously troublesome, the logic of the situation may call for conversion of the warfare into total war. Hence there is an incentive to live and let live, to cultivate a cooperative spirit, and to recognize priorities of interest in the hope of reciprocal recognition.[16]

Or as former Attorney General John N. Mitchell explained it, "if the food subsidiary of corporation A aggressively competes with the food subsidiary of corporation B, then the electrical subsidiary of corporation B may start a price war with the electrical subsidiary of corporation A. Thus, it may be in both A's and B's interest to maintain the status quo and not to engage in the type of aggressive competition which we expect in a free marketplace."[17]

That conglomerate interdependence exists, and that it militates against hard competition, is scarcely farfetched. For example, the evidence suggests that after Du Pont became a large diversified corporation in the early 1920s, it developed a community of interest with other national and international giants. When these concerns met as potential or actual rivals, recognition of their broader collective interests militated toward competitive restraint. As a Du Pont vice president explained his firm's policy in 1923 toward Britain's giant chemical conglomerate, Imperial Chemical Industries: "It is not good business sense to attempt an expansion in certain directions if such an act is bound to result in a boomerang of retaliation. It has been the Du Pont's policy to follow such lines of common sense procedure. . . ." Du Pont adopted this conciliatory stance, according to the firm, "on the broad theory that cooperation is wiser than antagonism and that in the matter of detail the chances in the long run were that the boot was just as likely to be on one leg as on the other." Or, as Irénée du Pont put it, "the great corporations of the country . . . should stand together without veiled threats from companies which are more predatory."[18] He did not have to explain that "standing together" was a gentlemanly euphemism for avoiding competition—either actual or potential.

Yet another example of conglomerate interdependence and competitive forbearance is the Standard Oil–IG Farben pact discussed in chapter 5. Pursuant to this "marriage" between America's largest petroleum company and Germany's giant chemical combine, the contracting parties agreed to divide the world between them. Standard described the agreement simply and forthrightly: "The I.G. are going to stay out of the oil business proper and we are going to stay out of the chemical business insofar as that has no bearing on the oil business."[19]

The point need not be belabored. There are instances where diversified giants—by explicit contract or, more frequently, by tacit understanding —agree not to invade each other's turf. From their private, profit-maximizing view, this makes much sense. Allocation of product markets and geographical division of territories reduce business risks by forestalling competition. "It is sound business procedure," a Du Pont executive once advised his colleagues, "to restrict ourselves to a certain degree to those markets in which we have advantage over foreign competitors so long as those competitors restrict themselves to other markets in which they have economic advantages."[20] The message is clear: Competition is contagious, and hence dangerous. Local skirmishes can quickly escalate into global confrontations. Prudence dictates restraint and forbearance. Rich are the rewards for superpowers versed in the art of peaceful coexistence!

THE BASIC POLICY ISSUES

Despite the creative apologetics concocted by academic theorists and disseminated by well-endowed think tanks, conglomerate power is not an optical illusion. It is a matter of public concern and a challenge for public policy. To conclude otherwise is to escape from reality—to flee from the evidence. As we have seen, conglomerate power can lessen competition and tend to create monopoly by mobilizing such weapons as cross-subsidization, reciprocal dealing, and competitive forbearance.[21] Section 7 of the Clayton Act—partly because of the way the law is written, partly because of its haphazard enforcement and interpretation—has not been effective in controlling conglomerate megamergers. Since such mergers, by definition, involve the union of firms engaged in unrelated operations, attention has necessarily been focused on the "relevant market" in which competition is lessened. At times this emphasis on the proper market definition has become an obsession distracting attention from the central issue of conglomerate power and the potential for its exercise. It is tantamount to straining at a gnat while swallowing a camel. Moreover, by concentrating on a particular merger, viewed in isolation, we have tended to lose sight of the aggregate effect of cumulative conglomeration and its structural impact on the economy as a whole. In the process, we have ignored the danger (against which *Fortune* warned) that with progressive conglomeration the United States might "end up completely dominated by conglomerates happily trading with each other in a new kind of cartel system."[22]

A clearer legislative mandate and stricter enforcement would seem to be in order. The risks, if any, are not substantial. A crackdown on conglomerate megamergers is not likely to compromise our quest either for operating efficiency, or innovation efficiency, or social efficiency. Indeed, an attack on conglomerate bureaucracies might yield positive benefits—not only by liberating closed markets from conglomerate control, but also by streamlining bloated corporate structures to enhance their productivity and competitiveness.

CHAPTER 15

THE LIMITATIONS
OF ANTITRUST

Of all the great evils now threatening the body politic and the political bodies, these cruel organizations of capital are perhaps the best example of what upright and earnest businessmen can do when they are let alone. They cannot be stamped out by laws or the decisions of courts or hostile legislation which is too friendly. Their destruction cannot be accomplished by demagogues.

The trusts are hideous monsters built up by the enlightened enterprise of the men that have done so much to advance progress in our beloved country. On one hand I would stamp them under foot; on the other hand not so fast.
— Finley Peter Dunne, *Mr. Dooley Says*

Eminent counsel . . . appear to have discovered in the Constitution a new implied prohibition: "What man has illegally joined together, let no court put asunder."
— Louis D. Brandeis, *The Curse of Bigness*

Forty years ago Walton Hamilton pondered the impact of American antitrust policy. Surveying the gulf between the ideal of antitrust as a "charter of liberty" on the one hand, and economic reality on the other, Hamilton asked:

Why has [antitrust] not been a success? Is the crux of the trouble the congressional failure to implement the law with adequate funds? Or is its weakness due to an insecure foundation? Is a statute enacted in the faraway nineties adequate to the problem of restraint five decades later? Is the machinery for its administration subject to the wear and tear of time, and has it become obsolescent? Can the basic issues of industrial government be transmuted into causes of action? Can the process of litigation be made to put an erring trade back on the right track? Have courts the distinctive competence to bring order and justice into the affairs of industry? Can a series of suits be depended upon to hold the national economy true to the competitive ideal? Are the sanctions of the statute of a character to induce compliance? In a word, can antitrust be made the answer?[1]

Unfortunately, the divergence between antitrust rhetoric and the competitive ideal is as real today—and as troublesome—as it was four decades ago. Antitrust has not succeeded in eliminating some of the basic obstacles to the operation of competitive markets. In key sectors of the American economy, it has failed to deter collusive restraints of trade; to dissipate monopoly; to cope with oligopoly; and, perhaps most important, to block mergers and arrest the trend toward concentration of power.

CONSPIRACY

To implement its prohibitions, the Sherman Act empowers the Justice Department to bring criminal charges against transgressors. Specifically, it provides that the violator "shall be deemed guilty of a felony, and, on conviction thereof, shall be punished by fine not exceeding one million dollars if a corporation, or, if any other person, one hundred thousand dollars or by imprisonment not exceeding three years, or by both said punishments, in the discretion of the court." Private plaintiffs are also permitted to file suit and, if successful in proving a violation, to recover from the defendant three times the damages suffered.

Criminal penalties—in antitrust as elsewhere—are designed to punish past transgressions in the hope of preventing future ones. The primary objective is deterrence. (As Lord Halifax noted some four hundred years ago, "men are not hanged for stealing horses; they are hanged so that horses shall not be stolen.") In theory, criminal penalties are particularly appropriate in the antitrust field because, unlike crimes committed in a fit of passion, antitrust violations are rational, premeditated acts often based on cunning cost-benefit calculations. Yet, in too many instances, the punishment does not fit the crime.

Antitrust fines are almost never commensurate with the profits derived from the violation, and hence are not effective deterrents. When General Motors was convicted in 1949 of having conspired to destroy a sizable portion of the nation's urban mass transit systems, the firm was fined a grand total of $5,000. On average, fines have represented a mere 0.05 percent of the value of commerce involved, and repeat violators have been dealt with no more severely than first offenders.[2]

The fear of imprisonment is an equally ineffective deterrent. Prison sentences are rarely imposed, are typically suspended, and in any event are usually less than six months in duration. In the eighty years from 1890 to 1969, for example, imprisonment was ordered in fewer than 4 percent of criminal antitrust convictions; through 1924, prison sentences were meted out only in cases involving labor unions; the first prison sentence ordered for "pure" price-fixing (involving neither labor unions nor acts of violence) was not imposed until the late 1950s;[3] and, ironically, prison terms in antitrust cases involving millions, even billions, of dollars have been incomparably less severe than those handed down for far milder offenses. As Mark Green found,

> A year after seven electrical manufacturers were sent to jail for 30 days apiece, a man in Asbury Park, New Jersey, stole a $2.98 pair of sunglasses and a $1 box of soap and was sent to jail for four months. A George Jackson was sent to prison for 10 years to life for stealing $70 from a gas station . . . and in Dallas one Joseph Sills received a 1,000 year sentence for robbing $73.10. Many states send young students, who are marijuana first offenders, to jail for five to 10 years. But the *total* amount of time spent in jail by all businessmen who have violated the antitrust laws [between 1890 and 1960] is a little under two years. Yet the electrical conspiracy alone robbed the public more than all other robberies and thefts in 1961 combined.[4]

The right of private plaintiffs to recover triple damages, while theoretically providing a more potent financial deterrent, is typically foreclosed by the government's willingness to accept *nolo contendere* pleas by defendants—a plea for punishment without contesting the charges, and without trial or adjudication of the facts. Proving an antitrust violation is a costly, time-consuming, and complicated matter. Moreover, the typical triple-damage plaintiff is a David confronting a Goliath, generally unable to make the full investigation and analysis needed to prove violation. Thus the private plaintiff usually depends on the government to have established an antitrust violation in a prior proceeding, which can then be used as prima facie evidence to carry forward claims for damages. But by accepting *nolo* pleas in nearly 90 percent of the criminal antitrust cases it files, thereby forestalling judicial determination of issues of facts and law, the government largely precludes the filing of private triple-damage actions. Thus a *nolo* plea becomes a protective device enabling the antitrust violator to short-circuit the threat of treble damages for the victims of his malfeasance.[5]

So it is hardly surprising that antitrust has fallen short as a deterrent to anticompetitive acts and schemes. One answer might be to substantially raise the monetary and prison penalties; Congress has done so twice since 1890. Perhaps the statutes should be amended to specify mandatory fines and jail sentences for various antitrust violations, analogous to state statutes on crimes committed with firearms. Perhaps the severity of penalties should be calibrated to the volume of trade restrained. Or a corporation violating the antitrust laws might be required to forfeit to the United States a sum equal to twice the total profits earned during the period of wrongdoing, while offending officers might likewise be required to forfeit double the compensation received, or be "separated" from their corporate offices for such malfeasance in the discharge of their fiduciary responsibilities. Since antitrust violations are premeditated and often reflect a cynical cost-benefit calculation, the deterrence of anticompetitive conduct could be made more effective by (in economic parlance) "increasing the cost of consuming delinquency."

Even without statutory changes, however, much can be accomplished. For example, the Reagan administration has compiled an admirable record in stamping out price-fixing conspiracies in the highway-paving industry. As a result of its concerted crackdown, the Justice Department has obtained almost three hundred convictions and prodded the courts to assess fines totaling $51,517,603, to impose jail sentences totaling nearly 46 years, to place offenders on probation for a total of over 192 years, and to "condemn" some of the defendants to a total of 10,032 hours of public service. While it is true that this harshness was directed primarily against "small business" offenders; while it has not (regrettably) been replicated with industrial giants, the success against the paving contractors shows what vigorous law enforcement can accomplish. Paltry penalties, it would seem, are not dictated by existing statutes.

This is not to deny that the "sentencing" problem may have deeper roots. Perhaps the government's failure to demand meaningful penalties reflects a proclivity to regard antitrust infractions as a harmless species of "civilized," "victimless," "white-collar" crime. What may be needed most, therefore, is a recognition that antitrust crimes are not inconsequential. They may be passionless in execution. They may be carried out by nonviolent means. They may be impersonal in character and indifferent in the choice of victims. But none of these considerations make antitrust offenses any less baneful, venal, or antisocial. As Edward A. Ross argued long ago, in his classic *Sin and Society*, "the villain most in need of curbing is the respectable, exemplary, trusted personage who, strategically placed at the focus of a spider-web of fiduciary relations, is able from his office-chair to pick a thousand pockets, poison a thousand sick, pollute a thousand minds, or imperil a thousand lives. It is the great-scale, high-voltage sinner that needs the shackle. To strike harder at the petty pickpocket than at the [white-collar criminal] . . . is to 'strain at a gnat and swallow a camel.' "[6] Or as Judge J. Cullen Ganey observed when sentencing the General Electric and Westinghouse executives for their role in the electrical-equipment conspiracy, antitrust transgressors do more than merely violate the law. These men, Judge Ganey said, "have flagrantly mocked the image of that economic system of free enterprise which we profess to the country, and destroyed the model which we offer today as a free world alternative to state control and eventual dictatorship."[7]

MONOPOLY

The government has since 1890 attacked and defeated monopolies in courtrooms across the country. Yet despite some notable successes, American monopoly policy in practice has fallen short of its promise.

Substantive structural relief is rarely obtained. Of the nearly four hundred monopolization cases brought by the Justice Department between 1890 and 1969, only thirty-two (or 8 percent) led to significant divestiture and reorganization.[8]

Structural relief is less than wildly successful even when it is obtained. Consider, for example, the Eastman Kodak Company.[9] Here is a classic monopolist that, through a panopoly of predatory practices and coercive and anticompetitive acts, monopolized fully 90 percent of the nation's amateur camera and film trade, and three-quarters of photographic paper sales, by 1904. After the government brought suit, the court ruled, in 1915, that trade had been "unjustly and abnormally restrained by the defendants by the formation of a monopoly, induced by wrongful contracts with regard to raw paper stock, preventing the trade from obtaining such stock, by the acquisition of competing plants, businesses, and stock houses, accompanied by covenants restraining vendors from re-entering the business, and by the imposition on dealers of arbitrary and oppressive terms of sale inconsistent with fair dealing, and suppressing competition." The court concluded, in unequivocal terms, that Kodak "attained, and now hold[s], an illegal monopoly . . . which in and of itself, as well as each and all of the elements composing it . . . whether considered separately or collectively, violates Sections 1 and 2" of the Sherman Act. It ordered the firm's assets to be "divided in such manner and into such number of parts of separate and distinct ownership as may be necessary to establish competitive conditions and bring about a new condition in harmony with the law."

The final "divestiture" order actually put into place, however, was ineffective. Not only were the Kodak properties to be divested trivial—

representing a mere 7 percent of the firm's sales and 5 percent of its profits—but they were drawn overwhelmingly from the obsolete *plate* photography field. Not surprisingly, Kodak's monopoly power has persisted down to the present. In 1944, for example, the Federal Trade Commission found that Kodak still had, for all intents and purposes, a monopoly in the production of amateur color film. In 1954 the firm entered into a consent settlement to avoid a second monopolization suit —a behavioral settlement that served to further *entrench* Kodak's monopoly power in significant respects. In 1972 the *Wall Street Journal* described Kodak as a company that "so dominates the world market for its products that it can, and does, call the shots for an entire industry." By the 1970s the Justice Department once again was investigating the industry's structure. In 1978 an economist retained by Kodak in a private monopolization suit conceded that the firm's shares of various photographic markets were essentially unchanged from those of three-quarters of a century earlier. And in 1979, Judge Irving R. Kaufman characterized Kodak as a firm that "stands, and has long stood, dominant."

The tobacco industry affords another case in point. The Supreme Court found the American Tobacco trust to have illegally monopolized trade and, in a landmark decision of 1911, ordered it dissolved. But rather than seeing that an effectively competitive industry structure was created, the Court merely divided the trust into three roughly equal parts, substituting a tight triopoly for a monopoly—a substitution that, by fostering high market concentration, had no substantive long-run economic impact on the industry. As might have been expected, the Supreme Court—in yet another landmark opinion three decades later— found the three lineal descendants (American Tobacco, Liggett & Myers, and R. J. Reynolds) to have collectively and unlawfully monopolized trade, in part through a remarkably parallel pattern of predatory pricing and leaf-tobacco purchases designed to crush independents whose competition threatened the Big Three's tacitly collusive price structure.[10] No structural relief was ordered in this second case; the highly concentrated structure of the industry remained intact; and the industry continues to exhibit extraordinarily uniform, noncompetitive oligopoly pricing.

Or consider the case of Standard Oil. Ordered dissolved by the Supreme Court in 1911, "the holding company distributed among its stockholders, on a pro rata basis, the shares of its subsidiaries. Though the successor companies were nominally independent, their owners were identical. These companies, moreover, were organized along state lines. A community of interest was thus maintained within a group of regional monopolies."[11]

Such examples can be multiplied.[12] They point up the failure of anti-trust to neutralize monopoly power and its structural base. They reflect undue judicial concern with the distinction between "good" and "bad" trusts—more emphasis on how a monopoly came into being and used its power than on the existence of the power and the potential of its abuse.

Monopoly prosecutions have to overcome three related obstacles:

1. The interminable legalistic wrangling over monopolistic "intent" and predatory "practices" causes endless delay. According to Geoffrey Shepherd, the duration of monopoly litigation "has lengthened, from about 6 years to about 20. The average interval from the original monopolization to remedy, which was already over 20 years in 1911 (35–40 years for Standard Oil), has now grown much longer. In the two major 1911 cases, Standard Oil and American Tobacco, a 'drastic' remedy was applied two or more decades after the monopoly was created. . . . In no case has an incipiency treatment been applied quickly enough to intercept a rising position of market power."[13]

2. As Senator Philip A. Hart noted, the search for evidence of predatory practices diverts attention from the central issue of monopoly power: "Government attorneys cull through the defendant firm's records in hopes of finding the hot document from which predation might be inferred, and the defendant recruits an army of satisfied users who extol the benefits of its products. Meanwhile, little or no attention is given to what ought to be the principal question: Does the defendant firm have a degree of economic power which should no longer be accepted in a competitive economy?"[14]

3. The emphasis on determining liability—that is, whether defendant has unlawfully monopolized—distracts attention from the economic remedy to be applied if the government wins the case. Remedy is almost an afterthought, and the temptation becomes almost irresistible to settle for (ineffectual) behavioral injunctions rather than insisting on structural change. In the end, the legal victory deals with the symptoms of monopoly rather than the causes.

To surmount these problems, the National Commission for the Review of Antitrust Laws and Procedures recommended in 1979 that Congress consider enacting "no-fault/no-conduct" legislation. Under this approach, the government would have the burden of proving that a firm possesses *persistent* monopoly power. Upon such showing, it would be spared the further obligation of proving that this power was obtained or maintained through predatory, exclusionary, or other forms of anticompetitive conduct. Instead, the proceedings would immediately turn to fashioning the structural remedies necessary to dissipate monopoly power, with the objective of creating as many economically viable competitors as possible. The monopolist, in turn, would bear the burden of demonstrating that such structural reorganization would entail the loss of significant economies of scale. These proceedings would involve neither a finding of fault nor the imposition of any penalties. This approach, the commission reasoned,

> would represent a logical solution to the several problems that today afflict monopolization litigation and would emphasize, as an independent antitrust goal, the elimination of persistent monopoly power. . . . By eliminating the conduct requirement, the monopolization proceedings would become forward-looking, rather than retrospective, and the talents of attorneys for both sides would not be devoted to lengthy battles over the existence and implications of alleged past conduct. Moreover, existence of the efficiencies defense would concentrate the efforts of both government and defense counsel on the issue of whether relief would harm consumer welfare by destroying efficiencies.[15]

OLIGOPOLY

Oligopoly, as we have repeatedly seen, is inherently incompatible with effective competition. Its noncompetitive structure militates toward non-competitive conduct—and ultimately to noncompetitive, and at times even disastrous, economic performance. Where market power is concentrated in the hands of a few and entry barriers are substantial, firms quite rationally recognize their interdependence. They understand that aggressive competition inevitably results in retaliation. They know that battle among giants can lead only to lower prices, cost controls, forced innovation, and eroded profits—all of which may be good for the public but not for the oligopoly. Hence, the central objective of the oligopoly game is to get ahead by getting along, to enjoy the quiet life without making waves.

Nevertheless, oligopolies in critical industries such as automobiles, steel, and energy have been virtually immune from structural antitrust. In automobiles, for example, most antitrust suits have been altogether peripheral in nature, and have never challenged the structurally rooted market power of the domestic auto oligopoly. The one exception, a "shared monopoly" investigation launched in the 1970s, was quashed by the Reagan administration. Of late, the government has not only spurned antitrust action against the automobile oligopoly, but has actively encouraged its entrenchment. It has sought to vacate past anti-

202 ■ THE BIGNESS COMPLEX

trust settlements and, as we have seen, has approved a rash of joint ventures and cross-ownership arrangements between the domestic oligopoly and its foreign rivals.

Likewise, there has been no serious antitrust challenge of the concentrated structure of the U.S. steel industry since 1920, even though the industry's woes stem largely from its noncompetitive structure. As economist F. M. Scherer has testified, the seemingly terminal maladies that today afflict the industry are due to the failure of structural antitrust over more than six decades.[16]

The oil oligopoly has enjoyed similar immunity. Since 1911, two major efforts were aimed at a comprehensive horizontal and vertical restructuring of the industry—the Justice Department's "Mother Hubbard" case of 1940, and the Federal Trade Commission's "shared monopoly" case of 1973. In both cases, the government's efforts languished and the proceedings ended without even token results. All in all, as Walter Measday has observed, the government's antitrust record is most noticeably characterized by "a marked reluctance particularly on the part of the Justice Department to get involved in any antitrust litigation involving the structure of the oil industry."[17]

Existing antitrust statutes may simply be inadequate to achieve a comprehensive restructuring of major oligopolistic industries. In the absence of outright collusion, overt predation, or collective predation, the enforcement agencies lack the ammunition they need to neutralize oligopoly power. Hence legislative proposals like the late Senator Hart's Industrial Reorganization Act, and the Neal Commission's Concentrated Industries Act have been put forward to deal with the structural oligopoly problem.[18]

Under the Neal Commission's Concentrated Industries Act, for example, the attorney general and the Federal Trade Commission would have been directed to investigate the structure of markets that appear to be under oligopoly control. "Oligopoly industries" would be defined as industries wherein "any four or fewer firms had an aggregate market share of 70 percent or more during at least seven of the last ten, and four of the most recent five base years," and where no substantial turnover had occurred in the ranks of the leading firms over a ten-year period. "Oligopoly firms" would comprise firms in oligopoly industries whose individual market shares exceeded 15 percent. Upon finding an oligopoly industry to exist, the government would be required to institute proceedings to obtain "a reduction of concentration such that the market share of each oligopoly firm in such oligopoly industry does not exceed 12 percent." This could be accomplished through provisions requiring the defendant firms (1) to modify contractual relationships or methods of distribution; (2) to grant licenses under or dispose of any patents, technical information, copyrights, or trademarks; or (3) to divest assets. To ensure achievement of effective structural relief, the Neal Commission proposed "a mandatory 'second look' every four or five years after the entry of affirmance of the original decree until concentration is reduced to the extent [called for in the act]. If relief granted in a decree has not had the desired effect, more drastic relief would generally be in order." Finally, in order to focus upon industries of substantial importance in the economy, the commission recommended that the proposed legislation be applied only to oligopoly industries with annual sales of at least $500 million.[19]

MERGERS AND ACQUISITIONS

Another important objective of antitrust is to arrest trends toward increased concentration in their incipiency—to nip them in the bud before they develop into full-blown concentrations of economic power. It was the failure of the Clayton Act as originally written to achieve this goal that impelled Congress to enact the Celler-Kefauver Amendment in 1950. Its legislative history and language made it clear that the chief goal was to block, even reverse, the tide of economic concentration—both in particular markets and industries and in the economy at large.

Once again, however, the merger provisions of the Clayton Act have fallen short of their full potential—despite some initially promising successes in *Bethlehem, Brown Shoe,* and *Von's Grocery.* Industrial organization specialist Willard Mueller explains: "Ironically, a vast merger movement commenced shortly after passage of [Celler-Kefauver Amendment] in 1950. Commencing in the early 1950s, merger activity registered progressive increases and reached a frenzied pace in 1967–70, when more than one of every five manufacturing and mining corporations with assets exceeding $10 million was acquired. For several years thereafter, the merger pace slowed to pre-1967 levels. But beginning in 1976, the pace picked up rapidly until today we are again in the midst of a great merger movement."[20] Activity has recently reached an all-time high. The total value of all acquisitions reached a record $122 billion in 1984, and a new record of $179 billion in 1985.[21]

In the petroleum industry, whose members rank as eleven of the twenty largest industrial concerns in the United States, and ten of the largest twenty worldwide, twenty major firms collectively control three-quarters of domestic crude oil production, and the sixteen largest control 82 percent of the nation's reserves, 75 percent of its refining capacity, nearly 70 percent of retail gasoline sales, and upward of 90 percent of total pipeline capacity. Here is an industry whose members dominate substitute, potentially competitive, fuels. And the energy field (oil, natural gas, coal, and uranium) is a field where, according to Federal Trade Commission calculations, economic concentration has "risen substantially between 1955 and 1970. For example, when measured in dollars, 4-firm concentration rose from 16.1 to 23.4 [percent], 8-firm concentration rose from 27.0 to 37.8, and 20-firm concentration rose from 43.3 to 57.2."[22]

Yet oil companies have engaged virtually unmolested in a spree of horizontal mergers, vertical mergers, and conglomerate mergers. Major crude-oil producers acquired 147 other other crude-oil producers between 1955 and 1970, while Mobil Oil (the second largest integrated producer) recently acquired Superior Oil, the nation's largest independent explorer and producer of oil and gas.[23] Approximately 40 percent of the increased refining capacity of the top 20 oil companies between 1959 and 1966 resulted from acquisitions of independent refiners.[24] Recent mergers of Occidental with Cities Service, Texaco with Getty, and Standard Oil of California (Socal) with Gulf united the industry's eleventh largest firm with its eighteenth, its third with its twelfth, and its fifth with its sixth. In taking over Consolidation Coal and Island Creek Coal, large petroleum companies obtained leading positions in coal, while conglomerate megamergers have included Mobil's acquisition of Montgomery Ward and Container Corporation, Exxon's acquisition of Reliance Electric, Occidental's acquisition of Iowa Beef Processors, and Sohio's acquisition of Kennecott. All told, the top twenty oil companies spent $26.6 billion on mergers and acquisitions in the short period 1978–81; for the years 1981–83, oil and gas company acquisitions totaled an additional $44.2 billion.[25] Obviously, antitrust has scarcely been a deterrent.

Nor has the Celler-Kefauver Amendment served to arrest the more general trend toward increased concentration throughout the economy. Despite an initial decline in 1950, the largest two hundred industrial firms continue to account for the bulk of large mergers and acquisitions. Indeed, both acquiring and acquired firms increasingly rank among the two hundred largest: In recent years, for example, Du Pont (fifteenth largest in the nation) has acquired Conoco (fourteenth); U.S. Steel (nineteenth) has acquired Marathon Oil (thirty-ninth); Occidental Petroleum (twentieth) has acquired Iowa Beef Processors (eighty-first); Allied Corporation (then fifty-fifth) has acquired Bendix (eighty-sixth); and most recently, Allied (by now twenty-sixth) has agreed to merge with Signal Companies (sixty-first). As a result of megamergers, control over more and more economic activity is being steadily concentrated into fewer, vastly larger, hands.

Beyond doubt, the 1950 amendment has failed to come to grips with merger-based increases in economic concentration. In no small part, this shortcoming is attributable to casual enforcement by Reagan antitrust officials who are ideologically wedded to the misguided belief that mergers and acquisitions "are essential to the nation's economic vitality," in the words of J. Paul McGrath, recent head of the Justice Department's Antitrust Division.[26] The concept of the "relevant market," wherein potentially anticompetitive effects of mergers must be shown, has provided a convenient subterfuge. Explains a recent chairman of the Federal Trade Commission: "If America's giants, Nos. 1 and 2 in an industry, prepare to join hands, the economist perceives that the relevant geographic market is not the United States, but the world. Should the No. 1 and 2 breakfast cereal manufacturers in the world become betrothed, our economists decide that the relevant market is far more commodious than had been thought: egg breeders, croissant bakers, Egg McMuffin vendors, lox and cream cheese purveyors—all are shepherded into one great breakfast market in which the cereal giants will be seen to occupy only modest market shares."[27] Cases such as *Brown Shoe, Bethlehem, Von's Grocery,* and the cement cases show that the existing statute can effectively halt potentially anticompetitive horizontal and vertical mergers in unconcentrated and concentrated fields alike. But instead of enforcing the law, the antitrust agencies in recent years have chosen to serve as cheerful "consultants" for merger partners in oil and other industries, helpfully suggesting minor adjustments that will permit the consolidation of American industry to proceed unencumbered—adverse economic performance consequences to the contrary notwithstanding.[28]

Even were the merger law to be enforced, however, antitrust would still be hamstrung in dealing with giant conglomerate mergers and the concomitant trend toward concentration of control in the economy at large. Here, too, the "relevant market" proof is a root cause: in attempting to block mergers of giants in unrelated fields, the government must prove, in each case, that a conglomerate megamerger may lessen competition in some narrowly defined geographic and product market. Thus, if Exxon, General Motors, and IBM were to merge, the government would have to demonstrate some anticompetitive overlap in some precisely identified "relevant market" before the merger could be stopped. But large conglomerate mergers and disproportionate firm size seem *inevitably* to exert a chilling impact on the entire competitive system. Almost unavoidably, they seem to create opportunities and incentives for cross-subsidization, reciprocity, conglomerate interdependence, and competitive forbearance. Cumulatively they thereby seem to undermine competition and its concomitant, good economic performance.

Furthermore, the strictures of Section 7 fail to comprehend the full measure of the power and influence wielded by gigantic conglomerates —to see that a consolidation of Exxon, General Motors, and IBM might well represent a concentration of economic power intolerable to a free society. Consider ITT, the twenty-first largest industrial corporation in nation, and in the world, which boasts that it is "constantly working around the clock—in 67 nations on six continents, in activities extending from the Arctic to the Antarctic and quite literally from the bottom of the sea to the moon."[29] Here is a firm whose officers and directors have included a former secretary general of the United Nations, a former premier of Belgium, two members of the British House of Lords, a member of the French National Assembly, a former president of the World Bank, and a former director of the CIA. And here is a firm that, over a four-day period, placed its aircraft at the disposal of two members of President Nixon's cabinet, three senators, five representatives, and two presidential candidates.[30] Given its gargantuan size, is it really surprising that ITT enjoyed sufficient access to the corridors of government to offer $1 million to the CIA and the National Security Council to overthrow the constitutionally elected Allende government in Chile?[31] Is it surprising that, when faced with government challenges to three of its proposed conglomerate acquisitions, the firm could bring to bear "a massive assault on every relevant area of government," crown its efforts with a $400,000 donation to finance the Republican National Convention, and then miraculously persuade the Justice Department to drop the cases?[32] The kaleidoscopic power of a giant conglomerate like ITT— virtually a state unto itself—cannot be seen in a narrow "relevant market." Nor does prohibiting mergers where they "may substantially lessen competition" come to grips with the essence of the problem.

THE FUTURE OF ANTITRUST

A number of alternative approaches have been proposed. For example, an outright ban could be imposed on mergers and acquisitions by any *Fortune* 500 firm unless the company could show—and the burden of proof would be on the firm, not the government—that the merger (1) would not substantially lessen competition or tend to create a monopoly in any line of commerce; (2) would enhance the operating efficiency of the acquiring and acquired firms; and (3) would promote technological progress not otherwise obtainable. Alternatively, a "cap-and-spin" restraint could be imposed on the nation's largest firms. Under this approach, firms larger than a specified size threshold would be prohibited from making any acquisition unless the acquiring firm spun off competitively viable assets equal in value to those which it sought to acquire. A key advantage of this option is that it would put an upper limit on the ability of corporate giants to short-circuit the market test for success through artificial, merger-based growth. At the very least, acquisitive industrial giants could be barred from floating bank loans or issuing "junk bonds" to finance their megamergers.

In discussing these alternatives it is important to recognize that none of them limits in any way the freedom of firms to expand through *internal* growth derived from better products and services, lower operating costs, or greater efficiency in innovation. Nor would they impair economic efficiency. They explicitly allow for efficiency defenses. And as the current deconglomeration and "small is beautiful" trends reveal, large conglomerate mergers more often than not have turned out to be economic disasters—not only for society but for private profits as well.[33] Thus it would seem that the private and public interests alike would not have been harmed—indeed, would have been advanced—had legislation along these lines been in place years ago.

Future enforcement of the antitrust laws undoubtedly will be fraught with some of the same difficulties that have limited its success over the last century.

Unlike agriculture or labor, antitrust does not have a powerful political constituency. This means that the budgets allocated to the Antitrust Division and the Federal Trade Commission will continue to be inadequate for the job of policing competition throughout the U.S. economy.

The antitrust authorities will continue to be bedeviled by the problem of case selection. Should they concentrate their scarce enforcement resources on price-fixing violations among small fry like the highway paving contractors, as the Reagan administration has done, while ignoring endemic structural problems like the wholesale consolidation of industry through merger and acquisition? Should they crush colluding producers of wood screws and wax crayons, while according benign neglect to mergers involving the nation's largest petroleum firms? Should they ruthlessly attack mergers among condom companies, while encouraging joint ventures among the world's largest automobile firms? In other words, should antitrust (as it has done under the Reagan administration) bravely sally forth in pursuit of rabbits while leaving elephants free to roam the Darwinian jungle?

Operating as it does in a highly politicized environment, antitrust will continue to be buffeted by the ubiquitous pressure of special interests and powerful influence peddlers. If antitrust strikes out against laundry operators in New Haven or wire-hanger manufacturers in Kansas City, the political fallout is minimal. If it were to launch an assault on a multinational colossus like General Motors, this would invite consternation (and chastisement) at both ends of Pennsylvania Avenue. This is not a matter of idle conjecture. When antitrust tried to slow down ITT's merger binge in the 1960s, its Washington lobby persuaded the administration that this would trigger nothing less than the collapse of Wall Street. In 1980, a coalition of cereal lobbyists, the AFL-CIO, and the Michigan legislature convinced candidate Ronald Reagan that continued prosecution of the FTC's shared-monopoly suit against the purveyors of corn flakes "would have a chilling effect on American industry." Alas, as Senator Philip Hart, chairman of the Senate Antitrust and Monopoly Subcommittee, once ruefully asked: "Have we now reached a point in our society where there has been permitted to develop a private concentration of power which, because of the enormity of their reach, makes impossible the application of public policy to them?"[34]

These institutional roadblocks are firmly embedded in our political economy. Yet, in evaluating antitrust it is well to maintain perspective. In the words of Walton Hamilton,

Antitrust is a symbol of democracy. It is an assertion that every industry is affected with a public interest. Quite apart from its operation, it keeps alive within law and public policy a value which must not be sacrificed or abridged. It asserts the firm, the trade, the economy to be the instrument of the general welfare. If the fact falls short of the ideal, the call is to amend the fact rather than abandon the ideal. It may be that in many industrial areas, the free and open market has been compromised or is forever gone. Still its norms of order and justice endure to serve as standards for performance under another arrangement. In matters where the market can be restored to its economic office, there should be caution in substituting administration. A hazard to the common good attends the enlargement of personal discretion.[35]

V

GOVERNMENT INTERVENTION AND PRIVATE POWER

In a free-enterprise economy, the competitive market is society's central decision-making mechanism—its surrogate for economic planning and social control. As long as the market performs its prescribed function, there is no need for direct government intervention in economic affairs. Government's role can be restricted to making the rules of the game and to enforcing them, serving as an arbiter and referee rather than a participant. In short, government's primary role is to uphold the market's authority as a governance system.

Even in a free-enterprise economy, however, the market cannot have unlimited sway as a decision-making mechanism. There are some tasks that can be entrusted only to government. "Revealed preference" in the market—consumers casting dollar votes to determine what goods are produced in what quantity—may be a felicitous process for deciding whether resources shall be used to make Hula-hoops or snowmobiles, but it is hardly a guide for stocking the nation's defense arsenal. Only government can provide society with such "collective" goods as battleships, missiles, and bombers. Only government can exercise the traditional police powers of the state—protecting the health, safety, and morals of the citizenry. The government, not the market, should make decisions about clean air, pure water, safe drugs, genetic engineering, and the disposal of toxic wastes.

And even in a free-enterprise society, there are some industries that are inherently incapable of operating under a regime of market competition. There are "natural monopolies," where enforced competition would entail prodigious inefficiencies and impose intolerable costs of duplication. A single electric company, for example, can deliver electricity to a community far less expensively than could multiple purveyors, each with its own system of lines and generators. Similarly, one large pipeline can transport petroleum between given points at a fraction of the cost that would have to be incurred by a myriad of small, parallel lines. In such "natural monopoly" situations, technological constraints militate against competition, and public policy must choose an alternative governance system. It may permit private ownership alone, trusting to the monopolist's sense of social responsibility not to exploit the public. Or it may subject private ownership to public control. Or it may put both ownership and operation of the natural monopoly in the hands of governmental authority.

These functions of government are rarely called into question except by ideological extremists. The practical problem arises when private interests importune government to transcend its necessary and proper functions. Then the problem becomes where to draw the line between legitimate intervention and blatant protectionism. For example, should the government extend "public utility" regulation to industries that are not natural monopolies—industries like trucking and airlines, endowed with inherently competitive characteristics? Would such intervention protect the public from exploitation or merely shield vested interests from competition? Should government intervene to protect major industries like steel and automobiles from import competition when the malaise of these industries is primarily a self-inflicted injury? Should it intervene to promote selected industries like nuclear power with massive subsidies? Should it intervene to bail out giant firms like Penn-Central, Lockheed, and Chrysler from imminent financial collapse? These are the issues on the cutting edge of public policy; they cannot be resolved by such simplistic slogans as "getting the government off the backs of business."

CHAPTER 16

THE REGULATION
OF POWER

Where competition is impossible and monopoly inevitable, there we must have state
regulation; but we should have greater faith in the workings of the competitive
system where it can be applied. It is far better for the government to try to preserve
and to restore competition and thus obtain a largely self-regulating economic system than to permit monopoly and then try to control and regulate it. If the latter
course is taken, there is grave danger that the monopolists will in the long run
control and regulate the government.
                              — U.S. Senator Paul H. Douglas (D-Ill.), 1952

The Supreme Power who conceived gravity, supply and demand, and the double
helix must have been absorbed elsewhere when public utility regulation was invented. The system is cumbersome, vulnerable to incompetence, and prone toward
becoming ingrown and co-opted.   — Professor F. M. Scherer, 1970

Toward the turn of the century, in that Gilded Age that Walt Whitman called "cankered, crude, su-
perstitious, and rotten," Lincoln Steffens reported on the ethics of city
government. He found that everything the cities owned—rights, privileges, franchises, and real property—was subject to sale by the people's
elected representatives. Boodling and corruption were widespread, and
their source was at the top, not the bottom of society. In St. Louis, said
Steffens,

with few exceptions, no ordinance has been passed wherein valuable privileges or franchises are granted until those interested have paid the legislators
the money demanded for action in the particular case. Combines in both
branches of the Municipal Assembly are formed by members sufficient in

number to control legislation. To one member of this combine is delegated the authority to act for the combine, and to receive and to distribute to each member the money agreed upon as the price of his vote in support of, or opposition to, a pending measure. So long has this practice existed that such members have come to regard the receipt of money for action on pending measures as a legitimate perquisite of a legislator.

In Pittsburgh, "the machine's idea was not to corrupt the city government, but to be it; not to hire votes in council, but to own councilmen." In other cities the pattern was substantially the same.

Most appalling about this corruption, according to Steffens, was that it involved "not thieves, gamblers, and common women, but influential citizens, capitalists, and great corporations." The big businessman, he found, was "buying boodlers in St. Louis, defending grafters in Minneapolis, originating corruption in Pittsburgh, sharing with bosses in Philadelphia, deploring reform in Chicago, and beating good government with corruption funds in New York. He is a self-righteous fraud, this big businessman," Steffens concluded. "He is the chief source of corruption, and it were a boon if he would neglect politics."[1]

In the Steffens era, municipalities were the prime target of opportunity for businessmen intent on controlling government for private gain. The reason was obvious: municipalities were the principal agency for dispensing privilege and favor. In this era of rambunctious, laissez-faire capitalism, the federal government was still a relatively small and insignificant factor in the economy. Its expenditures totaled a mere $600 million, which accounted for only 2 percent of the national income.

Today, by contrast, Washington exercises a pervasive influence over economic life. Its expenditures approach $1 trillion (or 1,638 times more than in 1900) and, if state and local expenditures are included, the total rises to $1.4 trillion—more than 35 percent of the national income. In this era of Big Government, government is no longer an impartial arbiter of economic activity but a principal participant.

The late Senator Paul H. Douglas of Illinois, a former professor of economics at the University of Chicago, had ample first-hand opportunity to observe Big Government in action. In his reflections on government-business relations, he points up the essence of the problem:

In a free market, prices are fixed impersonally by the forces of supply and demand, and, therefore, adjustments in quantities produced and hence in unit prices are made according to the schedules of costs and profits. There is little room for corruption or undue favoritism here. In contrast, when the government makes the decisions about prices, quantities produced, and what firms may enter an industry, the door is opened wide for the exercise of favoritism

and corruption. These matters are life or death to the businessman or industrialist. A hostile government may put him out of business, while a friendly
administration may give him great profits. Wherever government controls a
business, it becomes inevitable that the business should try to control the
government. . . .

When prices are fixed for an industry, the lobbyists will flock to the national capital. When the government determines which firms are to receive
steel, aluminum, or copper [as it customarily does in times of national emer-
gency] expediters and "fixers" will spring up like the dragon's teeth which
Cadmus was reputed to have sown. When the government decides which
firms are to enter an industry, as it now necessarily does in the case of radio,
television, and the airlines, it is certain that pressure and influence will be
applied by groups which wish to get the favored positions. When the government makes loans, there will be concerns which will hire men with influence
to obtain them. When it pays subsidies, the ranks of the government agencies
will be permeated by the secret agents of those who are subsidized.

In short, where economic decisions are made by the people and parties who
administer government, the decisions will not be on the lofty and abstract
grounds which are somewhat naïvely assumed by many economists who
favor pervasive and far-reaching economic controls. [Instead] the crucial
decisions will commonly be made in an atmosphere of pressure, influence,
favoritism, improper deals, and corruption. In short, the capitals of our de-
mocracies are likely to become even more sodden with corruption than was
Versailles under Louis XIV and Colbert and England under Charles I and
Archbishop Laud.[2]

Big Government, as we shall see, is in constant danger of being
transformed into a welfare state for powerful private interests and
constantly tempted to abdicate its function as a defender and promoter
of the public interest. This is particularly evident in the regulated sector
of the domestic economy and in international trade.

Regulation, as originally conceived, was to both supplement competition
and substitute for it. It was to be applied in those industries where the
cost of entry was so great or the duplication of facilities so wasteful that
some degree of monopoly was considered unavoidable. Here the visible
hand of public regulation was to replace the invisible hand of Adam
Smith in protecting consumers against extortionate charges, restriction
of output, deterioration of services, and unfair discrimination. This was
the rationale for creating state regulatory commissions and the Interstate Commerce Commission.

This regulatory concept, however, was first eroded and then extended. The regulatees themselves came to recognize that the better
part of wisdom was not to abolish regulation but to utilize it. Gradually

the public utility concept was transformed from consumer-oriented to industry-oriented regulation. By a process so brilliantly analyzed by Horace Gray,

> the policy of state-created, state-protected monopoly became firmly established over a significant portion of the economy and became the keystone of modern public utility regulation. Henceforth, the public utility status was to be the haven of refuge for all aspiring monopolists who found it too difficult, too costly, or too precarious to secure and maintain monopoly by private action alone. Their future prosperity would be assured if only they could induce government to grant them monopoly power and to protect them against interlopers, provided always, of course, that government did not exact too high a price for its favors in the form of restrictive regulation.[3]

Business interests gradually began to appreciate the virtues of public-utility status and to embrace government regulation as an instrument of protection from competition. As early as 1892, five years after Congress had passed the Interstate Commerce Act, Richard Olney, a former director of several railroad companies whom President Grover Cleveland had appointed to serve as U.S. attorney general, stated the proregulation position with Machiavellian clarity. In a letter to his old friend Charles E. Perkins, president of the Chicago, Burlington, & Quincy Railroad, who had implored Olney to spearhead a drive to repeal the Interstate Commerce Act, Olney wrote as follows:

> My impression would be that looking at the matter from a railroad point of view exclusively it would not be a wise thing to undertake. . . . The attempt would not be likely to succeed; if it did not succeed, and were made on the ground of inefficiency and uselessness of the Commission, the result would very probably be giving it the power it now lacks. The Commission, as its functions have now been limited by the courts, is, or can be made, of great use to the railroads. It satisfies the popular clamor for a government supervision of the railroads, at the same time that that supervision is almost entirely nominal. Further, the older such a commission gets to be, the more inclined it will be found to take the business and railroad view of things. It thus becomes a sort of barrier between the railroad corporations and the people and a sort of protection against hasty and crude legislation hostile to railroad interests. . . . The part of wisdom is not to destroy the Commission, but to utilize it.[4]

Unregulated industries, such as steel, for example, also sought government regulation—in the belief that regulation was a far less stringent taskmaster than competition. Thus, in 1911, after the U.S. Steel

Corporation had come under antitrust attack, its president, Judge Elbert H. Gary, host of the collusive Gary Dinners, told a congressional committee:

"I realize as fully, I think, as this committee that it is very important to consider how the people shall be protected against imposition or oppression as the possible result of great aggregations of capital, whether in the possession of corporations or individuals. I believe that is a very important question, and personally I believe that the Sherman Act does not meet and will never fully prevent that. I believe we must come to enforced publicity and governmental control, even as to prices, and, so far as I am concerned, speaking for our company, so far as I have the right. I would be very glad if we had some place where we could go, to a responsible governmental authority, and say to them, 'Here are our facts and figures, here is our property, here our cost of production; now you tell us what we have the right to do and what prices we have the right to charge.' I know this is a very extreme view, and I know that the railroads objected to it for a long time; but whether the standpoint of making the most money is concerned or not, whether it is the wise thing, I believe it is the necessary thing, and it seems to me corporations have no right to disregard these public questions and these public interests."

"Your idea then," said Congressman Littleton of the committee, "is that cooperation is bound to take the place of competition and that cooperation requires strict governmental supervision?"

"That is a very good statement," replied the judge.[5]

Obviously, U.S. Steel was persuaded that it could more assuredly preserve its power and continue to lead the "quiet life" under the gentle surveillance of an ICC-style regulatory commission than under the competitive strictures of the Sherman Act.

By 1940, protectionism by regulation had become both a popular and respectable governmental control mechanism. Independent regulatory commissions had been entrusted with the oversight of motor carriers, inland waterways, airlines, communications, and natural gas—despite the fact that some of these industries hardly conformed to the structural prototype of "natural" monopolies. "Public convenience and necessity," not the dictates of the competitive market, had become the standard for determining entry, rates, and quality of service. Most important, this great transformation had been accomplished, not over the objection of business interests, but with their approval and (sometimes enthusiastic) support.

Eventually, experience with regulation revealed what public interest advocates had long ago predicted.[6] Empirical evidence accumulated to show that regulation in some industries was not a device to protect

consumers from exploitation but to protect vested interest from competition. At the hands of some regulatory commissions, the power to license
had become the power to exclude; control over rates had turned into an
instrument of price supports; and authority over mergers had become a
mechanism for fostering industry concentration. The regulatory commissions, according to former FTC Chairman Lewis Engman (a Republican appointee serving during the Nixon administration), had transmuted
the industries under their jurisdiction into "federal protectorates, living
in the cozy world of cost-plus, safely protected from the ugly spectres
of competition, efficiency, and innovation." In short, under the aegis of
the "independent" commissions, regulation was essentially a neomercantilist device of protectionism in which industry, labor, and government regulators had an abiding interest—to the detriment of the general
public.

Donald Baker, a former chief of the Antitrust Division, underscores
this point with the following anecdote. The Charles River Bridge, Baker
reports, was built in 1786 by a private company, which was given a
seventy-year charter by the State of Massachusetts; but the state legislature, eager to encourage competition for lower fares, chartered a new
bridge in 1828. The first company brought suit, and in 1837 the Supreme
Court upheld the second charter, saying that while private property
rights should be "sacredly guarded," the public interest must prevail.
"Imagine," says Baker,

> this case coming before a modern regulatory agency. Squadrons of attorneys,
> economists, businessmen, engineers, and accountants would present volumes
> of briefs, statistics, charts, and multiple regression analyses showing why the
> second bridge was bad. They would argue that there is no public need for the
> new service, that it would lead to overcapacity, "cream skimming" and cut-
> throat pricing, that economies of scale require a bigger first bridge (not a
> second bridge), that the safety and quality of the second bridge was in doubt,
> and that an integrated and balanced transportation system, looking toward
> future needs, requires just one bridge run by one bridge authority. QED.
> Against this array of (speculative) horribles would be the idea of competition.
> But given the weight of evidence, the constitution of the regulators, and their
> fear of uncharted waters, it can be doubted whether today's decision would
> be the same as in 1837.[7]

In the next two chapters, we shall examine the U.S. experience with
government regulation in two major industries—airlines and trucking.
It was an experiment in mercantilist statecraft that was fraught with
fatal defects.

CHAPTER 17

AIRLINE REGULATION

Here an agency of Government has proved itself a willing instrument of vested carriers seeking to maintain a closed industry.
— Walton Hamilton,
The Politics of American Industry

Increased competition should make for a leaner, more efficient scheduled operation in more than one way. Filling empty seats with discount fares reduces average costs. Even more important, I think, increasing intensity of price competition should exert powerful pressures on airlines, who have for too long been operating in a regime of protectionism and cost-plus pricing, to intensify their efforts to rationalize their operations, hold down input prices, and improve the efficiency with which they use those inputs. — Alfred E. Kahn, former chairman of the
Civil Aeronautics Board, 1978

Thoroughgoing federal regulation of the commercial airline industry commenced in 1938 with the passage of the Civil Aeronautics Act. The new law created the Civil Aeronautics Board (CAB) and entrusted it with regulating interstate air transportation so as to promote a high degree of safety, sound economic conditions, and the proper adaptation of air transportation to the nation's commercial, postal, and defense needs.

To carry out its mandate, the board was given four key powers: (1) The entry power: the power to grant or to deny "certificates of public convenience and necessity," which an airline would need in order to fly interstate. (2) The rate power: the authority to set air fares. (3) The merger power: the power to approve or deny mergers involving certificated carriers; approval would confer immunity from the antitrust laws.

(4) The antitrust power: the power to approve (or disapprove) agreements among air carriers; again, approval would confer immunity from the antitrust laws.

Initially, unlike the regulation of such "natural monopolies" as telephone and electric service, competition was to play an important role in achieving the goals set out for the CAB. For example, a commission established in 1935 studied the industry and made recommendations that decisively shaped the final regulatory legislation; it urged, "There must be enough competition to serve as a spur to the eager search for progress, but there must not be so much as to raise costs materially through the duplication of facilities. There must be no arbitrary denial of the right of entry of newcomers into the field where they can make an adequate showing of their readiness to render a better public service than could otherwise be obtained. There must be no policy of a permanent freezing of the present air transport map, with respect either to the location of its routes or the identity of their operators. The present operators of airlines have no inherent right to a monopoly of the routes that they serve."[1]

This initial attention to the role that competition was expected to play was not misplaced. As Assistant Attorney General for Antitrust, Thomas E. Kauper, has explained, the air transport industry is *not* naturally monopolistic; rather, it is innately competitive:

> Evidence is quite abundant that there are no important economies of scale in air transportation; that is, larger firms are not more efficient or less costly simply because of their size. In fact, other things being equal, the largest air carriers tend to have a *higher* level of unit costs, and there are some indications that these increased costs are caused by the difficulties of managing an airline of very large size.
>
> The reasons for this are apparent—the airlines' "right of way" is the air itself, and their "tracks," if any, are the air traffic control guideways maintained by the federal government. Well over 80 percent of the airlines' investment is in flight equipment, which is among the most mobile of assets, rather than in fixed assets, as is the case in the classical "natural monopoly." Not only does this make competitive service economically feasible, but it makes duplication of routes far less risky, because competitors can more easily adjust their operations by rescheduling an aircraft from one city-pair to another.[2]

In practice, however, regulation of commercial aviation diverged from the competitive ideals and assurances offered by its proponents. Ostensibly undertaken to promote and protect the public interest, regulation soon became the instrument for protecting the private interests of the regulatees. A new field bursting with prospects for economic growth and opportunity was blocked off as the exclusive preserve of a privileged few. Most important, the burden of cartelized protectionism was borne by the public in whose interest the industry was first regulated. "The practical lessons," the Justice Department later concluded, "have been that present economic regulation of our domestic airlines has a serious, built-in tendency to waste scarce resources, deprive many consumers of the benefits of air transportation, and withhold commercial opportunities in the aviation industry from many individuals and firms."[3]

REGULATION IN PRACTICE

Let us examine regulation of airline entry, rates, mergers, and antitrust exemptions to see how the CAB actually functioned.

ENTRY

Prior to 1938, there was no legal barrier to entry into commercial aviation. With the advent of regulation, however, a certificate or license to operate was required for admission. The CAB was instructed by law to issue an operating certificate if the applicant was found to be "fit, willing and able to perform such transportation properly," and if the proposed service was deemed to be "required by the public convenience and necessity."

Presumably, the certification requirement reflected Congress's decision that, owing to its newness and hazards, air transportation was "affected with a public interest" and entry should therefore be monitored. But the certification requirement did not in and of itself indicate how much entry—and, therefore, competition—should be permitted, by whom, or how rapidly.

In practice, the board used the power to control entry in three significant respects. First, by virtue of a "grandfather clause" contained in the Civil Aeronautics Act, the eighteen carriers operating as of 1938 (including TWA, United, American, Eastern, Braniff, Continental, and Delta) were automatically certificated to serve the trunk lines between major metropolitan areas that they had already staked out for themselves. The board thereafter fastened upon these carriers as its chosen—and privileged—instruments for serving the nation's most heavily traveled and most lucrative air markets. Subsequently, the CAB refused to certify a single new domestic trunk-line carrier beyond those originally grandfathered into the industry. As the Senate Select Committee on Small Business reported in 1953, "In the 15 years since the act was passed, the

Board has refused to certificate any new carrier to perform common carriage of passengers on trunk routes"—this despite a twentyfold increase in the volume of air traffic.[4] In 1962, economist Richard Caves concluded: "The Board's policy toward the entry of new trunk-line carriers is easy to summarize: none has been certified since the 'grandfather' carriers."[5] And in 1975—four decades after the industry had been regulated with assurances that there would be nothing to prevent "a little fellow with a new idea" from entering the field—the CAB acknowledged that between 1950 and 1974 it had received seventy-nine applications by companies who wanted to enter the domestic scheduled airline industry. Not one was granted![6]

Although some new firms were permitted to provide air service, it was minimal—usually in newly created service classes (local or "feeder" service, supplemental or charter service), which were tightly circumscribed by the CAB to prevent competition with grandfathered trunk-line carriers. Not insignificantly, new entry typically required explicit congressional intervention.

The extent of the CAB's solicitude for trunk-line carriers, and its refusal to use competition to promote the public interest, were dramatized by its response to irregular, or "nonscheduled," carriers. Carriers providing nonscheduled flight services were initially exempt from entry controls and hence free to enter the industry. But right after World War II, the number of "nonskeds" increased substantially, as former war pilots began entering with surplus military aircraft. Most importantly, the nonskeds pioneered low-fare "coach" service, bringing air travel within reach of a vastly larger public. With fares averaging one-third less than those of certificated carriers, sparking a surge in the demand for air transportation, the irregular carriers had "a shattering effect on the concept that air travel must necessarily be an elite type of luxury."[7]

Rather than embracing these low-fare pioneers and encouraging them, the CAB instead moved to eliminate irregular carriers as a viable competitive force in long-haul trunk-line air transportation. In 1950, for example, the board held the operations of nonscheduled carriers to be against the public interest because "substantial diversion from the certificated carriers has occurred." The following year, the CAB denied entry to a number of irregular carriers seeking to offer low-fare service, because to permit them to enter would pose "a serious threat to the future orderly progression toward cheaper air transportation for the Nation." It was only under heavy congressional pressure that the board consented to certificate nonscheduled operators as supplemental, or charter, carriers. Yet the restrictive web of regulations within which these carriers were forced to operate was (according to Lewis Engman, former chairman of the Federal Trade Commission) tantamount to permitting charter carriers to operate only if the traveler "is leaving on a Wednesday morning, plans to remain at his destination for precisely 53 days, is carrying no luggage and is a charter member of the Flat Earth Society."[8]

Furthermore, the CAB tightly restricted the number of grandfather trunk-line carriers permitted to compete directly on the same routes. Between 1965 and 1975, out of 1,800 applications for authority to serve the 100 most heavily traveled city-pairs, only 8 percent were approved. According to a Government Accounting Office (GAO) study, "123 applications were filed to serve major routes between 1964 and 1969. Of these, 14, or 11.4 percent, were granted. Between 1969 and 1974, 49 were filed, and 2, or 4 percent, were granted. The remainder were withdrawn, dismissed as stale, dismissed for some other reason, or remained pending at the end of the period."[9]

Impact on incumbent carriers—not service and choice for the flying public—seemed paramount in the CAB's decision-making calculus. With few substantive exceptions, the board's power to monitor entry was transmuted into the power to block entry, and a policy of "controlled entry" became a policy of "all control and no entry."[10]

FARES

Section 404(a) of the Civil Aeronautics Act required carriers "to establish, observe, and enforce just and reasonable individual and joint rates." In deciding the lawfulness of air fares, the board was instructed to consider, *inter alia*, the effect of rates on the movement of traffic, the public interest in adequate and efficient air transportation, and the carriers' needs for revenues sufficient to enable them to provide efficient and adequate service.

In practice, CAB regulation of fares failed to promote these objectives. First, the board seemed uninterested in the appropriateness of fare levels. It initiated general fare investigations on only two occasions. Instead, the bulk of its efforts focused on the amount of air-mail subsidies paid to the carriers—even though these subsidies soon accounted for only 10 percent of total carrier revenues. It was only with the advent of low-fare nonscheduled carriers that the board began to consider the possibility that the demand for air travel might be price-elastic, and that price might be used as a tool to stimulate air travel.[11]

The CAB served primarily as a forum where carriers could discuss rates, with the resulting fares validated and enforced by the board. This was typically done in informal *ex parte* conferences held without benefit of public access.[12] The process became so flagrant that in the late 1960s, when the CAB permitted fares to rise "after closed sessions with carrier representatives, without statutory public hearings," Judge Skelly Wright chastised the board and reminded it of its duty to the public. "While we recognize," he said, "that under the statute the Board has an obligation to afford the carriers sufficient revenues, that obligation cannot become a *carte blanche* allowing the Board to deal only with the carriers and disregard the other factors, such as the traveling public's interest in the lowest possible fares and high standards of service. . . . There is more to rate-making than providing carriers with sufficient revenues to meet their obligations to their creditors and to their stockholders."[13] The board was quite respectful of carrier—as opposed to public—interests; it was willing to modify rates when the carriers so desired, and to terminate fare investigations when carriers wished to shield embarrassingly high profits.[14]

Throughout, the board apparently abhorred price competition. It rejected fares lower than those already set by other carriers, and fares that threatened to reduce the profits of incumbent carriers. The CAB drove low-fare nonscheduled carriers from the industry in the early 1950s, despite the tremendous increase in air travel they produced. At the same time, the board exhorted certified carriers to raise their fares and eliminate discounts.[15] In 1974, "the Board suspended one of Allegheny's tariffs because the tariff was lower than Allegheny's competitors, and the Board considered Allegheny to be too small a factor in the market to be allowed to cut prices."[16]

The CAB's procedures often seemed expressly designed to deter price competition. According to the Justice Department's evaluation,

The existence of the tariff filing and protest mechanism discourages price changes which would be opposed by other airlines, primarily price cutting. The requirement that carriers give advance notice of their price changes and the justifications for them exposes firms to peer group pressures to avoid upsetting industry price stability. . . . Also, any attempt to cut prices in the regulated airline industry is exposed to before-the-fact litigation by competitors, and the possibility of lengthy suspension by the Board. . . . The expense, delay and marketing difficulty which a suspension order brings are such that carriers are very reluctant to risk filing tariffs below the level which their competitors find comfortable, even if they believe that marketing considerations alone would justify lower rates.

Other CAB procedures had the same effect.[17]

MERGERS AND CONSOLIDATION

Sections 408(a) and (b) of the Civil Aeronautics Act charged the CAB with determining the lawfulness of mergers involving certificated carriers. Mergers and combinations receiving the board's sanction were exempted from the antitrust laws.

Board oversight of mergers did little to encourage competition. First, in evaluating mergers, the CAB used standards that were significantly more lenient than the antitrust standards under Section 7 of the Clayton Act. For example, the board permitted United Airlines to acquire Capital Airlines in 1961, even though, as airline specialist Lucille Sheppard Keyes has pointed out, the merger "eliminated competition in nineteen city-pair markets accounting for almost one million passengers a year and including four major city-pairs: New York-Cleveland, Cleveland-Chicago, Philadelphia-Detroit, and Philadelphia-Cleveland," and further, as board member G. Joseph Minetti protested, "this merger of the Nation's second and fifth largest airlines . . . create[d] a system between 15 and 30 percent larger than the then biggest carrier, and was contrary to the board's long-standing efforts to effect a more equitable distribution of traffic among the trunk lines." On the other hand, the board blocked mergers involving small local carriers when it feared that the combined firms might be better able to compete with certificated trunk carriers.[18]

The board permitted and at times actively encouraged mergers between carriers as a means of compensating for failures in its attempts to regulate other aspects of airline operations. In one policy statement, for example, carriers were invited to point out "uneconomic route pattern situations" that could be corrected through merger and consolidation—patterns resulting, as we shall see, from CAB-imposed restrictions and regulations.[19] Ruling out fare reductions as one response to cyclical, recession-induced downturns in the demand for air travel, the board instead prescribed merger medicine as a quick fix for carriers' financial ailments.[20]

ANTITRUST IMMUNITY

The CAB's power to sanction anticompetitive agreements between regulated carriers, and to immunize those agreements from the antitrust laws, was set forth in Sections 412 and 414 of the Civil Aeronautics Act. Under Section 412, any agreements between carriers involving earnings, losses, traffic, service, equipment, rates, and scheduling had to be filed with the board. Under Section 414, board approval of an agreement made it immune from antitrust attack.

The board's use of this power was notable in two respects. First, the board had the power to approve "anticompetitive agreements among air carriers without the necessity for finding that the anticompetitive effects of such agreements are clearly outweighed by any overriding public interest, and without requiring carriers to seek less anticompetitive ways of achieving any legitimate objective sought to be achieved by the agreement." In considering these agreements, the board rarely held full evidentiary hearings, even where there was a strong possibility of anticompetitive effects.[21]

Second, the board steadily accorded broader antitrust immunities. The Justice Department reported in 1975 that the CAB had moved into an "area it previously had largely avoided—the approval and even promotion of anticompetitive agreements such as pooling, capacity restraint agreements and 'route swaps,' which in reality amount to enforceable agreements not to compete." The common goal in each of these agreements "has been to decrease or at least stabilize competition and increase the rate of return in the industry."[22]

THE CONSEQUENCES OF REGULATION

The CAB's use of its powers of regulation had at least five significant effects:

EXCESSIVE CONCENTRATION

The CAB's regulation of entry, and thus its control over the number of firms serving particular routes, kept the structure of the airline industry incredibly stable and highly concentrated for almost thirty years. In 1938, predecessors of United, American, TWA, and Eastern carried 82.5 percent of all domestic revenue-passenger miles. By 1972, they still carried 60.5 percent, and there were very few changes in the size ranking of the domestic carriers. This was all the more surprising in view of the fact that traffic had grown about 24,000 percent![23]

Most analysts agree that concentration was neither natural nor inevitable. Had there been no entry control, "between 4 and 12 times the actual number of certificated carriers could have existed in the industry."[24] Moreover, had the board been less permissive about mergers, it is doubtful that the number of trunk-line carriers would have declined from nineteen to ten.[25]

INEFFICIENT ROUTE STRUCTURE

The CAB's policies created a static route structure, inducing route inefficiencies. In the mid-1970s, for example, Pan American was forbidden to carry passengers between New York and San Francisco—even though it already operated between them on its international routes. It was obviously wasteful—injuring both traveler and airline—to require Pan Am to turn away willing customers while flying its planes nearly empty from coast to coast.

Such inefficiencies are almost inevitable when carriers are denied the freedom to enter and leave routes in response to market conditions, and instead must go through expensive, time-consuming, and unpredictable legal processes before rearranging their operations. The Justice Department found that this generates "waste, inflexibility, and insensitivity to the desires of consumers."[26]

Moreover, despite claims by the certified carriers and their regulators, small communities were not well served by the CAB's route-allocation policy. "During the twenty years from 1955 to 1975 the number of certificated points in the United States decreased from 539 to 394. Small air carriers that were exempted from CAB economic regulations added 355 points to the air transportation system during this period, more points than the regulated carriers dropped. Less regulated, more competitive state carriers added major points to the system in California and Texas, and developed markets the certificated carriers had not been able to develop."[27]

INFLATED RATES
Fares on regulated interstate routes were substantially higher than they would have been had carriers been permitted—or required—to compete on prices. This was evident when regulated interstate fares were contrasted with rates in comparable *intra*state routes in California and Texas—states where entry and pricing were largely unregulated. Thus, in 1975, a traveler could fly the 338 intrastate miles from San Francisco to Los Angeles for $18.75, but had to pay $38.89 for the 339 miles from Chicago to Minneapolis. Within Texas, Senator Kennedy's Judiciary Committee found a coach seat for the 248-mile trip from Dallas to San Antonio cost $23.15 on day flights and $13.89 on evening and weekend flights. But the 191 miles across state lines from Boston to New York cost $24.07 during the day and $19.00 at night. Overall, unregulated intrastate fares were "approximately 50–70 percent of the CAB fares for approximately the same distances and kind of routes."[28]

WASTEFUL NONPRICE COMPETITION
Inflated fares were not translated into high profits, however. Rather, as the Kennedy Committee explained, "the airlines—prevented from competing in price—simply [channeled] their competitive energies toward

costlier service: more flights, more planes, more frills. Thus, the skies [were] filled with gourmet meals and Polynesian pubs; scheduled service [was] frequent. Yet planes [flew] across the continent more than half empty."[29] Consumers got "large numbers of flights and empty seats instead of cheaper transportation."[30]

The board's attempts to control this wasteful nonprice competition merely compounded the problem, engulfing the industry in an everexpanding morass of regulation. Said the Department of Justice: "Once it begins to regulate the terms of service offerings, the Board is tempted into further and further intrusion into the details of service offerings because as it eliminates competition with respect to one amenity, competition crops up in the provision of another. Thus, even after the Board set seating configuration and load factor standards, it found itself considering coach lounges, carryon luggage bins and free alcoholic drinks."[31]

DENIAL OF ECONOMIC FREEDOM

Finally, airline regulation denied freedom of choice to consumers and freedom of opportunity to potential competitors. In the words of the Justice Department, "Unnecessary or overbroad economic regulation shuts business—particularly small, new businesses—out of opportunities to serve new markets and find new outlets for their competitive energies and creativity. It can deprive consumers of options they want and could have. So excessive economic regulation costs society more than just dollars and cents. It costs us a certain amount of our freedom."[32]

WHICH DIRECTION IS FORWARD?

In the airline industry, pervasive economic regulation fell far short of the objectives of the 1938 legislation. As an experiment in economic statecraft, it suffered from two basic, perhaps congenital, defects. First, the symbiotic identification of the board with the carriers tainted the regulatory process, and eventually led to the capture of the process by those who were to be subject to it. In the end, the trunk-line carriers were allowed to operate a cartel created, sanctioned, and protected by the government. Second, the CAB never managed to compel good economic performance through regulation. It could not command the regulated firms to innovate, to develop new services, or to initiate new marketing concepts. As the Justice Department observed, "Only the proper incentive structure can spur that kind of business creativity, and those incentives generally can be created only by a greater degree of economic freedom and competition—the carrot of profits and the stick of competition."[33]

Congress ultimately elected to turn to the competitive option. Phased deregulation of the industry was launched by the Airline Deregulation Act of 1978—passed, as we shall see in chapter 23, over the vociferous opposition of airline management and organized labor.[34] While airline safety was still to be regulated (under the Federal Aviation Administration), the law mandated the eventual elimination of CAB control over routes, rates, entry, and mergers. It called for the "sunset" of the CAB by 1985.

Experience under deregulation indicates that in an innately competitive industry like airline transportation, competition is a far more effective public control mechanism than regulation. Since 1978, for example, the number of certified scheduled carriers offering passenger service has grown from 36 to 98; in real terms after accounting for inflation, air fares averaged 13 percent lower in 1982 than in 1973; the proportion of travelers flying on discount fares grew from 48 percent in 1978 to 80 percent by 1982; air travel has expanded at average annual rates significantly higher than before deregulation; industry load factors have risen to their highest level in fifteen years; the industry's productivity has increased by an estimated 80 percent, with an estimated cumulative cost saving of nearly $10 billion; air service has increased for large and small communities alike; and the share of grandfather trunk-line carriers has fallen. Even the carriers' own Air Transport Association concedes that "the management flexibility made possible by deregulation has enabled the airlines to cope with [periodic adversity] far more quickly and effectively than if the cumbersome regulatory apparatus had still been in operation."[35]

Thus there is reason for optimism and confidence in the industry's future. Nevertheless, a caveat is in order. Once an industry has been liberated from comprehensive government regulation, it must be subjected to the control mechanism of competition. This does not happen "naturally" or automatically. The competitive market is a human artifact that has to be nurtured and preserved by vigilant enforcement of the rules of the game. This means that an industry, once it is deregulated, must be subject to strict antitrust surveillance—particularly with respect to pricing, mergers, and competitive practices.

With respect to pricing there is the ever-present danger of collusion and conspiracy. On February 21, 1982, some four years after deregulation, the following telephone conversation took place between Robert L. Crandall, head of American Airlines, and Howard Putnam, head of Braniff:

Mr. Crandall: I think it's dumb as hell for Christ's sake, all right, to sit here and pound the [expletive] out of each other and neither one of us making a [expletive] dime.

Mr. Putnam: Well . . .

Mr. Crandall: I mean, you know, goddamn, what the [expletive] is the point of it? . . .

Mr. Putnam: Do you have a suggestion for me?

Mr. Crandall: Yes, I have a suggestion for you. Raise your goddamn fares 20 percent. I'll raise mine the next morning.

Mr. Putnam: Robert, we . . .

Mr. Crandall: You'll make more money and I will too.

Mr. Putnam: We can't talk about pricing.

Mr. Crandall: Oh [expletive], Howard. We can talk about any goddamn thing we want to talk about.

In such cases, strict enforcement of the *per se* rule under Section I of the Sherman Act is an obvious imperative.[36]

With respect to mergers, deregulation will inevitably trigger a massive restructuring of routes. However, the way this restructuring is accomplished is of vital importance. It makes sense for traditional point-to-point routing systems to be replaced by the hub-and-spoke concept of feeding passengers from outlying points to one central city for long-distance flights. It makes sense to supplement the seven major hubs (Chicago, Dallas, Denver, Atlanta, San Francisco, Los Angeles, and New York) with new minihubs (say Pittsburgh, Miami, Dayton, and Charlotte) to serve smaller markets. This makes sense because it is cost-effective and therefore bound to enhance the industry's operating efficiency. However, restructuring implemented by mergers or acquisitions must be subjected to the test of Section 7 of the Clayton Act. Such restructuring must be blocked wherever it "may have the effect of substantially lessening competition" or where it "may tend to create a monopoly." Currently, this is of special relevance in view of the massive merger movement that seems to be undermining the industry's competitive structure: Pan Am merging with National (1980), Republic with Hughes (1980), Texas Air with Continental and Eastern (1981, 1986), People Express with Frontier (1985), Northwest Orient with Republic (1986), and TWA with Ozark (1986).

Other competitive practices must also be under constant antitrust surveillance. It is important to permit coordination between carriers where necessary, while preventing coordination from being used to forestall competition. The reservation system is a case in point. There is some question whether the very largest carriers—or indeed any—should be allowed to control the computerized scheduling system and to use it to the disadvantage of other carriers; or whether this scheduling system should be jointly owned by a consortium of *all* domestic and international carriers—a consortium to which new entrants would have to be admitted as a matter of right.

In sum, deregulation is not synonymous with anarchy. It means the substitution of one regulatory mechanism (competition) for another (government). Nor, as we shall see in chapter 19, does the end of *economic* regulation mean the abandonment of *safety* regulation.[37]

CHAPTER 18

TRUCKING REGULATION

The cruellest of our revenue laws are mild and gentle, in comparison of some of those which the clamour of our merchants and manufacturers has extorted from the legislature, for the support of their own absurd and oppressive monopolies.
— Adam Smith, *The Wealth of Nations*, 1776

In the absence of public intervention, the trucking industry would be the quintessential embodiment of the economist's dream of "perfect" competition. Capital costs for starting a trucking company—a truck and a chauffeur's license—are extremely low, hardly a barrier to entry. More than 90 percent of annual expenses are variable; fixed costs and overhead are relatively modest. Equipment can be shifted easily from one route to another, which makes price discrimination unlikely and unattractive. There are no significant economies of scale. This, combined with the large number of competing firms, makes the prospect of monopolization (or oligopolization) most improbable. In short, given the industry's inherent technological and economic characteristics, trucking would—in the absence of public intervention—be a highly competitive industry.

Yet since the passage of the Motor Carrier Act in 1935, and with but two exceptions (carriage of agricultural commodities, and private not-for-hire transport), entry, routes, freight to be carried, rates, and mergers were regulated by the Interstate Commerce Commission. The ostensible reasons given in the act's preamble were to recognize and preserve the inherent advantages of, and foster sound economic conditions in, such transportation and among such carriers in the public interest; promote adequate, economical, and efficient service by motor carriers, and reasonable charges therefor, without unjust discriminations, undue preferences or advantages, and unfair or destructive competitive practices; improve the relations between, and coordinate transportation by and regulation of, motor carriers and other carriers; develop and preserve a highway transportation system properly adapted to the needs of the commerce of the United States and of the national defense.

However, the primary impetus for regulation seems in fact to have sprung from the railroads' desire to protect themselves from motor-carrier competition, and from the desire of established motor carriers to eliminate competition among themselves and to foreclose competition from new entrants.[1] In the words of the Senate report recommending enactment of the act, the carriers wanted "some restraining hand."[2]

The resulting cartel—created, maintained, and enforced by the government acting through the ICC—was reminiscent of the earlier Elizabethan monopolies. According to Professor Fritz Machlup, "The results of the restriction of entry and the regulation of rates in the trucking industry have been to reduce the number of trucking firms; to encourage the growth of larger size firms; to facilitate, nay, render necessary, collusive trade association activity, especially with regard to rate making; to restrict independent action on the part of smaller truckers; and to increase the level of rates. . . . In this field," he concluded, "it is public policy to restrain competition, to suppress it through thoroughgoing regulation by government agencies and private associations."[3]

REGULATION IN PRACTICE

As in the preceding chapter, let us first examine government regulation with respect to entry, rates, mergers, and antitrust immunities. We shall then analyze the major consequences of regulation.

ENTRY

As later with airlines, the Motor Carrier Act of 1935 prohibited interstate operation of any for-hire motor-carrier service without a certificate of "public convenience and necessity." The Interstate Commerce Commission was empowered to issue certificates for operating authority if it held the applicant to be "fit, willing, and able properly to perform the service proposed" and, further, if it deemed the service to be "required by the present or future public convenience and necessity." The act required that operating certificates be intricately detailed, specifying "the service to be rendered and the routes over which, the fixed termini, if any, between which, and the intermediate and off-route points, if any, at which, and in case of operations not over specified routes or between fixed termini, the territory within which, the motor carrier is authorized to operate." Carriers in regular operation by June 1, 1935, were grandfathered into the industry, their operations and services automatically certified by the commission. The act exempted two types of operations from ICC regulation: (1) motor vehicles used exclusively to transport agricultural commodities; and (2) private, not-for-hire vehicles used solely to transport goods owned by the operator.

How did the commission use its power to control entry and the number of motor carriers? Virtually from the outset, "the public need test took on protective considerations."[4] In a key 1936 opinion that controlled for the next forty-five years, the commission specified three criteria that would have to be simultaneously satisfied before an operating certificate would be issued. The prospective entrant had to prove (1) that the new operation or service would serve a useful public purpose; (2) that this purpose could not be served as well by existing carriers (regardless of whether they actually were providing the service); and (3) that the proposed service would not impair the operations—including profitability—of existing carriers.[5]

This three-tier entry hurdle was a curious interpretation of "public convenience and necessity." It showed more concern for the protection of established firms than for shipper needs, more concern for maintaining the status quo than for promoting efficient, economical, and flexible transportation service for the consuming public. Public convenience was subordinated to public necessity, and public necessity was defined in narrow physical terms rather than meaningful economic ones. As long as service over a given route was physically adequate, the ICC seemed satisfied, even though service could be improved and costs reduced by certifying additional competitors.[6]

In one application hearing, for example, the ICC held that "existing carriers normally should be accorded an opportunity to transport all of the traffic they can handle . . . without the added competition of a new operation." In another, it ruled that "the mere existence of monopoly, standing alone, is not a sufficient justification for the establishment of a new operation."[7] In a third instance, a carrier was denied operating authority to serve a number of small towns because these towns had only "limited transportation needs" and the existing service—despite shipper testimony to the contrary—was not "so inadequate as to justify a grant of additional authority."[8] Indeed, there were "many instances in which the ICC denied temporary authority applications, even though existing authorized truckers were unable, or unwilling, to meet the shippers' needs."[9]

The ICC encouraged applicants for new operating certificates to limit their applications to as few commodity and route authorizations as possible. It did so, not only to protect incumbent carriers but to minimize their protests against new competition (which typically would take two or more years to resolve.)[10] An early congressional study found that 62 percent of all regulated truckers were limited to carrying only special kinds of goods, with 40 percent of these restricted to one commodity or commodity class and 88 percent restricted to six or fewer; about 70 percent of all regular route common carriers were not authorized to provide full service to intermediate points on their routes, and 10 percent were prohibited from serving intermediate points altogether. In 1975, transportation specialist Thomas G. Moore reported that these restrictions were substantially undiminished.[11]

The commission (together with established motor carriers and railroads) consistently tried to curtail the regulatory exemption that permitted free entry and rate competition in the hauling of agricultural commodities. For example, in disregard of expert testimony by the Department of Agriculture, the ICC ruled that redried tobacco leaf, dressed poultry, shelled nuts, flowers and bulbs, and frozen fruits and vegetables were *manufactured*, not agricultural commodities, and hence could not be transported under the regulatory exemption for agricultural products. On appeal, the courts regularly overturned these bizarre rulings —often with overtones of ridicule. One judge wryly noted that "a chicken which has been killed and dressed is still a chicken," another that "after shelling, a nut is still a nut."[12] Such decisions, as well as constant congressional vigilance, preserved the hauling of agricultural commodities as an island of competition in a sea of regulation.[13]

FARES

Section 216 of the Motor Carrier Act directed that rates for motor carrier transportation be "just and reasonable," and become effective only upon formal acceptance by the ICC, which was empowered either to sanction or set rates, whether precise, maximum, or minimum. The ICC was to give due consideration to the inherent advantages of motor-carrier transport and the impact of rates upon the movement of traffic; to the public's interest in adequate, efficient service at the lowest practicable cost; and to the carriers' need for revenues sufficient to support such service. Finally, it was to investigate any rate "upon complaint of any interested party."

In practice, the regulation of rates was almost immediately shot through with protectionism; perhaps most notably, the ICC prohibited applicants seeking new operating authority from justifying their proposed service on the basis of lower rates. In a 1937 opinion, the commission held that the offer of lower rates to shippers by a new applicant could *not* be considered as a relevant factor in evaluating the adequacy and efficiency of existing service and operators.[14] Note this exchange between Senator Edward Kennedy and the chairman of the ICC, Daniel O'Neal, at a 1978 Senate hearing:

Sen. Kennedy: Do you mean cost evidence isn't presently considered?
Mr. O'Neal: It is not considered when a carrier applies for authority under the Interstate Commerce Act. It cannot introduce evidence as to the rates that it will charge.
Sen. Kennedy: If they can haul it and haul it for less, the ICC doesn't at the present time give weight.
Mr. O'Neal: That is not a factor that is considered in these application cases.[15]

Further, rates for hauling various commodities were set at a level designed to yield a "compensatory" return to all carriers certified to carry them; the standard was typically based on the average costs of a sample of carriers, not those of the most efficient carriers or of any individual carrier.[16]

The commission also permitted "any interested party"—including other carriers—to challenge rates—particularly reductions in rates. James C. Nelson found that protests by carriers against rate competition rose "from 227 in 1946 to 4,712 in 1962, or from 40 percent to more than 90 percent of the total."[17] Given the nature of the regulatory process, the Justice Department observed, an attempt to lower rates was not merely a business decision; it was "a decision to go to war" with competing carriers, who would present a united front against the reduced rate. The protesters, of course, shared their litigation expenses, while the competing carrier trying to lower fares had to bear the burden of litigating the other side by itself.[18]

MERGERS AND CONSOLIDATION
Under the Motor Carrier Act, mergers and acquisitions required prior approval by the ICC, contingent upon a finding that the combination

would be in the public interest. Once sanctioned by the ICC, the merger was immune from the antitrust laws.

In practice, the ICC seemed to proceed on the assumption, candidly stated before a Senate committee, that "there hasn't been enough concentration" and that "we need more concentration than has occurred if we are going to have a healthy, vigorous motor carrier industry."[19] Untroubled by the lack of evidence supporting these assertions, the commission approved most of the merger proposals that came in—90 percent in 1969 and 88 percent in 1977.[20] Moreover, it did so in a distinctively discriminatory fashion—it approved some acquisitions (usually by large carriers) because nothing was adduced to show them *contrary* to the public interest; it rejected other acquisitions (usually by small carriers) because they were not shown to be *consistent* with the public interest.[21]

Second, the commission seldom considered less restrictive alternatives to mergers, such as granting route or commodity extensions to existing carriers or admitting new entrants. Some years ago it approved the combination of seven large eastern carriers into Associated Transport, Inc., which thus became the largest trucking company in the country. The merger not only eliminated competition between the participating carriers over roughly one-third of their routes but also made Associated the only carrier to provide single-line, through-service from Florida to the Northeast. The commission insisted that this diminution of competition would result in improved service, greater efficiency of operation, and substantial operating economies. It apparently ignored the alternative of granting the merging carriers (and others) the right *independently and separately* to provide the admittedly superior through-service, thus giving the public all the alleged benefits of the merger without sacrificing competition. In any event, the commission's decision did not stand the test of time: thirty-five years after the merger was approved, Associated Transport declared bankruptcy.

ANTITRUST IMMUNITY

The most significant antitrust immunity granted by the ICC pertained to rate bureaus—"carrier-owned organizations, formed by agreement between and among regulated common carriers, for the purpose of joint or collective ratemaking activities."[22] The Reed-Bulwinkle Act of 1948 empowered the commission to approve rate bureaus if it judged that they would further the national transportation policy. Carriers would then be free to join together and decide the rates to be submitted for ICC approval. This collective rate-fixing was immunized from the antitrust laws. However, individual member carriers were to be free to take independent action, and bureaus were required to publish among their tariffs any rate that a carrier acting on its own initiative might wish to charge.[23]

In practice, the rate bureaus and their surveillance by the ICC often acted in conflict with the public interest. A rate bureau is a sophisticated mechanism for price-fixing—a cartel whose activities are protected and reinforced by government regulatory policy. As James C. Miller III explained to the Kennedy Committee,

> It is a forum in which members can "communicate" and "get to know" each other. It is also a forum in which the competitive initiatives of various members are exposed for all to see, thus making it easier to "police" activities which do not "fit." The kinds of behavior that may come out of such an environment include an "understanding" not to solicit traffic from a shipper using a competitive carrier; an "understanding" not to offer a lower rate to a shipper when this might have adverse effects on a competitor in the form of demands that that competitor also reduce its rate; and an "understanding" not to reduce a rate when the effect might be to cause a shipper to shift its traffic to the initiating carrier.[24]

All this, of course, would be less troublesome if entry were free, and newcomers could undercut rates fixed by the bureaus.

Also, the commission actively encouraged collective action by the rate bureaus as a "necessary" part of the rate-making process. Given the hundreds of thousands of rates filed, and the commission's limited staff of sixty rate investigators, it was perhaps inevitable that the commission routinely approved the rates submitted. During fiscal year 1977, for example, 221,874 trucking rates were proposed to the commission; of these only 0.8 percent were rejected.[25] As a result, associations of carriers acting through rate bureaus, not the ICC, in effect controlled the cost of regulated motor carrier service.[26]

The ICC did little to ensure that rate bureaus and their members adhered to the terms of the approved agreements. Not until 1972—a quarter-century after rate bureaus were legalized—did the commission seriously inquire into their operations. In spite of evidence of flagrant violations, these investigations involved no careful economic analyses and resulted in few changes.[27] No rate bureau ever lost its antitrust exemption because it inhibited competition.[28]

The "right" to file rates independently—an option cited by the industry as proof that collective rate-making did not suppress price competition—was little more than a sterile privilege. An arsenal of weapons, from subtle to blatant, was ever ready to deter independent rate filing.

Most important were the procedural disincentives built into the regulatory process. Competing carriers had the right to protest an independent rate cut, and the commission could automatically suspend the "independent rate proposal" for a period of seven months. The rate-cutter had to bear the expense and delay of extended proceedings with no guarantee of ultimate victory. Moreover, once his proposed rate was protested by his competitors, he bore the burden of proving that the lower rate was "compensatory"—that it covered his full costs of operation.

Not surprisingly, independently filed rates governed only 3 percent of all general freight shipments.[29] This meant that on all other shipments, a shipper had the "freedom to choose" a single rate collectively fixed by rate-bureau members, largely unchecked by the ICC, and totally uncontrolled by competitive market forces.

THE CONSEQUENCES OF REGULATION

The economic consequences of ICC regulation of the trucking industry are remarkably similar to those in the airline industry.

INEFFICIENT ROUTE STRUCTURE

Motor-carrier regulation fostered a frozen, fragmented, and inefficient transportation system enmeshed in a tangle of inordinately detailed operating restrictions. According to the Senate Judiciary Committee, some certificates authorized carriers "to haul crated, but not uncrated machinery," or "2-gallon paint cans, but not 5-gallon cans." One permitted a carrier "to haul bananas and pineapples—provided the pineapples are mixed with the bananas. If only pineapples—or 5-gallon cans— [were] available for the return trip, then the carrier [had to] either lease himself out to a regulated carrier or return empty."[30]

Detailed specification of routes and of intermediate points that could and could not be served resulted in inefficiently circuitous routings. A carrier seeking to eliminate nearly 40 percent of excessive mileage on its routes between Minneapolis–St. Paul and Dallas during the height of the 1974 energy crisis was prevented from doing so by the ICC on the grounds that this would permit the carrier to better serve shippers and thus adversely affect competing carriers.[31]

Trucks were forced to return empty due to limited backhaul authority. President Jimmy Carter noted that "as recently as 1975, only half the operating certificates awarded contained authority to haul goods on a return trip."[32] The implications for fuel conservation and efficiency are too obvious for comment.

Finally, route restrictions created further inefficiencies by forcing excessive interlining, or transfers of freight, between carriers. Where no single carrier had the authority to carry a shipment its entire journey, it had to be interchanged to another carrier at least once along the way. This raised costs and often added substantially to transit times.[33]

EXCESSIVE CONCENTRATION

Under the commission's restrictive entry policy and its encouragement of mergers, the number of motor carriers declined drastically, increasing concentration in the industry.

In 1935, there were more than 25,000 carriers of property. By 1966, that number was down to 17,000, and by 1974 down to 15,000. Most of the survivors were firms originally grandfathered into the industry. Only 5 percent of all new operating authority was awarded to new firms entering the industry.[34] The commission's reluctance to grant new operating rights, and the severe restrictions written into those granted, encouraged mergers and consolidations. Virtually the only way for a carrier to expand, or to adapt its route pattern to changing market conditions, was to obtain extensions of authority via merger.[35]

Inevitably, concentration increased. The Kennedy Committee found that 6 percent of all regulated motor carriers accounted for more than 75 percent of all revenues.[36] Only a dozen general-commodities carriers were allowed to provide regular through-service on long-distance, transcontinental routes.[37] And, most relevant in an economic context, the four largest carriers collectively controlled an average of 50 to 60 percent of all traffic between major city-pairs.[38]

INFLATED RATES

Regulation and the antitrust immunity extended to rate bureaus raised the cost of motor-carrier transportation, eliminated incentives for efficiency, created a built-in inflationary bias, and enabled carriers to enjoy excessive returns.

Comparisons of regulated and unregulated (or deregulated) trucking markets document this conclusion. One study—in what can be considered a controlled before-and-after experiment—compared trucking rates for various goods when they were classified as "regulated" commodities and after they became (as a result of court decisions) "exempt" agricultural commodities. Deregulating the transportation of these goods resulted in dramatic price declines: 12 to 59 percent in particular markets for fresh and frozen poultry, and a weighted average of 19 percent for frozen fruits and vegetables.[39] A second study, based on a survey by the National Broiler Council, compared the rates on *fresh* poultry shipped by exempt carriers with rates on *cooked* poultry shipped by regulated carriers; over the same routes, between the same points, the unregulated rates were some 33 percent lower.[40] Rates were lower in states and nations where trucking was unregulated or had recently been deregulated. In New Jersey, where the rates of intrastate motor carriers were unregulated, prices were found to be 10 to 15 percent—and in some cases as much as 60 percent—below comparable regulated interstate rates.[41] Other examples could be cited, from Maryland to Great Britain.

The ICC's regulatory machinery almost inevitably promoted an inflated rate structure. Efficient carriers would refrain from setting rates at competitive, cost-based levels, because the difficulty of overcoming rate-bureau protests and obtaining commission approval was not worth the effort. And the ICC's practice of basing allowable rates on *industry*-wide, as opposed to *individual*, carrier costs removed the incentives for effective cost control. Indeed, it provided a strong incentive to increase costs, because under ICC rules, higher costs meant higher profits. The rate structure was thus based on an upside-down incentive system: trucking firms could earn higher returns on a constant investment whenever their costs were increased.[42]

The inflated rates were reflected in the profits of the regulated carriers. In 1971–76, the Senate Judiciary Committee found, "the average rate of return on shareholder's equity earned by the top eight trucking firms, measured by book value, was almost twice that earned by corporations listed in the *Fortune* 500"—a pattern that existed across and within all major rate bureaus. Not surprisingly, the operating certificates required to earn these magnanimous profits increased in value spectacularly. The American Trucking Association freely acknowledged "that operating rights increased at an annual compound rate of 16 percent between 1962 and 1972; by 1974, trucking operating authorities were selling for between 15 and 20 percent of a firm's gross annual revenue"; they were "the single most important asset" of any motor carrier.[43] Their value, one might add, reflected rates of return in excess of those required to attract capital into the industry, and can certainly be considered a capitalized return on cartelized power.

WASTEFUL NONPRICE COMPETITION

Regulatory elimination of price competition encouraged excessive, wasteful nonprice rivalry. It also created excess capacity, which further inflated rates and the cost of motor carrier service. Because the ICC regulated the number of trucking firms, but not the number of trucks, operating on particular routes, one form of nonprice rivalry between certified carriers consisted of providing overfrequent service. This raised costs because trucks tended to run with less than full loads. While the added service may have been of value to some shippers, others were forced to pay more and to receive more service than they would choose to receive if carriers were free to offer lower rates.[44]

SMALL TOWNS AND SMALL SHIPPERS

Not insignificantly, small towns and small shippers—always trotted out by the industry as the primary beneficiaries of trucking regulation— suffered under the system.

Although common carriers could be prosecuted for *total* failure to serve a class of traffic or a geographic region they were authorized to serve, they were not obligated to provide a *level* of service adequate to shippers' needs. In spite of their "common carrier obligation," they could choose to provide poor service or to minimize unprofitable traffic. Many did precisely that. A memo from a terminal manager of Consolidated Freightways, one of the nation's largest, explained how it worked: "For customers who have been, or are giving us freight to undesirable lanes, we are using a negative sell. . . . We are actively discouraging this freight by informing the customers that, due to service problems, we cannot give them the service they need and deserve in these areas at this time." A study by the Wyoming Public Service Commission of sixty-six towns found that only half of the carriers authorized to serve any one of them were actually doing so. A study of service to small towns in nine Western states revealed that while many carriers are certified to serve the terri- tory, "their actual presence at a 'grass-roots' level is not great." The Kennedy Committee concluded, "the current regulatory system leaves carriers essentially free to abandon service to small communities they find unprofitable. And many of them do."[45]

Small *shippers* fared no better. Unlike the *Fortune* 500 companies, small firms could not avoid dealing with regulated carriers by doing their own trucking, nor, given their limited volume, could they secure the services of a contract carrier or force regulated carriers to negotiate with them individually for commodity rates on less-than-truckload ship- ments.[46] As a result, small shippers under regulation typically had to pay higher rates than their larger rivals.

THE IMPACT OF "DEREGULATION"

Nearly half a century of motor-carrier regulation could boast of one major achievement. It had created a government-sanctioned and govern- ment-enforced freight cartel. Entry was restricted, mergers encouraged, concentration increased, rate-fixing tolerated, and competition harassed—all on the false assumption that trucking was akin to a "natural monopoly" and therefore had to be regulated like a public utility. Whatever the original objectives, trucking regulation—like any legalized cartel—ultimately became a system for dispensing private privilege and protecting vested interests.

Eventually Congress decided to reverse course and to deregulate the industry—partly. In the Motor Carrier Act of 1980, it did not—as it had in airlines—abolish the regulatory commission altogether. But it did significantly curtail the ICC's powers. In entry proceedings, for example, the burden of proof was shifted from the applicant to protestors. No longer did a newcomer have to prove that his proposed service was *consistent* with the public interest; instead, those who would deny him entry had to show that the proposed service was *contrary* to the public interest. The act also narrowed the class of firms permitted to protest applications for operation authority; it broadened existing operating authorities; it established "zones of pricing freedom" within which rates could be varied without ICC approval; and it restricted the antitrust immunity accorded to collective rate-fixing.

The Motor Carrier Act of 1980 has now been in effect for six years, and there can no longer be any doubt that even partial deregulation has been an enormous success.[47] This should not be surprising: in an inherently competitive industry, performance ought to be superior under competition.

With free entry permitted, applications for operating authority have jumped from 6,746 in fiscal year 1976 to 29,311 in the first year under deregulation—with the approval rate exceeding 95 percent.

The number of regulated carriers has increased from 18,000 in 1981 to 33,000 in 1984.

Established carriers have become more efficient and innovative. They have restructured their gerrymandered route patterns and reduced empty backhauls.

With increased competition, rates have been reduced and shippers have benefitted from new price and service options. Independent rate actions—proposed price reductions—have increased from 27,141 in calendar year 1979 to more than 230,000 in fiscal year 1983!

Finally, contrary to the warnings of proregulation Cassandras, deregulation did not lead to the abandonment of small communities and rural areas. According to a Department of Transportation survey, "96.3 percent of all respondents thought that post-deregulation service was as good or better than before. Moreover, shippers and receivers in very remote areas were as satisfied with their truck service as were small community respondents in more accessible areas: 97.3 percent . . . reported that overall service quality was as good or better than pre-deregulation service."[48]

In short, increased competition has had a salutary effect. Yet more needs to be done. Perhaps total deregulation and abolition of the ICC are not politically feasible. But removal of antitrust immunity from the collusive activity of rate bureaus would be a helpful first step. If collusive price-fixing is a *per se* antitrust violation for contractors in the highway-paving industry, is there any reason why 33,000 trucking companies should be allowed to engage in collective rate-making and enjoy antitrust immunity?

CHAPTER 19

THE LIMITS OF
DEREGULATION

Deregulation [of airlines] was all to a traveler's benefit; chalk up points for deregulation. But it doesn't necessarily follow that total deregulation of airline operation would be even better. We still need the air-control system, not an untrammeled right for every airline pilot to follow his own route in the sky and land or take off when he pleases. The abandonment of all maintenance standards, leaving each carrier to its own devices, would in the end separate safe airlines from unsafe ones, but until the public found out which was which it would hardly contribute to the air traveler's peace of mind.

So too with some other areas.... We don't want the government stopping doctors or drug companies from exploring new ways to save lives through new operations or new medicines. It doesn't follow that we should permit anybody to pick up a scalpel and chop out an appendix or market some new nostrum for cancer untested for hazards.   — Vermont Royster, *Wall Street Journal*

In 1981, shortly after its inauguration, the new administration in Washington launched a major attack on government regulation. President Reagan declared that he wanted to get the government "to stand by our side, not to ride on our backs." Secretary of Commerce Malcolm Baldrige stated that "we should deregulate from top to bottom" because "we're overregulated everywhere." Budget Director David Stockman wrote an "economic Dunkirk" memo, warning of a "ticking regulatory time bomb," set to explode in the next 18 to 40 months, which would hit American companies with more than $100 billion in added costs, inevitably fueling further inflation. Professor Murray Weidenbaum, the new chairman of the Council of Economic Advisers, promised that the Reagan administration would seek a fundamental change in government policy by appointing

245

more regulators who did not like regulation and who would pay greater heed to business complaints about excessive rules. The message was clear: regulation produces nothing but private-sector headaches and public-sector jobs.

Such indictments, couched in flaming rhetoric, have broad appeal. Yet they are based on little more than unenlightening, simplistic generalizations. "Regulation" is in fact a catch-all category that comprises quite different types of government intervention, designed for quite different purposes, and undergirded by quite different rationales. Most fundamental is the distinction between *economic* regulation and *social* regulation, each of which must be further subdivided in order to arrive at analytically meaningful conclusions.

Economic regulation comprises thoroughgoing government control of all aspects of a particular market or industry, including control of the number of firms, entry and exit, price, profits, investments, capital structure, and service quality. At times, this type of regulation has been applied to inherently competitive industries like airlines and trucking. In these cases, as we have seen, economic regulation is not conducive to good economic performance; *de*regulation is, in fact, the appropriate public policy. However, economic regulation is also applied to "natural monopolies" (like the local distribution of natural gas and electricity) where—for technological and economic reasons—competition cannot serve as a socially effective regulatory mechanism. In these situations, there are no attractive alternatives to direct government regulation (or government ownership).

Social regulation, on the other hand, is essentially synonymous with the police powers of government—the obligation to protect the health and safety (and, once upon a time, the "morals") of the citizenry. This involves government's responsibility to protect the purity of the air we breathe, the water we drink, the foods we eat, and the medicines we use, and the safety of the cars we drive. In these areas, social regulation is a response to two major market "imperfections" or "failures": (1) consumers' lack of sufficient information or technical expertise to enable them to make rational purchasing decisions; and (2) the gnawing problem that economists call "externalities."

In this chapter, we shall discuss the three types of market failures that necessitate some form of government regulation. Our discussion should make it clear why "the market" cannot—and cannot be expected to—cope effectively with the problems generated by natural monopoly, imperfect information, and externalities.

NATURAL MONOPOLY

"Natural monopoly" refers to fields where economies of large-scale production are so great, and the costs of duplication of facilities so wasteful, as to render competition unworkable, unsustainable, and socially undesirable. When these technological conditions are present, as Professor Charles F. Phillips explains, competition "may exist for a time, but only until bankruptcy or merger leaves the field to one firm. Competition is self-destructive and results in a waste of scarce resources. Conceivably, two or three firms could make an agreement to share the market. Neither the firms nor the public would benefit should this occur. The firms would be high-cost producers, and the consumers would be denied the benefits derived from economies of scale. Moreover, non-price rivalry between inefficient plants does not lead to an efficient allocation of resources. When economies of scale permit only one optimum-size producer in a market, it is highly desirable for public policy to allow a monopolist supplier to operate. But the mere fact that a monopolist is allowed to exist does not assure the public of obtaining the benefits of whatever lower costs are achieved. In fact, the monopolist might absorb not only the benefits resulting from the lower cost but might also raise prices."[1]

Pipeline transportation of petroleum is a case in point.[2] Petroleum pipelines are characterized as naturally monopolistic on four grounds:

1. They are endowed with dramatic economies of scale. In part, these economies result from the engineering fact that the cost of building a pipeline is proportional to the radius of the pipe, while the line's capacity is proportional to the *square* of the radius. According to calculations by Charles E. Spahr, chairman of the board of Standard Oil Company of Ohio, a single 20-inch-diameter line would cost about four times as much to build as a 4-inch line, but could transport fully forty-eight times as much petroleum.
2. Pipelines are extremely capital-intensive, requiring eight times more net plant investment than the average industrial corporation, and eight and a half times more investment per employee than the railroad industry. Because most pipeline costs are fixed and do not vary with the quantity of petroleum shipped, the average *total* cost to transport a barrel of petroleum declines sharply as the size of the line and the quantity of petroleum carried are increased. This is evident in Chart 1, presented to a congressional committee by Exxon: We can see that a single 40-inch-diameter line can transport a million barrels of petroleum much more cheaply than could four 10-inch lines. Thus a single

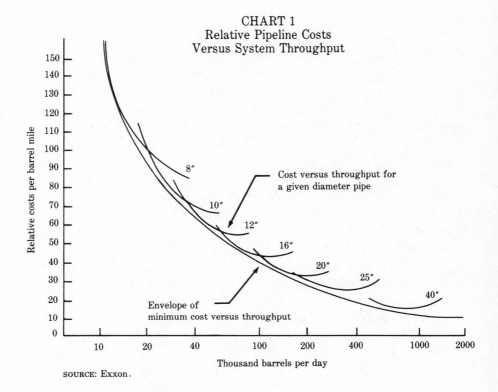

CHART 1
Relative Pipeline Costs
Versus System Throughput

SOURCE: Exxon.

large line can obviously operate far more efficiently than can a number of smaller, parallel lines.

3. It costs far less to expand existing pipelines to increase capacity than to construct entirely new lines. As a result, new competitors are unlikely to enter existing pipeline corridors, and rarely do.
4. These factors, together with additional advantages such as stability of rates and continuity of operation, effectively insulate petroleum pipelines from competition by other transport modes. The cost to ship petroleum by rail is *five* times greater than by pipeline. Truck rates are often *twenty-five* times more expensive. And barges and tanker ships are increasingly unable to compete with large pipelines. Moreover, pipelines "are able to operate 24 hours a day, 7 days a week, and are almost entirely insensitive to external conditions such as adverse weather and rail, waterway, or highway traffic congestion."[3] Pipelines thus are the main mode for transporting petroleum; 75 percent of crude oil arrives at refineries via pipeline, and almost 90 percent of domestically refined gasoline flows directly into pipelines for distribution and marketing.

So petroleum pipelines can legitimately be said to constitute a natural monopoly wherein, on the ground of operating efficiency, competitive market structure is neither workable nor economically desirable. Moreover, access to pipeline transportation by producers, refiners, and distributors decisively affects conditions of competition at these other stages of the petroleum industry. Hence regulation of rates, terms of service, and profits are necessary in order to obtain the operating efficiencies of monopoly in pipelines, while still preventing monopolistic exploitation and control of shippers dependent on access to them.

IMPERFECT INFORMATION

At a news conference in 1981, the newly appointed chairman of the Federal Trade Commission, James C. Miller III, told reporters that "imperfect products" should be available on the open market because, as he perceived it, consumers have "different preferences for defect avoidance." He said: "Those who have a low aversion to risk—relative to money—will be most likely to purchase cheap, unreliable products."[4] According to this line of reasoning, the roster of products provided by markets free from government intervention reflects a socially optimal blend of goods demanded by consumers, who have carefully and knowledgeably weighed risks and dangers against costs, and made purchases according to their own (perhaps perverse) schedule of personal preferences. In Dr. Miller's universe, there would be no need for government regulation of product safety; indeed, government intervention would reduce social welfare by restricting the hazard-cost trade-offs available to perfectly informed customers.

Of course the assumption that consumers are perfectly informed does not always hold true. Information on product risks and dangers may not be available. Certainly those with best access to product safety information—the producers—have little incentive to publicize such information, or even to collect it in the first place, because it obviously would do little to enhance their sales. Even if full product-safety information were available, consumers might still lack the technical knowledge or sophistication needed to assess its significance. In that event, buyers' choices would not be "rational," nor would the mix of goods produced be "socially optimal." In such circumstances, government would have a legitimate role to play in protecting consumer health and welfare.

This is clearly the case in the field of medicines and pharmaceuticals. For example, in its thorough study of the drug industry, Senator Estes Kefauver's Antitrust Subcommittee pointed to Diabinese as "a striking example of the failure by a company to disclose to physicians essential information on side effects which it had in its possession." This particular drug—a potent substitute for insulin in the treatment of diabetes—was marketed by Pfizer in 1958 and promoted as having an "almost complete absence of unfavorable side effects."[5] Yet a number of medical specialists found evidence to the contrary. One authority in the field, Dr. Henry Dolger, stated that Diabinese exhibited "an increase in serious side effects and toxicity, especially in liver damage."[6] Another specialist found "the side effects are distinctly of sufficient importance to be carefully brought to the attention of any physician who plans to use it." He concluded that other drugs, with far fewer side effects, should be used instead of Diabinese.[7]

In fact, the producer knew before marketing it that the drug produced serious side effects in 27 to 31 percent of the test cases examined— including jaundice, exfoliative dermatitis, gastrointestinal effects such as nausea and vomiting, and severe hypoglycemia. "Despite the substantial information known to Pfizer with respect to side effects as early as the summer of 1958," the Kefauver Committee discovered, "the company made no attempt to supply this essential material to physicians in its advertising."[8] Given these circumstances, neither the prescription of Diabinese by physicians nor its consumption by patients can be construed as a rational exercise of consumer sovereignty or a socially optimal trade-off between risk, cost, and product reliability.

The recent Dalkon Shield affair, which involves an intrauterine birth control device produced by A. H. Robins Company, underscores the point. Here, too, one could hardly argue that consumer decisions were based on a fully informed cost-risk calculus. Between 1971 and 1975, the firm distributed over 4 million Dalkon Shield IUDs in eighty countries, with false claims of efficacy and safety. In the United States alone, more than 2 million women were fitted with the device by doctors who believed the misleading claims. To date, tens of thousands of women have suffered physical damage caused by the Shield, ranging from pelvic infections to sterility, miscarriage, and even death[9]; and A. H. Robins has negotiated settlements with some nine thousand damage claimants for more than $300 million. The company has been found guilty of outrageous and reckless misconduct (including the destruction of evidence) by seven juries, which returned punitive damage awards against it totaling more than $13 million. (In April 1985, company officials announced that they had set aside a $615 million reserve fund to pay for future compensatory damages, but they acknowledged that this would not be enough to cover punitive damages or law suits brought in foreign countries by women who had used the Dalkon Shield). Chief U.S. District Judge Miles

W. Lord was so outraged by the evidence in the case that he told officials of the firm: "Your company, without warning to women, invaded their bodies by the millions and caused them injuries by the thousands. . . . Under your direction your company has in fact continued to allow women, tens of thousands of them, to wear this device, a deadly depth charge in their wombs, ready to explode at any time." It was, Judge Lord found, "corporate irresponsibility at its meanest."[10]

Clearly, the "market" does not by itself generate all the information that consumers need to make "rational" decisions in maximizing their purchasing power. To assume that competition rewards those who provide the information desired by consumers, and that the fear of damage suits will assure acceptable product quality, is to assume away the problem—to mistake a fanciful model for the real world. To be sure, information is not a free good. There is a cost to disseminating it to those who might find it useful. Nevertheless, as economists Robert E. Litan and William D. Nordhaus suggest, "Where the benefits of having information outweigh the costs of providing it, economic efficiency could be improved, in principle, through regulations that make it available."[11] This is especially so with respect to food, drugs, and health—areas that, as Arthur Okun put it, may well lie outside "the domain of dollars." Here it may be far "better to prevent consumer harm than to compensate it later."[12] Here government has a clear obligation to protect consumers from products whose hazards are not likely to be disclosed fully, and, if disclosed, cannot be "rationally" assessed even by knowledgeable consumers.

Nevertheless, in spite of the voluminous evidence of market failures caused by inadequate information (or outright misinformation), some "libertarians" are still reluctant to concede the need for regulation. They see hope in "voluntary" arrangements between cooperative business firms intent on doing the right thing and a nonadversarial, nonconfrontational government willing to accomplish the goals of regulation without saddling business with the burdens of regulation. Without gainsaying the virtues of "voluntary compliance," we doubt that such a policy, if relied on exclusively, offers sufficient safeguards to the public.

A case in point is the ten-year battle by General Motors against air bags. Although the Department of Transportation estimated that equipping all cars on American roads with air bags would save at least nine thousand lives a year and prevent hundreds of thousands of serious injuries, and although GM promised—in August 1970—to make air bags available on all its cars by the 1975 model year, General Motors "pursued a policy of withholding that technology from the public, encouraging delay of federal passive restraint requirements, and discouraging consumer interest in the handful of air-bag-equipped cars it produced in the mid-1970s." At least that was the testimony of Ben Kelley, senior vice-president of the Insurance Institute for Highway Safety (IIHS) before a congressional committee investigating motor vehicle safety.[13] The following chronology, excerpted from Kelley's testimony, documents his conclusion:

- *August 1970:* In a submission to the National Highway Safety Bureau (NHSB) and a letter to eighty-two members of Congress, General Motors pledges to voluntarily provide air bags, first as options and then as standard equipment, on all its cars by the 1975 model year.
- *November 1970:* NHSB issues its standard requiring passive-restraint protection effective 1 July 1973—a six-month delay from the date that it had been proposing.
- *1971:* General Motors learns, in a survey it would not make public until 1979, that between 40 and 50 percent of customers surveyed by the company would pay some significant amount for air-bag protection. GM's summary of the survey results states that "the Air Cushion Restraint concept is a viable one to the consumer" and was "preferred over the passive harness system because it afforded equal protection, but was judged far superior in all areas of style and convenience."
- *March 1971:* The National Highway Traffic Safety Administration (NHTSA) grants a two-year delay in the passive-restraint standard—until the 1976 model year—because of Nixon administration fears about its economic impact on the auto industry.
- *October 1973:* Allstate Insurance Company, subsequently followed by many other insurers, announces a 30 percent discount on medical and no-fault personal-injury coverages for air-bag-equipped cars.
- *February 1974:* A GM spokesman acknowledges to the Insurance Institute for Highway Safety *Status Report* that it is unlikely the company will build even 150,000 air-bag-equipped cars in the 1974–75 model years. (As it turns out, only about 10,000 were built during the 1974–76 model years.)
- *May 1974:* Two former GM officials tell an NHTSA meeting that air bags for front-seat occupants should cost about $148 per car, not $225 to $335 as auto companies have claimed.
- *September 1974:* Ed Cole, a strong supporter of air-bag technology, retires as president of GM.
- *December 1974:* NHTSA issues cost-benefit analyses showing that air bags are superior to lap-shoulder belts.

■ *August 1976:* An IIHS poll finds that "a great majority of car-buying Americans prefers automobiles with increased crash protection that is completely or at least partly automatic—such as air bags, or belts and bags in combination," rather than active protection.

■ *November 1976:* A front-page exposé in the *Wall Street Journal* examines GM claims that consumers do not want air bags. The air bag "received no wholehearted promotion," the *Journal* reports. "Instead, the company and its dealers actively discouraged sales."

■ *January 1977:* Former GM president Ed Cole, in letters to the IIHS president, says: "I firmly believe the air cushion system can be made to work successfully at a reasonable cost. . . . The technology is available and the need is there. I think the only way passive restraints are going to get to first base is to make them mandatory. Another test will prove nothing. Let the passive air cushion evolve like all other systems." Cole also lists numerous reasons why belt systems cannot protect as effectively as inflatable systems in crashes.

■ *September 1977:* At a Senate hearing, IIHS provides the results of its analysis of GM's own data comparing real-world crashes of GM air-bag-equipped cars with those of non-air-bag cars. The analysis shows that "serious head, face, neck, and torso injuries (that is, injuries that produce the overwhelming bulk of fatal and disabling conditions) are down 44 percent" in cars with bags.

■ *1978:* A GM study involving more than a thousand GM car owners— not made public until 1979—concludes: "The air cushion restraint system . . . received the highest ratings on all operation, comfort, and appearance items evaluated."

■ *March 1980:* GM informs NHTSA that, its earlier commitments to the contrary, it "does not plan to offer inflatable restraints on medium- or small-size cars" in the 1982–86 model years, but may still offer them on full-size 1982 cars.

■ *April 1980:* A GM memo circulated on Capitol Hill says the company plans to "accommodate" a level of air-bag demand in 1982 models involving about 250,000 full-size car purchasers, a reduction from previous plans to produce 400,000.

■ *June 1980:* GM announces that it has canceled plans to provide air bags as options in its large 1982 models—despite having promised to do so only a few months earlier both in its "1980 Public Interest Report" and in a filing with NHTSA.

■ *1984:* General Motors spearheads a lobbying campaign to persuade states to enact mandatory seat-belt laws as an alternative to the mandatory air-bag regulations of the Department of Transportation.

Alas, "voluntary compliance" is often a code word for letting an industry engage in self-regulation—a euphemism for letting powerful economic interests in the political economy decide what is necessary to protect the public's health and safety.

EXTERNALITIES

Externalities constitute a third kind of market failure that necessitates government intervention and regulation. "In a market economy," Professor Allyn Strickland explains, "consumers and producers pursue their own self-interests through their private market decisions. The model of perfect competition implicitly assumes that these decisions are completely independent of one another. Each consumer and each producer solely incurs all the costs and receives all the benefits associated with his or her economic activities. This, of course, does not always happen. An action by one individual can impose costs or bestow benefits on other individuals. These effects are called *externalities.* "[14]

Where negative externalities and costs are involved, there is no assurance that decentralized competitive market decision-making will produce socially optimal results. This is because nontrivial costs will be imposed on innocent third parties and "bystanders"—costs that are not taken into account by those making economic decisions. Environmental pollution, such as the dumping of toxic wastes, is a classic example of the problems posed by negative externalities.

"Sometime in the 1940s," investigative reporter Michael H. Brown recounts, "the Hooker Chemical Company, which is now a subsidiary of Occidental Petroleum, found an abandoned canal near Niagara Falls, and began dumping countless hundreds of 55-gallon drums there. In 1953, the canal was filled in and sold to the city for an elementary school and playground . . . and modest single-family dwellings were built nearby." Occasional signs of trouble (collapses of earth where drums had rotted through, skin rashes in children and pets) were largely ignored until 1978. By then, many of the homes were found to be deteriorating rapidly and to be infiltrated by highly toxic chemicals that had percolated into basements. An investigation by the New York State Health Department uncovered startling health problems among the residents—birth defects, miscarriages, epilepsy, liver abnormalities, bleeding, and headaches. In August 1978, President Carter declared Love Canal to be a federal disaster area and 240 families were evacuated from their contaminated houses.

Since then, Brown explains,

new dumping grounds have been reported in several precarious places. Under a ball field near another elementary school in Niagara Falls health officials have found a landfill containing many of the same compounds. . . . Officials have discovered, too, that Hooker disposed of nearly four times the amount of chemicals present in the Love Canal several hundred feet west of the city's municipal water treatment facility, and residues have been tracked inside water-intake pipelines. Across town, near Niagara University, a 16-acre Hooker landfill containing such killers as Mirex, C-56, and lindane—essentially chemicals that were used in the manufacture of pest killers and plastics —have been found to be fouling a neighborhood stream, Bloody Run Creek, which flows past drinking-water wells. About 80,000 tons of toxic waste are said to have been dumped there over the years. . . . Still worse, as the company recently acknowledged, Hooker buried up to 3,700 tons of trichlorophenol waste, which contains one of the world's most deadly chemicals, dioxin, at various sites in Niagara County between 1947 and 1972. Investigators immediately sought to determine whether dioxin had seeped out and, indeed, the substance was identified in small quantities within leachate taken from the periphery of the Love Canal, an indication that it may have begun to migrate.

As much as two thousand pounds of dioxin may be deposited near the Niagara River, which flows into Lake Ontario, and which, in turn, serves as the source of water supplies for a number of cities, including Syracuse, Rochester, and Toronto. Most sobering is the fact that (according to chemists) as little as three *ounces* of dioxin are sufficient to kill more than 2 million persons.[15]

Unfortunately, the toxic-waste hazards that have surfaced at Love Canal and, more recently, at Times Beach, Missouri, and Hamilton, Ohio, are not unique. In 1983, the Office of Technology Assessment estimated that one ton of hazardous waste is generated annually for every person in the United States. The Environmental Protection Agency fears that more than 90 percent of these wastes are disposed of in environmentally unsound ways, including haphazard land disposal, improper storage, and illicit dumping.[16] Currently more than eight hundred waste dumps are listed (or proposed for listing) on the EPA's "national priority list" of high-risk sites.[17] Though concentrated in the Northeast, the worst toxic dumps are sprinkled across the country.

"The effects of poor disposal methods and abandoned waste disposal sites," the Senate Committee on Environment and Public Works has found, comprise "the contamination of surface water and groundwater, causing contamination of drinking water supplies, destruction of fish, wildlife and vegetation, and threats to public safety due to health hazards and threats of fires and explosions."[18] To suppose that the "market" is capable of resolving such problems is the height of naïveté. Here, clearly, government regulation is essential to protect public health and safety.

REGULATORY ENDS AND MEANS

Even if there were agreement that government must play an active role to intervene in the aforementioned areas of market failure—natural monopoly, inadequate information, externalities—difficult questions remain. There would still be vexing issues of benefits and costs, of ends and means.

There is the question of *benefits*—whether government intervention to counteract market failure has, in fact, served to provide benefits for society. Undoubtedly regulation in all the foregoing areas has been far from perfect. Nevertheless, given the unpalatable alternatives, much has been accomplished. In automobiles, for example, safety features mandated by the NHTSA since 1966 include laminated windshields, collapsible steering assemblies, dashboard padding, improved door locks, and dual braking systems, among others. According to Department of Transportation studies, taking into account reduced speed limits nationwide in 1974, automobiles are 25 percent safer today because of these features, and more than eighty thousand lives have been saved since 1968. Approximately 27 fatalities have been avoided for each dollar increase in new-car prices caused by automotive-safety regulation.[19] The changes have been justified, but they wouldn't have come about through market forces. Even Henry Ford II—hardly an enthusiast for NHTSA programs—acknowledged on *Meet the Press* (October 1977): "We wouldn't have safety programs without the federal law, we wouldn't have emission controls without the federal law, and we wouldn't have as much fuel economy without the federal law."

Similarly, as Chart 2 shows, air-pollution controls have produced substantially cleaner air, with reductions in various air pollutants ranging from 7 to 68 percent from 1970 to 1980. Likewise, water-pollution controls have helped maintain or improve water quality nationwide.[20] Estimates of the value of the benefits of air- and water-pollution controls range as high as $67 billion per year, including such gains as increased health, reduced water-borne disease, and increased agricultural production.[21]

The benefits of regulation by the Consumer Product Safety Commission are also impressive. They include a 90 percent reduction in poisoning fatalities among children as the result of rules requiring childproof caps on drugs, pesticides, cleaning solvents, and other toxic substances.[22]

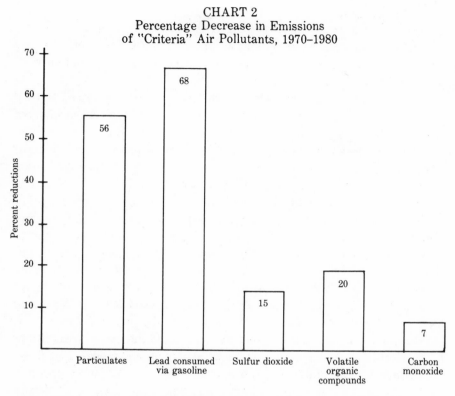

CHART 2
Percentage Decrease in Emissions
of "Criteria" Air Pollutants, 1970–1980

SOURCE: U.S. Government Accounting Office, *Cleaning Up the Environment: Progress Achieved but Major Unresolved Issues Remain*, vol. 1, July 21, 1982, p. 11.

Next, what should the *goal* of regulation in areas of market failure? How clean should air and water be? How safe should products be? In other words, what should be the targeted ends of regulation? The benefits of regulation are not without costs; the two must be balanced. Obviously, the zero-risk society is unattainable. It is economically unaffordable. And as we have just seen, information can never be perfect. Thus society must collectively decide on the ends toward which regulation strives. In reaching that decision, it may rely to some extent on consumer preference revealed in the market, but ultimately it must turn to voter preference revealed in the political arena.

Then there is the question of what *means* should be utilized to reach these targeted ends. We have seen that "enlightened voluntarism" is a defective instrument of social control. But should regulation proceed primarily on the basis of government commands? Or should it seek to rely more on creating economic incentives that would induce producers to act in accordance with the public interest? For example, should the government command firms to reduce their air pollution to some specified level? Or should a pollution pricing system be implemented whereby producers are free to pollute, but must pay an "effluent fee" per unit of pollutants in excess of targeted levels?

Some "libertarians" suggest that the market system, acting in conjunction with the legal system, will create sufficient incentives to deter antisocial behavior on the part of producers. After all, they reason, the victims of pollution or hazardous products can obtain redress by suing offenders for damages. "Libertarians" are confident that these penalties would be adequate to compel firms to control pollution and reduce hazards without government intervention.

Sadly, reality refutes this argument. As Mark Green and Beverly Moore have pointed out, the "victim's ability to collect is persistently undermined by the difficulty of calculating damages, imperfect substantive liability rules, restrictions on class actions, dilatory practices of defendant corporations, 'ethical' prohibitions against lawyers informing consumers of their right to sue, similar rules against lawyers' financing and purchasing consumer causes of action, and the general high cost of legal representation."[23] How, for example, could individual responsibility for contaminated drinking water be assigned, when dozens of firms may generate pollutants in a particular area? Could a low-income family really afford to carry a defective-product case against General Motors through to the Supreme Court? Who compensates the cancer victim, when the firm responsible for dumping carcinogenic wastes has long since ceased to operate? How could the victim ascertain that the cancer was caused by those particular wastes? What about asbestos, where exposure to the material finally triggers cancers many years later on so monumental a scale that compensating the victims would bankrupt even Johns-Manville? Alas, the blind cry for deregulation is singularly unhelpful in resolving these problems, which are endemic in a modern industrial society and which are not likely to disappear under the onslaught of ideological sloganeering.

GUIDEPOSTS FOR REGULATORY POLICY

Where industries are inherently competitive (trucking and airlines), economic deregulation combined with strict antitrust surveillance is the appropriate policy—but not the abandonment of safety regulation. We must continue to rely on government to provide a system of air-traffic control, to assure the proper maintenance of aircraft, to promulgate standards for training and licensing pilots, and to oversee surveillance procedures to protect travelers against terrorism. Such social regulation is clearly consistent with the maintenance of competitive markets.

Where industries are "natural monopolies," there are no credible alternatives to comprehensive government regulation or outright government ownership. Nevertheless, a caveat is in order. Natural monopoly stems from production technology, and technology is dynamic. It may transform the natural monopoly of yesteryear into the competitive industry of today. Seventy-five years ago, for example, long-distance telephone calls between New York and Chicago had to be transmitted over a cable laid between the two cities; economies of scale made such communication a natural monopoly. Today voice can be transmitted by cable, microwave, or satellite. Long-distance telephony is no longer a natural monopoly, and public policy should no longer treat it as such.

In "hybrid" industries, parts of which are inherently competitive and others monopolistic, economic regulation should be strictly confined to the latter. If efficiency is the goal, it is not necessary for a holding company like AT&T to control *both* the supply of local telephone service (a monopoly field) and the manufacture of telephone equipment (inherently competitive). Once the two are divorced, the service function should continue to be regulated, and manufacturing be opened to competition.

In markets where freedom of choice is hampered by inadequate information, or where rational choice requires extraordinary expertise, there is no acceptable alternative to government regulation. Contrary to libertarian preachments, it would be imprudent to expect an air traveler to do research required to avoid unsafe airlines, or for the automobile buyer to find out which cars are afflicted with rear-wheel lockup, or for the pregnant woman to conduct chemical tests to avoid drugs that may kill or deform her unborn child. Here social regulation is imperative, either by providing indispensable information to consumers or by prohibiting hazardous products outright. Here the privilege of free choice in a free market is the freedom to play Russian roulette with health and safety, and to impose the cost of death or injury on families or on society.

In markets fraught with externalities, again there is no alternative to regulation—whether by command, incentive, or a combination of both. Here again we must recognize that nobody willingly buys automobile pollution or rationally risks radiation from nuclear reactors. The market cannot control negative externalities effectively, and cannot be expected to do so.

Finally, under the best of circumstances, even if there were universal agreement on the need for social regulation, we would still confront the specter of bigness. In the field of social regulation, as elsewhere, bigness is not inert. It does not willingly submit either to the rules of the competitive market or to the requirements of regulation. To avoid the penalties for producing a life-threatening and cancer-causing products, asbestos giants lobby for legislation curbing consumer rights to recover damages. To evade fuel-efficiency requirements promulgated nearly a decade ago, General Motors and Ford argue for a change in regulations that will permit them to produce the kinds of cars they choose to supply—irrespective of any national concern for fuel conservation or safety. They know that their size—their economic impact on employees, parts suppliers, dealers, and municipalities—gives them substantial immunity from public sanction. They know that disregard of regulatory requirements will not precipitate a shutdown of their facilities. They know that flaunting a current law will likely result in the change of that law by a compliant government. In short, just as bigness can mobilize its power to obtain protection from competition, so too can it wield power to subvert social regulation.

CHAPTER 20

THE PROTECTION
OF POWER

Once given a fair trial and equal opportunity to compete in overseas markets, and once subject to healthy competition from overseas manufacturers for our own markets, American management and labor will have additional reason to maintain competitive costs and prices, modernize their plants, and increase their productivity. The discipline of the world marketplace is an excellent measure of efficiency and a force to stability. To try to shield American industry from the discipline of foreign competition would isolate our domestic price level from our world prices, encourage domestic inflation, reduce our exports still further, and invite less desirable government solutions.   — John F. Kennedy, message to Congress, January 25, 1962

W ith the internationalization of markets and the liberalization of world trade since World War II, the threat of foreign competition has revived the age-old cry for protection—to protect domestic industry from the depredations of "unfair" competition, to protect domestic labor from "import-induced" unemployment, to protect the nation's balance of payments, and, of course, to protect national security. These arguments are especially appealing during recessions and sound eminently reasonable to politicians in election years. They are particularly irresistible when voiced by corporate giants whose fortunes affect the lives of millions.

Foreign competition is a serious challenge to firms that must struggle for profits and growth in a free market. It forces them to innovate and to produce efficiently. It is a disruptive force that undermines monopoloid market control and cartellike pricing schemes. It promotes the defection of mavericks from collusive pricing arrangements and threatens industries luxuriating in delinquent performance behind formidable barriers to new competition. Foreign competition, the nemesis of "orderly marketing," becomes a prime target for neomercantilist governments and the interest groups that manipulate them.

In recent years, import quotas have become a favorite tool of protectionism. The scenario is roughly as follows: imports capture a growing share of the domestic market. The industry affected is joined by its trade union in demanding protection from foreign competition. Complaints are filed under statutes against "dumping," "subsidization," or the like. In case of failure—more common than not—legislative action is then requested to impose mandatory restraints on the "injurious" imports. Exporting countries are informed that mandatory restraints are likely unless they practice "voluntary" self-limitation. The typical result is the "voluntary" quota—usually only a temporary solution. If the quota applies to cotton textiles, the import problem will shift to wool or man-made fibers. If the quota applies to steel mill products, the import problem will crop up in higher-priced steel products, and eventually in finished products of steel. If the quota restrains one country (say Japan), new producers (Hong Kong, Taiwan, Korea) will enter the protected (high-price) market. Bilateral negotiations must then become multilateral. Broad import controls over an entire industry or segment must be refined, made increasingly specific. Moreover, exporting countries, responsible for monitoring their side of the bargain, are obliged to reorganize their export trade to encourage collective action among competing companies and form export associations (that is, export cartels). These new producer groups must allocate quotas and divide markets—and inevitably raise prices to the importing country. They are also constrained to negotiate with counterparts in other exporting countries to develop a *modus vivendi* for competition in the import market. Finally, under the auspices of their respective governments, and under the threat of legislated trade restrictions, the exporting firms and the domestic industry are encouraged to work out orderly marketing agreements, designed to prevent "injury" or "potential injury" to industry and labor in the importing country.

In practice, such agreements are little more than a euphemism for international cartels, organized and operated by special-interest groups with the connivance of governments. They are the politico-economic prototype of neomercantilist statecraft—the analog in the international arena of regulatory protectionism in domestic public utilities. Like public-utility regulation, they create a private-industry–government complex immunized from the disciplinary control of competition. But unlike public-utility regulation, import protectionism is not subject even to nominal regulatory oversight aimed at ensuring acceptable (not to say progressive) industry performance.

In this chapter we shall examine the steel industry as a representative case study of the political economy of protectionism. We leave other aspects of protectionism to our analysis of the management-labor complex in chapter 23.

THE POLITICAL ECONOMY OF PROTECTIONISM: STEEL

For decades the steel industry in the United States has been afflicted by the typical maladies of bigness and oligopoly. As noted in chapters 3 and 4, innovation has been lethargic, hampered by the dry rot that tends to accompany corporate giantism and noncompetitive industry structure. Bigness has shackled the dominant integrated firms with bloated, uncompetitive costs. Price policy in the industry has been uniform and inflexible, except when prices rise; and though leadership has rotated among the big-steel oligopolists, the level of product prices has been anything but market-determined.

Into this well-ordered preserve surged a rising tide of imports, first responding to the long labor dispute of 1959. Once the industry grasped that these imports were not a temporary aberration—that they were disturbing accustomed price relationships and procedures, indeed undermining the very foundations of the domestic oligopoly—U.S. steelmakers organized for a counteroffensive. As an alternative to meeting foreign competition in the marketplace, the industry sought government protection under existing "antidumping" and "countervailing duty" statutes.

After successive defeats before the U.S. Tariff Commission (now the U.S. International Trade Commission), the domestic industry launched a major campaign on a new front—Congress. Beginning as early as 1967, a succession of bills surfaced in Congress providing statutory limits on steel imports. Other industries that also faced intense foreign competition for the first time in the 1960s then joined forces with steel. These protectionist efforts peaked when Representative James Burke, the Massachusetts champion of the embattled footwear industry, and Senator Vance Hartke, the indefatigable spokesman for Indiana's steel industry, submitted an omnibus bill that included mandatory import quotas on a number of products.

THE 1968 VOLUNTARY RESTRAINT AGREEMENT

By 1968, the forces supporting legislative quotas had gathered such strength that the State Department panicked. To undercut support for congressional quotas, the department persuaded the major steel exporting countries—Japan and the members of the European Economic Community (EEC)—to enter into a Voluntary Restraint Agreement (VRA). Steel imports from Japan were limited to 5.8 million tons a year and from the EEC to 5.8 million tons, compared with their then current levels of 7.5 million and 7.3 million tons, respectively. The agreement also provided for an annual growth factor of 5 percent in the allowable quotas.

Within three years, however, the domestic industry found the VRA unsatisfactory.[1] One reason was that the VRA was expressed in terms of tons, so that foreign producers could expand their shipments of stainless steel and other high-value products to the U.S. This "upgrading," combined with the inevitable increase in the price of imported steel, meant that the total *value* of steel imports was as high in 1970 as in 1968 —despite a 25 percent decline in the tonnage.

To plug such "loopholes," the three-year extension of the agreement in May 1972 contained specific tonnage limitations on three categories of specialty steels (stainless, tool, and other alloys), and set the quotas below the level of 1971 imports. Fabricated structural steel and cold-finished bars were specifically included, and the participants agreed to maintain their product mix and their customary geographic-distribution pattern. Finally, the annual increase in the allowable import tonnage allocated to Japan and the EEC was reduced from 5 percent to 2.5 percent.

To enforce the extended VRA, the United States installed a monitoring system to be administered by the Treasury and the Customs Service. The exporting countries not only had to agree among themselves to observe the VRA, but also had to set up machinery for the producers within each country to arrive at mutually satisfactory export quotas to the United States. In other words, Japanese and European steel producers, under U.S. pressure, were obliged to set up cartels in order to arrange for their share of the U.S. market. More important, however, the connivance between the domestic industry, the State Department, and foreign steel producers to limit imports triggered an antitrust suit by Consumers Union, which charged that the VRA constituted a prima facie conspiracy under the Sherman Act. While the court eventually ruled only on the State Department's authority to insulate the agreement from the antitrust laws, the decision was clear enough to persuade all concerned that the VRA should not be renewed when it expired in May 1975.

THE 1978 TRIGGER PRICE MECHANISM

Disenchanted with previous import-restraint devices, the industry persuaded the government to institute the so-called Trigger Price Mechanism (TPM) beginning on 1 January 1978. A thinly veiled floor price for nearly all imported steel products, the TPM was calculated quarterly by the Treasury Department (and later the Commerce Department) on the basis of Japanese production costs, plus all exporting costs from Japan to the United States, plus a margin for profits.

The pricing freedom that TPM accorded to the domestic industry was significant. On 7 December 1977, one day after the concept of trigger pricing was announced by President Carter, a steel executive stated that U.S. steel prices would be increased in the first quarter of 1978. Shortly thereafter, a 5.5 percent increase in the domestic price of basic steel products was posted. This was followed by a further price rise of 1.1 percent in April 1978. On 8 May 1978, the Treasury raised trigger prices by 5.5 percent on sheet, plate, wire, and cold-finished bars, 13.9 percent on angles, 14 percent on reinforcing bars, and 14.5 percent on flat bars. Two months later it raised trigger prices once again. Thus, the total increase of trigger prices for 1978 amounted to 10.6 percent.

Initially, domestic steel companies were quite pleased. Foreign producers unexpectedly applauded this new import restraint. M. Jacques Ferry, head of the Common Market's steelmakers' group, stated: "We don't have any problems" with the trigger price mechanism. "It has raised steel prices all around the world."

After less than two years, though, the domestic industry found TPM wanting. The initial cause for TPM's "success"—a rapid strengthening of the Japanese yen against the dollar—in the end brought about TPM's demise. Once the yen-dollar exchange rate was stabilized, the constancy of Japanese production costs meant that there would be no further increase in trigger prices—the consummation the domestic industry so devoutly desired.

Hence the U.S. steelmakers—in spite of government warnings—once again began to file massive antidumping, unfair-competition, and export-subsidization complaints against their foreign competitors. The TPM was first suspended, and then abandoned.

THE RETURN TO QUOTAS

The domestic industry then mounted an all-out assault on foreign competition, pushing protectionism both before the International Trade Commission and in Congress, especially during election years.

In a subsidization complaint filed with the International Trade Commission, and involving all five major European producers, the commission ruled that the steel imports in question benefited from an export subsidy and were sold in the United States at "less than fair value"— even though in at least five of the sixteen instances cited, the subsidy was clearly far too small to account for lower import prices. With carbon steel plate, for example, the evidence showed that "Belgium benefitted from a weighted average subsidy margin well under 2 percent, but undersold domestic producers by 5–15 percent," and that "Germany enjoyed a subsidy evaluated by Commerce at 0.000, but undersold domestic products by 10–15 percent." Similarly, on structural shapes, "Luxembourg benefitted from a subsidy ranging in size from 0.5 to 1.5 percent . . . but undersold domestic producers by generally wide margins, ranging from 2 to 38 percent," and "one German exporter was deemed to benefit from a subsidy of 1.131 percent, while another's was officially listed as 0.000. . . . The margin by which these German exporters undersold their U.S. rivals ranged from 1 to 28 percent."[2] In short, the commission majority ignored the smallness of the subsidies, even where the Commerce Department had determined the margin to be zero —carried to the third decimal place! Moreover, one commissioner aptly pointed out in dissent that allegedly subsidized imports were not the crux of the problem: "To an industry plagued by prolonged, deep recession, delayed modernization, a noncompetitive cost structure, and an over-valued dollar," she wrote, "the duties for which I have voted . . . are no panacea." She concluded that in the steel industry, "the Great Depression II has already arrived and to blame subsidized imports for any significant share of the problems would be to deceive."[3]

Nevertheless, the domestic oligopoly successfully utilized this decision to "induce" European and Japanese producers to "voluntarily" restrain their carbon-steel exports to the United States.

As the 1984 election drew nigh, the industry unleashed yet another fusillade against foreign competition. Producers and steelworkers lobbied both houses of Congress to obtain protective legislation. In the House, the Fair Trade in Steel Act of 1984 was introduced, which aimed to establish specific quotas in forty-four product groups, with the objective of limiting imports to fifteen percent of the U.S. market. It would have directed the secretary of commerce to develop detailed forecasts of U.S. steel consumption, and to apportion allowable import tonnages in every product class among every country exporting steel to the United States. No discomfiting questions of "fair" versus "unfair" competition would have been required. And the legislation would have remained in effect for five years, with a possible three-year extension.[4]

Simultaneously, the industry (led by Bethlehem Steel and the Steelworkers) returned to the International Trade Commission with yet another complaint. A majority of the commission accepted most of the industry's charges, despite evidence that several other factors seemed far more important than imports in explaining the plight of domestic producers. These included long-term declines in the demand for steel; the worst recession (or depression) since the 1930s; intense *domestic* competition from nonintegrated mini-mills and other small rivals; and the increasingly uncompetitive cost structure of Big Steel, as well as its deplorable record for innovation. Indeed, Commissioner Paula Stern observed that Big Steel had taken important steps to become competitive during the years 1980 to 1983—"a period when the U.S. steel market was relatively open and U.S. steel producers were subject to import pressure"—and she recommended against import restraints because they "are more likely to inhibit rather than enhance the overdue efforts of U.S. steel producers to adjust to conditions of competition of the 1980s." Nevertheless, the majority of the commission advised the president to impose a variety of tariffs and quotas, covering nine major steel product categories and accounting for approximately 70 percent of all U.S. steel imports.[5]

As an alternative to the commission's recommendations, President Reagan—in the midst of his reelection campaign and beset by steel-industry pressures—directed his special trade representative to negotiate comprehensive "voluntary" restraint agreements with all countries exporting steel to the United States market. To lend urgency to these talks, the White House indicated it would block access to the American market by any countries refusing to participate. The threat did not go unheeded. The resulting agreements, starting in late 1984 and covering more than a dozen countries, were aimed at holding total steel imports to 18.5 percent of the U.S. market (down from about 25 percent in 1984). They covered imports of all finished steel products and were scheduled to remain operative for five years.[6]

So revitalized was the industry by these arrangements that it soon moved to raise prices and to file another twenty-eight trade petitions against eight more steel-producing nations. By November 1985, six more nations were governed by the agreement, extending the "voluntary" agreements to 90 percent of American steel imports.[7]

EFFECTS OF PROTECTIONISM IN STEEL

There are several economic consequences of the steel industry's tireless maneuverings to obtain protection from foreign competition:

First, the succession of antidumping complaints, countervailing-duty charges, mandatory-quota threats, the VRA, the TPM, and the import-injury proceedings must have had a chilling effect on the intensity of import competition. Import sales were probably reduced, simply to avoid the appearance of an "excessive" inflow during the period when remedies were being considered. The artificial restriction of supply almost inevitably meant an increase in price.

Second, there is hard evidence that the various protection stratagems profoundly affected steel prices. According to one study, the composite steel price index rose 4.1 points between January 1960 and December 1968—or 0.45 point per year—indicating the moderating effects that imports had on domestic prices. By contrast, between January 1969 and December 1972, while the VRA was in effect, the steel price index rose 26.7 points—or 6.67 per year—twice as much as the index for all industrial products (including steel). Steel prices rose 14 times as fast in the four years after the import quotas went into effect than in the nine before. Another study showed that steel prices increased by $26 to $39 per ton under VRA, meaning that they would have been 13 to 15 percent lower without VRA.

Predictably, the TPM had similar effects. Considering only the original trigger prices announced by the Treasury in January 1978, the Federal Trade Commission estimated the direct cost increase to steel consumers at $1 billion. An official of the Council on Wage and Price Stability estimated the direct price effect as between $800 million and $1.2 billion. Kurt Orban, an international expert on steel markets, estimated that the trigger-price system increased steel costs to consumers by $4 billion. Finally, if the domestic steel industry is to be believed in its claim that imports caused transaction prices to be $60 per ton below list prices, then estimates of increased steel costs could range up to $6 billion.[8]

And the evidence suggests that the most recent round of "voluntary" restraints, limiting imports to 18.5 percent of the market, will significantly raise prices. The Congressional Budget Office calculates that steel prices will be about 7 percent higher over the five-year term of the restraints than they would be otherwise, with a total cost to the U.S. economy of $18 billion; Federal Trade Commission economists anticipate increases of as much as 8.8 percent.[9]

Third, the use of quotas, or threat of quotas, to reduce competition from foreign steel has profound implications for the fight against inflation. It may be difficult to specify the precise importance of steel in the producer price index, but there can be little doubt that price increases in steel trigger and "justify" concomitant price increases in a host of other products. As Dr. George Eads observed in the Council on Wage and Price Stability's report on steel prices (1975): "Throughout this report, the crucial role that import competition plays in moderating domestic steel price increases has been continually stressed. . . . While we must protect against unfair foreign competition, there is a tendency on the part of many industries to consider *all* foreign competition 'unfair.' Domestic firms cannot be allowed to take advantage of their market power to raise prices [perversely] during periods of weak demand and then expect the government to protect them from the consequences."[10]

Fourth, import restraints tend to undermine competition and cement collusive market controls. Quotas, as we have seen, mean that the U.S. market for imports must be parceled out to exporting countries in precise percentage terms, and that each exporting country must allot specific portions of its national quota to its exporters. This militates toward an elimination of competition among the exporters of any given country, the elimination of competition among exporting countries, and ultimately, the elimination of competition between exporting countries and domestic producers. In short, competition in the U.S. market is stifled because exporting countries (and companies in them), prohibited from increasing their allotted market, lack the incentive to cut prices.

Restraints implemented through minimum-price mechanisms have similar effects. The TPM required the publication and elaborate enforcement of minimum prices. It provided wholly reliable, government-certified, minimum-price lists, subject to quarterly adjustment. Thus every domestic producer of wire rod at all times knew the minimum price at which this product could be imported at every major port in the United States. So did importers. To allow—or, in this case, virtually to compel —foreign steel producers to observe price floors on every major steel product carries to the extreme the use of publicity to solidify conscious parallel action among tacitly colluding oligopolists. Through the intercession of government, therefore, oligopolists were in a much better position to pursue a policy of concerted action and price escalation than if they had had to depend on private means to achieve that objective and still remain within the strictures of the antitrust laws.

Fifth, the various steel import restraints imposed by the United States are significant because they help lay the groundwork for comprehensive multinational agreements controlling world trade in steel. Such agreements, of course, are the dream of influential members of the world steel community. In July 1976, for example, Jacques Ferry, president of the French Steel Industry Association, stated that "a world steel pact is urgently needed to stave off chaotic market conditions." Such a pact, he said, would "involve major steel-producing countries agreeing to orderly marketing procedures, with rules for resorting to production controls and import restrictions when these are justified by previously agreed criteria on levels of investment, employment, deliveries and the like." He claimed "considerable support from U.S. steel circles for such a pact." Similar statements, couched in euphemisms like "fair trade" and "orderly marketing agreements," crop up in international steel discussions with remarkable regularity. Regardless of their avowed purpose, their effect may well be to reconstitute the international steel cartel that operated between the two world wars.[11]

Sixth, the government installed successive import restraints without exacting a quid pro quo from the steel oligopoly. It did not obligate the industry—in return for protection—to modernize its facilities or to take stipulated measures to improve its competitiveness.[12] Thus protection from foreign competition has left the steel giants free to squander their admittedly inadequate financial resources on mergers and acquisitions —U.S. Steel's $6.3 billion purchase of Marathon Oil, Armco's disastrous multimillion-dollar foray into insurance,[13] and LTV's (to date) indigestible acquisition of Republic, a combination unlikely to enhance either operating efficiency or efficiency in innovation. Successive periods of "breathing space" have also left the industry free to arrange buying foreign steel slabs (as U.S. Steel is reportedly doing) instead of refurbishing its plants to produce them in the United States.[14]

Finally, and ironically, quantitative import restraints do not necessarily handicap foreign steel producers. Instead, they may well *enrich* foreign firms by permitting them to raise prices and profits. In the case of South Korea, for example, the *Wall Street Journal* points to the likelihood that higher prices for the country's steel products "will eventually offset the volume loss" occasioned by U.S. trade restraints.[15] Foreign producers do not necessarily regard worldwide quotas and "orderly marketing agreements" as drawbacks. They understand that such arrangements have all the virtues of an international cartel. Like their confrères everywhere, they, too, prefer private arrangements to the discipline of competitive markets. The impact of such arrangements on the U.S. economy, however, is quite a different matter.

SOME PUBLIC-POLICY IMPLICATIONS

The experience in steel is not unique. Essentially the same process is observable in automobiles, another major American industry. Here, too, import competition has been the result—not a cause—of deficient, noncompetitive performance by the domestic auto oligopoly. Here, too, powerful oligopolists (together with organized labor) have fought foreign competition in the corridors of Congress rather than in the marketplace.

And the effects of voluntary restraint agreements restricting Japanese auto imports into the U.S. during the 1980s have not been insubstantial. They have artificially inflated car prices by as much as $2,500, cost consumers an estimated $15.7 billion, reduced consumer choice, retarded the offering of innovative new cars—and *strengthened* Japanese car companies by vastly enhancing the profitability of their desirable but artificially scarce products in the U.S. market. Yet at the same time, the Big Three U.S. automakers have used the "breathing space" bought by the restraints to arrange for increased *foreign* production of cars, parts, and components, frequently in concert with their former foreign rivals.[16]

Thus an analysis of the political economy of protectionism suggests these public-policy implications:

1. It is crucial to recognize that the alleged depredations of foreign competition and the associated demands for import protection can be, fundamentally, *symptoms*, not causes. They can be deeply rooted in noncompetitive industry performance and, at bottom, systematic consequences of bigness and noncompetitive industry structure. For example, our earlier analysis of operating, innovation, and social efficiency reveals steel and autos to be industries wherein oligopolistic giantism has long predominated, and where effective competition has been absent and performance correspondingly poor. These consequences of bigness and noncompetitive structure were largely obscured until the advent of efficient, innovative foreign competitors glaringly exposed them.

2. A study of the protection of power thus underscores the important role of antitrust policy, particularly as regards the maintenance of competitive industry structure. If public policy on the antitrust front had sought to block bigness in steel and autos, and to render industry structure in these fields competitive, would foreign competition be a policy "problem" at all? Would competitive structure, enforced by antitrust action, have spurred domestic steel and auto firms to be so efficient in production and so innovative as to preclude any need for protectionism? Alas, public policy did not take this course. Instead, protectionism has become an instrument for bailing out bigness, for sanctioning noncompetitive industry structure, and thus for validating ongoing, deficient industry performance.

3. Protectionism cannot remedy recessionary macroeconomic conditions and their adverse effects. To do this adequately is the task of counter-cyclical fiscal and monetary policy. Indeed, to the extent that import restraints enable domestic oligopolies to *raise* prices during economic downturns (as in steel and autos), protectionism aggravates reces-

sionary conditions by reducing sales, production, and employment in protected industries, as well as in a range of related fields.

4. Protectionism alone is unlikely to be effective. The proponents of import restraints—in a curious perversion of Friederich List's "infant industry" argument—justify their demands as providing a breathing spell that will allow corporate giants in senescent oligopolies to re-form themselves to meet international competition. Given temporary relief, the argument runs, bigness will be able to "stand on its own feet" and compete with the world's front-runners, including the Japanese.

Unfortunately, as experience demonstrates, the right moment never seems to come. Instead, and at considerable social cost, "temporary" relief degenerates into permanent protection. But is this really surprising? After all, import restraints alone do not exact any quid pro quo in return for government protection from foreign competition. They offer no assurance that the higher profits will not be invested in foreign facilities or anticompetitive joint ventures with foreign rivals, or spent on megamergers that further increase bigness and exacerbate delinquent performance. Protectionism provides no spur for technological progress, modernization of domestic facilities, or enhanced production efficiency at home. Nor does it provide the discipline needed to curb an industry's proclivity for constant, pervasive price escalation. Events also show that quantitative import restraints need not necessarily handicap foreign rivals, and instead may well strengthen them by making them more profitable and even more formidable opponents—thereby rendering the continuation of "temporary" restraints virtually an assured outcome.

5. Protectionism in basic fields such as steel raises the price and hence the cost of key inputs to a variety of other industries. It thus triggers demands for protectionism in other fields. For example, the *Wall Street Journal* reports that "steel represents 58 percent of the total cost of producing a hammer, according to Stanley Tools. International Harvester . . . says steel accounts for 25 percent of its manufacturing costs. And just a 7 percent rise in steel prices could add more than $30 million in annual expense for Caterpillar Tractor Co., which . . . faces fierce foreign competition of its own."[17] Protectionism in one field thus can undermine the international competitiveness of other industries and expand the demand for, and social costs of, protectionism generally.

Needless to say, nations must be permitted to defend themselves against massive dumping attacks by their foreign rivals and trade-distorting subsidization by foreign governments. They should also have the right to grant adjustment assistance to industries and workers suffering import hardships. But public policy ought not embrace "solutions" to the import "problem" that are based on flawed diagnoses, which treat symptoms rather than causes, and which provide no structural basis for correcting poor industry performance.[18]

In the final analysis, the protectionism issue points up the critical role of competition and procompetitive public policy, as well as the essence of the political economy of power.

Our study of the causes and consequences of protectionism strongly suggests that vigilant enforcement of antitrust may be the best policy to promote international competitiveness in American industry. Conversely, to permit noncompetitive industry structure to persist domestically—to permit, if not encourage, megamergers and bigness—is to encourage what eventually tend to become invitingly easy targets for more competitive foreign producers.[19]

The miraculous performance of the Japanese economy since World War II underscores this proposition. The Japanese "miracle," we submit, is largely attributable to the fact that Japanese industry was compelled to export in order to survive and prosper, and that it was constantly subject to the ruthless discipline of competitive international markets that it could neither manipulate nor control. In order to be successful, Japanese industries were compelled to produce goods wanted by consumers in competitive world markets; and they had to sell those goods at prices that buyers with competing alternatives were willing to pay. Contrary to the conventional wisdom, the Japanese did not forge their economic miracle by promoting corporate giantism, immunity from antitrust, or a symbiosis between government, industry, and labor. Their success was not due to insulation from competition, but to mastery of the competitive discipline to which international markets subject rival participants.[20]

The lesson is clear. Protectionism is not the key to enhanced productivity and international competitiveness. It does not remedy—indeed, it perpetuates—the structural problems that make industries vulnerable to foreign competition. As a public policy, protectionism is little more than an exercise in suicidal self-deception.

CHAPTER 21

THE PROMOTION
OF POWER

Through year after year of cost overruns on nuclear power, America's electric utilities have added, by some estimates, an extra $100 billion in interest and other costs to the nation's electric power bill and placed ratepayers, shareholders, creditors and taxpayers between the proverbial rock and a hard place. Even at that high price, many customers will be left with nuclear-generated power that is overpriced compared to fossil fuel alternatives and that represents more capacity than is necessary to fill power needs into the 1990s. Worse still, a minority of users must help finance multibillion-dollar shells of nuclear reactors unlikely—at least for the next five-to-ten years—to generate enough power to run a toaster, let alone replace or supplement fossil fuel–based plants. — *Dun's Business Month*, 1984

O nce upon a time, the prospects of the nuclear-power industry seemed roseate, its horizons unlimited. Harnessing the atom to generate electricity would produce power "too cheap to meter." Forty years later these forecasts have turned to dross. An enormous investment in what was to be a miracle source of electrical power has left in shambles an industry that has been spawned, nurtured, and protected by government.

Consider, for example, the nuclear-plant project of Consumers Power Company.[1] In 1967, Consumers Power announced plans to build a two-unit nuclear-power plant in the city of Midland, Michigan. The estimated cost of the combined units was $256 million, with Unit 1 to be completed in 1974, and Unit 2 in 1975. By 1977, the cost estimate had grown to $1.67 billion. At the end of 1979, the cost estimate leaped to $3.1 billion; by this time, $1 billion had already been invested in the plant, leaving a "to go" cost of $2.1 billion, the largest "to go" cost in the history of the project.

Although objections began to be raised by the Michigan attorney general and others, the company was confident that the $3.1 billion estimate was realistic. The Michigan Public Service Commission authorized continuation of the project and declined to make findings concerning either the need for the Midland plant or its cost-effectiveness; the commission thought it "impractical" to review the economics of a project already under construction. In February 1982, estimated costs rose to $3.39 billion. In March 1983, they were revised to $4.43 billion; the completion was now scheduled for 1985. In April 1984, Consumers Power announced new, and what proved to be the final, figures: Unit 2 was to be completed in 1986 at a cost of $4.1 billion, while Unit 1 (in which $1.5 billion had already been invested) would be indefinitely suspended. Finally, in July 1984, the project was scrapped. By then, $4.1 billion had been spent, with no net salvage value anticipated by the company. Consumers Power stock plummeted to $4.50 per share, from $21 a year earlier. Lines of bank credit were canceled. The loss on the project was equivalent to $3,000 for each of the company's electric customers.

As Table 3 shows, Midland is not grossly atypical. According to the Department of Energy, 84 percent of operating nuclear plants built during the last thirteen years cost at least twice as much as initial estimates, and at least four times as much in 30 percent of the cases. Industry experts estimate that nuclear plants now nearing completion will produce electricity at costs far greater than those of comparable coal-fired plants and, in some cases, at costs equivalent to electricity generated from oil priced at $100 per barrel.[2] "Any [nuclear] plant which is less than 50 percent complete today should definitely be canceled," concludes energy analyst Irvin C. Bupp. "Plants in the 50 to 80 percent range probably should be canceled."[3] Abandoned atomic power plants— Marble Hill in Indiana, Midland in Michigan, Washington Public Power Supply System ("Whoops") in Washington, and Zimmer in Ohio—stand as silent monuments to waste.

Energy, Einstein found, equals mass multiplied by the square of the velocity of light. This formula permitted mankind to split the atom. It was the nucleus of the bombs that destroyed Hiroshima and Nagasaki and brought an end to World War II. But could atomic power be turned to peaceful uses? In particular, could it be utilized as a new source for electricity? Would this be technologically feasible? Could it be economically viable? How should these determinations be made? And by whom?

These were the questions confronting government just after World War II. Atomic weaponry and nuclear technology had been developed

TABLE 3
Nuclear Plants under Construction, February 1984

	Percent Complete	Due In Service	First Cost Estimate	Current Estimate
ALABAMA				
Bellefonte 1	83	4/88–4/89	$725 million	$5.2–5.6 billion
Bellefonte 2	63	4/90–4/91	for both	for both
ARIZONA				
Palo Verde 1	99	12/84	$2.8 billion	$5.7 billion
Palo Verde 2	98	9/85	for three	for three
Palo Verde 3	81	1987		
CALIFORNIA				
Diablo Canyon 1	100	3/84	$620 million	$4.5 billion
Diablo Canyon 2	99	5/85	for both	for both
CONNECTICUT				
Millstone 3	80	5/86	$400 million	$3.54 billion
GEORGIA				
Alvin W. Vogtle 1	61	3/87	$2.5 billion	$6.6 billion
Alvin W. Vogtle 2	20	Fall 1988	for both	for both
ILLINOIS				
Braidwood 1	70	4/86	$934 million	$3.575 billion
Braidwood 2	54	4/87	for both	for both
Clinton 1	82	11/86	$430 million	$2.85 billion
KANSAS				
Wolf Creek	90	3/85	$783 million	$2.67 billion
LOUISIANA				
River Bend 1	80	12/85	$350 million	$2.5 billion
Waterford 3	99	12/84	$230 million	$2.6 billion
MICHIGAN				
Midland 2	83	Mid-1986	$350 million	$4.43 billion
Enrico Fermi 2	98	12/84	$229 million	$3.075 billion
MISSISSIPPI				
Grand Gulf 1	100	Late 1984	$400–$500 million	$3 billion
MISSOURI				
Callaway 1	95	12/84	$550 million	$2.85 billion
NEW HAMPSHIRE				
Seabrook 1	86	7/85	$900 million	$5.8 billion
(Future of Unit 2 uncertain)			for both	for both
NEW JERSEY				
Hope Creek 1	76	12/86	$600 million for twin units	$3.79 billion for one
NEW YORK				
Shoreham	100	7/85	$261 million	$4.1 billion
Nine Mile Point 2	81	10/86	$382 million	$4.2 billion

TABLE 3 *(Continued)*

	Percent Complete	Due In Service	First Cost Estimate	Current Estimate
NORTH CAROLINA				
Shearon Harris 1	85	10/86	$1 billion for four units	$2.8 billion for one
OHIO				
Perry 1	92	5/85	$632 million	$5.2 billion
Perry 2	44	5/88	for both	for both
PENNSYLVANIA				
Beaver Valley 2	76	5/86	$321 million	$3.07 billion
Susquehanna 2	98	12/84	$1.1 billion	$4.1 billion
(Unit 1 in service 6/83)			for two units	for two units
Limerick 1	92	4/85	$1.7 billion	$6.45 billion
(Future of Unit 2 uncertain)			for two units	for two units
SOUTH CAROLINA				
Catawba 1	99	Early 1985	$320 million	$1.95 billion
Catawba 2	65	Early 1987	$320 million	$1.95 billion
TENNESSEE				
Watts Bar 1	96	Fall 1984	$621 million	$3.4 billion
Watts Bar 2	61	Mid-1986	for both	for both
TEXAS				
South Texas 1	50	6/87	$1 billion	$5.5 billion
South Texas 2	25	6/89	for both	for both

SOURCE: *New York Times,* 26 February 1984.

during the war by the government and in utmost secrecy. The safety and health hazards of atomic power were obvious; the public would have to be protected and regulation would be necessary. But given this, how should the government proceed to determine if nuclear electrical power was commercially viable? Should it limit its role strictly to regulation to protect the public welfare, while making the technology that it had developed available to private firms? Or should it take the far more significant step of actively promoting nuclear electrical power by offering subsidies, incentives, and bounties? If the latter, could the government simultaneously promote *and* effectively regulate the field? Or would it, by the very act of promotion, become indissolubly wedded to nuclear power as subsidizer and protector? Once begun, and once investments were made, could the program be stopped it if proved uneconomic? What of the alchemy between governmental promotion and subsidy on the one hand, and the monopolized public-utility environment of electric-power production on the other? What cost constraints, if any, could be expected under these conditions? And, finally, what about the public interest in efficient and safe power?

The government chose—at the prodding of manufacturers and utilities—to promote nuclear power. By the terms of the Atomic Energy Acts of 1946 and 1954, the Atomic Energy Commission (AEC) was established to develop, encourage, and regulate peaceful uses of the atom.[4] "We do not believe that the efforts of free enterprise, using its own resources and moneys, are by themselves adequate to achieve the speediest possible attack on the goal of peacetime power," the Joint Committee on Atomic Energy reported to Congress. "Neither do we believe that maximum progress toward this objective will be afforded by an effort relying exclusively on governmental research and development, using the public's moneys. We believe, rather, that teamwork between Government and industry . . . is the key to optimum progress, efficiency, and economy in this area of atomic endeavor. In other words, our legislative proposals aim at encouraging flourishing research and development programs under both Government and private auspices."[5]

The government thereafter poured billions of dollars into the atomic energy program. It sang the siren song of the "private" beneficiaries of the program—that commercially viable power was always just around the corner and, with a little more public largesse, would be realized. Together with industry and the utilities, it suppressed safety problems that threatened to raise the costs of nuclear power or to undermine public confidence in the industry. It tolerated constant delay in resolving critical problems, such as the disposal of atomic wastes. And it denigrated competitive alternatives such as conservation and solar power.

The nuclear-power episode graphically demonstrates the problems that almost inevitably arise when government moves beyond its legitimate role and attempts to promote a particular industry. It shows how the very act of promotion can create, conjoin, and unleash powerful vested interests, public as well as private, and how these special interests can subvert the public interest. At a minimum, a study of government-industry promotionalism and its consequences in nuclear power provides a sobering antidote for today's industrial "targeting" proposals.

GOVERNMENT SUBSIDIZATION OF NUCLEAR POWER

"If you were to inquire whether Westinghouse might consider putting up its own money" to construct a nuclear power plant, an official of the firm told a congressional committee in 1953, "we would have to say 'No.' The cost of the plant would be a question mark until after we built it and, by that sole means, found out the answer. We would not be sure of successful plant operation until after we had done all the work and operated successfully. This is still a situation of pyramiding uncertainties." For the committee's benefit, he explained: "There is a distinction between risk-taking and recklessness."[6] Based on such reasoning, the government construed its prime responsibility to be one of showering private industry with magnanimous financial subsidies and incentives.

REACTOR RESEARCH, DEVELOPMENT, AND PRODUCTION
The government subsidized the research, development, and production of civilian nuclear-power reactors in a variety of ways. It sponsored research and development of military reactors, including propulsion systems for nuclear submarines and aircraft, which underlay and directly contributed to the design and construction of civilian atomic-power plants. It expended funds directly for the research and development of civilian nuclear power systems. Under various "rounds" of its Power Reactor Development Program begun in 1955, for example, government performed at no charge R&D work requested by the industry, made lump-sum R&D grants, waived nuclear-fuel-use charges for utilities, and built reactors whose power was fed into utility power grids. To top this off, government bore the risks as well as the costs of constructing and operating the plants.

Government further subsidized domestic producers of nuclear power plants and equipment through a variety of programs designed to enhance the construction abroad of plants built by U.S. firms. These subsidies included loans, loan guarantees, grants, gifts, supply of nuclear materials and waiver of fuel-use charges, research grants, and the financing of training courses, schools, symposiums, and conferences. Eleven of the seventeen large nuclear reactors sold by General Electric and Westinghouse before 1965 were sold abroad. "They would be out of business if it wasn't for us," a spokesman for the U.S. Export-Import Bank has said. All told, these subsidies amounted to perhaps $20 billion.[7]

URANIUM PRODUCTION
Early U.S. uranium needs were supplied almost exclusively from foreign sources. Beginning in 1948, the government launched financial incentives to create a domestic uranium industry—guaranteed prices for uranium ores, bonuses paid for discoveries of uranium deposits, payment of haulage and development allowances, access to public lands (including the construction of 1,500 miles of roads), and guaranteed prices for

vanadium (a mineral found together with uranium). The government also explored extensively for uranium deposits, developed methods to assay and process uranium ore, and blocked the importation of foreign uranium in order to protect domestic producers and prices.[8] Cumulative subsidies on this score are estimated at $2.5 billion.[9]

URANIUM ENRICHMENT

Uranium must be "enriched" before it is suitable for fueling reactors. The government does this at three plants in Kentucky, Ohio, and Tennessee. Through its pricing of these services, the government has further subsidized the industry: the government's prices have been below those that would be set by private suppliers because the government's prices include no allowance for a rate of return, taxes, insurance, or the costs involved in the eventual decommissioning and cleanup of enrichment plants. Moreover, the government buys the electric power used for enrichment at prices significantly below what a commercial plant would pay, and its depreciation charges are understated. Thus, the Energy Research and Development Administration estimates that a fair market value for enrichment would be about one-third greater than the actual fees set by the government. Cumulative subsidies to the industry from this source may exceed $7 billion.[10]

WASTE DISPOSAL

In its treatment of nuclear waste disposal, the government has subsidized the industry in a variety of ways.

First, it has spent more than $2.3 billion researching the management and disposal of nuclear wastes.[11]

Second, the government's assumption of ultimate responsibility for waste disposal has absolved producers and utilities from ensuring (at their own expense) that nuclear wastes will be disposed of in a socially acceptable and safe manner. Under the Uranium Mill Tailings Act of 1978, government assumed responsibility for funding 90 percent of the costs of safely cleaning up waste tailings at twenty-five abandoned uranium-milling sites across the country. By the terms of the Nuclear Waste Policy Act of 1982, the government (and the public) assumed responsibility for transporting and insuring used nuclear fuel rods, including the cleanup of any accident that might occur during transit.[12]

Third, as a rule, costs of disposing spent nuclear fuel have not been incorporated into utility rate structures and rates. Because no environmentally sound method of fuel disposal has yet been devised, estimates of these costs vary substantially; they are conservatively placed at $2.1 billion. In addition, utilities have not been required to provide for future costs of decontaminating and decommissioning nuclear power plants now in operation when they reach the end of their serviceable lives. While these costs are also largely unknown, a conservative estimate is nearly $2 billion.[13]

All told, then, cumulative waste-disposal subsidies amount to perhaps more than $6.5 billion.[14]

LIMITATIONS OF DAMAGE LIABILITY

Finally, the largest, but least quantifiable, subsidy of the industry stems from the government's assumption, and limitation, of liability for the damages that would result from a nuclear reactor meltdown.

"The gravest problem now facing the atomic-energy business," a General Electric official explained to Congress in 1956,

> is that of liability for the consequences of an atomic accident. . . . It is . . . one thing to say that you will take your chances of sustaining losses, even substantial losses, and quite another thing to say that you will embark on a course where the entire assets of your stockholders are at stake, a course which might affect the stability of your company or its very existence.
>
> The testimony you have already heard is to the effect that a serious reactor incident is very unlikely but possible and that, if one occurred, it could be of catastrophic proportions. The insurance pools which have been organized to provide atomic hazard liability coverage are at present talking of limits which in combination amount to about $60 million. Compared to normal liability coverage this amount is high, but there is no use making any bones about the fact that it does not meet the major concern of many of us. . . . It seems to me a fair assumption that we could have an incident where the extent of the harm exceeded both the insurance liability coverage and the assets of the company which might be legally responsible for it.[15]

Without government protection on this front, he concluded, a domestic nuclear-power industry would not be viable.[16]

Congress responded to the industry's importunings with the Price-Anderson Act of 1957. By the terms of this act, which subsequently has been reenacted, the government limited the liability of reactor manufacturers and utilities to $60 million and assumed liability for any additional damages that might result from a nuclear reactor accident up to a maximum of $500 million (regardless of the actual damages that might occur).[17]

GOVERNMENT POLICIES TOWARD
NUCLEAR SAFETY

"Source and special nuclear material, production facilities, and utilization facilities are affected with the public interest," declared the Atomic Energy Act of 1954, "and regulation by the United States of the production and utilization of atomic energy and of the facilities used in connection therewith is necessary in the national interest . . . to protect the health and safety of the public." By this act, the AEC assumed the twin duties of promoting the development, construction, and operation of nuclear power plants, and of regulating their safety.

A crucial, and inevitable, dilemma thus arose: Having committed itself to encouraging the commercialization of nuclear power, could the government afford to be unduly concerned about safety problems that might threaten the program's viability, either by raising costs or undermining public confidence and acceptance? Where the desire to promote the industry collided with the duty to protect public welfare, how would the conflict be resolved?

The answers, perhaps, were predictable. According to Carroll Wilson, the first general manager of the AEC, "nuclear power proponents had something similar to a war mentality. . . . There was a whole set of forces moving in one direction with no one saying anything against it. The further it went, with all the commitments, and all the reputations, and all the investments at stake, you got an enormous snowballing of everybody defending the way it is."[18]

First, the government and the industry ignored serious safety problems that arose, or halted particular lines of research when serious safety problems began to be uncovered. For example, the AEC's Advisory Committee on Reactor Safety recommended in 1956 against construction of the Enrico Fermi nuclear power plant to be built by a consortium of utilities in an area bordered by Detroit, Dearborn, and Ypsilanti, Michigan, Toledo, Ohio, and Windsor, Ontario, on the basis of the plant's particularly volatile design. The committee chairman reported, "there is insufficient information available at this time to give assurance the reactor can be operated at this site without public hazard."[19] The AEC ignored the report, however, and issued a construction permit; when the plant subsequently suffered a partial meltdown, one engineer remarked, "We almost lost Detroit."[20] On other occasions, research that threatened to uncover similar safety problems was actively discouraged.[21]

Second, unfavorable information about reactor safety was suppressed or distorted. A study of the risks posed by the gigantic reactors scheduled for construction in the 1960s was quietly begun within the AEC in 1964, for example. One researcher called the results "frightening": Under a worst-case scenario, radioactive contaminants would be released from the plant over an area the size of Pennsylvania, as many as 45,000 deaths could result, and upward of $250 billion in property damage might follow. After reviewing the study, the industry's major trade association, the Atomic Industrial Forum, urged the AEC not to publish the study. The commission assented; "an important factor" in the decision, according to one AEC official, was "public relations considerations." Similarly, concerns regarding the efficacy of emergency cooling systems were suppressed by AEC task forces on which industry representatives held majority positions. Instead, industry representatives reviewed their own designs and, not surprisingly, found them "satisfactory." More generally, the government and industry hesitated to call attention to defects in future plants utilizing existing designs because to do so would have been to admit safety deficiencies at existing plants.[22]

Third, in discharging its regulatory duties, the government typically adopted a hands-off approach and permitted the industry to regulate itself, to evaluate its own safety, to write many of its own standards, to veto unfavorable reports, and to police its own construction work.[23]

Fourth, regulatory procedures and processes were structured in a manner that assured that serious (and, thus, potentially costly) safety problems would be dismissed, ignored, or covered over. If a particular plant being reviewed for licensing approval suffered a safety defect shared by other plants, for example, the problem was classified as a "generic unresolved issue," and the plant was approved on the grounds that it suffered no *special, unique* safety defects. According to the Kemeny Commission, appointed by President Carter to examine the Three-Mile Island accident, labeling a problem as "generic" was "a convenient way of postponing decision on a difficult question." As for the AEC's hearing procedures, a 1973 study by the National Science Foundation stated: "The only consensus among all of the parties to the [AEC's hearing process] appeared to be a general evaluation that the whole process as it now stands is nothing more than a charade, the outcome of which is, for all intent and purposes, predetermined."[24]

Fifth, government and industry smothered dissent by those most knowledgeable in the field. After reviewing internal documents leaked by AEC employees, for example, one reporter concluded that government officials "were apparently more concerned about the possible public relations impact of safety studies than the actual safety of reactors."[25] At times, the government used its control of security clear-ances to mute efforts by physicists to debate the effects of radiation on human health. Before testifying in public, AEC staff members were instructed, "Never disagree with established policy." Staffers who disagreed with "established policy" found themselves "reassigned" to more innocuous, less influential positions. Similarly, industry staffers were told that while they were free to testify in investigations, they could not be assured of continued employment with their firms if they "abused" their freedom of speech. Public critics found themselves under the surveillance of private detectives hired by utilities, or were branded as suffering from "emotional" problems.[26]

In an attempt to rectify this situation, Congress passed the Energy Reorganization Act of 1974, which abolished the AEC and severed the promotion of nuclear power from its regulation. Mindful of "a growing criticism of the mixture of the developmental and regulatory functions within the AEC," and the "weak and undernourished" condition of the regulatory arm of the commission, Congress transferred the promotional role to the Energy Research and Development Administration (later subsumed within the Department of Energy), while assigning the regulation role to the newly created Nuclear Regulatory Commission (NRC).[27] Judging by later events, though, these changes were primarily cosmetic: AEC personnel were transferred to the NRC; the NRC adopted without review the safety and licensing regulations of its predecessor; and curtailing safety-review processes became the NRC's highest priority, with safety reviewers (according to an NRC staffer) evaluated "on speed rather than on the depth of the review."[28] "The bare fact," the House Committee on Government Operations recently reported, "is that important, identified inadequacies in reactor safety have not been remedied by operating utilities on time and the NRC has failed to adequately pursue those failures."[29]

GOVERNMENT'S APPROACH TO NUCLEAR-WASTE DISPOSAL

In their collective promotional zeal, the government and the industry traditionally also delayed dealing with the problem (and costs) of safely disposing of lethal, radioactive nuclear wastes.

Atomic reactors are powered by "cores"—bundles of sealed metal tubes, typically half an inch in diameter and twelve feet long, containing pellets of enriched uranium. A portion of the fissionable uranium isotope U 235 is "burned" during reactor operation, and fragments of fissioned atoms begin to accumulate. As this occurs, the fuel becomes less efficient. Approximately one-third of the fuel core in the reactor must be replaced every year. Because they are highly radioactive—and toxic for as long as 250,000 years—these wastes must be disposed of safely. Moreover, after operating a number of years, the power plant itself is highly radioactive; some wastes in the plant's structure emit hazardous levels of radiation for 200,000 to 500,000 years. Hence, the site of the plant must be cleaned up, and the radioactive rubble safely removed.[30]

Apparently these problems have not given serious concern either to government or the nuclear industry. Reported the House Committee on Government Operations in 1978: "Radioactive waste is a significant and growing problem—at least 3,000 metric tons of spent nuclear fuel are now being stored at commercial reactor sites, with an additional 17,000 metric tons expected to accumulate in the next decade—yet there is still no demonstrated technology for permanently and safely disposing of this waste. . . . Neither the Federal Government nor the nuclear industry has prepared reliable cost estimates for the ultimate disposal and perpetual care of radioactive wastes and spent nuclear fuel."[31] Temporary waste storage efforts to date have been less than reassuring. For example, more than 400,000 gallons of highly radioactive liquid wastes have leaked from tanks at the Hanford Reservation site in Washington State; owing to corrosion of underground tank walls, more than 50 million gallons of waste may be irretrievably lost.[32] At the same time, every commercial attempt to safely and economically reprocess spent nuclear fuel in the United States has failed. As a result, the states have been saddled with the task of cleaning up reprocessing sites abandoned by their commercial operators.[33]

Decommissioning of radioactive generating plants has been accorded a like degree of indifference. In his 1977 investigation of the problem, the comptroller general found that the Nuclear Regulatory Commission "had done relatively little to plan for and to provide guidance for decommissioning of commercial nuclear facilities. Studies sponsored by the Commission on acceptable alternative methods to decommission are several years from completion. It does not require owners of nuclear facilities—except for uranium mills—to develop plans or make financial provisions to cover the cost for future decommissioning."[34] The comptroller's reinvestigation of the problem five years later concluded: "progress has been slow and many of the same weaknesses still exist. More importantly, the United States still does not have a national policy or strategy for decommissioning nuclear facilities or sites."[35]

In sum, it would appear that, as California's energy commissioner told Congress, "the foremost theme of waste disposal . . . has been, and continues to be, to defer decisions to another time and place."[36]

THE CONSEQUENCES OF PROMOTION

What, then, are the consequences of the alliance between government, manufacturers, and utilities to promote nuclear power? After forty years of this experiment with governmental promotion-cum-regulation, at least four major consequences are apparent.

NUCLEAR POWER IS NOT ECONOMICALLY COMPETITIVE

Despite continual massive subsidization over four decades—at a cumulative cost amounting to $54 billion or more—nuclear power is still not an economically competitive source of electrical power.[37] Even if these subsidies are *not* taken into account, and the costs of nuclear power thereby *understated* by as much as one-half, the utility industry's own Electric Power Research Institute concedes "the average new nuclear plant coming on line between 1985 and 1992 will produce electricity at a cost that is 25 percent to 50 percent higher than the typical new coal plant."[38]

In fact, nuclear power has over the past decade become progressively *less* competitive. The costs to construct nuclear power plants have increased at a rate far greater than the costs to construct conventional power plants. Since the 1960s, reactor construction costs have skyrocketed ten times faster than the Consumer Price Index, and two to three times faster than the costs to construct comparable coal-fired plants.[39] Second, nuclear power plants incur far greater operating and maintenance expenses than conventional plants, and operate at significantly lower capacity utilization rates. In their study, Richard and Caroline Hellman find operating and maintenance expenses for giant nuclear plants (the plants the industry promised would be most efficient[40]) to be approximately *double* those of comparable coal-fired plants.[41] Industry expert Charles Komanoff estimates that large nuclear plants operate, on average, at 55 percent of their designed capacity, compared with a 70 percent rate for comparable coal plants.[42]

It is important to point out that this record is *not* attributable primarily to burdensome, misguided intervention by government or by radical environmentalists. Instead, studies by the Rand Corporation, the Engineering Department of the Massachusetts Institute of Technology, and others indicate that the prime cause is mismanagement.[43] "Inadequate management has been one of the major causes of construction cost overruns and erratic operation," the Congressional Office of Technology Assessment recently concluded. The conservative business periodical *Forbes* agrees, characterizing the U.S. nuclear power program as "the largest managerial disaster in business history, a disaster on a monumental scale."[44] In the case of the Midland plant, for example, poor management performance included construction of the plant in a swampy area, on top of improperly compacted fill material, thereby requiring a $400 million tunneling project to shore up the foundations; distorted sales growth projections; flawed cost analyses; and the unwillingness of the utility to consider less costly alternatives of buying power from other utilities on the ground that these sources of supply would be "unreliable."[45]

Nor are state regulatory commissions—charged with overseeing utility managements, ostensibly in order to protect the public interest—blameless. For example, the Michigan Public Service Commission for many years permitted utilities to charge customers for virtually the full cost of all completed plants, regardless of their usefulness. "Utility management's knowledge that on a worst case scenario, where a project must ultimately be aborted, it will probably be permitted to recover its investment from ratepayers . . . encourages the commencement of a project. The knowledge that the cost of a project will be fully ratebased upon completion, regardless of its value, is a powerful incentive to continue construction. . . ."[46]

But is this really surprising? What cost constraints could be expected to be operative in the monopolistic world of public utilities? What penalties are there for inefficiency and managerial misfeasance? Is this not the same generic problem we saw in the airline and trucking industries under regulation? When combined with complacent state regulatory commissions, did government-industry promotionalism not afford a tantalizing billion-dollar, cost-plus bonanza for giant equipment producers like General Electric and Westinghouse, construction companies, engineering "consultants," and organized labor? As the Michigan attorney general's office points out, "Anticompetition statutes give comfort to utility managers embarked on high-cost construction projects that whatever the rate consequences of those projects, there will be little, if any, potential competition from a low-cost producer."[47]

INDUSTRY'S DEPENDENCE ON SUBSIDIES HAS INCREASED
Precisely because nuclear power is not commercially viable, the industry demands "more government involvement in financing the development of commercial nuclear power" (but, of course, "less government involvement in safety regulation").[48] Indeed, the industry now variously proposes that government (that is, the taxpayers) buy and operate nuclear plants; that government make low-cost loans to utilities to construct nuclear reactors; and that government—and taxpayers—assume responsibility for reactor cost overruns.[49] The industry thus is unable to withdraw from the public largesse to which it has become addicted. Nor

does there seem to be a threshold "under which this industry is willing to reverse itself and consider that there may be a better alternative, or even that their portion of the supply side of the pie should be diminished or restrained in the light of other alternatives and considerations."[50]

THE NUCLEAR POWER PROGRAM HAS RESULTED IN ENORMOUS WASTE

"By year-end 1982," the Department of Energy reports, "the electric utility industry had cancelled 100 nuclear units, totaling 109,754 mega-watts-electric (MWe) of capacity. These cancellations represented 45 percent of the total commercial Nuclear Steam Supply System (NSSS) capacity previously ordered. By comparison, only 39 fossil fuel–fired generating units, totaling about 23,000 MWe, have been canceled since 1972, the year of the first nuclear cancellations. The costs associated with these nuclear plant cancellations have been substantial. It is es-timated that about $10 billion was expended on the 100 nuclear units canceled since 1972. . . ." Moreover, the Energy Department has iden-tified a number of additional nuclear power plants in various stages of completion as being vulnerable to cancellation, involving additional abandonment costs of $4.5 billion to $8.1 billion. And, not insignificantly, the department finds that "the great majority of cancellation costs have been levied upon utility ratepayers and taxpayers, who had little or no control over the planning and construction of power plants."[51]

THE "OPPORTUNITY COSTS" OF THE PROGRAM HAVE BEEN SUBSTANTIAL

The nuclear power debacle has been enormously expensive, not only in direct outlays and subsidies, but also in terms of the "opportunity costs" of monies *not* spent on perhaps more promising (and less risky) energy alternatives, such as solar power and conservation. As one congressional committee has found, the potential benefits of these alternatives could have been substantial: "Solar power—including wind, waste wood, bio-mass, ocean thermal—is one of the most attractive energy alternatives to nuclear power. If the Federal Government spent only a small portion of what it has already spent on nuclear power development for the commercialization of solar power, solar generated electricity would be economically competitive within five years, in the view of many experts. . . . The United States could meet a substantial portion of its new energy needs for the next twenty-five years through energy conservation." Moreover, in an era of stubborn, persistently high unemployment rates, the committee pointed out, alternative energy strategies would yield an important fringe benefit: "Nuclear plants are capital-intensive and thus produce few jobs. Renewable-energy sources such as solar and conser-vation are not capital-intensive, and are expected to produce many jobs

—500,000 constructions jobs for solar hot water installation alone—or three times as many jobs as produced by the nuclear industry."[52]

PIVOTAL PUBLIC-POLICY ISSUES

The government's role in the promotion and regulation of nuclear power, as well as the role of the powerful vested interests created in the process, highlight some major public-policy issues.

First, who shall pay for the failure of nuclear power? Cost estimates of this failure are substantial—"roughly $15 billion invested in plants that have already been abandoned, $20 billion to $40 billion in plants likely to be canceled before completion, and $30 billion to $40 billion for plants that will come on line after sustaining such huge cost overruns that their electricity will cost much more than that from fossil-fueled plants."[53] Should these costs be passed on to consumers in the form of sharply higher electricity rates? If so, this has serious consequences not only for households, but for the economy of particular states and regions; high rates for electricity obviously influence location decisions by industry and business, driving existing plants out of a state and discouraging others from coming in; the effects on production and employment in the state may be devastating. Alternatively, should the costs of failure be imposed on the stockholders and creditors of local public utilities? If so, this too has adverse consequences. By increasing the risk of investing in such utilities, it would increase the cost of raising capital and eventually lead to higher rates or to deterioration in service, quality, and reliability, or both. Or should taxpayers—themselves blameless for the nuclear-power fiasco—be saddled with the financial burden? In that event, we would see yet another example of government subsidies and bailouts to correct the mistakes of incompetent managements. We shall see more fully in the next chapter that enterprises that have grown to gigantic proportions are assured survival—however egregious their lack of vision, judgment, and leadership. Perhaps here, too, the greatest advantage of giant size is an insulation from failure.

Second, are there not broader consequences of the power and influence inherent in the government-industry nuclear complex? Do they not go beyond the commandeering of sizable amounts of public monies? One would think so. As energy analyst Amory Lovins points out, guarding long-lived nuclear wastes necessitates a significant expansion of the police power of the state. Forcing communities and states to accept nuclear waste dumps means the spread of eminent domain and the coercive power of the federal government. The existence of nuclear power plants, fuels, and hazardous wastes enhances the possibilities (and opportunities) for terrorism. The social consequences, it seems, are not trivial—"a world of subsidies, $100 billion bailouts, oligopolies, regulation, nationalization, eminent domain, corporate statism."[54] In other words, promotionalism is planning. But, once again, the crucial questions arise: Planning by whom? For what? With what consequences? For whom? And with what accountability?

Finally, there is a related issue, and that is whether government-industry promotionalism in this field has met the test of open and informed decision-making in a democratic society. In the words of industry expert Mark Hertsgaard: "The question at hand is not whether nuclear power is a tolerably safe energy source today, but rather whether Americans, if given all the available information about the potential dangers of nuclear power production in the 1950s, would have given their approval to the sort of all-out commercial nuclear program envisioned by the Atomic Brotherhood. The men of the Brotherhood apparently believed they would not, and so they conspired to keep the full truth of nuclear energy from the public."[55] Viewed from this perspective, the nuclear debacle testifies to the consequences of power unrestrained either by the competitive market or in the political arena. These consequences, we have seen, are not necessarily beneficent or insubstantial—or temporary.

CHAPTER 22

THE BAILOUT OF POWER

Uncle Sam's gold—meaning no disrespect to the worthy old gentleman—has . . . a quality of enchantment like that of the Devil's wages. Whoever touches it should look well to himself, or he may find the bargain to go hard against him, involving, if not his soul, yet many of its better attributes; its sturdy force, its courage and constancy, its truth, its self-reliance, and all that gives emphasis to manly character.
— Nathaniel Hawthorne, *The Scarlet Letter*, 1850

The old saying holds: Owe your banker a thousand pounds and you are at his mercy. Owe him one million and the position is reversed.   — John Maynard Keynes

Confronting imminent bankruptcy in 1971, the Lockheed Aircraft Corporation—then the largest defense contractor and the nation's thirty-third largest industrial company—petitioned the federal government for a financial bailout. The firm's plea elicited extensive economic criticism. "It is the very threat of bankruptcy which jolts firms, large and small, from inefficient practices," economist Alan Greenspan told Congress. "To have the possibility of falling back on a guarantor of last resort must inevitably remove this very valuable prod to efficiency and productivity." Said Professor Milton Friedman: "Our private enterprise system is a profit and loss system. The loss element is at least as important as the profit element. The fundamental principle of this system is that private industry assumes risks and takes the consequences of its actions. This principle guards our freedom by distributing and disbursing power. If government is to guarantee against losses, it is entitled to determine what ventures enterprises undertake and how they prosecute them. This would be a step away from the free enterprise society and toward a collectivist society." In all, more than twenty economists counseled Congress against bailing Lockheed out. Their case was rigorously reasoned, cogently presented—and uninfluential. Lockheed got $250 million in federal loan guarantees.[1]

Eight years later, in 1979, the Chrysler Corporation—the nation's tenth largest industrial concern—petitioned for a bailout. Chrysler, too, faced financial collapse. Once again, the plea elicited strong protest from economists. "The basis of our free enterprise system is that individuals and corporations risk their own capital in producing products or services for the market," economist Thomas Gale Moore testified. "If they are successful, they earn profits which they can keep. . . . If unsuccessful, they [and their investors] may lose. Thus our system is based on a carrot and stick approach to providing goods and services." Removing the discipline of failure through government bailouts, he explained, "can only lead to a less vigorous economy and a less enterprising one."[2] Professor Friedman again pointed out that bankruptcy due to mismanagement "is highly beneficial for the community as a whole. It assures that resources are directed toward those enterprises that can use them most effectively."[3] William E. Simon, former secretary of the treasury, warned that if government bailouts continued, "we will become an inefficient, bungling nation. . . . And our self-description as a free-market economy will simply be a sham."[4] Once again, the economic case against bailout was logical and articulate—and ignored. Chrysler got $1.5 *billion* in guarantees.

In the early 1980s, billions of dollars of risky loans, extended to developing countries by the nation's largest banks, began to sour. The banks promptly petitioned for an $8.4 billion increase in U.S. government contributions to the International Monetary Fund as a means of assuaging their financial difficulties. Professor Friedman counseled: "Banks made loans to the debtor countries at terms they considered profitable, taking full account of the risks involved. Had all gone well, they would have reaped the profits. If any loans go sour, the banks (i.e., their stockholders) should bear the loss, not the taxpayers. If government socializes the losses, it will inevitably end up socializing the profits." He concluded: "Neither the banks nor the rest of us can have our cake and eat it."[5] But big banks proved Dr. Friedman wrong, and obtained government support.

Then, in 1984, Continental Illinois—the nation's eighth largest bank holding company—experienced a devastating run of withdrawals by depositors and investors disillusioned with the bank's risky growth strategy.[6] But in sharp contrast with the vast majority of smaller banks, which were permitted to disappear ignominiously (after depositors were compensated up to statutory limits), Continental Illinois was bailed out with more than $8 billion in transfusions and unlimited access to government monies. An official of the avowedly "free market" Reagan administration justified this preferential treatment on the grounds that a large bank's failure would have greater consequences than would the collapse of a smaller bank.[7] Indeed, the comptroller of the currency conceded under congressional examination that the government realistically could not permit any of the nation's eleven largest banks to fail—prompting Congressman Stewart B. McKinney to remark: "We have a new kind of bank. It is called too big to fail, TBTF, and it is a wonderful bank."[8]

In the preceding six chapters, we have explored different aspects of government intervention. We have noted how the pressure of powerful private interests has perverted the role of government into a mechanism to create and protect privilege—an instrument for shielding firms from the penalties of inefficiency and mismanagement, a method for guaranteeing corporate survival despite delinquent economic performance. We have seen evidence of the government playing the role of an indirect bailout agency.

In this chapter, we shall focus on *direct* government bailouts. Our detailed review of the Lockheed and Chrysler affairs will highlight the fact that once firms attain giant size, they are no longer allowed to fail, because government feels compelled to guarantee their survival almost regardless of how inefficient, unprogressive, or mismanaged they may be. Bigness, we shall see, confronts government with an intractable dilemma: if corporate giants are rescued from the consequences of their self-inflicted injury, this subverts the carrot-and-stick discipline of a free market economy; if ailing giants are allowed to fail, this produces unfortunate "externalities" for millions of people whose fortunes are intimately tied to the survival and success of those giants. In the end, government is forced into a painful trade-off between free-enterprise ideals and political reality. It is forced to pay the price for its toleration of concentrated economic power and the political influence that accompanies it. It is forced to recognize a pivotal fact of economic life—typically finessed by the economic Darwinists—that giant firms are protected from failure, not by being better, but by being bigger.

LOCKHEED

As noted, in 1971 Lockheed faced financial collapse. The crisis confronting the firm seemed to be due to three main factors.[9] First, costs on four
of the company's major defense contracts were escalating almost out of
control—especially on the C-5A military transport jet (a contract first
awarded to Boeing, but reassigned as a result of successful lobbying by
Lockheed). In 1968, cost overruns on this project alone were disclosed to
be about $2 billion. Although the Defense Department provided for what
were euphemistically known as "unfunded deficiencies" on the contract,
although it successfully petitioned Congress for an additional $200 mil-
lion "contingency fund" for Lockheed, and although it guaranteed that
this special aid would minimize the firm's losses, Lockheed's defense
operations were still consuming cash at prodigious rates.

Second, as its defense problems mounted, Lockheed tried to decrease
its dependence on defense contracts by reentering the commercial-air-
craft market, to exploit what it perceived to be the strong demand for
wide-body jets.[10] Here, too, though, the firm's management under-
estimated the costs of developing and producing its L-1011 TriStar. As
a result of cost overruns on both its defense and its commercial projects,
Lockheed incurred a loss of $86.3 million for 1970. At this point, the firm
began to negotiate with its twenty-four-bank lending consortium for
additional credit.

Third, in early 1971, Rolls-Royce, selected to produce jet engines for
Lockheed's TriStar, failed and was placed in receivership. The collapse
of Rolls-Royce further delayed the L-1011 project and aggravated Lockheed's dire and deteriorating cash position.

In the face of this development, banks and prospective customers
broke off negotiations for the $600 million in financing that Lockheed
needed. Without government loan guarantees of $250 million, Lockheed
claimed, its lenders would refuse to continue financing the firm's operations. Said Lockheed's chairman, Daniel J. Haughton: "If we cannot
obtain the necessary financing, the TriStar program will have to be
abandoned, and if the TriStar program is abandoned I know of no way
to save Lockheed from going bankrupt."[11]

Given the firm's immense size, support for a government bailout was
impressive and wide-ranging. It included President Nixon; his secretary
of the treasury, John B. Connally; the Department of Defense; banks,
including the Bank of America; Transworld Airlines, Eastern Airlines,
and the air carriers' trade organization, the Air Transport Association;
and labor unions, including the International Association of Machinists
& Aerospace Workers, and the AFL-CIO. These bailout advocates ar-

gued that a Lockheed bankruptcy would have devastating consequences —for the aerospace industry, defense production, aircraft manufacturing, airlines, the country's international trade position, and the economy generally.

Lockheed's chairman pointed out: "The L-1011 at the end of January 1971 employed more than 34,000 persons in 35 states. Of these, about 17,800 were employed by Lockheed and more than 16,000 by L-1011 suppliers. Weekly payroll totaled about $9 million. Applying a conservative multiplier, however, the L-1011 is responsible for more than 60,000 jobs that would be affected by termination of the program." AFL-CIO president George Meany emphasized to Congress that the employment loss would "be felt far beyond the corporate structure of Lockheed and also far beyond the boundaries of Southern California. . . . At least 156 companies in 25 states are directly producing parts for the L-1011. These prime contractors are in turn buying from suppliers in at least 10 more states." This meant, he warned, that government failure to support Lockheed would be felt "in scores of communities in every corner of the nation." Indeed, Treasury Secretary Connally advised Congress, the repercussions of a Lockheed bankruptcy "could severely dampen and perhaps even thwart the business recovery."[12]

Bailout advocates argued that the country's defense could be imperiled. By means of a "domino effect," the deputy secretary of defense told Congress, the collapse of Lockheed could jeopardize the national defense "because many suppliers and subcontractors of the L-1011 commercial program were and are also important suppliers and subcontractors for Lockheed on defense programs. Many of these firms could have serious financial problems if the L-1011 commercial program failed at this time." Moreover, competition in defense contracting could also be seriously damaged, Secretary Connally said. "You can't have a corporate organization of this type go under without seriously and adversely affecting future competition among suppliers to the defense establishment."[13]

Airlines, too, could be sucked into the economic maelstrom. The Treasury Department advised that "among the creditors of Lockheed are three large U.S. airlines [TWA, Eastern, Delta] which have made advance payments of $240 million toward the purchase of L-1011 aircraft. The questionable value of these unsecured claims against Lockheed would obviously hamper efforts of these airlines . . . and this could endanger their competitive position among domestic air carriers." Airline officials suggested that the financial collapse of Lockheed would have serious anticompetitive consequences for the production of commercial jet aircraft in the United States. It would, they said, portend domination of the tri-jet field by a single firm (McDonnell-Douglas), and thus mark "the loss to the Nation of the great competitive manufacturing base which has generated so much progress over the years and such benefits in international trade."[14]

The cost to the Treasury would also be substantial: "Included in this aggregate economic loss, in addition to lost disposable income of workers and the gross product of capital, is a Federal income tax loss estimated to be $65 to $95 million. . . . Additionally, loss recognition by creditors, shareholders and suppliers of Lockheed will result in a short-run Federal revenue loss . . . [aggregating] from $275 to $340 million, depending on the realization rate of creditors and their tax status, in the few years immediately following the bankruptcy of Lockheed. Finally, additional unemployment compensation paid out to displaced workers will amount to $50 to $75 million."[15]

Finally, bailout advocates pointed to a history of federal support for large aerospace producers:

> Presently there is on loan or committed [from the U.S. Export-Import Bank] $600 million outstanding in guaranteed loans and credits to finance foreign purchases of 71 Boeing 747s, and there is $190 million outstanding or committed to finance foreign purchase of 29 McDonnell-Douglas DC-10s. . . . Further, the Douglas Co., prior to its merger with McDonnell obtained in 1967 guaranteed loan authority totaling $75 million through V-loan procedures. It is true that V-loan procedures are intended to aid companies with defense business, but the origin of the Douglas problem was clearly stated as being caused by the commercial portion of Douglas activities—the DC-8 and DC-9 programs at that time.[16]

Bailout proponents contended that the case for government support of Lockheed, as Secretary Connally put it, was not "simply a concern for a particular company or a particular industry. . . . Rather, the primary motivation is a deep concern for the well-being of the American people." In this respect, they were sure that Lockheed was "a very unusual situation which I do not think we will see once in a decade, perhaps once in a lifetime."[17]

Of course, evidence pointing *against* a government bailout surfaced during the course of congressional hearings: given their heavy investments in the firm, banks had a strong incentive to continue to provide credit to keep Lockheed financially solvent; Lockheed possessed profitable properties that could be pledged as collateral for further loans; the employment consequences of a Lockheed financial failure seemed to be significantly exaggerated; Lockheed's defense programs would in all likelihood continue as the firm was financially reorganized under bankruptcy proceedings; and Lockheed had knowingly gambled on Rolls-Royce's ability to supply jet engines at the costs contracted for.[18]

Nevertheless, Congress responded to the powerful pressures exerted on it by the Nixon administration and other influential officials of government, industry, and organized labor. After conducting hearings on the issue, the Senate Committee on Banking observed: "It is possible for large, well-established, and credit-worthy enterprises to experience difficulty in obtaining needed credit. Failure to provide credit to such enterprises could have serious and adverse effects on the nation's economy or on the economy of a region of the nation. The failure of the enterprises could be extremely costly in terms of jobs destroyed, confidence impaired, income lost, and goods not produced." The committee found "a need to avoid serious disruptions of this character" and expressed the belief "that legislation with standby authority and general standards and procedures to deal with these problems is absolutely necessary."[19]

Congress accepted these recommendations and, in August 1971, passed legislation intended to provide Lockheed with up to $250 million in federal loan guarantees. To administer the program, a three-person board was created consisting of the secretary of the treasury, the chairman of the board of governors of the Federal Reserve System, and the chairman of the Securities and Exchange Commission. With this support Lockheed was able to obtain a $750 million financing package from banks and airline customers. It built the L-1011 and C-5A (although as we shall see in chapter 23, the C-5A was plagued by seemingly insuperable problems, including the persistent refusal of its wings to remain firmly attached to the fuselage). And the government's guarantee was voluntarily terminated two months ahead of schedule in October 1977.[20]

CHRYSLER

On 31 July 1979, officials of the Chrysler Corporation announced a loss of $207.1 million in the second quarter of 1979, the largest quarterly loss in the company's history, greater than its loss for the entire previous year. Total losses for 1979 were expected to approach $700 million.

Accompanying the announcement was a statement that Chrysler would request financial assistance from the federal government—a $1 billion cash advance through tax credits against future profits—in addition to its previous requests for relief from federal regulatory requirements. Chrysler officials said the corporation must have direct federal assistance in order to continue operating until it could regain financial health.

At the time, the Chrysler Corporation was the third largest automobile manufacturer in the country, after General Motors and Ford. As of the end of 1978, it ranked tenth among industrial companies in the United States in terms of sales, which amounted to $13.6 billion, and thirteenth in the world.

Chrysler attributed its plight largely to "three key factors over which it had no control." These included: (1) federal regulatory requirements in the areas of pollution control, safety, and fuel economy, which were claimed to put a "small" company like Chrysler at a competitive disadvantage; (2) gasoline shortages, which cut severely into the market for Chrysler's most profitable vehicles—large cars, vans, and light trucks; and (3) economic recession accompanied by a relatively large decline in car and truck sales across the board.

However, at a congressional hearing, the chairman of the corporation admitted that Chrysler's problems to a large degree stemmed from a record of poor management decisions. These included (1) the company's expansion into often doubtful overseas operations in the 1960s, which became a financial drain in the 1970s; (2) the decision to redesign its large cars in the early 1970s and delay the development of smaller cars; and (3) a persistent pattern of delays in production and in the introduction of new models.[21]

On August 9, Treasury Secretary G. William Miller delivered the Carter administration's initial public response to the Chrysler request. He stated that the administration was opposed to tax credits but would consider loan guarantees to Chrysler "in amounts considerably less than the $1 billion suggested by the company." Secretary Miller went on to indicate that the "Administration's willingness to consider aid will depend upon Chrysler's submission of an acceptable overall financial and operating plan." He insisted that this plan "should include substantive contributions or concessions from all those who have an interest in Chrysler's future—management, employees, stockholders, creditors, suppliers, other business associates and governmental units."

On 15 September, Chrysler officials submitted to the Treasury Department a "Proposal for Government Assistance" in the form of $1.2 billion in federal loan guarantees. Then in October, Chrysler announced its largest quarterly loss, $460.6 million, bringing total losses for the year to date to $721.5 million. Chrysler, it seemed, was on the verge of going "belly up."

Congressional hearings were convened, and bailout proponents described the economic catastrophe they foresaw if Chrysler went bankrupt.

Treasury Secretary Miller provided a clinical assessment. "Chrysler is the tenth largest industrial corporation in the United States. Its 1978 revenues were $13.6 billion, generated almost entirely from the sale of 1.2 million cars and 490,000 trucks. Its employment at the beginning of this year was 131,000 and today approximates 113,000. Approximately a quarter of a million others are employed by Chrysler dealers and principal suppliers."[22] He then delineated the economic ramifications of a Chrysler failure.

A "Chrysler bankruptcy could cost the Federal Government more than $1.5 billion in 1980 and 1981 alone. We estimate the Federal cost for those years at a total of at least $2.75 billion, an amount that includes loss of revenues, unemployment claims, welfare costs, and other incidental costs. Furthermore, there would be a substantial cost to the state and local governments. Moreover, this does not take account of any cost to the Pension Benefit Guarantee Corporation on Chrysler's unfunded vested pension liabilities of approximately $1.1 billion, which would ultimately be borne by other pension fund sponsors."

There would be a "serious direct impact on the people that work for Chrysler, its dealers, its suppliers, and for their families. There are now approximately 113,000 Chrysler employees, about an equal number of employees of its dealers, and 150,000 employees of its suppliers. Many would be affected. Conservatively, unemployment would increase by 75,000–100,000 during the 1980–81 period."

There would be a "serious impact on Detroit, the State of Michigan, and other areas in the Midwest region, as well as specific localities around the country—not only where Chrysler has plants, but in places where automotive suppliers and dealers operate."

He cited "the need to maintain a competitive domestic auto industry. Without Chrysler, the two remaining major domestic producers would represent a very narrow competitive base. This would be especially troublesome given current concerns about the strength of the competitive process and the high barriers to entry. Chrysler has exercised an important competitive role in challenging GM, Ford, and others throughout the market, despite its current lack of profitability. Its recent success in the subcompact market is indicative of its competitive importance."

He also pointed to "potential loss of Chrysler's current, and planned, increases in capacity in the small-car market, at a time when the amount of small-car, domestic capacity is critical for trade, environmental and other reasons."

There would, Mr. Miller said, be important "negative effects on the

U.S. balance of payments because Chrysler's production would be displaced by substantial foreign imports. The negative impact could be up to $1 billion per year through 1981 from increased imports, largely of subcompacts but also of other models."[23]

Douglas Fraser, president of the United Auto Workers, whose members were threatened with layoffs and possibly permanent unemployment at a time when the auto industry was languishing, testified: "I am more concerned with the 600,000 workers in the United States threatened with short- and long-term unemployment should Chrysler fail than I am with the hand-wringing of those worried about protecting the 'free enterprise system.'" With government loan guarantees, he said, "Chrysler can meet its short-term capital needs and return to health by producing the kind of small, fuel-efficient, nonpolluting, safe, and attractive cars the American consumer wants to buy. The Chrysler workers met their responsibilities by agreeing to concessions that provide $403 million in improved cash flow for the company. The UAW has made it clear that it is open to providing further help to Chrysler outside the bargaining contract. Now Congress should enact the loan guarantees to ensure equity of sacrifice for those with the most at stake."[24]

Not surprisingly, William G. Milliken, then governor of Michigan, a state suffering from the most virulent recession since the 1930s, supported the bailout. "Chrysler paid $2.4 billion in wages in Michigan in 1978, and paid an additional $2.4 billion to Michigan-based suppliers," he explained. "The initial shock to the Michigan economy of a Chrysler bankruptcy would throw 165,000 individuals out of work either from Chrysler or from suppliers. . . . It would cost the State more than $200 million in revenue annually. At the same time, the two-year period following a bankruptcy would see welfare costs in Michigan [rise] some $460 million, with roughly half paid by the State and half by the Federal Government." He reported that the state had devised a $150 million aid package for the firm, which, together with an additional $61 million in local government tax abatements, would be provided contingent on federal support.[25]

Coleman A. Young, mayor of Detroit, explained that "Chrysler employs approximately 37,000 Detroiters, providing some 7 percent of the City's total employment. In the Metropolitan area, Chrysler employs approximately 74,000 persons. In addition, many of the company's statewide supplier and dealership employees are residents of the City of Detroit. It has been estimated that the loss of these jobs could effectively double Detroit's unemployment rate which, as of September 1979, stands at 10 percent." He pointed out that "Chrysler pays approximately $1.1 billion in wages, salaries, and fringe benefits to its Detroit employees, making it by far the largest private income generator in the City." He stressed the obvious—namely, the "impact of a Chrysler shutdown on the City of Detroit's budget would be severe."[26]

Mayor Young hastened to add that Detroit was not unique:

> In Delaware, the Wilmington-Newark metropolitan area could lose 14,000 jobs and have its unemployment rate doubled. In St. Louis, more than 25,000 jobs could be lost, together with nearly a $2 billion economic loss. Metropolitan Syracuse would have its unemployment rate doubled, as would Huntsville, Alabama. Perhaps hardest hit would be the smaller cities of Kokomo and New Castle, Indiana. In New Castle, one-third of all jobs might be lost. In Kokomo, 40 percent of all jobs would be affected by the direct and secondary effects of a Chrysler shutdown. . . . In Toledo, total income and property tax losses would amount to nearly one million dollars. In Indianapolis, the figure is over one-and-a-half million. For St. Louis, tax losses would be two-and-a-half million. In Kokomo, a much smaller city, nearly two million dollars in Chrysler-related taxes could be lost.[27]

In support of these contentions, the U.S. Conference of Mayors submitted a policy resolution calling upon "the Administration and the Congress to recognize the significance of a Chrysler shutdown for national and regional economies" and to enact "immediately into law federal assistance in the form of loans, loan guarantees, tax credits, or other measures which would restore Chrysler to profitability, and ensure the long-term viability of the enterprise."[28]

Wendell Miller, Dodge dealer and first vice president of the National Automobile Dealers Association, straightforwardly warned Congress "the real story is that 4,700 [Chrysler dealers] in every congressional district in this country will be out of business in a very short period if Chrysler is not given the cash-flow assistance it needs to carry it over the one-year transition period between energy, economic and management problems to a period of viability and profitability."[29]

Benjamin L. Hooks, executive director of the National Association for the Advancement of Colored People, presented an NAACP resolution to Congress highlighting the racial implications of a Chrysler failure. He emphasized that "the disproportionate unemployment rate for Blacks in the United States is compounded by the current recession" and, further, that the "Chrysler Corporation has a higher employment rate of Blacks than the average industrial corporation and a higher number of Black employees in urban areas where the majority of Blacks reside and the unemployment figures of Blacks are excessively high." Therefore, on behalf of the NAACP, he called upon "the executive and legislative branches of government to provide a program of federal financial assistance to the Chrysler Corporation. . . ."[30]

Finally, Senator Donald Riegle reassured his colleagues that the rescue of Chrysler would not represent a departure from past congressional practice—indeed, that the cost of job protection in the Chrysler case would be less onerous than similar support accorded to ailing steel producers: "The fiscal 1978 State-Justice Appropriation Act, for example, authorized . . . up to $550 million in loan guarantees for steel companies. Three objectives were identified. Steel companies would be helped to modernize so that they 'could better face foreign competition,' to 'meet Government mandated environmental standards,' and to retain jobs in the U.S. steel industry. . . . Since early 1978, five firms have received a total of $364 million in loan guarantees under the program." This meant, according to Senator Riegle's calculations, that the administration paid $6,800 in loan guarantees for each job retained in the steel industry. If the government were to spend the same amount per worker to protect jobs in the automobile industry, Riegle said, this would justify a loan guarantee to Chrysler ranging in size from $1.4 to $4.1 billion.[31]

Taking all this into account, Chrysler's charismatic chairman, Lee Iacocca, summarized what he and others saw as the choice confronting the country. "If government wants to do something about unemployment," he said, "if it wants to keep the nation's urban areas and cities alive, if it wants to prevent increased welfare dependency and government spending, if it wants to offset an $8 billion imbalance of automotive trade with Japan, let it approve Chrysler's legitimate and amply precedented request for temporary assistance."[32]

And so, after lengthy hearings and negotiations, Congress passed the Chrysler bailout bill by comfortable margins in both the House and the Senate. The overwhelming lobbying pressure from diverse interest groups—labor and management, state and municipalities, dealers, suppliers, and creditors, Democrats and Republicans—carried the day. The fact that leading economists of different ideological and philosophical persuasions—ranging from Milton Friedman and Alan Greenspan to James Tobin, John K. Galbraith, and Robert Eisner—vigorously opposed the rescue mission obviously made little difference.

Based on estimates submitted by the administration, Congress determined that approximately $4 billion should be made available to meet the corporation's financing needs through December 1983. The total amount of $4 billion was to be made up of three basic components specified by Congress as follows: Up to $1.25 billion would consist of federal loan guarantees, administered by the Chrysler Corporation Loan Guarantee Board; $1.43 billion would be financial commitments and concessions from parties with an economic stake in the health of the corporation (e.g., banks and other creditors, suppliers and dealers, stockholders, labor unions and employees, and state, local, and other governments); and a three-year freeze on wages and benefits of all Chrysler employees, both union and nonunion workers, including management, would yield about $1.32 billion.

As a result of the program, Chrysler was in effect reorganized without going through bankruptcy. The company used $1.2 billion of the $1.5 billion in loan guarantees authorized by Congress, and it was afforded all of the additional concessions required from other parties. On June 15, 1983, Chrysler redeemed $400 million of government-guaranteed notes; the rest were redeemed two months later.[33] Aided by restraints on Japanese imports, the firm thereafter enjoyed record profits in 1984—so much so that, in 1985, it began to play the corporate-acquisition game by offering to purchase the Gulfstream Aerospace Corporation. Thus the government bailout of Chrysler seemed to be a triumph of what Mr. Iacocca has penetratingly described as "democracy in action."[34]

THE POLICY ISSUES

Narrowly construed, the Lockheed and Chrysler bailouts seemed to be "successes." Lockheed's profits in 1984 were $344.1 million, Chrysler's $2.4 billion. Neither loan guarantee resulted in losses to the government; indeed, the government earned a modest profit in both. Yet these and other bailouts leave several public-policy issues unresolved.

To begin with, is a federal loan guarantee an appropriate remedy for the distress of giant companies that have been victimized by managerial incompetence, technological lethargy, or insensitivity to changing market conditions? At Chrysler, for example, a source of continuing concern was the age and inefficiency of a number of its plants. Seven of its forty-four automobile plants and five of its twenty-two plants in the Detroit area were over fifty years old. This problem was further compounded by other management failures dating back at least a decade. According to Alfred Dougherty, chief of the bureau of competition of the Federal Trade Commission, miscalculations included: "Chrysler's chronic production and quality control problems; its failure to modernize its U.S. plants, now among the oldest and least efficient in the industry; its preoccupation with overseas operations, which received disproportionate amounts of investment capital and have now been largely sold off; and the decimation of its engineering staff as a cost-cutting move during the 1974 recession, which has been linked to some of Chrysler's subsequent design and engineering problems."[35] Two design and marketing mistakes cited most frequently were Chrysler's failure to introduce a subcompact in the mid-1970s, thus "defaulting" this entire market to General Motors, Ford, and the imports, and its maintenance of a manufacturer's inventory, or "sales bank"—a practice unique in the industry whereby it manufactured automobiles before any dealer or customer had committed to purchase.

Similar managerial misfeasance and malfeasance were apparent in the Lockheed case, as Treasury Secretary Connally and even the firm's own chairman conceded.[36] For example, Congressman William S. Moorhead pointed out that Lockheed's decision to enter the commercial jet-aircraft market when it was experiencing substantial cost problems with its major military contracts seemed to constitute "gross irresponsibility toward its stockholders."[37] *Business Week* agreed, observing that each new development in the case demonstrated that the firm suffered heavily from "bad judgment."[38]

Situations like these, long in the making and resistant to short-run palliatives, raise the question whether a one-shot infusion of government-guaranteed loans is sufficient to ensure the long-run viability and survival of giant companies bedeviled by poor performance.

If corporate behemoths can confidently expect government bailouts from the adverse consequences of their own ineptitude, what are the effects on the incentive structure of a free-enterprise economy that is supposed to reward successful firms with profits and punish poor performers with losses? To what extent can the operation of the profit-and-loss mechanism be compromised without subverting the motivational essence of a free-enterprise economy?

In a free-enterprise economy, it is inevitable that some firms, large and small, will experience financial difficulties—a normal consequence of a dynamic market economy. It is inevitable that some firms will be less expertly managed than others; that some will seriously miscalculate costs or product demands; that some—due to shifting economic circumstances—will find themselves in uneconomic locations; that, given the limited supply of loanable funds, some will be unable to obtain those funds when they need them. In other words, some firms will simply fail the market test in the competition for capital.

It seems obvious, as Professor Donald F. Turner observed during the Lockheed hearings, that protection of corporations from such risks cannot be achieved "without eradication of a competitive, free enterprise economy, and without incurring a high economic cost of inefficiency and serious misallocation of our productive resources. If the threat of bankruptcy were removed or substantially moderated, by what process would scarce capital funds be allocated among competing demands, by what process would efficiency, both in allocation of resources and among individual firms, be maintained?"[39] Unless corporate managements are held to account for their policies—unless they are forced to expect to pay for their mistakes—how can the discipline of the competitive market yield the efficient and progressive performance that society demands? Once the penalty of failure is removed, what incentives remain to survive in the competitive struggle purely on the basis of merit and without the prospect of artificial resuscitation when the need for it may arise? The option of falling back on the government as a guarantor of last resort must almost inevitably remove this spur to efficiency and productivity—especially in large, bureaucratic, somnolent corporations.

We must also ask if the insolvency of a major corporation necessarily means the total shutdown of a viable enterprise, with attendant losses to employees, to suppliers, to customers, and to the economy of a region or the economy as a whole. Is a government bailout the *only* remedy for the situation or are alternative (perhaps preferable) solutions available, such as bankruptcy proceedings?

Insolvency—in the accounting sense—does not mean that the physical and human assets of an ailing corporation are condemned to disappearance. If the corporation is economically viable, the private capital market can be expected to find the means of keeping it afloat—on the condition that the corporation agrees to certain (perhaps painful) terms and conditions. What is at stake is not the shutdown of the enterprise, but rather the resolution of who shall own and manage it and under what constraints. And that, as Dean Phil C. Neal of the University of Chicago noted in the Lockheed hearings, is the function of the reorganization provisions of the Bankruptcy Act. These are specifically designed to avert the liquidation of an enterprise that is economically useful—that is, an enterprise that has reasonable prospects of being operated profitably. They allow for "the necessary alterations in the existing interests of stockholders and creditors, even to the point of finding, if necessary, that the existing stockholders have no equity and the existing creditors cannot be paid in full." In other words, under provisions of the Bankruptcy Act, the ailing but economically viable corporation may be subjected to drastic reorganization; its deficient management may be ousted and replaced by a court-appointed trustee or a team designated by senior creditors; its owners may suffer losses in the form of reductions in the value of their equity. But the corporation as a going concern would not disappear. It would be reorganized in order to enhance its prospects for long-run survival.

Clearly, proceedings under the Bankruptcy Act would entail compre-

hensive changes in a corporation's structure, personnel, and policies—
all designed to avert in the future the mistakes of the past. By contrast,
government subsidy in the form of a loan guarantee tends simply to
preserve the status quo by preserving and protecting existing vested
interests. It thus creates a windfall benefit that relieves present management, stockholders, and creditors of the consequences of risks they have
taken and ought to sustain. In short, a government bailout may be
counterproductive; it may fail to stimulate the fundamental changes in
a corporation necessary to prevent a temporary malaise from turning
into a chronic disease.

If the government grants special loan guarantees to one ailing corporation, by what criteria can it deny the same privilege to other corporations in similar distress? For example, should one firm with ten thousand
employees be given special aid, while ten firms with a thousand employees each are denied aid? Should a firm whose ten thousand employees constitute 30 percent of the total labor force in a particular
region be accorded aid, while another firm whose ten thousand employees are only 5 percent of the labor force in its region is left to its
fate? In short, are corporate size and regional impact to be the primary
determinants in a modern version of governmental triage?

During the Chrysler debate, former Secretary of Transportation
Brock Adams put the issue squarely. Observing that Chrysler's problems were not unique but generic, and that other large corporations are
afflicted by aging plants, technological lethargy, and shrinking markets,
Adams urged Congress to start asking the hard questions: "Does the
government save all industries that are big and sick? If not, what determines salvation—number of employees, kinds of products and service,
effect on the total gross national product? Do we have appropriate measures of national interest? Unless we begin to face these unhappy questions now, the Congress will limp from bailout to bailout without any real
understanding of where we are going or why."[40] These questions become particularly relevant if Congress creates a loan guarantee mechanism that is generally available rather than targeted to particular
corporations on an ad hoc basis.

Are bailouts of bigness, as proponents have often suggested, a preferred policy instrument for providing jobs and employment? Asked
what performance would be demanded of Lockheed in return for government support, for example, Secretary Connally replied: "What do we
care whether they perform? We are guaranteeing them basically a $250
million loan. What for? Basically so they can hopefully minimize their
losses, so they can provide employment for 31,000 people throughout the
country at a time when we desperately need that type of employment.

That is basically the rationale and justification." But as Senator Adlai E. Stevenson pointed out, "the $250 million in government credit extended to Lockheed would go a long way toward creating or preserving jobs . . . by building mass transit facilities as opposed to other airplanes, or schools or hospitals."[41]

Furthermore, do big-firm bailouts undermine competition in another, more subtle way by, as Turner has pointed out, encouraging lenders to extend credit to those corporations that are large and influential enough to be likely to obtain government assistance if they flounder?[42] Are not the competitive hurdles already confronted by small businesses thereby further raised?

Finally, does government rescue of corporate giants because of their size, impact, and influence constitute an objectionable, and perhaps eventually, intolerable unfairness? Senator McIntyre pointed up the essence of this problem during the Lockheed hearings. "There are many small companies in my own State of New Hampshire which are in a desperate state of finance," he said.

> These companies have asked the Government for help and have not received it. There are many other companies that are in difficulty with inadequate financing. When these companies come to their own Government in Washington they are told time after time that this is the way the system of capitalism works, this is the way that capitalism penalizes those whose management has been inefficient, whose costs are high, whose products can no longer command adequate markets. . . . All of these companies are small and relatively poor, but we apply the test of capitalism and free enterprise to them. Now we have Lockheed, a large company, with platoons of representatives in Washington, backed by the biggest banks in the world. Our Government, it seems to me, is not applying the rules of capitalism to Lockheed. We seem to be setting up a double standard which provides socialism for the rich and powerful.[43]

Nor does it suffice to say that managements of tottering giants have suffered unforeseen circumstances and events beyond their control; after all, how many of the tens of thousands of firms that fail annually do so deliberately? Apart from economic desirability, then, the question arises whether it is fair to reserve the painful principles of free enterprise exclusively for the small.

In the final analysis, the bailout issue dramatizes the dilemma of corporate bigness in a free-enterprise democracy. It casts the political economy of power in bold relief. For once a corporation has attained the size of a Lockheed, a Chrysler, or a Continental Illinois, its fortunes reverberate throughout the economy. The possible demise of such a firm is no longer a private failure; it is a social disaster. Once society permits itself to become dependent on the success of such corporate giants, it becomes the captive of its chosen instruments. Then government is in the position of the bank so deeply committed to a borrower that it cannot permit the client to default for fear of jeopardizing the solvency of the bank itself.

Obviously, as we have seen, the political economy of bigness radically —albeit subtly—transforms the nature of the economic system and shatters the delusion that economic affairs are hermetically sealed off from decisions in the political realm. It obviously repudiates simplistic Darwinian admonitions that only efficient firms survive, that megamergers and bigness are at worst benign, and the corollary that an antitrust policy is neither necessary nor desirable. So, too, does it create a further dilemma—how to insulate government from the political pressures that corporate giants and their trade unions, their private and public dependents, are bound to mobilize in their hour of need and putative collapse, *and* how to do so in a way that preserves representative democracy. Finally, and ironically, the bailout of bigness suggests the possibility that the engineers of modern socialism may be big industrialists and big banks, not bearded revolutionaries—Darwinian ideologues and "friends" of free enterprise, not devotees of Marx and Lenin. Viewed from this perspective, the political economy of power seems to transcend superficial labels of "conservative" and "liberal," "right" and "left," and to render them obsolete.

Lockheed and Chrysler may have returned to financial health, but in the light of these issues their recovery is hard to cheer as a social "success." Periodic government bailouts of corporate giants remains an embarrassing perversion of private-enterprise principles.

VI

THE COALESCENCE
OF POWER

The competitive market, as we have repeatedly emphasized, controls power through a pervasive system of checks and balances. The presence of many firms—sellers competing against sellers, buyers competing against buyers—restrains the ability of any one firm (or a small group of firms) to dominate the decision-making process. Under a regime of competition, economists are wont to say, the individual firm is a price-taker, not a price-maker.

But some economists—notably John Kenneth Galbraith—have argued that concentration of power among sellers (or among buyers) is not the social evil that advocates of competition suppose it to be. Galbraith, for example, contends that the real restraints on a seller's market power are vested not in its competitors but in its customers. They are imposed, not from the same side, but from the opposite side of the market. In this view, "private economic power is held in check by the countervailing power of those who are subject to it." Power blocs among sellers beget power blocs among buyers, and vice versa. The power of sellers to exploit buyers, or buyers to exploit sellers, is neutralized. The operation of countervailing power, it is claimed, provides society with a more effective system of checks and balances than classical competition. It obviates the erstwhile concern about excessive concentrations of economic power.

In this section, we shall examine the validity of the countervailing-power thesis. We shall observe that the confrontation of Big Business and Big Labor, both in the regulated industries and in the private sector, results more often than not in the coalescence of power rather than in countervailance of power. We shall observe that, in the weapons-acquisition process, the confrontation of a monopolistic buyer (the Pentagon) and oligopolistic sellers (the defense industry), there is a similar tendency toward a coalescence of power—what President Dwight D. Eisenhower called the "military-industrial complex." We shall find that great power blocs on opposite sides of the market tend to join together, through overt or tacit collusion, and that the public is the ultimate victim. In short, the proliferation of great power blocs and their symbiotic coalescence creates "states within a state," largely immune from social control either by the market or public authority. As we shall see in the final section, it exacerbates the problem of dealing with concentrated power in a free society.

CHAPTER 23

THE LABOR-INDUSTRIAL COMPLEX

The temptation to hold on to jobs that are being competitively bid away is politically very strong. Often, what protection involves is a subsidy by the median American workers who earn $10 an hour or less compared to the aristocrats of the labor market who under collective bargaining earn over $20 in the auto and steel industries. That is not good microeconomics, or macroeconomics, or defensible social philosophy.
— Professor Paul A. Samuelson,
Nobel Laureate, 1983

In his classic book *American Capitalism*, John Kenneth Gailbraith argued that countervailing power, not classical competition, was the instrument for keeping concentrated power in check. The real restraints on a firm's market power are imposed from the opposite side of the market, by its customers and suppliers. Thus, "private economic power is held in check by the countervailing power of those who are subject to it. The first begets the second." A monopoly offers an inducement to both suppliers and customers to develop the power with which they can defend themselves against exploitation. Thesis gives rise to antithesis, and there emerges a system of checks and balances that makes the economy as a whole workable, a modus operandi that lends stability to American capitalism. Most importantly, this system of checks and balances relieves the government of its obligation to launch any frontal attack on concentrated economic power. No longer need the government be concerned about the decline of competition or the sparsity of sellers in a particular market. Countervailing power will eliminate the danger of any long-run exploitation by a private economic power bloc.

Put differently, countervailing power operates primarily through the creation of bilateral monopoly or oligopoly situations. A monopoly on one side of the market finds its power neutralized by the appearance of a monopoly on the other side of the market. Thus a system of checks and balances is built on the foundation of bilateral power concentrations.

Galbraith cites the labor market as an area where the operation of countervailing power can be observed with the greatest clarity, for it is in the labor market that giant unions bargain on a national, industry-wide scale against groups of employers acting jointly either through a trade association or an ad hoc bargaining committee. Galbraith sees countervailing power at work in highly concentrated industries like the steel, rubber, and automobile-manufacturing industries and points out "Not only has the strength of the corporations in these industries made it necessary for workers to develop the protection of countervailing power, it has provided unions with the opportunity for getting something more as well. If successful they could share in the fruits of the corporation's market power." Thus Galbraith justifies bilateral monopoly in the labor market because it prevents unilateral exploitation, while simultaneously allowing one monopolist to share in whatever exorbitant gains may accrue to the other.[1]

But bilateral monopoly in the labor market has further consequences. According to pure economic theory, this type of market structure is characterized by what Heinrich von Stackelberg aptly called *Gleich-gewichtslosigkeit*—an incapacity to achieve a stable equilibrium. The inherent and irreconcilable conflict between the bilateral monopolists can be rationally resolved (in the best interests of both parties) only if they agree to enter into a vertical combination or conspiracy. Such coalescence, of course, represents a compromise—a case of mutual for-bearance—in order to jointly maximize profits. And, says Stackelberg, profits will be maximized for the bilateral monopolists if, for example, in labor-management confrontations, the employer enjoys a monopoly in the sale of his products.[2] In other words, market control or market dominance in the product market serves not only the best interests of management but also the best interests of labor. Hence a bilateral monopoly naturally militates toward coalescence of power between management and labor, not antagonism or countervailance of power.

Understandably, this insight (which is neither profound nor esoteric) was used by the exponents of industrial cartels as a prime argument to persuade workers that cartels were in labor's best interests. Robert Liefmann, for example, pointed out that cartels were in a better position than competitive firms to grant wage increases, because they could pass the resulting cost increases on to consumers in the form of higher prices:

> Where the firms are in a cartel, they are more inclined to concede the workers higher wages than in a state of free competition, because they find it easier to pass the increased costs on to their customers by charging higher prices. The workers will therefore, generally speaking, find it easier to impose higher wages upon organized firms, and it is in their power, at least if they can form strong trade unions, to demand wages increasing with the cartel's prices, i.e., a "sliding wage-scale."[3]

Thus, said Liefmann, market dominance and market control were in the best interests of labor as well as management, because the greater the market control, the more ample the fruits to be shared through a system of vertical cooperation.

The consequence of such cooperation from the viewpoint of the public interest is, of course, another matter. In a prescient article written in 1890, Alfred Marshall observed that traditionally the public was protected by labor-management antagonism. Employers and employed

> have seldom worked together systematically to sacrifice the interests of the public to their own, by lessening the supply of their services or goods, and thus raising their price artificially. But there are signs of a desire to arrange firm compacts between combinations of employers on the one side and of employees on the other to restrict production. Such compacts may become a grievous danger to the public in those trades in which there is little effective competition from foreign producers; a danger so great that if these compacts cannot be bent by public opinion they may have to be broken up by public force.[4]

In short, the absence of effective competition in product markets, when combined with vertical collusion between management and labor—whether tacit or overt—poses a central problem for public policy. Put differently, countervailing power is not a suitable substitute for antitrust policy, because countervailing power tends to be subverted by coalescing power and thus makes the problem of controlling market power more intractable than ever.

The virulence with which management and labor in recent years have fought for protectionism in the public as well as private sector affords a striking illustration of tacit vertical collusion and coalescing power in action. It also reflects the common perception by both management and labor that immunity from competition confers private benefits on both groups, and that, therefore, government protection from competition is in their rational—albeit, short-run—mutual self-interest. In the longer run, as we shall indicate, the exercise of coalescing power constitutes a tacit mutual suicide pact between management and labor. It tends to exacerbate delinquent industrial performance and to undermine the implementation of an effective macro-stabilization policy.

In this chapter, we shall review the operation of coalescing power (and some of its effects) in four major industries—two in the regulated sector, and two in the private sector of the American economy. We shall then sketch some implications for both micro- and macroeconomic policy that, we submit, run counter to the newly emerging, currently fashionable precepts of "neoliberalism" and the advocates of "industrial policy."

THE REGULATED SECTOR

In the regulated sector of the economy, the operation of coalescing power is dramatically illustrated by management's and labor's battle— side by side and in a variety of forums—against the deregulation of the airline and trucking industries. The arguments advanced by both management and labor against deregulation were so uncannily parallel— between each other, and between industries—as to border on what might be called "echolalia monopolistica."

In the case of both airline and trucking, the labor-industrial coalitions maintained that deregulation would have the following deleterious results:

1. Service to smaller communities would deteriorate or disappear altogether.
2. Competition would be wasteful and inefficient.
3. Deregulation would usher in a state of abject chaos.
4. Deregulation would stimulate predatory conduct and eventually result in excessive industry concentration.
5. Deregulation would cripple the affected industry's ability to obtain capital.
6. Deregulation would undermine the position of organized labor.
7. Deregulation would produce negative side effects on related industries.
8. Deregulation would pose a serious threat to public safety.

To get the flavor of the cooperation between management and labor in their fight for government protection from competition, consider the following (typical) extracts from the deregulation debate.[5]

AIRLINES

A major argument made by airline management and labor against deregulation was that increased competition would cause severe deterioration of air service to small and medium communities across the country. They argued that with free entry and exit, airlines would concentrate on the most densely traveled (and most lucrative) routes between major metropolitan areas. Competition in these corridors, in turn, would eliminate the excess profits required to subsidize service to smaller communities. Thus, they argued, hundreds of communities would suffer from a reduction in (or complete elimination of) air service, along with an increase in fares, thereby creating bleak prospects for further economic growth and development, given the importance of air service in modern society.

As uncontrolled, profit-maximizing carriers focused upon the most lucrative, highest-density markets, Continental Airlines argued, their "marginal markets, namely shorter-haul and lower-density markets . . . are bound to suffer." "In this trial by fire," a United spokesman added, "the small cities and marginal segments will be burned." Nor would the victims of the portended maelstrom be limited to the smallest communities: "Any legislation that allows the more lucrative branches from the airline tree to be snipped off," Mr. Borman argued on behalf of Eastern Airlines, "is going to result in a severe impact on Nashville and Raleigh/Durham and in medium-sized cities in this country." Speaking for all major airline carriers, the Air Transport Association (ATA) concluded that only a handful of major cities would continue to be served adequately. "Accordingly, the real choice to be made," the ATA warned, "is between either a continuation of the extensive air network we have today, with constantly improving service to all segments of the public, or a concentration of operations in the high-density air markets, with an accompanying reduction of services to the smaller, less productive markets."

Organized labor was in complete agreement with the position taken by airline management. The Airline Pilots Association argued, "It doesn't take much imagination to visualize what profit-oriented airline managements would do in a liberalized entry environment. The opportunity to get into the more lucrative, high-population markets would be too much for most airline marketing executives to resist. . . . The unfortunate consequence of this development would be . . . a reduction or loss of service now enjoyed by the smaller cities of America whose traffic-generating potential is limited. . . ." The Airline Clerks concurred: "It is obvious that airlines will have to concentrate on the major population centers in order to survive. If they direct their resources to these population centers, smaller communities which are not profitable will eventually be dropped or at the least, service to those cities will be greatly curtailed." Similarly, the executive council of the AFL-CIO concluded that deregulation would "threaten air service to many cities."

Ultimately, the ATA argued, the deregulation of air service would discourage economic development of small- and medium-sized communities while limiting the access of residents in these areas to the world. The Airline Pilots agreed: "A city in today's world without adequate air service is in the same dire shape as one without rail service 50 years ago. It is isolated and dying."

TRUCKING

As in airlines, another major argument against deregulation advanced by both trucking management and labor was the contention that competition would be wasteful and inefficient. In this, management and labor agreed with each other as well as with their colleagues in the airline industry. The argument comprised two elements. Free entry, it was alleged, would merely lead to wasteful excess capacity and fuel consumption as more carriers competed to haul a fixed volume of traffic. Concentration of entry in the most lucrative routes would destroy the efficiencies of balanced freight hauling, which management and labor claimed to have been engineered into the industry by the Interstate Commerce Commission (ICC). Ironically, they concluded, competition would impair—not promote—economic efficiency.

"Unlike potential volumes of passenger traffic," the American Trucking Association (ATA) opined,

> freight traffic is a pie of relatively fixed dimensions. Its size is controlled by the general level of the economy and not by the number of people willing to carry freight. The market for transportation is a derived demand. Carriers do not create freight. They can only carry what the economy produces. . . . The elimination of entry controls and the ensuing entry into the industry of thousands of new truck operations, the need for which had not been established through application of the test of "public convenience and necessity," would create excess capacity. The inevitable result would be a marked increase in empty truck mileage.

Moreover, Mr. Herold, speaking for the Middle Atlantic rate conference, stated: "If entry was free to anyone . . . then the full-service carriers who are trying to provide a full transportation service to all points in the country are going to have less traffic to handle and they are going to have higher costs and, therefore, higher rates." The outcome, according to the testimony of carrier representatives, would be "wasted mileage coming from too many trucks chasing a limited amount of traffic," presenting "the real danger of excess capacity with resulting inefficiencies, particularly in fuel usage."

Organized labor's position on this point was, at times, virtually indistinguishable from that of management. "The volume of traffic to be moved by motor carriers is relatively stable," a Teamster spokesman claimed, "and, even if the rates were lowered, the volume would not increase appreciably." "Because everybody and his brother is going to buy a truck," another Teamster testified, "there will be more trucks running empty than Carter has pills." The adverse effect of free entry upon the alleged balance of freight movement accomplished under regulation—an effect cited by management—was also emphasized by Teamster President Frank Fitzsimmons: "Permitting the nonregulated carriers who do not have the obligation to serve all shippers and all communities, large or small, to take selected backhauls of commodities would disrupt the balanced movements that the regulated carriers have laboriously achieved, thereby making the for-hire carrier service less efficient and more costly to the general public." "And in an energy-starved nation," another labor spokesman claimed, "deregulation would put thousands more trucks, all burning critically short fuel, out on the road chasing the same amount of freight and greatly increasing the empty truck miles. With the problems this Nation is going to have in meeting our basic needs with increasingly short energy supplies, the logic of that totally escapes me." Thus organized labor agreed with management that "empty mileage would increase, equipment would be underutilized and our scarce supplies of fuel would be wasted."[6]

THE PRIVATE SECTOR

In the private sector, the operation of coalescing power is illustrated by the joint battle waged by management and labor to obtain government protection from import competition. In the case of both automobiles and steel, the coalition attempted to justify its demands by arguing that (1) there exists a symbiotic government-business relationship in exporting countries; (2) world exports are being diverted to an unprotected U.S. market; (3) the domestic industry needs "breathing space" to make adjustments that will enable it to stand on its own feet in international competition; and (4) the cost of protection is less than the cost of inaction.

Consider the following typical excerpts from the debate over import restraints.[7]

AUTOMOBILES

A prime justification advanced by management and labor to support their demands for restriction of Japanese automobile competition was that rampant protectionism in the world's major markets diverted Japanese exports to an unprotected United States market and thus focused the full brunt of Japanese expansionism on American companies and their workers. Import restriction, they agreed, was a necessary offset and belated defense to an ostensibly ubiquitous protectionism abroad.

In its petition for protection before the International Trade Commission, the Ford Motor Company contended that "the size of the U.S. market, the unusually low U.S. auto tariffs, and high import barriers in Europe and elsewhere made it clear that the United States would be the primary target for a surge of Japanese exports." The following month, a Ford spokesman, commenting on the necessity of import restrictions on Japanese products, exclaimed: "Everyone else has done it." "The other countries of the world have already set up barriers against more Japanese products," Chrysler added. "There is no place those products can go but in here."

Here, too, the union was in complete agreement with management. Appearing before the House Subcommittee on Trade, UAW President Douglas Fraser charged, "Practically every country exercises import restraint on autos in one form or another—through high tariffs, outright quotas, orderly marketing arrangements, 'gentlemen's agreements,' and various forms of nontariff barriers. . . . As the biggest, most open market in the world," he insisted, "the U.S. auto market has been targeted by the Japanese for the lion's share of its exports." In contrast to U.S. policy, explained Mr. Fraser, "when Japanese autos have threatened to take a significant segment of the market in various European countries, they have been frozen at levels by gentlemen's agreements." According to the union, "Other countries have dealt with similar trade problems in a more sophisticated manner," while the United States receives "the leftovers from other countries' plans." "Given the auto policies of the rest of the world and the present disarray of the industry in North America," the union agreed with management, "immediate measures to redress the balance are required," and it, too, warned that "the U.S. can no longer afford to be the lone sitting duck in this situation."

STEEL

Another major argument propounded by the management-labor complex in steel (and in autos) was that foreign competition deterred sorely needed domestic investment. Only with suitable protection by the government, steel companies and the steelworkers warned, would moderni-

zation of the U.S. steel industry proceed. Repeatedly, the argument
paralleled that of the auto industry.

Testifying before the House Ways and Means Committee in 1973, the
American Iron and Steel Institute (AISI) declared that an "adequate
guarantee against both continuing and spasmodic disruptive increases
in imports stimulated by the domestic policies of other countries is essential to the health of both the economy and the industry" and warned
committee members that the "threat of such increases is a serious deterrent to expansion of capacity in this country in view of the large sums
of capital and the long planning and construction time involved."

When next it resurfaced, the argument underscored the importance
of "breathing space." "During the long lead time, 5 to 8 years, individual
steel companies will need to plan and carry out the needed modernization
of their plants and equipment," AISI President Robert Peabody contended before the House Subcommittee on Trade, "the Government
must take action to assure that imports do not continue to disrupt our
domestic markets through either quantity or price. . . . Only with assurances of this type," he warned, "will our competitive market system
commit sufficient capital to steel on the scale required to maintain a
modern industry in this country."

Union officials, again, dutifully reiterated and reemphasized management's arguments in a succession of public forums. In 1970, the union
called for an extension of voluntary restraint agreements "or for legislative protection to accomplish one of the stated purposes for the restraint,
namely, to provide a lead period for the industry to modernize." Mr.
I. W. Abel, president of the union, reiterated the argument in his testimony before the Senate Finance Committee in 1973: "You do not build
a steel mill for $1 million. It now runs $500 million to build a modern
integrated steel mill. This is just an awful lot of capital to raise and to
invest and, when there is the danger of foreign competition taking all of
the business from you, it is hard to raise that kind of money." Union
spokesmen insisted, as had management, that import protection was
essential if modernization was to occur. "We need immediate relief,"
USW President Lloyd McBride urged in 1977, "so that the industry can
undertake the task of modernization without having its domestic markets stolen during the process." Citing the "desperate need to modernize
some of the older mills, particularly in older steel communities," a 1977
union policy statement argued that "imports have not only cost us jobs,
they have caused so much idle capacity in our mills, in most of the last
15 years, that our industry has had no incentive to modernize and expand, and many companies have lacked the capital to modernize."

Finally, in 1980, in testimony before the International Trade Commission, management and union agreed that "disruptive" steel imports have a deleterious effect on "the rate of modernization, the addition of new capacity, and the ability of our industry to generate necessary investment capital," and that such imports constitute "a significant discouragement to capital investment."

SOME EFFECTS OF COALESCING POWER

The battle for government protection from competition, waged jointly by management and labor, reflected a rational recognition of mutual (short-run) self-interest by the coalition partners. Both understood that monopolistic or cartelized product markets yielded special benefits not obtainable under competitive conditions.

AIRLINES

In the airline industry, as we noted in chapter 17, Civil Aeronautics Board (CAB) regulation protected management from competitive entry and price competition. But organized labor also found remunerative security under the protective umbrella of CAB regulation. Regulation permitted the carriers not only to charge exorbitant fares but to accede to persistent wage escalation for various categories of airline employees represented by the Airline Pilots Association, the Transport Workers Union, and the International Association of Machinists. In 1963, airline employees as a group received an average salary of $7,781—1.7 times more than the $4,625 average earned by all workers in the economy; by 1976, the average salary for airline employees had risen to $21,500, or more than double the level of workers generally. The rate of increase over the 1963 to 1976 period ranged from 168 to 217 percent for airline workers in contrast to 117 percent for workers generally.[8]

Clearly, collective bargaining in a government-regulated industry, protected from "unbridled" competition, yielded succulent fruits for labor, as well as for management.

TRUCKING

In trucking, the same pattern is observable. As we found in chapter 18, ICC regulation gave management protection against competitive entry and competitive price cutting. Predictably, organized labor also benefitted from the operation of this government-created and government-protected cartel. Aside from the benefits derived by drivers from the additional mileage covered as a result of "deadhead" hauls and circuitous routes, regulation-unionization seems to have resulted in significant wage increases in the industry. Thus, according to one study, compensation paid to drivers was more than 30 percent higher than that of their unregulated counterparts.[9] According to another study (1973), the typical owner-operator (unregulated and not represented by a union) would earn about $11,125 for a 250-day work year, while the average compensation received by the unionized driver for a regulated Class I intercity hauler of general freight was $17,249. After surveying these and other studies, Thomas Gale Moore concluded that "a conservative estimate of the impact regulation-unionization has on wages of truckers, helpers, and platform workers would therefore be about 50 percent. Some of the evidence suggests the gain could be as large as 55 percent; the most conservative estimate is 37 percent. This implies that the gains to Teamster members would have been between $1 billion and $1.3 billion in 1972."

When the "rents" received by the owners of ICC certificates and permits ($1.5 to $2 billion in 1972) are added to the above figures, it becomes obvious that the stake that management and labor had in continued regulation of trucking was substantial. It meant excess revenues for the industry of about $3.4 billion in 1972, of which, according to Moore, between 74 and 97 percent constituted monopoly "rents" accruing to capital and labor.[10]

AUTOMOBILES

Since the end of World War II, automobile prices have followed a typical oligopoly pattern—their outstanding characteristics being uniformity between producers at any particular point in time and steady escalation upward over time. Thus the average retail price of new domestically produced automobiles increased from $3,310 in 1967 to $11,059 by 1984, or 234 percent. And the domestic oligopoly has raised new car prices regardless of demand shifts, sales levels, or macroeconomic conditions.[11]

Organized labor's compensation policy during this period was strikingly parallel to management's pricing policy. Between 1967 and 1980, hourly compensation in the motor vehicle industry increased 214 percent compared to a 179 percent increase in manufacturing as a whole; output per worker increased 39 percent compared to 35 percent in manufacturing; unit labor costs increased 127 percent compared to 107 percent in manufacturing.[12]

Charles L. Schultze, a former chairman of the President's Council of Economic Advisers, summarized the implications of this wage escalation record:

In the mid-1960s hourly costs (wages and fringe benefits) in the major auto companies were about 20 percent above average for manufacturing industries. Every three years since, the labor contract negotiated between industry and the union has widened the gap. By 1978 wages and fringes at the major auto companies had risen to almost 50 percent above the all-manufacturing average. Those extra costs were passed on in higher prices.

Finally, in 1979—faced with mounting interest rates, an incipient recession, sharply higher gasoline prices, growing resistance to large American cars and increased imports from Japan—what did the industry do? It negotiated a contract that by 1980 put auto wages and fringes about 60 percent above the manufacturing average.[13]

Obviously the exercise of coalescing power brought consistent short-run gains to both management and labor. But, as one might have predicted, these gains were tenable in the long run only so long as effective competition could be restrained successfully in the final product market. Hence, as Schultze ruefully observed in 1981, "the UAW and the auto industry, calling attention to what is undoubtedly a serious problem of import penetration, are urging the government to validate these gains, and to make possible the price increases necessary to pay for them, with import protection."[14]

In short, price-wage escalation, effectuated through the exercise of coalescing power, was possible only if markets could be artificially shielded from the impact of competition.

STEEL

In steel, the story is much the same. As we have already seen, restraints on import competition—in the form of mandatory quotas, voluntary quotas, and the Trigger Price Mechanism—have enabled U.S. producers to raise prices with virtual impunity. Organized labor, of course, also derived short-run gains from this protectionism. Between 1964 and 1980, hourly compensation in iron and steel increased by 282 percent compared to 212 percent in manufacturing as a whole; output per hour increased 19 percent and 40 percent, respectively; and unit labor cost increased 221 percent and 123 percent, respectively.[15]

As in the case of the automobile industry, the gap between hourly employment costs in the steel industry and manufacturing as a whole widened; according to Charles Schultze, the cost differential rose from 25 percent in the mid-1960s to 60 percent in 1980. This record, when superimposed on constantly escalating prices, meant declining competitiveness for the steel industry and militated toward protectionist governmental restraints on foreign competition—a bailout from the self-inflicted injury wrought by the exercise of coalescing power.

SOME PUBLIC-POLICY IMPLICATIONS

The case studies we have examined in this chapter illustrate the efforts of labor-management coalitions to secure governmental restraints on competition. The coalition partners advocated positions that were uncannily parallel and substantively indistinguishable. They advanced and endlessly reiterated arguments that were couched in virtually identical rhetoric.

Unless these case studies are egregiously unrepresentative of American industrial structure, some general conclusions and public-policy implications are appropriate:

1. In industries where producers possess monopoly, oligopoly, or cartel power in the product market, and where powerful trade unions dominate the relevant labor markets, there is an almost irresistible tendency toward tacit (if not overt) vertical collusion. Countervailing power—ostensibly a structural safeguard of the public interest—is transmuted into coalescing power, a ready instrument for subverting the public interest.[16]
2. Tacit vertical collusion and coalescing power are sustainable only where product markets are immune from effective competition. Hence a paramount objective of the labor-industrial complex is to obtain or preserve governmental protection from competition in the form of entry controls, minimum rate regulation, immunity from the antitrust laws, import restraints, etc.
3. The exercise of tacit vertical collusion and coalescing power has both microeconomic and macroeconomic consequences. On the microeconomic level, it militates toward noncompetitive structure in the affected industries that in turn leads to noncompetitive conduct that ultimately produces deficient industrial performance.
4. On the macroeconomic level, the most serious consequence of tacit vertical collusion is a seemingly uncontrollable process of cumulative price-wage-price escalation—an engine of cost-push inflation that undermines the effectiveness of macrostabilization policies. As Professor Henry C. Simons of the University of Chicago recognized over three decades ago, the efficacy of such macroeconomic tools as monetary and fiscal policy vitally hinges upon an economy's underlying

microeconomic market structure. "No amount of monetary or fiscal stimulation," he wrote,

will give us adequate employment or investment, if strategically situated unions and enterpriser monopolists insist upon utilizing improved demand conditions to increase their wages and prices rather than to increase employment, investment, and output—or to hold up prices where improved technology is markedly reducing costs. And there is no reason why organized producer groups, holding adequate organizational and political power, should, acting in their separate interest, forego the opportunity to improve their relative position in such circumstances. They may, to be sure, injure themselves along with the community, all or most of them being worse off by virtue of their restrictive measures than if none had practiced them. But each group may be better off than if it alone had behaved less monopolistically; and short of dictatorship at one extreme and real competition at the other, there would appear to be no means for getting coordinated or cooperative action from such groups as a whole.[17]

Simons concluded that "the inherent conflict of interest between each producer group and the community . . . must be reconciled or avoided, either by the discipline of effective intragroup competition or by the dictation of absolute authority from above."[18]

The only viable policy option, it would seem, lies in vigorous enforcement of the nation's antitrust statutes to obtain and maintain structurally competitive markets—for the sake of industry-specific performance, for macroeconomic stability, and perhaps not insignificantly, for freedom from dictation of absolute authority from above.

CHAPTER 24

THE MILITARY-INDUSTRIAL COMPLEX

The Congress must constantly bear in mind the growing autonomy of the federal bureaucracy, the increasing lack of control by the Congress, and the bureaucratic tendency to make accommodations with industrial corporations.

If a close partnership between government and industry is actually necessary, then a great responsibility rests on the Congress and on the executive branch to see to it that these giant organizations do not become, in effect, a fourth branch of government—a fourth branch, but with men exerting power without political or legal responsibility. — Admiral Hyman Rickover

By the early 1960s, the military's need to quickly transport troops and equipment outstripped the capacity of existing aircraft. So the air force launched a program to procure a giant new jet transport. Lockheed—then the nation's largest defense contractor—was ultimately selected to produce the C-5A, and a contract was completed in late 1965. Lockheed would supply 120 planes for $3.4 billion.[1]

Within four months, the C-5A program began to exhibit signs of cost overruns. By midsummer of 1966, costs of key components and work in progress were running 27 to 30 percent over budget. These overruns were concealed by the responsible air force officers and by Lockheed officials. Accurate information became almost impossible to obtain. Air force officers who objected, or who sought to expose the full extent of the overruns, received less than enchanting reassignments—such as Vietnam. A. E. Fitzgerald, an expert defense auditor previously cited by the military for his outstanding systems analysis and cost-control work, was fired for attempting to call attention to the C-5A situation.

But in 1968 the extent of cost overruns on the C-5A began to surface. Congressional hearings revealed the program's costs to be running $2.2 billion over budget. The projected cost per plane had escalated from $28 million to $60 million.

Lockheed's chairman thereafter told Defense Department officials that owing to cost overruns, the firm was financially incapable of completing the C-5A as originally contracted. Because the Defense Department considered the plane essential, it was willing to renegotiate Lockheed's contract. Under the restructured contract, the firm's costs on the project would be reimbursed in order to ensure that it would lose no more than $200 million on the program. But as we have seen in chapter 22, even this was not enough to extricate the firm from its financial morass, and the government eventually bailed out the entire Lockheed organization.

The C-5A continued to be plagued by a number of what the comptroller general characterized as "significant deficiencies." These included malfunctions and performance failures in the landing gear, navigational gyros, hydraulic systems, and radar. In a 1972 report, the General Accounting Office found that, on average, the C-5A suffered a major technical breakdown during each hour it was airborne; a randomly selected C-5A had forty-seven major defects, including fourteen that impaired the aircraft's capability to perform all or part of six missions that it was intended to carry out. Although the plane was originally intended to have an air life of thirty thousand hours, air force fatigue tests conducted in 1974 indicated that the C-5A would last only sixty-five hundred to ten thousand hours. Perhaps most disturbing, however, was the rather alarming tendency of the plane's wings to crack. In 1975, Lockheed received a new billion-dollar contract to strengthen the structure and correct the problem. The contract involved no competitive bids, as the air force concluded that Lockheed alone possessed the expertise required to perform the work. "In a $1.6 billion program still going on at the Lockheed-Georgia plant, and paid for by the U.S.," the *Wall Street Journal* reported in 1983, "the company is rebuilding the entire center section of the fuselage on each C-5A in the fleet and attaching stronger wings—merely to bring the planes up to original specifications."

Most recently, Lockheed has all but abandoned the private sector. The reason, according to one account, is to enable the firm to "concentrate on what it knows best, selling weaponry to the Pentagon."

The Pentagon is the nation's largest single purchaser of goods and services. Its spending for weapons totaled $61.9 billion in 1984, forecast to rise to $110 billion by 1988.[2] Entire manufacturing industries depend heavily on military sales, including aircraft, radio and communications equipment, ordnance, and industrial chemicals.[3] For many products, the Pentagon is the only buyer. Moreover, the Defense Department supports as many as one-third of all scientists and engineers in the United States, spending about $10 billion a year on research and development.[4]

A few firms get most of the Pentagon's weapons money. The twenty-five largest contractors account for slightly more than half of all prime contracts, the hundred largest for 70 percent. Moreover the biggest contractors also rank among the largest industrial firms in the nation and depend on defense contracts for a substantial portion of their total revenues (see Table 4). More often than not, these firms are weapons "conglomerates," manufacturing several systems for the various services (see Table 5). For example, General Dynamics, the nation's largest military contractor, produces fighter planes, submarines, missiles, and tanks; defense contracts account for 96 percent of its total revenues.

The government wields vast power procuring its weaponry. But so, too, do the corporate giants who supply the weapons. Hence the questions arise: Do these power blocs oppose—and effectively neutralize— one another from *across* the military market? Or instead have they been mutually attracted to each other, as the labor-industrial complexes have in steel, autos, and the regulated sectors of the economy? Does the military hold in check the powerful private interests lusting after billion-dollar bonanzas? Or have private interests coalesced with and come to dominate the national interest in security? In other words, does the mere existence of two potentially opposed power concentrates protect the public interest? Is it an acceptable substitute for competitive economic organization?

President Eisenhower was not sanguine. The World War II commander in chief of Allied forces in Europe warned the nation of what he called the "military-industrial complex" and its potential for abuse. "Our military organization today bears little relation to that known by any of my predecessors," he explained in 1961 in his presidential farewell address. The nation had been compelled to create "a permanent armaments industry of vast proportions." This conjunction "of an immense military establishment and a large arms industry is new in the American experience." And he warned: "In the councils of government, we must guard against the acquisition of unwarranted influence, whether sought or unsought, by the military-industrial complex. The potential for the disastrous rise of misplaced power exists and will persist."

We shall now examine some evidence of coalescing power in the military-industrial complex, some of its major consequences, and some public-policy options for dealing with the problem of coalescing power.

TABLE 4
The Ten Largest Defense Contractors (Fiscal Year 1983)

Company	Rank Among Defense Contractors	Fortune 500 Rank	Prime Defense Contracts Received (Billions)	Defense Share of Company Sales (Percent)
General Dynamics	1	46	$6.8	96
McDonnell-Douglas	2	42	6.1	75
Rockwell	3	43	4.5	56
General Electric	4	10	4.5	17
Boeing	5	27	4.4	40
Lockheed	6	50	4.0	62
United Technologies	7	18	3.9	27
Tenneco	8	19	3.8	26
Hughes	9	na	3.2	na
Raytheon	10	59	2.7	46

SOURCES: Department of Defense, "100 Companies Receiving the Largest Dollar Volume of Prime Contract Awards" (Washington, D.C., Fiscal Year 1983), p. 4; *Fortune,* 30 April 1984.

SOME EVIDENCE OF COALESCING POWER

Taken together, the following factors suggest the presence of coalescing power in the operation of the military-industrial complex.

EXCESSIVE NONCOMPETITIVE WEAPONS PROCUREMENT

The public and the private interest obviously collide in the conditions under which weapons are procured. Profit-maximizing contractors would prefer, of course, to supply the military under monopoly conditions as long as possible. Monopoly clearly would serve their private interest, guaranteeing (possibly excessive) revenues and profits, while protecting them from competitive pressure to keep costs and prices low, and to keep productivity and innovation high.

Despite Congress's intent—in the Armed Services Act of 1947—to obtain the maximum possible competition in procurement, most Defense Department contracts are awarded without effective competition. The General Accounting Office recently found that only one-third of the value of all defense contracts are competitively awarded—and moreover, that the statistics it used significantly *overstated* the proportion of military contracts competitively assigned. "In the final analysis," the GAO concluded, "only about 10.5 percent of the total amount of [Department of Defense] procurements were for price competitive" contracts.[5]

Clearly the design and procurement of technologically complex new weapon systems may require negotiation and acquisition processes different from those used to buy household items. Nevertheless, the evidence suggests that the military's disdain for competition and its preference for monopoly often exceed constraints imposed by the nature of the weaponry.

The military frequently permits itself to become locked into a single producer by permitting the firm that develops and designs a weapon to monopolize the technology developed at the public's expense, and thus to monopolize the subsequent *production* of the weapon. Defense expert Jacques S. Gansler explains: "In defense, there customarily is a fierce rivalry during the initial competition for an award of a research and development contract. After this initial competition . . . the winner becomes the sole developer and producer for the military system over the next 20 years. Thus, a program—such as a missile system—may once have had an initial competition, but after that first step there is no alternative source for this much-needed piece of equipment. Therefore, the sole-source producer increases the price, the government has little choice but to attempt to 'negotiate,' and basically to accept the cost increases."[6]

TABLE 5
Weapons Produced by Large Defense Contractors

Company	Major Products
General Dynamics Corp.	F-16 and F-111 fighter aircraft, nuclear submarines, Tomahawk and Stinger missile systems, MK-15 close-in weapon system, M-1 tank.
McDonnell Douglas Corp.	F-18 Hornet, F-15 Eagle, AV-8 Harrier, and KC-10 aircraft; Harpoon missile system.
Rockwell International Corp.	B-1 bomber; RDT&E for aircraft, and missile and space systems; space vehicles; various electronics and communications equipment.
General Electric Co.	Nuclear reactors for submarines and aircraft carriers; J-79, J-85, TF-34, and F-101 turbofan and turbojet engines; space vehicle components; guided missile subsystems; transmission components for M-2 infantry fighting vehicles; armament training devices.
Boeing Co.	C-135 Stratolifter, B-52 Stratofortress, and E-3A aircraft; miscellaneous electronics for B-1 bomber; ZAGM-86 missile system; AWACS; RDT&E for electronics and communication equipment, aircraft, missile and space systems, and space transportation systems.
Lockheed Corp.	C-5 Galaxy, C-130 Hercules, and P-3 Orion aircraft; Trident and Polaris missile systems; amphibious assault ships; RDT&E for missile and space systems, aircraft, and electronics and communication equipment.
United Technologies Corp.	F-100, TF-30, TF-33, and J-52 turbofan and turbojet aircraft engines; UH-60 UTTAS, CH-53 Sea Stallion, and SH-60 Seahawk helicopters.
Tenneco, Inc.	Aircraft carriers, nuclear submarines.
Howard Hughes Medical Institute	TOW, Maverick, and Phoenix missile systems; radar equipment and guided missile systems for F-14, F-15, AH-1J, B-52, and SR-71 aircraft; RDT&E for electronics and communication equipment, missile and space systems, and ammunition; equipment for M-1 combat tank and M-2 infantry fighting vehicle.
Raytheon Co.	Patriot, Hawk, Sparrow, NATO Sea Sparrow, and Sidewinder missile systems; various electronics and communication equipment.
Grumman Corp.	F-14 Tomcat, A-6 Intruder, E-2 Hawkeye, C-2 Greyhound, and EA-6B Prowler aircraft;

TABLE 5 *(Continued)*

Company	Major Products
	electronics for F-16 Fighting Falcon; RDT&E for aircraft, electronics and communications equipment, and missile and space systems.
Martin Marietta Corp.	Pershing and Titan missile systems, AH-64 Apache aircraft, guided missile cruisers, operation of government ammunition facility, RDT&E for missile and space systems and electronics and communication equipment.
Litton Industries, Inc.	Guided missile cruisers, battleships, and destroyers; various electronics and communications equipment.

SOURCE: Department of Defense, "100 Companies Receiving the Largest Dollar Volume of Prime Contract Awards" (Washington, D.C., Fiscal Year 1983), pp. 5–6.

Rather than "breaking out" components of weapons systems for competitive bidding, the Defense Department typically awards a sole-source contract giving the supplier a monopoly over much of the system and most of its components. The technical data required for component break-out and bidding is paid for and, presumably, owned by the public. But a congressional investigative staff reports: "Many manufacturers are reluctant to sell technical data to [the Defense Department] as it would result in their losing their sole-source status and, in turn, would force them into a competitive situation." The expense of procuring technical data from contractors, the staff concludes, "plus the reluctance of the procurement officer to initiate such action, has deterred [the military's] breakout program and hindered competitive procurement." In some instances the military dispenses millions of dollars to contractors for parts and components on which no price has even been negotiated.[7]

Defense analyst James R. Kurth finds that major defense contracts are awarded in a manner that appears designed to keep the largest contractors' production lines operating, rather than on the basis of competitive merit. He characterizes this as the "follow-on imperative." By this process, defense contractors are treated as chosen instruments—as national resources—and the concentrated industrial structure is thereby entrenched. The imperatives of this process in aerospace are reinforced, he notes, "by the imperatives of the political system. Six of the production lines are located in states which loom large in the Electoral College: California (Lockheed-Missiles and Space, Rockwell, and Douglas division of McDonnell-Douglas), Texas (General Dynamics and Vought), and New York (Grumman)."[8]

In these ways, then, power appears to coalesce as the military favors a few giant firms and frees them from effective competition for billions of dollars of public funds.[9] This noncompetitive, cost-plus environment is well suited to monopolistic contractors' private interests. But its consequences for the public interest seem to be an entirely different matter, as we shall shortly see.

TESTING, PERFORMANCE DEFICIENCIES, AND MISSION REDEFINITION

As a buyer, the military not only buys weapons, it also (presumably) ensures that the weapons meet the performance standards contracted for. If they fail to meet the standards, the military can (1) force the contractor to meet performance levels contracted for and withhold funding until standards are met; (2) contrive "tests" sure to make the weapon a "success"; (3) lower performance requirements by redefining the weapon's mission; or (4) dispense with testing altogether. Contractors, of course, would prefer any of the latter three options, and the military's apparent predilection for the same three further suggests the operation of coalescing, rather than countervailing, power.

Appropriately orchestrated "tests" ensure that producers will receive funds tied to performance levels. For example, the staff of one congressional committee assigned to investigate a key "test" of the navy's $40 billion F-18 fighter jet found that

> either the contractor or the Navy, aware of the aircraft's range deficiencies, attempted to structure [the test] to provide the aircraft with extra advantage. This conclusion is based on the following: (1) the mission was flown by a contractor's employee rather than a navy test pilot (as directed by the Secretary of the Navy); (2) the F/A-18 was "towed" into takeoff position for engine start on the runway to conserve fuel; (3) the interdiction profile was not conducted and attack was made on the target at "idle" power setting on the aircraft, which also conserves fuel; and (4) the approach into Patuxent River was made in the "minimum fuel condition."[10]

Similarly, a recent "test" of a heat-seeking antitank missile system comprised an attack on fifteen obsolete gasoline-powered tanks on a bulldozed, treeless New Mexico desert, with the tanks' guns turned backward and with metal baffles installed over the exhaust to increase the targets' heat signature (recognized by the missile). The weapon was proclaimed a "success," even though in battle it would be deployed in the heavy forests of Central Europe, and the targets would be moving tanks powered by diesel engines, which emit far less heat.[11]

As an alternative to contrived testing, the military has proven willing to downgrade performance standards when weapons fail to meet contracted levels. When the F-18 fighter failed to meet contracted acceleration standards, for example, the "Navy could choose one of two alternatives: (1) fix the airplane, or (2) 'fix' the specification. . . . The Navy's solution, in the face of having to admit a large acceleration performance gap, was simply to adjust the contractual acceptance level to [that] where the aircraft performs best."[12] Likewise, when the army's Viper antitank weapon proved incapable of penetrating the front armor of modern tanks, its mission was redefined as "attacking" enemy tanks from behind, despite the rather obvious problems this would pose for combat troops.[13]

Or tests can simply be dispensed with altogether. When prototypes of the army's Sergeant York (DIVAD) air-defense gun appeared unlikely to meet performance requirements, tests of reliability, availability, maintainability, and durability were canceled—although production of the weapon continued apace until 1985, when the project was finally canceled, after nearly $2 billion had been spent.[14]

More generally, the comptroller general reports, "major weapon systems . . . are being fielded without fully demonstrating that they will meet performance expectations." Indeed, Russell Murray, former assistant secretary of defense, concludes that no defense problem "is as serious as our lack of rigorous and forthright operational testing to make sure that our new weapons will live up to expectations if we have to fight a war with them," and that we "have nourished an attitude of contempt on the part of weapon system promoters, whose glittering promises at the start of a development are literally encouraged by our reluctance to put them to the test at its conclusion"[15]—a situation hardly compatible with the notion of countervailing power in the public interest.

RESISTANCE TO EFFECTIVE AUDITING OF CONTRACTORS

"Since the bulk of major defense contracts are awarded without competition," Senator William V. Roth points out, the Defense Department "must thoroughly review prices proposed by contractors to ensure that the Government does not accept any contracts that are not reasonably priced and supported by firm cost or pricing documentation." Ostensibly, this is the task of the Pentagon's Defense Contract Audit Agency (DCAA)—"to go in with a finely chiseled pencil and analyze the prices suggested by contractors for weapons systems, spare parts and other equipment and services."[16]

In actuality, the military has permitted this auditing function to be rendered ineffectual in a variety of ways.[17] The DCAA cannot compel contractors to provide relevant information. Contractors—particularly the largest ones—are frequently permitted to deny auditors access to essential information—even though virtually all defense contracts contain a clause granting the Defense Department the right to examine books, records, documents, and accounting practices. Sometimes, auditors are even denied access to production facilities owned by the government. Military procurement officers are permitted to waive adverse or inadequate auditing reports, even where auditors advise that proposed contract costs and prices cannot be meaningfully evaluated. Moreover, DCAA seldom stops payments to contractors who refuse access to salient data, even though it is empowered to do so. And auditors' performance is rated according to a system that implicitly tends to institutionalize timidity.

Generally the DCAA has exhibited "an excessive emphasis on the concept that DCAA is a member of the procurement team," and to display a pervasive attitude "that reflects undue regard and solicitude for the concerns of contractors and procurement officials in the audit process." Thus when one auditor, George Spanton, reported questionable charges of more than $100 million by one contractor, the "Pentagon sent criminal investigators to check out the auditor, kept mum about his findings, lowered his job performance ratings, attempted to transfer him, then pressured him to quit." In the opinion of veteran defense auditors, the DCAA—ostensibly the protector of the public interest, in the front line of presumably countervailing power—has come "to specialize . . . in finding no evidence of violations by contractors. . . . It is what they do best."[18]

CONTRACTING OUT KEY DEFENSE FUNCTIONS

Contracting out key defense functions to weapons producers is another sign of coalescing power. It suggests a gradual capturing of defense management and decision-making by the firms who stand to benefit from the decisions, a tendency of private power and interest to commingle with, and perhaps dominate, the public interest.

A congressional investigative staff report prepared in 1981 points to the "apparent loss of in-house expertise evidenced by contracting for work that should be done by [Defense Department] in-house personnel," and cites instances where expensive decisions were unduly influenced by outside contractors. The staff found that "operational reliance on [outside contractors] has reached the point that navy air wings, and to some extent the [air force's] Tactical Air Command (TAC) do not have the capability to operate at full combat mission readiness without civilian contractual support."[19]

More generally, the military is willing to have major defense producers analyze the performance capabilities of enemy weapons, as well as study the feasibility of weapons that the firms produce. Six of the top ten companies already holding contracts for multi-billion-dollar "Star Wars" weaponry also have contracts to determine the system's feasibility.[20] Where the government has private contractors assess the performance capabilities of enemy weapons, one high-ranking Defense Department official points out, "the government ends up contracting out to counter an emerging threat to the very people who benefit from it." A former CIA official draws the obvious conclusion: "Companies that produce the weapons will always inflate the threat to maximize their sales."[21]

In short, coalescing power potentially permits giant defense contractors to significantly influence the demand for weaponry in accordance with their private—as opposed to the public's—interest.

JOINT PROMOTION AND PROTECTION OF WEAPONS SYSTEMS

"A contractor can not be expected to passively accept the cancellation of his principal product," defense expert Franklin C. Spinney has explained. "Even if cancellation is clearly in the national interest, the contractor's survival *still* depends on continued production; and therefore, he must try to combine his interest with compatible interests of other actors to override a cancellation decision. If he succeeds, the general interest is sacrificed for a coalition of special interests."[22] In such cases, there would seem to be, once again, a clear coalescence of power.

For example, the navy articulated its desire for a long-range, air-to-surface missile in 1962.[23] Development commenced in 1965, and Rockwell was named prime contractor the next year, promising lucrative returns for Rockwell. Later, the Condor program was severely criticized by the General Accounting Office (GAO) and the Office of Management and Budget (OMB), among others, on the grounds of cost effectiveness, vulnerability, mission effectiveness, operational suitability, and reliability. Nevertheless, the interest of the navy's procurement office conjoined with that of Rockwell in promoting the system. The Joint Congressional Committee on Defense Production found that "the Navy Project Manager and the contractor considered themselves to be, in essence, teammates cooperating to overcome their adversaries at [the Office of the Secretary of Defense], the General Accounting Office, and the Congress." The committee discovered that military procurement officers "showed an unusual degree of interest in the continued survival of the program," including advising Rockwell on how to approach members of Congress during its consideration of the military budget.

And apparently, the Condor is not an isolated instance of explicit collusion between procurement officers and weapons suppliers. Requested by Congress to investigate Lockheed's recent C-5B cargo carrier program, the comptroller general reported,

> After the defeat of the C-5B program in the Senate, the Director of the Air Force Legislative Liaison initiated, organized, and directed an intense legislative liaison and lobbying effort to promote the C-5B program in the House. The effort included numerous visits to Congressmen by Air Force, Army, and Marine officials, other Congressmen, Lockheed Corporation officials, and representatives of other companies that had an interest in the C-5B program or did business with Lockheed or the Department of Defense. . . . A computer was used by Lockheed to monitor the progress of the legislative liaison and lobbying effort.

Despite the comptroller's finding of "unlawful" lobbying pressure, Defense Department officials said that "the actions taken to promote the C-5B program were similar to those taken for other large Defense programs."[24]

PERSONNEL TRANSFERS AND THE "REVOLVING DOOR"

The movement of high-ranking officials between military employment on the one hand, and employment with major defense contractors on the other, also points to coalescing power. This "revolving door" represents the institutional absorption of buyer and seller as integral elements of an organic whole, and it blurs the distinction between the "public" and "private" sector. It thus raises the question whether the public interest is distinguishable from private advantage.

The interflow of personnel within the military-industrial complex is not insignificant. Table 6 shows, for example, that nearly 400 persons moved between Boeing (currently the nation's fifth largest defense contractor) and defense agencies during the 1970s. Professional incest is substantial for other major contractors, including General Dynamics, McDonnell-Douglas, Lockheed, Northrop, and Rockwell.

Furthermore, large contractors are heavily represented on defense-agency "advisory committees." In its 1976 investigation, a congressional committee staff found that twenty-nine of the thirty largest defense contractors held positions on Defense Department advisory committees. Participation by large contractors was extensive: Lockheed (then the largest contractor) had eleven employees on twelve committees, while Boeing (second largest) had twelve employees on fourteen committees. The congressional staff further noted that many "of these contractor representatives are retired generals, former high-ranking civilian offi-

TABLE 6

The Revolving Door between the Defense Department and its Contractors
(DOD 1970–79 and NASA 1974–79)

| Company | Total Flow | FLOW TO COMPANY | | | FLOW TO GOVERNMENT | |
		from DOD Military	from DOD Civilian	from NASA	to DOD	to NASA
Boeing	398	316	35	3	37	7
General Dynamics	239	189	17	1	32	0
Grumman	96	67	5	1	16	7
Lockheed	321	240	30	6	34	11
McDonnell-Douglas	211	159	12	2	29	9
Northrop	360	284	50	9	16	1
Rockwell	234	150	26	6	47	5
United Technologies	83	50	11	3	12	7
Total	1942	1455	186	31	223	47

SOURCE: G. Adams, *The Iron Triangle: The Politics of Defense Contracting* (New Brunswick, N.J.: Transaction Books, 1982), p. 84.

cials of the Department of Defense or the individual services, and former congressional staff."[25]

This institutional fusion between buyer and seller appears to be neither random nor haphazard. For example, over two-thirds of Boeing personnel transfers involved the air force (which accounts for most Boeing military sales); more than 80 percent of General Dynamics transfers involved the air force (which buys the firm's missiles and aircraft) and the navy (which buys its ships and missiles). Some affiliations are even more sharply targeted: the manager of Rockwell's laser program later moved to the Army Missile Command—as a general engineer in the army's laser-project office.[26]

Contractors also supply a large number of persons for key defense policy positions. In the Reagan administration, for example, Boeing has provided the assistant secretary of the navy for research systems and analysis, the deputy undersecretary for strategic theater nuclear forces, the deputy director of the Defense Department's Office of Intelligence and Space Policy, the assistant secretary of defense for international security policy, the associate director of presidential personnel in the national security field, and the deputy head of the president's transition team for the Department of Defense.[27] Other direct links include the undersecretary of defense for research and engineering (formerly of TRW); an undersecretary of the navy (former chairman of Bath Iron Works, one of the forty largest military contractors); and the deputy undersecretary of defense for communication, command, control, and intelligence (formerly a division vice president of RCA, one of the twenty-five largest defense contractors).[28]

Conflicts of interest would seem unavoidable. As Senator William Proxmire points out, it "can have a subtle, but debilitating effect on an officer's performance . . . in a procurement management assignment. If he takes too strong a hand in controlling contractor activity, he might be damaging his opportunity for a second career following retirement. Positions are offered to officers who have demonstrated their appreciation for industry's particular problems and commitments."[29]

The foregoing considerations—excessive noncompetitive procurement, performance deficiencies and mission redefinitions, ineffective auditing, contracting out key functions, joint promotion and protection of weapons, and the "revolving door" in employment—suggest that power on the buyer side of defense markets has coalesced with, rather than effectively countervailed, the power on the seller side.

―――

SOME CONSEQUENCES OF COALESCING POWER

Coalescing power is not inert. Nor is it benign. It has consequences; in the defense industry, it has at least three important ones.

OVERRUNS AND EXCESSIVE WEAPONS COSTS

Current cost overruns for major weapons programs are familiar enough and require no extended discussion. The magnitude of these overruns, however, is breathtaking when they are considered on a unit basis. For example, the cost for each of the army's Roland missiles is now estimated at $43.9 million—143 percent above original estimates of $18.8 million. The navy's F-18 fighter has quadrupled in price, from $10.4 million to $42.1 million per plane.[30]

The monopoly pricing discretion afforded by coalescing power extends to the mundane—as shown in Table 7, comparing the cost of a kit of tools if bought at retail with the price charged by defense contractors. For comparative purposes, Senator Roth pointed out that the total taxes paid by an American family earning $25,000 would cover only two-thirds of the tool kit.[31]

Coalescing power also permits corporate giants to raise prices virtually at will. One study found that "approximately 65 percent of the

TABLE 7
Prices of Ordinary Tools: Retail versus Defense Contractors

Tool	Retail Price	Contractor's Price
Hammer	$ 7.66	$ 435.00
Wrench, end box, 1 set	4.99	768.00
Pliers, slip joint, 6	3.77	430.00
Pliers, slip joint	5.97	449.00
Pliers, vise grip, 2	7.94	486.00
Wrench, socket set, ⅜th	12.88	545.00
Bar extension	1.99	430.00
Bar extension	2.19	431.00
Socket, ½-inch	1.49	456.00
Screwdriver, square-blade, 1 set	1.69	265.50
Screwdriver, jeweler, 1 set	1.97	232.00
Screwdriver, phillips, 1 set	1.69	258.06
Screwdriver, offset	2.79	225.00
Crimping tool	3.96	729.00
Superjust wrenches	4.88	1,150.00
Wrenches	1.57	234.00
Drill set	1.69	599.00
Hex driver	3.99	469.00
Feeler gauge	4.27	436.00
Circuit tester	3.39	489.00
Tool box	11.67	652.00
	$ 92.44	$ 10,168.56

SOURCE: U.S. Congress, House Committee on Armed Services, *Hearings on H.R. 5064 and H.R. 4842*, 98th Cong., 2nd sess., 1984, pp. 9–10.

15,000 spare [aircraft engine] parts sampled experienced cost growth in excess of 50 percent between 1980 and 1982. During this same period, more than a quarter of these parts increased in price by over 500 percent."[32] The Consumer Price Index rose 27 percent over the same period.

The enormity of the cost escalations and overruns is almost incomprehensible. "The entire 1981 farm bill—with four years' worth of price supports, loans, and Government-purchase options—would cost $2 billion less than the cost overrun of the Army's XM-1 heavy tank program," one defense analyst calculates. "Since 1933, taxpayers have anted up about $36 billion to support dairy farmers and farmers who grow corn, wheat, cotton, tobacco, and peanuts. Yet the cost overruns on the Navy's current submarine, frigate, and destroyer programs come to $42 billion."[33]

DEFICIENT WEAPONS PERFORMANCE
Deficient weapons performance appears to be a second consequence of coalescing power in the military-industrial complex.

For example, the army's M-1 tank program was begun in 1972. In February 1982, the tank's performance deficiencies included deficient system reliability, deficient combat-mission reliability, excessive power-train breakdowns, excessive maintenance requirements, excessive fuel consumption, and an unfortunate tendency for engines to "drown" during fording exercises.[34]

Similarly, the GAO recently reported on the navy's $38 billion F-18 jet fighter program: "The most serious problem the testers identified was the deficiency in the F/A-18's combat radius or range. Other deficiencies identified included the lack of an electronic warfare system, the excessive amount of wind-over-deck required to launch the aircraft on most carriers, the rapid descent rate of the F/A-18 parachute, locking of the aircraft's leading edge flaps, problems in the delivery of high-drag weapons, wing oscillation, the inadvertent jettison of a Sparrow missile, and arrestment weight problems in carrier landings."[35]

Unfortunately, these faults are not unique, or even exceptional. The crucial sighting and firing system of the army's $50-million AH-64 attack helicopters is fully mission-capable only 35 percent of the time. The air force's $28-million F-15 fighter requires 27 maintenance man-hours per flight hour (compared to a desired rate of 11 hours) and suffers a mean time between system failures of 1.2 hours (compared to a desired rate of 5.6 hours). The Sparrow missile, originally projected to score "kills" in 90 percent of its firings, reportedly has achieved a kill rate of only 8 percent; more recently, GAO investigators found one-quarter to one-third of the navy's Sidewinder and Sparrow missiles to be "unserviceable" for combat.[36]

With such a record, it is perhaps not surprising that defense contractors are lobbying Congress to repeal recent legislation requiring suppliers to guarantee that their products meet contract standards and that they are free from defects. And in the light of coalescing power it should not be surprising that the Pentagon has joined with contractors in resisting Congress's demand for weapons warranties. But as Admiral Steven A. White points out, the navy has demanded and obtained a weapons warranty before—from the builder of the *Monitor,* the Civil War ship that battled the Confederacy's *Merrimack.*[37]

TECHNOLOGICAL "GOLD-PLATING" AND THE DECLINE OF
DEFENSE CAPABILITY

Finally, the issue now being raised is whether the private interest of contractors in building extravagantly expensive, ultrasophisticated weaponry has distorted military strategy into a drive for "technology for technology's sake"—a drive that maximizes contractors' profits but may well impair the nation's security.

The capacity of monopolistic contractors to overrun costs and to raise prices has meant sharp cutbacks in the numbers of current and planned weapons actually bought. These cutbacks range from 21 to 82 percent for various weapons systems.[38]

TABLE 8

Comparative Cost and Military Effectiveness: New versus Old Weapons

Weapon	New System	Old System	Ratio of Military Effectiveness (New to old)	Ratio of Real Cost (New to Old)
Tanks	M-1	M-60	1.278	1.583
Armored personnel carriers	FVS	M113	3.500	7.500
Attack helicopters	AH-64	AH-1S	1.600	4.085
Lightweight fighter	F-111	F-105	1.300	4.250
Fighter bomber	F-15	F-100	3.400	15.000
Intercontinental ballistic missile	MX (projected)	Minuteman I	5.000	6.200

SOURCE: National Marine Engineers' Beneficial Association, *Waste in the Defense Department* (Washington, D.C., March 1985), p. I-21.

Although new weapons are more effective than older weapons, they are far more expensive and, in a number of cases, less reliable. Table 8 shows one set of calculations comparing relative military effectiveness and relative costs for new weapons and their predecessors. For example, while an F-15 fighter is 3.4 times more effective in a military sense than the F-100, its predecessor, it is fully *fifteen* times as expensive, suggesting that the amounts currently spent on F-15s would be far more cost-effective spent on F-100s. Likewise, "the army is now spending roughly the same amount on new tanks as it did during the Korean War. But that amount buys one-tenth the tanks it used to—700 today compared to almost 7,000 in 1953. Similarly, we built over 6,000 fighter planes in 1951 with $7 billion, but can build only about 300 with $11 billion today."[39] (*This after adjusting for inflation!*) Moreover, new weaponry involves significantly greater operating costs. "The Army's new M-1 tank costs

$58.90 per mile to operate, for example, compared with $27.51 per mile for the older M-60A1. The new Bradley Fighting Vehicle is said to cost $44.47 per mile to operate compared with $12.93 per mile for its predecessor, the M-113 armored personnel carrier. And these estimates do not include repair costs."[40] Thus the paradox of coalescing power is that more and more is spent to obtain less and less—a phenomenon that Marine Lieutenant Colonel David Evans describes as "self-imposed disarmament" whereby U.S. forces "will be increasingly outnumbered as we reluctantly spend more on defense."[41]

"High-tech" weapons may well be less reliable and less effective in actual combat. Reporters for the *Los Angeles Times* found that career military officers were among the most caustic critics of a weapons strategy requiring "more and more operator training, more field support and, in most cases, more sophisticated maintenance."[42] Oversophisticated weapons, analyst Peter Navarro points out, "break down more often than their simpler counterparts. Fixing them requires equally sophisticated and expensive diagnostic testing equipment, more highly trained and skilled repair personnel, and a more expensive inventory of spare parts."[43] Further, high-tech weaponry may present insuperable logistical problems in the field; the army's supersophisticated, gas-guzzling M-1 tank, for example, requires what one veteran tank commander calls a "rolling traffic jam" of fuel trucks, technicians, and spare parts vans.[44] Indeed, weapons may have become so complex as to necessitate a perilous dependence on contractors to operate and maintain them—a rather sticky problem in actual combat.[45]

All this raises the question of whether coalescing power best serves the public interest in a sound, secure national defense. A recent report by the *Wall Street Journal*, based on internal Pentagon documents, is sobering: "Despite more than $600 billion in defense spending during the first three years of the Reagan administration, military-unit combat readiness has declined significantly."[46]

SOME PUBLIC-POLICY OPTIONS

In defense, as elsewhere, power blocs on opposite sides of the market tend to coalesce with—rather than check—one another. As a result, society suffers from poor economic performance. Once society permits itself to become dependent on bigness as its chosen instrument, then bailouts—subsidies, funding of cost overruns, relaxation of performance standards—are almost inevitable. Then society no longer has any viable options. In the defense sector, this is perhaps most evident in cases involving fraud and malfeasance, where small suppliers are expendable and hence severely punished for even minor transgressions, while corporate giants like General Dynamics and General Electric are too important to punish with anything more than a "feather bomb," no matter how egregious their excesses.[47] The private interests of bigness doubtless are well served in this noncompetitive, cost-plus environment, where payment is virtually divorced from performance. But, as we have seen, the consequences for the public interest in an effective national defense are an entirely different matter.

What are the public-policy options?

Outright nationalization of major defense contractors is one option. Indeed, this would seem to be a relatively minor step, given current structure and conduct in the defense sector.[48] Yet the ramifications are troubling. Nationalization would formalize and legitimize coalescing power in the military-industrial complex. Removing the last vestiges of competition from the field would render the government and the public even more dependent on a few giant contractors, might well degrade their already deplorable performance, and thus might render coalescing power more intractable than ever. And nationalization would raise questions about the wisdom of concentrating political and economic power in the same hands—subject to even less oversight and accountability than the present military-industrial complex.

Second, giant defense contractors might be regulated by a kind of public-utility commission independent of the Pentagon. Yet experience with airlines, trucking, and nuclear power teaches us that regulatory agencies are prone to capture by their regulatees. Even where regulatory bodies clearly know what correct conduct is, they have rarely been able to induce powerful firms to comply with their prescriptions. At best, public regulators have been able to enjoin bad practices, without being able to define efficient, productive, and innovative performance, much less compel it. The powerful forces and interests at play in defense, and the vast economic stakes, could be expected to exacerbate the congenital infirmities of public-utility regulation.

Third, a policy of *effective* competition can be adopted. Here the overarching principle would dictate that the government, like any rational buyer, contract in a manner calculated to secure a maximum number of options and alternative sources of supply at all stages of the weapons-acquisition process. It would counsel the government to capitalize on its position as the sole buyer of weaponry in order to obtain and maintain a competitive supply industry and thereby to avoid depending on one or a few monopolistic contractors. It would, in short, attack the problem of coalescing power at its structural roots.

The gains would be substantial. Knowledgeable analysts variously calculate that effective competition could reduce weapons costs by 50 percent or more[49]—which, given projected weapons expenditures, would certainly help reduce the seemingly uncontrollable federal deficits. It would neutralize monopoly power by setting one private interest against another and channeling them into the socially beneficial avenues of reducing costs and prices, and advancing productivity and innovation. And it would prevent society from being dependent upon, and thus susceptible to capture by, a handful of corporate giants.

Professor Murray Weidenbaum, former chairman of the President's Council of Economic Advisers, has proposed the following planks of an effectively competitive policy platform in defense:

1. Broaden the competitive base. This could be accomplished by encouraging defense companies to diversify into commercial markets and, conversely, encouraging commercially oriented companies to consider military work as a possible source of diversification for them. This would reduce the tendency for a relatively small number of companies to become primarily dependent on government business.
2. Emphasize production rather than R&D as the major point of competition. This could be done by doing more of the design work in federal laboratories and making the designs available to the various private companies who would bid on the production work. Alternatively, the design and development work could be done in the private sector but the companies doing this kind of work would not be permitted to bid on production contracts.
3. Break out more subsystems for competition. Even during the heyday of the weapon system contractor concept, key subsystems were supplied separately, notably aircraft engines. More attention to breaking out major elements, either during the development or production stages, might increase the number and types of firms competing for prime contracts.
4. Widen the participation in subcontracts. Much of the subcontract dollars go to companies that are prime contractors on other systems. More attention in the award of subcontracts could be paid to small business and other industries not actively participating in the military market as primes.
5. Reduce the competitive advantage of using government assets. Some thought might be given to reducing the competitive advantages that accrue to the dominant primes that hold on to government-owned plant and equipment for long periods of time. The free provisions of these assets also explains much of their high profit rates.

6. Tighten patent policies. In general, contractors get to keep free of charge the patent rights they obtain from research on government contracts. This of course puts the "ins" at a competitive advantage over the "outs." It is interesting to note the double standard. When these same contractors award contracts to research institutes, they insist that the client and not the contractor retain the patent rights.[50]

Admittedly, implementing the competitive approach to weapons procurement would not be easy. It would demand effort, energy, imagination, and innovation in contract design and management. Yet as we are now discovering, the public interest in defense may permit no other choice.

VII

PUBLIC-POLICY
ALTERNATIVES

CHAPTER 25

INDUSTRIAL POLICY: THE NEOLIBERAL VISION

Foreigners may argue over which Industrial Policy option is best but never over Industrial Policy itself. For them it's the third leg on the policy stool, as critical as monetary and fiscal policies for economic growth and stabilization.
— Professor Robert B. Reich, Harvard University

When you strip away the philosophical paraphernalia, industrial policy is a mechanism by which the politically powerful get their hands in the till.
— Alan Greenspan, Townsend-Greenspan & Co.

In response to the devastating 1981–83 depression, in an effort to arrest the "deindustrialization of America," and under the guise of promoting the international competitiveness of the American economy, the AFL-CIO spearheaded a movement to institute an industrial policy for the United States. The rationale was this:

America cannot hope to achieve full employment for the 1980s without coherent strategies for revitalizing basic industries and supporting emerging industries that can generate new job growth for the future.

The hope for a more equitable, balanced society will likewise hinge on industrial policy and related efforts aimed at stabilizing and expanding middle-income jobs for growing numbers of people.

It has become abundantly clear that exclusive reliance on macroeconomic policy—manipulation of monetary and fiscal levers alone—cannot revitalize industry or lead to full employment. This country has tried several macroeconomic variants in the past fifteen years—Keynesian, monetarist, and supply-side—with the uniform result of escalating unemployment, recurrent

351

inflation, and continuing industrial disinvestment. Specific problems facing individual industries and regions will not necessarily respond to an overall improvement in the economic climate—particularly if "micro" problems of technology, training, international trade, or industrial organization are the real issues. The first step, certainly, is to implement a balanced, macroeconomic policy oriented toward growth, but this must be supplemented by targeted measures that can respond productively to the needs and potential of specific sectors and regions. America's very successful "industrial" policies for agriculture and aerospace need to be extended to other, equally important, industrial sectors.

The twin challenge of industrial policy is to: (1) stabilize and modernize the traditional industrial base; and (2) promote the development of new industries.

Ranking *Fortune* 500 manufacturing firms and powerful trade unions joined in this call for an industrial policy.[1] Politicians embraced it. So did a number of academic economists.[2]

It should be obvious that a macroeconomic stabilization policy must be supplemented with a micropolicy designed to strengthen the supply capabilities of the economy and, where necessary, to promote a structural transformation of industry. But do we need a full-blown industrial policy to do it?

To be sure, the United States—since Alexander Hamilton's *Report on Manufacturers*—has had an arsenal of microeconomic policies. These consisted of (1) protection of the domestic market from foreign competition; (2) tax policies, including special depreciation rules, depletion allowances, offsets for foreign taxes, tax deferral for export profits, etc.; (3) antitrust exemptions for specific price-fixing and price-support programs, industry-wide cartels, joint research and development projects, export associations, and selected mergers and acquisitions; (4) patent privileges and other forms of assistance to science and technology; and (5) financial assistance, including loan guarantees, loans at preferential terms, export financing, and even total bailouts of failing companies. All these measures are a form of microeconomic policy. But, the neoliberals say, these measures are isolated, makeshift devices to deal with microeconomic problems. What is needed, they argue, is a coherent, systematic national plan—a long-run strategy, a comprehensive industrial policy.

The neoliberal style of industrial policy rests, we contend, on dubious facts; it is flawed in its theory; and, when previously tried in the United States, it has been an abysmal failure.

DUBIOUS FACTS

The neoliberals' case for industrial policy typically proceeds from a number of questionable presuppositions.

THE "TARGETING" MYTH

In the United States, it is fashionable to point to Japan as a country that has achieved economic miracles by implementing a sound industrial policy. Japan is smaller than California and almost devoid of natural resources. Japan imports 99.8 percent of its oil. Almost half of its food is imported. It must export enough of what it produces to pay for the imports necessary for survival. Yet Japan has become one of the world's premier industrial nations. Why? Because, say the neoliberals, she has fashioned an industrial policy that substitutes cooperation for confrontation between management, labor, and government, and that targets entire industrial sectors for broad, coordinated, systematic assistance.

The centerpiece of this industrial policy is alleged to be Japan's Ministry of International Trade and Industry (MITI), which exercises broad powers. MITI, Professor Robert S. Ozaki reports:

> is responsible for shaping the structure of industry and making necessary adjustments for industrial dislocations as they occur, properly guiding the development of specific industries and the production and distribution of their products, managing Japanese foreign trade and commercial relations with other nations, ensuring an adequate supply of energy and raw materials to industry, and managing particular areas such as small business policy, patents, and regional development. To achieve these diverse goals, MITI plays many roles ranging from that of broad policy architect to ad hoc working-level problem-solver, and from formal regulator to regional policy arbiter or informal administrative guide. In some areas MITI holds strong statutory authority; elsewhere it has only a broad and weak influence.[3]

Frequently, it is charged, the industries that MITI targets for support receive government assistance through the Japan Development Bank.

Placed in perspective, however, targeting has not played the crucial role that the "victims" of Japan Inc. like to attribute to it. In a landmark study, for example, Professor Gary Saxonhouse of the University of Michigan has found that both the general and sectoral support provided by the Japanese government is quantitatively far less significant than is popularly supposed:

> In striking contrast with the policies of some European countries where large sectors of the economy are publicly owned and where large subsidies may be

given . . . there is very little in the way of direct subsidies and grants given
to manufacturing industries in Japan. In a study done on Japanese government subsidy policy, for 1977 and 1978, for thirteen major manufacturing
sectors in Japan, only one of these sectors received direct subsidies greater
than 0.1 percent of gross domestic product originating in that sector. This
single manufacturing sector which was targeted for special attention was
food processing, which received subsidies equal to 0.6 percent of gross domestic product originating in that sector. Where there are large subsidies given
by the Japanese government they go to agriculture, mining and to transportation utilities. . . . In absolute amount, the actual subsidies given agriculture
are greater by almost 50 percent than the total amount of subsidies given the
rest of the Japanese economy. The rate of subsidy given agriculture is fully
12.3 percent of gross domestic product originating in that sector.[4]

Moreover, Saxonhouse reports, "what is true about direct subsidies,
in general, is also true specifically about research and development
grants from the Japanese government. In the late 1970s the Japanese
government funded no more than 1.9 percent of all research and development undertaken by private sector industry. This contrasts with West
Germany funding 15.8 percent of private sector R&D, France funding
25.3 percent, the United Kingdom funding 30.9 percent and with the
United States so actively involved in private sector R&D as to fund fully
35.3 percent of all research and development undertaken by the private
sector in the American economy."[5] Saxonhouse reports that the communication and electronics industry receives contracts, grants, and subsidies from the Japanese government equal to 1.03 percent of its R&D
expenditures, while the comparable figure for pharmaceuticals, machinery, and precision equipment are 0.3, 1.4, and 0.5 percent, respectively.
Japanese government expenditures on biotechnology come to no more
than $35 million, between one-tenth and one-fifteenth the amount spent
by the U.S. government. In 1982, the Japanese government spent $15
million on R&D in flexible manufacturing systems—in contrast to the
U.S. Department of Defense, which alone spends an average of $225
million annually on CAD/CAM systems, robotics, and flexible manufacturing systems. Finally, according to Saxonhouse, the Japanese government spent $48 million in 1982 on contracts, grants, and subsidies to the
private sector for R&D in computers and semiconductors. By comparison, U.S. government funding for semiconductor research alone averaged $90 million in the early 1980s, while an additional $310 million was
spent annually on computer-related research by the Department of Defense, the National Science Foundation, and NASA.[6]

Thus it is difficult to accept the claim that Japanese targeting explains
either the phenomenal success of its industries in world markets or the

"harm" inflicted on nations that lack an industrial policy. It would seem that other factors must have played a more decisive role in the Japanese "miracle."

THE "ANTITRUST" MYTH

Another claim is that the antitrust laws have had a crippling effect on American industry, and that enforcement of these laws has put the United States at a distinct disadvantage in international competition with countries not burdened by antitrust inhibitions.

Professor Lester C. Thurow, a neoliberal economist from MIT and a vociferous advocate of industrial policy, states the proposition in its bluntest form:

> America should abolish its antitrust laws. The time has come to recognize that the techniques of the 19th century are not applicable in getting ready for the 21st. An economy where growth is stopped and living standards are falling behind those of its competitors cannot afford a legal system that cripples its industrial future.
>
> The United States is no longer richer and more technologically advanced than its competitors. It cannot afford to waste billions of dollars in lengthy court battles. Those resources should be going into investment. It cannot afford to force American companies to independently invent the same wheel when they should be engaging in cooperative research and development projects. It cannot hope to compete in world markets if Americans are unable to respond to Japanese trading companies with American trading companies.[7]

Curiously, at the other end of the political spectrum, President Reagan's secretary of commerce espouses roughly similar arguments.

This claim that antitrust is a costly and counterproductive anachronism is stale wine in old bottles, an assertion almost totally devoid of empirical support. As we have noted earlier, the mere increase of firm size does not guarantee greater efficiency, promote technological progress, or improve the social allocation of resources. Moreover, there is no evidence that tolerating interfirm conspiracies—overt or tacit—improves industrial performance or serves the national interest.

More important, can anyone seriously suggest that overzealous antitrust enforcement is in any way responsible for the current malaise of our basic industries, particularly steel? Did antitrust succeed in undoing the mammoth mergers that created U.S. Steel and laid the foundation for the industry's concentrated structure at the turn of the century? Did antitrust in the mid-1960s block the acquisition of Jones & Laughlin by LTV and of Youngstown Sheet & Tube by Lykes—mergers that were supposed to provide the acquired companies with capital to modernize their antiquated facilities? Did antitrust, in the mid-1970s, block the merger of LTV and Youngstown after the latter had been milked dry by its conglomerate owner and had been reduced to a "failing company"? Did antitrust, in the early 1980s, block the merger between LTV and Republic? In short, did antitrust stand in the way of the succession of mergers between major steel companies, all ranking among the eight largest in the industry, and thereby prevent a massive restructuring ("rationalization") of the American steel industry? No. Yet did this inaction by antitrust induce the modernization of the industry's superannuated facilities or the construction of new "greenfield" plants à la japonaise? Did this antitrust inaction foster industrial efficiency or better performance by merger-bloated American steel producers? Ironically, as we have seen, the one time antitrust did block a major merger, between the second and sixth largest steel companies, the result was the construction of a new, modern, integrated steel plant by a major steel company.[8]

In oil, is not the record similarly replete with inaction by the antitrust authorities? In the 1980s, in the face of megamergers like Texaco's acquisition of Getty ($10.1 billion), Socal's of Gulf ($13.2 billion), and Mobil's of Superior ($5.7 billion), was not antitrust a policeman looking the other way? Did antitrust prevent oil giants from acquiring coal, uranium, and solar-energy properties potentially competitive with petroleum? Yet is there any evidence that these mergers and acquisitions— and the failure to challenge them—have in any way contributed to realizing any vaunted economies of scale? Or that they have accelerated the exploration for *new* petroleum reserves? Or that they have hastened the development of synthetic fuels? In short, what are the public benefits of this massive escalation of firm size and industry concentration that have been allowed to proceed unobstructed?

In automobiles, did the antitrust authorities stand in the way of the joint venture between General Motors and Toyota—the world's largest and third-largest auto producers? Has it stymied Ford's joint venture with Mazda, or Chrysler's with Mitsubishi? Yet how are these quasi-mergers and agreements likely to prevent the deindustrialization of America or improve the ability of American companies to compete more effectively against their foreign rivals? Is antitrust the villain, or must we look elsewhere?

What about conglomerate mergers? Has antitrust been a significant force in interdicting the progressive conglomeration of American industry and its untoward performance effects? The answer is, once again, no.

The Japanese experience is enlightening. The *Wall Street Journal* notes that "in almost every industry where Japanese companies have done well in export markets, they have honed their teeth in fierce domestic competition." The fields include cameras, color TVs, hi-fi audio equipment, copying machines, automobiles, and steel.[9] The struggle in competitive markets, it seems, has not hindered the Japanese "miracle."

THE "PROTECTIONISM" MYTH

Yet another question central to the industrial-policy debate is what to do about aging manufacturing industries and how to reverse their loss of international competitiveness. "Before 1960," reports Lane Kirkland, president of the AFL-CIO, "manufactured imports were insignificant for most American industries. In 1960, for example, imports of shoes, apparel, steel, autos, major consumer electronic products, and machine tools represented 6 percent or less of total U.S. consumption for each of these product areas. In 1982, the import share of the U.S. market for these products ranged from 23 percent for steel to 95 percent for consumer electronics." The impact was devastating: "Between July 1973 and July 1983, there has been about a 46 percent decrease in the number of people employed in [America's] basic manufacturing industries, representing the loss of about 850,000 jobs."[10] Moreover, these job losses have been concentrated in certain areas—primarily the industrial heartland of the Midwest.

To deal with this problem, an industrial policy would provide guidance and support to lagging sectors of American industries, to help them "in catching up with international competitors by modernizing and adopting advanced technology."[11] Industrial policy would also protect these lagging industries from "the determined onslaughts of unfair trade practices" employed by other countries inundating the U.S. market with dumped or subsidized imports. The mechanisms for accomplishing these goals would be a Council for Industrial Competitiveness—including representatives of industry, labor, and government, to do the planning MITI supposedly does in Japan—and a National Bank for Industrial Competitiveness, modeled on the Reconstruction Finance Corporation of the 1930s, to grant low-price loans, guarantees, and, where necessary, outright subsidies. In addition, the lagging industries would be protected from injurious imports while they revitalize and modernize themselves to catch up with their foreign competitors.

Here again, however, a number of troubling factual questions arise. Has not protectionism in steel, in force almost continuously for nearly two decades, failed to resuscitate the industry? Has not U.S. protection of the auto industry served largely to enrich Japanese car companies and enhance *their* competitive superiority? Has not foreign competition proved so problematic in key smokestack industries primarily because they were noncompetitive in structure, noncompetitive in conduct, and delinquent in performance? In other words, are imports the *causes* or merely the symptoms of a structural malaise in some of our domestic industries?

It is doubtful whether an industrial policy as generally perceived is the optimum technique for revitalizing old industries or stimulating new ones. As Charles L. Schultze, Brookings economist and past chairman of the Council of Economic Advisers, points out, "One does not have to be a cynic to forecast that the surest way to multiply unwarranted subsidies and protectionist measures is to legitimize their existence under the rubric of industrial policy. The likely outcome of an industrial policy that encompassed some elements of both 'protecting the losers' and 'picking the winners' is that the losers would back subsidies for the winners in return for the latter's support on issues of trade protection."[12] A policy designed to assist "losers" and pick "winners" may turn out to be little more than a new form of pork-barrel politics, institutionalized protectionism, and lemon socialism.

FLAWED THEORY

Beyond its dubious factual presuppositions, neoliberal industrial policy also seems to be fatally flawed in its theoretical constructs. It is based on the precepts of what Theodore Lowi calls "interest-group liberalism"[13]—the belief that the public interest will be best served when the power to make policy is parceled out to organized interest groups. Interest-group liberalism relies on bargaining and logrolling among organized groups to determine what is in the collective best interest of the nation, and provides a mechanism for achieving it. But the fact that there is a mechanism that sanctifies wage escalation by powerful trade unions and price escalation by monopolistic corporations does not mean that the resulting wage-price spiral is consistent with the public welfare.

As the blueprint for industrial policy, interest-group liberalism suffers from some critical flaws. First, it mistakenly presumes that logrolling between a few powerful interest groups will, in fact, accurately define society's best collective interest. That is, it presumes that superficially consensual arrangements like "pluralism," "creative federalism," "partnership," "participatory democracy," and "countervailing power" adequately define and safeguard the public interest. But, as we have seen earlier, power coalesces rather countervails, and interest-group complexes—industry and labor, military and industry, regulators and regulatees—are hardly a surrogate for the public interest, properly defined.

Interest-group liberalism makes pragmatic accommodation, peaceful co-existence, and preservation of the status quo among vested interests the ultimate end of public policy. It is cartelization of political economy writ large.

Second, interest-group liberalism more often than not undermines accountability: "Parceling out policy-making power to the most interested parties tends strongly to destroy political responsibility. A program split off with a special imperium to govern itself is not merely an administrative unit. It is a structure of power with impressive capacities to resist central political control." Programs constructed on this principle, Lowi points out, "cut out all of that part of the mass of people who are not specifically organized around values salient to the goals of that program" and "there tends to be a self-conscious conspiracy to shut out the public."

Third, policy constructed this way tends "to create and maintain privilege; and it is a type of privilege particularly hard to bear or combat because it is touched with a symbolism of the state. Interest-group liberalism is not merely pluralism but is *sponsored* pluralism." It is interest-group collusion under the aegis of the state and with its blessing.

Finally, interest-group liberalism promotes inflexibility, rigidity, and resistance to change, because powerful groups strive to protect, maintain, and defend the bargains they strike among themselves. The overarching defect, as Lowi concludes, is that this approach to policy-making provides stability "by spreading a *sense* of representation at the expense of genuine flexibility, at the expense of democratic forms, and ultimately at the expense of legitimacy."[14]

A HISTORICAL FLASHBACK

These defects are not merely theoretical. Contrary to popular belief, industrial policy is not novel to the American economic scene. The National Industrial Recovery Act (NIRA), enacted during the depths of the Great Depression, was the most comprehensive attempt in peacetime to institutionalize a system of management-labor-government cooperation in the United States—just what contemporary industrial-policy advocates want.

The NIRA was essentially a political deal that offered diverse interest groups something that each of them wanted. Business wanted self-government, the elimination of "destructive" competition, and immunity from the antitrust laws. Labor wanted machinery to guarantee minimum wages, maximum hours, and the right to organize and bargain collectively. Government wanted to arrest the depression-induced downward spiral of wages and prices and thus to restore business confidence and resuscitate mass purchasing power. These objectives, many New Dealers believed, could be achieved only by scrapping an "anachronistic" regime of competition and replacing it with a "modern" system of planning along individual industry lines—sectoral planning jointly designed by business and labor and supervised by government in the public interest.[15]

Under the NIRA each industry was to draft a "code of fair competition," which had to include guarantees to labor on collective bargaining, maximum hours, and minimum wages. Once approved by the government, the code became the standard of "fair competition" for the industry it covered; violations were deemed "unfair methods of competition" within the meaning of the Federal Trade Commission Act, punishable by fine and subject to cease-and-desist orders. The president also had the power to impose codes upon industries that failed to submit one of their own drafting, as well as to license business enterprises to operate, if that was necessary to make the codes effective. Finally, the president could limit imports of foreign goods if necessary to carry out the purposes of the NIRA. Needless to say, all NIRA codes, licenses, and agreements were exempt from antitrust laws.

In practice, the codes were drafted by business, implemented by business, and enforced by business, with government playing only a *pro forma* role. The codes of "fair competition" were little more than euphemisms for "no competition." Their provisions were couched in terms of eliminating "cut-throat" competition and "chiselers," but their purpose was combination, conspiracy, and restraint of trade. General Hugh S. Johnson, the NIRA administrator, admitted as much. There is a question, the general wrote, *"whether the consumer has a right to the lowest prices that any kind of competition can provide.* The Anti-Trust Act says yes. NIRA says no. . . . The Anti-Trust Acts prohibit combinations in restraint of trade. But NIRA specifically permits such combinations with government sanction and supervision. *There is not one single Code that is not a combination in restraint of trade,* and if Codes are not permitted so as to restrain trade then NIRA ought to be repealed tomorrow. It [wouldn't] mean a thing."[16] General Johnson did not mince words: "It is industrial *self-government* that I am interested in. The function of this [National Industrial Recovery] act is not to run out and control an industry, but for that industry to come to this table and offer its ideas as to what it thinks should be done."[17] In other words, NIRA's task was not to impose codes but to accept them. Clearly the very purpose of this experiment in business-labor-government coop-eration was the compulsory cartelization of American industry under the banner of the Blue Eagle.

Industrial-organization experts did not mourn the demise of NIRA—for a number of good reasons. In the first place, the essence of NIRA was regulation of industry by industry. It was carried out in the name of the state, but not necessarily in the interest of its citizens. It was the exercise of social control by private interests, but without social account-ability or responsibility. In the words of Clair Wilcox, NIRA provided the "country with a demonstration of the character and the consequences of cartelization. It showed that industry, when given the power of 'self-government,' could not be trusted to exercise it in the public interest; that enterprise would be handicapped and vested interests protected, progress obstructed, and stagnation assured."[18] Neither, one might add, could industry be trusted with self-government when it exercised such power in symbiotic unison with organized labor.

Also, NIRA delegated virtually unchallenged power to organized business without providing more than nominal safeguards to protect consumers from exploitation. During the 1920s, trade associations had functioned as a voluntary device to regulate markets; under NIRA they became legally ordained and sanctified instruments of market control. Trade associations drafted the codes; trade-association representatives, more often than not, were the government officials who enforced the codes; and these officials exercised the power to punish violators of the codes. Consumers served on "advisory" committees, but their role was cosmetic and their influence at best marginal.

Further, NIRA posed the problem of how to define cost, and how to make cost the basis for "fair" competition (also a central problem in the regulated industries and in international trade). Accounting is as much an art as a science, and costs cannot be scientifically ascertained with impersonal objectivity. Moreover, as Wilcox observed, NIRA's cost-pro-tection philosophy ignored the economic function of cost and price. It rested on the false assumption that cost is immutable and price adjusta-ble—that cost, therefore, must always be taken as cause and price as effect. In fact, however, causation may operate the other way around:

If price falls below cost, it is possible that cost may be reduced. New materials may be employed, new methods discovered, wastes eliminated, and efficiency increased. The cost of capital may be reduced, by writing down excessive valuations, or by putting overvalued assets through the wringer of bank-ruptcy. This, after all, is the disciplinary function of the cost-price relation-ship. If price were never permitted to fall below cost, there would be no business failures, no compulsion to adjust production to changing demands, no penalty for waste and inefficiency. Business under a system of private enterprise is driven by the carrot of profit and by the stick of loss. Cost protection would leave the carrot, but it would take away the stick.[19]

Policymakers intent on protecting domestic industries against foreign competition might well take note of this insight.

Finally, the NIRA revealed the difficulties of grafting business-labor-government syndicalism onto a system of free-market economics. The NIRA experience highlighted the dangers of permitting vested interests to set the rules by which the economic game shall be played, and thus to usurp the functions of government itself. As Lionel Robbins pointed out in the 1930s, "the problem of planning is not to be solved by giving each industry the power of self-government (i.e., restriction of entry and production). This is not planning, it is syndicalism. It merely extends to whole industries the right to make plans for themselves similar to the right already enjoyed by individual entrepreneurs. But by eliminating competition, or potential competition, it creates a state of affairs much less likely to be stable—much more likely to be restrictive—than the so-called chaos of competitive enterprise."[20]

INDUSTRIAL POLICY EVALUATED

In abstracto, it would not be impossible to formulate a systematic, coherent, organically consistent government policy of trade protection and investment assistance to "mature" industries. This would be feasible if two implicit central assumptions of industrial-policy advocates were valid—that is, if a sectoral government policy were designed and administered by Platonic philosopher-kings on the basis of rational economic (rather than political) criteria, and if the substitution of labor-management-government cooperation for confrontation were in fact likely to improve economic performance. But alas, to paraphrase John Dewey, saints dream of brave utopias, while burly sinners rule the world. Contrary to the pious hopes of industrial-policy advocates, powerful vested interests—more intent on lessening the pains of economic change than on improving economic performance—would almost inevitably politicize the best mechanism and transmute it into a system of neomercantilist protectionism.

Industrial-policy proposals can be properly assessed only in a political-economy context, considering economic power groups, their dynamic interaction, and their ability to mobilize political power to protect their vested interests. If this be done, we are likely to find that industrial policy is not the way to improve economic performance.

It is crucial to recognize that industrial policy is built on a foundation of market control, jointly exercised by labor and industry, and validated by government. Each group is motivated by self-interest to support the scheme:

1. Market control is a tantalizing objective of business policy. The reason is obvious: market control confers immunity from competition. Immunity yields exorbitant profits, or the quiet life, or both.
2. Market control for business holds parallel attractions for organized labor. Where firms are monopolized, oligopolized, or cartelized, they are more inclined to give high wages and fringe benefits than in a state of free competition, because they can pass the increased costs on to their customers. As a general rule, the greater an industry's market control, the more ample are the fruits to be shared by labor and management through a system of vertical cooperation and vertical collusion. This militates toward a coalescence of power between monopolistic management and organized labor.
3. But market control is subject to uncertainty. It is in constant danger of erosion. It is forever threatened by new firms, new ideas, and new technology. It can be fortified on a stable, permanent basis only if government validates the collusive bargain between management and labor, and only if government stands ready to bail out firms performing poorly as a result of such labor-management bargains.

In sum, when stripped of euphemism and persiflage, industrial policy means the formation of a labor-industry-government complex, organized by industry, to suppress competition and protect vested interests. It is a prototype for the corporate state.

CHAPTER 26

THE OPPORTUNITY SOCIETY: THE NEO-DARWINIST VISION

The entire modern deification of survival *per se*, survival returning to itself, survival naked and abstract, with the denial of any substantive excellence in *what* survives, except the capacity for more survival still, is surely the strangest intellectual stopping place ever proposed by one man to another. — William James

The neo-Darwinist vision, like its neoliberal counterpart, is fatally flawed as a guide to public policy. It, too, is based on mythical assumptions. It, too, lacks a sound theoretical infrastructure. It, too, almost deliberately disregards evidence born of experience.

The "opportunity society" is more an ideological belief than a policy guidepost. It is a slogan—a code word for pristine, unadulterated laissez-faire. Its central policy prescriptions can (with only modest exaggeration) be stated succinctly: The best government policy is *no* government policy. A good antitrust policy is *no* antitrust policy—at least no structural policy aimed at mergers, monopolies, and oligopolies. Good economic regulation is *no* economic regulation, even in sectors controlled by natural monopolies. Appropriate social regulation is virtually *no* social regulation. Free markets—defined as markets free from government intervention—will solve society's most important problems. Free markets, the neo-Darwinists assure us, will create unbounded opportunity and unleash a now dormant reservoir of entrepreneurial talent. Consumers will be blessed with a socially optimal mix of goods and services, produced with the most efficient technologies, by optimally

sized firms, in optimally structured industries. However, this happy outcome is possible only so long as "natural laws" are given free play to
work toward their ineluctable, "natural," and hence optimal ends.

This vision is not without appeal. In an age of tumultuous complexity,
its message is comforting and reassuring: don't meddle, don't interfere
with the natural order of things, *tout s'arrangera!* Forget about industry and market imperfections, about pollution of air and water, about the
safety of foods and medicines! The market will provide all the protection
that is necessary. This message is simple enough to attract the masses;
it can be elaborated and adumbrated to suit the academic taste for
sophistication and sophistry; most important, it promises relief and se-
renity to all weary of the struggle—the lotus eaters tired of striving. It
grants us respite from the need to act, the imperative of making choices.

Alas, this "vision" is rooted not in fact but in fantasy. Laissez-faire
is not automatically conducive to superior economic performance. Permitting corporate giants to roam the Darwinian jungle does not guarantee that their pursuits will produce a *summum bonum.* To argue that,
without government intervention, economic performance will be at a
maximum is to indulge in a sterile tautology. Thus it borders on the
preposterous to argue that efficiency is at a maximum, because if it could
be increased, it would be increased, and the fact that it has not been
increased proves that it cannot. In the light of the evidence, which we
need not recite yet again, it seems absurd to argue that firms are big
because they are efficient—that they would not be big if they were not
efficient. In this book we have seen enough to cast doubt on the assertion
that bigness is the guarantor either of operating efficiency or of efficiency of innovation or social efficiency.

The neo-Darwinist "vision" contains no structural mechanism for
compelling good performance. It holds out no reliable system of durable checks and balances that can *ensure* that the discretionary power of
corporate giantism will be directed *solely* to socially desirable ends,
utilizing socially beneficial means. Modern-day Darwinists extol the private profit motive. They ceaselessly celebrate the "invisible hand." But
in their dithyrambic zeal, they forget that private interest and social
service are not necessarily synonymous. It is undeniably true that profits
and growth can result from greater operating efficiency or superior
innovativeness. But neo-Darwinists conveniently ignore the fact that
profits and size can also be attained in antisocial ways—that is, monopolization, oligopolization, collusion, and anticompetitive mergers and acquisitions. That is, untrammeled market "freedom" includes the freedom to
subvert the market—to destroy it as an effective regulatory mechanism.

The competitive market, contrary to ideological preachments, is *not* a gift of nature. It is a man-made institution that, in the absence of public supervision, can be eroded by powerful private interests unwilling to submit to its disciplining constraint.

As a man-made device, the competitive market is not perfect. It cannot solve all economic problems. It cannot create competition in situations like "natural monopoly," where effective competition is technologically infeasible and unworkable. Consumers are not omniscient, information is not perfect. Nor can the "free" market resolve externality problems of unclean air and water and lethal toxic wastes. To maintain otherwise, as neo-Darwinists do, is as Dr. Johnson said of second marriages, a triumph of hope over experience.

Finally, the neo-Darwinist "vision" is based on the supremely naïve assumption that bigness and economic power have no political consequences—that the economic sphere and the political arena are hermetically sealed off from one another. Neo-Darwinists presume that the economic giantism that can be expected to flourish in their laissez-faire regime would dutifully respect the boundary between "economics" and "politics." They assume that bigness would voluntarily confine itself to the former and disdain the latter. But as the editors of the *Wall Street Journal* remind us, "Adam Smith understood well that capitalism has to be protected from the capitalists, each of whom will seek government protection from the rough-and-tumble competition that makes the system work."[1] They realize—unlike the neo-Darwinists—that in reality, as opposed to ideology, bigness strives to shape public policy to its own ends, rather than to necessarily social ends, and seeks to avoid the sanctions of the "free" market in favor of incompetence and inefficiency. Bigness can demand, and is likely to obtain, government protection from superior foreign competitors through tariffs, quotas, "voluntary" restraints, and the like. Confronting financial collapse, whether due to mismanagement or a failure to meet the market test, bigness will not submissively cast itself on the scrap heap of failure; instead, it can demand, and is likely to obtain, protection from market failure through government bailouts—subsidies, loan guarantees, privileged dispensation from social regulations, and so forth. In a neo-Darwinist world, the only way to escape this dilemma and avoid the political influence of bigness, it seems, would require that government be unresponsive to pressures exerted upon it, a stratagem more palatable to a corporate state than to a democratic society steeped in the traditions of representative, accountable government.

In the final analysis then, the most glaring defect of the neo-Darwinist "vision" is that it ignores the political economy of power. As a result, the "free" market and the "opportunity society" so alluringly described by its apostles are, more likely than not, doomed to degenerate into freedom and opportunity for a powerful few to the detriment of the general welfare.

CHAPTER 27

A PUBLIC PHILOSOPHY

In an economy of intricate division of labor, every large organized group is in a position at any time to disrupt or to stop the whole flow of social income; and the system must soon break down if groups persist in exercising that power or if they must continuously be bribed to forgo its disastrous exercise.
— Henry C. Simons, *Economic Policy for a Free Society*

Centralization: Father knows best.
Decentralization: Then again, maybe Father doesn't know best.
— Stuart Jackson, *Business Week*

Imbued by the brute facts of their colonial experience, the Founding Fathers understood that power and the control of power pose the greatest challenge to a free society. In drafting a constitution for the political governance of the new nation, therefore, they embraced two transcendental principles: it is the *structure* of government, not the personal preferences and predilections of those who govern, that is of paramount importance; and, in Jefferson's words, that "it is not by the consolidation or concentration of powers, but by their distribution, that good government is effected."

These principles, we contend, are as relevant to the structure of economic institutions as they are to political affairs. They are as relevant today as they were two hundred years ago.

THE CHALLENGE OF ECONOMIC STRUCTURE

The challenge is to find a suitable framework—a framework attuned to the precepts of a democratic society—to deal with the core questions of political economy: Who shall make what decisions, on whose behalf, at whose cost, with what benefits, for whom, and with what social accountability? The challenge is to design and preserve a framework that has a built-in mechanism for compelling the kind of economic decision-making that is most likely, in the long run, to promote the public interest. The challenge is to construct and maintain an economic system that provides for the maximum degree of individual freedom consistent with the greatest collective liberty. The challenge is to construct an organizational framework that, at the same time, has a built-in means for detecting and correcting the bad decisions that inevitably will occur, a system of organization that in its operation will lead to a minimum of economic problems, while rendering the problems that do arise more susceptible to rational resolution. Finally, the challenge is to fashion an economic system endowed with public accountability, responsibility, and legitimacy.

In confronting these challenges, the major obstacle is the Bigness Complex. The reasons, as we have tried to demonstrate, are manifold.

Despite the hubris in which it has come to be cloaked, economic power militates against good economic performance. Whether in its horizontal, vertical, or conglomerate guise, whether wielded by business, labor, or government—or all three in coalition—it tends to undermine efficiency and to obstruct progressiveness. It creates bloated bureaucracies that are an inadequate instrument of social planning and interfere with an intelligent utilization of society's resources. It is unproductive at best and dangerous at worst. As Henry Simons pointed out long ago: "Political insight reveals that concentration of power is inherently dangerous and degrading; economic insight reveals that it is quite unnecessary."[1]

The unpoliced "free" market does not automatically restrain economic power. The competitive market system of decentralized economic decision-making is not an immutable artifact of nature. Economic power, as we have repeatedly seen, does not arise solely because of superior economic performance, nor does it persist solely by dint of economic superiority. Through monopolization, oligopolization, mergers, and sheer bigness, power tends to subvert the competitive market as a social control mechanism.

Economic power, and the threats it poses, is inherently—and unavoidably—both political and economic in nature. Power does not dutifully confine itself to the "economic" realm, narrowly construed. It does not passively submit to "the market." It does not submissively play according to an unalterable set of rules for survival and success. Instead, it reaches out to change the rules of the competitive game—or to dispense with them altogether—by capturing the state and perverting it to private (often antisocial) ends. It does so in a variety of ways: obtaining, or striving to retain, government cartelization of inherently competitive fields (e.g., airlines and trucking); pleading for government protection from foreign competition (e.g., steel and automobiles); seeking privilege, preferment, and promotion at the hand of government and at society's expense (which, as the flirtation with nuclear power shows, can entail far more than monetary costs); demanding government bailouts as a means of avoiding the consequences of self-inflicted injury and delinquent performance.

Economic power almost inevitably militates toward increasing government intervention in the economy. On the one hand, the Bigness Complex "invites" government to save it from itself—to help it avoid paying the costs of its nonfeasance or misfeasance. On the other hand, government feels compelled to intervene, in order to protect society from the adverse consequences of such nonfeasance or malfeasance. In either case, this confronts policymakers with increasingly intractable trade-offs and irreconcilable dilemmas: job preservation through import restraints (which inflate the input costs of other producers and lead to additional pleas for protection) versus tolerating the demise of some of the nation's basic industries; bailouts of collapsing corporate giants versus the threat of widespread economic devastation; tolerating the cost-push inflation induced by the wage-price spiral in oligopolized or cartelized industries versus attacking inflation with monetary/fiscal measures that would result in recession and unemployment. The difficulty of resolving such dilemmas is further compounded by the ability of the Bigness Complex to defy society—in effect to hold it hostage—by threats of massive shutdowns, layoffs, and plant closings unless its demands are validated and legitimized by government action.

Economic power is not a unidimensional phenomenon. Power blocs do not exist in isolation. They do not neutralize or countervail one another. Instead, they tend to coalesce into power complexes. Thus, the Big Three and the United Automobile Workers, the steel oligopoly and the United Steel Workers, join hands in demanding government protection from foreign competition; the major airlines and their multiple trade unions, the certificated truckers and the Teamsters Union, form a solid phalanx in opposing deregulation of their industries and the competitive entry of newcomers; the military-industrial complex is an *imperium in imperio*.

Such coalitions of power blocs, and the economic and political power they wield, compound the difficulty experienced by policymakers in dealing with problems ranging from deficient industry performance and declining international competitiveness to fighting economic instability and the seemingly congenital tendency to stagflation. Above all, they challenge the capacity of democratic government to govern in the public interest.

In the final analysis, economic power, and the problems it poses, are primarily structural in nature. They are fundamentally rooted in disproportionate size. It is disproportionate size, for example, that undermines operating, innovation, and social efficiency. It is disproportionate size in particular markets that erodes effective competition and good economic performance. It is disproportionate size that permits the Bigness Complex to manipulate the state and public policy. Many of today's most pressing economic problems, we contend, are to a crucial degree symptomatic of basic structural maladies. They are, as economist Ben W. Lewis has observed, problems of economic architecture, and not "goodness" or "badness" in the conventional moral sense.[2] They are, in short, products of the Bigness Complex. As such, they cannot be finessed with superficial palliatives; left untreated, they become more, not less, intractable.

AN AGENDA FOR ACTION

If our analysis is correct, if our economic problems are structural in nature, we must face up to the political economy of the Bigness Complex. We must confront the unpleasant fact that concentrated power exists and that it has social consequences.

The prominent "isms" that currently dominate our political debates —neoliberalism on the left, and neo-Darwinism on the right—are not the answer. They may be alluringly packaged to attract divergent constituencies; they may promise monistic (and relatively painless) solutions; they may have ideological appeal and command organized political support. But neither provides a system for controlling power. They differ only over who should be allowed to have power and to exercise it. The neoliberals would trust a coalition of Big Business, Big Labor, and Big Government. The neo-Darwinists would put their faith in the select few anointed by an untrammeled laissez-faire marketplace. Yet, neither "ism" offers a persuasive answer to Lord Acton's warning that power corrupts and absolute power corrupts absolutely. Neither provides a reliable social control mechanism.

There is, we contend, a nonideological, pragmatic alternative—an integrated, coherent public policy founded on the principle of decentraliza-

tion. Its objective would be to promote an economic architecture in which
power is dispersed to the maximum extent feasible, subject only to the
constraints of technological and economic imperatives. The virtues of
such a policy should by now be obvious: a structure in which power is
subject to automatic checks and balances and therefore provides *sys-
temic* safeguards against potential abuse; a structure that disperses
power among multiple centers of initiative and therefore fosters an
environment receptive to imagination, creativity, and progressiveness; a
structure that provides incentives for individual initiative and efficiency
and sanctions against bureaucratic lethargy and managerial arterio-
sclerosis; a structure in which power and performance are constantly
subject to social accountability; and, above all, a structure that tends to
frustrate the politicization of economic power and the manipulation of
the state by vested interests.

Without attempting to present an all-inclusive catalog of measures to
be included in such a policy, some illustrative examples may be in point.

MERGERS

The current merger mania is clearly out of control. Billion-dollar mega-
corporations are roaming the Darwinian jungle, making helter-skelter
acquisitions or merging with one another. Generally these consolidations
are unproductive at best and counterproductive at worst. They seldom
promote efficiency or enhance international competitiveness or stimulate
technological breakthroughs. They do not result in the creation of *real*
values, the building of *new* factories, the development of *new* products
or processes, or the employment of *new* workers. The vast majority of
these megamergers are a form of paper entrepreneurialism, a means for
reshuffling *existing* assets, an exercise in financial razzle-dazzle that
benefits the merger midwives of Wall Street (to the tune of more than
$150 million in 1985 for First Boston Corporation alone), but not the
American economy.

When conservative business journals like *Forbes* write that the mint
made out of takeovers by Wall Street's merger and acquisition shops
does "more to explain the current merger mania than all the blather
about synergy and diversification"; when *Business Week* in a single
year prints successive cover stories with suggestive titles like "Small Is
Beautiful," "Small Is Beautiful Now in Manufacturing," "Do Mergers
Really Work? Not Very Often—Which Raises Questions About Merger
Mania," and "Splitting Up"; when corporate executives like Martin S.
Davis, president of the giant conglomerate Gulf & Western, states that
"Bigness is not a sign of strength. In fact the opposite is true"; when
the "urge to purge" among debt-burdened acquisitors has become al-

most as powerful as the "urge to merge"—then the time for action is clearly at hand.[3]

One quick way of slowing down the pace of megamergers and acquisitions would be to pull out one linchpin of the hot corporate takeover game by controlling "junk bond" financing. This has been suggested by Federal Reserve Chairman Paul A. Volcker. It would prevent corporate raiders from financing their takeovers by, in effect, using the stock of the acquired company as collateral for loans. A similar proposal would bar the financing of megamergers by bank loans or similar debt obligations.

Our own preference would be an amendment to Section 7 of the Clayton Act barring all corporate mergers involving corporations with assets of more than $1 billion, *unless* the acquiring corporation could affirmatively demonstrate—say, before an expert tribunal like the Federal Trade Commission—that the proposed merger would not be likely to lessen competition in any line of commerce; that it would enhance operating efficiency and contribute substantially to the firm's international competitiveness; and that it would promote technological progress in demonstrably specific ways. Such legislation would, of course, permit any firms, *regardless* of size, to grow by internal expansion—by building rather than buying. It would even permit growth by acquisition, but only on the basis of proven social advantage rather than on the basis of public relations claims and media hype. Its most positive benefit would be to refocus management's attention on creative entrepreneurship and away from unproductive financial shell games.

REGULATION

In many sectors of the economy, the lodestar of public policy should be comprehensive *de*regulation—the dissolution of a government-industry-labor power complex. A policy of deregulation is eminently sensible in those sectors of the economy where inherently competitive industries have been subjected to the bureaucratic control of government regulatory commissions. In trucking and airlines, for example, regulation was not an instrument for protecting consumers from exploitation but a means of protecting vested interests from competition. Regulation was synonymous with a government-created, government-administered, and government-protected cartel that permitted regulated firms to charge exorbitant rates and labor unions to extract exorbitant wages. It gave consumers a harvest of substandard economic performance.

The deregulation of airlines in 1978, and the partial deregulation of trucking in 1980 represent a felicitous application of our decentralization principle. They are case studies worthy of imitation, in whole or in part, in other sectors of the economy where inherently competitive industries are still under the heel of bureaucratic regulation. A note of caution, however, is in order. It is not enough to deregulate an industry and then permit the deregulated firms to go on a merger and acquisition spree. Deregulation must be supplemented by strict antitrust enforcement to preserve competition and to prevent deregulation from becoming a hand-maiden of monopolization, oligopolization, and laissez-faire cartelization.[4]

Two other caveats deserve mention. First, deregulation is clearly inappropriate in cases of "natural monopoly." In such cases, deregulation would not result in the substitution of the unseen hand of the competitive market for the dead hand of bureaucratic regulation, but the exposure of consumers to the whim and caprice, the arbitrary discretion and exploitative predilection, of an uncontrolled monopolist. Second, *economic* deregulation must be carefully distinguished from *social* deregulation. The competitive market has prodigious virtues as a regulator of economic activity, but these virtues are not without exception. There are some regulatory tasks—the assurance of pure foods and drugs, clean air and water, automobile safety, and protection from toxic or otherwise hazardous wastes—which must, for better or worse, be entrusted to government. No matter how strong a society's commitment to free enterprise and competition, only ideological zealots would do away with the government's police powers to protect the health and safety of its citizens.

FOREIGN COMPETITION

We have repeatedly seen that in the typical oligopoly, a noncompetitive industry structure comprising a few large firms militates toward non-competitive industry behavior which, in turn, tends to yield unsatisfactory industry performance.

Foreign competition, of course, is (from the oligopoly's perspective) an unwelcome challenge to oligopoly power and its concomitant, deficient economic performance. Foreign competition disrupts the harmony among ostensible domestic rivals. It injects uncertainty and instability —that is, competition—into the very foundations of oligopoly structure and conduct. It is the nemesis of price maintenance schemes and "orderly" marketing arrangements. In short, it promotes the public interest in good industry performance.

Understandably, then, oligopolies strive to promote their private interest over that of the public, and seek to immunize themselves from this challenge, by petitioning for government protection. They demand (with the support of their trade unions) that the government impose barriers to foreign competition in the form of tariffs, import quotas, and government-sanctioned international cartels. The proper response to such demands should be obvious: to the extent that, in oligopolized or monopolized industries, imports constitute the only source of effective competition; to the extent that imports in such industries are a symptom and not a cause of delinquent industry performance; to the extent that imports, therefore, provide a necessary stimulus for the industry's reform and revitalization, the government should clearly refrain from interfering. Here, indeed, is a clear case for laissez-faire—except, of course, where foreign firms or governments are proven guilty of predatory competition or convicted of violating the GATT rules for international trade.

WAGE-PRICE SPIRALS

Concentrated economic power has not only microeconomic, but also macroeconomic consequences. In industries where firms exercise economic power in the product market, and where dominant trade unions control the labor market, there is an inevitable tendency for the two power blocs to combine forces. Each gains from the arrangement. Workers can obtain higher wages and more generous fringe benefits, while the firms are free to pass these higher costs on (after adding an appropriate "kicker" to their profit margin) in the form of higher prices. The two power blocs, acting in unison, either tacitly or overtly, can play this wage-price escalation game in seeming perpetuity, but only so long as the industry is immune from outside competition or the entry of newcomers.

The result of this process of wage-price escalation is a tendency toward persistent, ratchetlike cost-push inflation that is difficult to control, unless the government is willing to tighten the monetary-fiscal noose sufficiently to induce a recession. Short of such Draconian measures, or the imposition of government wage and price controls, there is only one alternative: to promote enough competition in product markets so that firms will be unable to grant exorbitant wage demands or to raise prices with impunity. That such a policy is both feasible and effective has been demonstrated in industries impacted by foreign competition and in competitive industries liberated from government cartelization.

DEFENSE CONTRACTING

Coalescing power in the military-industrial complex has consequences far more serious than $7,000 coffee brewers and $600 hammers. Endemic multibillion-dollar cost overruns exacerbate an unprecedented federal budget deficit. They represent an enormous waste in the American economy at a time when funds are sorely needed for world-class plants, productivity, and products. And ironically, but perhaps most significant, coalescing power jeopardizes national security and undermines the country's defenses, as weapons become less reliable, as cost overruns shrink the number of weapons that are affordable, and as funds necessary for combat readiness and support are consumed by weapons procurement. As President Reagan points out, "waste and fraud by [defense] contractors are more than a ripoff of the taxpayer—they're a blow to the security of our nation."[5]

Handwringing and moral outrage are not the answer. Nor can the problem be resolved by spawning a multitude of watchdog agencies and grafting them onto an already bloated bureaucracy. Instead, a competitive industry structure must be put into place that can keep costs in check and promote good economic performance. The Project on Military Procurement advocates legislation mandating "that the present 6 percent competitive procurement in [the Department of Defense] be slowly increased each year by say, one quarter, until 70 percent of all procurement is based on competitive bids." As an incentive, they suggest, "noncompetitive procurement would be cut back proportionally in any year that the Pentagon fails to reach the mandated percentage."[6] Instead of one-shot "winner-take-all" procurement, bids could be regularly recompeted for, and contracts parceled out among competing firms on the basis of their submitted prices. This approach—experimentally adopted with great success in ammunition procurement,[7] and recently proposed for the acquisition of fighter jet engines—would foster continuous competition through "repeat sales," while at the same time sustaining rivals capable of competing as bids are periodically relet.[8] In addition, weapons production facilities built with public monies should be dispersed widely to create a large competitive base of contracting firms rather than, as has been the case since World War II, frequently permitting them to become concentrated (free of charge) in the hands of the dozen largest contractors.[9] Similarly, rather than being permitted to entrench monopoly, technology developed by contractors at public expense should remain in the public domain and made as widely available as possible. Finally, government production could serve as a valuable tool for compelling good economic performance, as well as a means for breaking the stranglehold of monopoly; as Josephus Daniels, secretary of the navy from 1913 to 1921, discovered after outfitting the navy with its own shipbuilding facilities, private "builders found they must compete to get orders, and Navy Yards understood they must do as well or better than outside concerns."[10]

Steps such as these, we contend, constitute a necessary structural solution to what is, at bottom, a structural problem of coalescing power.

Once in place, these steps can be bolstered in a variety of ways, including requirements that contractors guarantee their weapons to be free from defects and capable of meeting standards contracted for; establishing an independent weapons-testing capability; and enactment of sanctions blocking the "revolving door" between monopolistic suppliers and military procurement offices.

BAILOUTS

Public bailouts of collapsing bigness complexes seem to have become the order of the day: Penn-Central, Lockheed, Chrysler, Continental Illinois, and possibly the entire farm credit system. Yet we contend that this trend represents a perversion of sound public policy. Failure as the price for poor performance is an indispensable mechanism by which a decentralized, competitive market system disciplines economic decision making. It is a vital means for harnessing self-interest and rendering it accountable to, and congruent with, the public interest—a means for ensuring that resources are utilized in accordance with society's wishes by hands best suited to this task.

Bailouts of bigness from the consequences of its misfeasance and malfeasance are profoundly unwise. They blatantly discriminate against the thousands of small businesses permitted to fail every year. They are tantamount to a perverse "lemon socialism," whereby profits are privatized while costs are publicly born. By rewarding bigness, public bailouts almost inevitably ensure that poor economic performance will persist—if not proliferate—into the future. And perhaps most disturbing, they render the Bigness Complex even more powerful, and even less accountable, to society.

Instead of bailouts, bankruptcy is a competitive market society's preferred method for dealing with financial insolvency. Bankruptcy proceedings do *not* in any way destroy *physical* plant and equipment; factories are not toppled over, nor is machinery smashed. Rather, such proceedings bring about a necessary and desirable readjustment in (artificial) accounting and financial values in order to permit economically productive properties to remain in operation—either in their existing field of employment, or in other activities more highly valued by society. Hence, bankruptcy is a competitive market society's ingenious resolution of the problem of preserving physical assets and keeping them intact, while at the same time realigning the financing of those assets, the management of them, and the uses to which they are put.

In the final analysis, the bailout problem highlights how disproportionate size fundamentally alters an economic system and renders it more vulnerable. It underscores the importance of keeping firms to a size where society can tolerate their failure—a size that prevents private tragedies from becoming social catastrophes, and that thereby prevents the public from being hostage to bigness.

The foregoing are illustrative of the ways in which a structure of economic decentralization can be implemented and maintained. Such steps as these—and the list is suggestive rather than exhaustive—are integrally linked with antitrust as mutually reinforcing elements of a set of unified, and, we contend, viable and acceptable guideposts for economic policy in a free society.

Above all, these policies, anchored in the principle of decentralization, represent a reorientation of current thought—a reorientation of our public philosophy. As Henry C. Simons, the great libertarian of yesteryear, wisely observed,

> The great enemy of democracy is monopoly, in all its forms: gigantic corporations, trade associations and other agencies for price control, trade-unions—or, in general, organization and concentration of power within functional classes. Effectively organized functional groups possess tremendous power for exploiting the community at large and even for sabotaging the system. The existence of competition within such groups, on the other hand, serves to protect the community as a whole and to give an essential flexibility to the economy. The disappearance of competition would almost assure the wrecking of the system in the economic struggle of organized minorities; on the political side, it would present a hopeless dilemma. If the organized economic groups were left to exercise their monopoly powers without political restraint, the result would be usurpation of sovereignty by these groups. . . . On the other hand, if the state undertakes to tolerate (instead of destroying) such organizations and to regulate their regulations, it will have assumed tasks and responsibilities incompatible with its enduring in a democratic form.

"Thus, for one who prizes political liberty," Simons concluded, "there can be no sanguine view as to where the proliferation of organization leads."[11]

THE CHOICE: SELF-DELUSION OR REALISM?

Unfortunately for the nation, the hold of the Bigness Complex remains as powerful as ever among some prominent economic policymakers. Even in late 1985, officials in the Reagan administration continue to be beguiled by bigness. They persist in discerning in bigness some secret alchemy for inducing productivity, innovation, and international competitiveness.

For example, Attorney General Edwin Meese III declares to have discovered "that big is not necessarily bad and that small and many [firms] are not of themselves necessarily good."[12] Similarly, Commerce Secretary Malcolm Baldrige characterizes antitrust as "based on economic theories with no relation to the present and future." He proposes that Congress repeal entirely the antimerger provisions of the Clayton Act because, he believes, such a step "will increase the efficiency of U.S. firms and strengthen their competitiveness in world markets."[13] The President's Commission on Industrial Competitiveness, too, warns that "U.S. antitrust law must recognize the potential efficiency of mergers and other business combinations."[14]

These pronouncements are alarming, not only because they are predicated on what Professor Phillip Areeda describes as the astonishing suggestion "that the thing that prevents the American automobile industry from competing effectively with Japan is that General Motors is *too small.*"[15] They are not troubling just because they surrealistically posit that antitrust has been too strictly enforced, despite the fact that the nation's economy is in the throes of the most massive merger and consolidation movement ever. They are not unsettling merely because they are devoid of scientific proof or because they run counter to the "new learning" in business that—perhaps—"small is beautiful." These policy perorations now emanating from Washington are most depressing, because they attest to the durability of mythological belief and the addiction to ideological dogma, even at the highest levels of government.

A cynic once said that establishments reward the lies that sustain them and punish the truths that embarrass them. More unfortunate, perhaps, they also believe the myths that undermine them.

NOTES

PREFACE

1. See Kenneth Minogue, *Alien Powers: The Pure Theory of Ideology* (New York: St. Martin's Press, 1985). On the role of myth and ritual, see Bronislaw Malinowski, *Myth in Primitive Psychology* (New York: W. W. Norton, 1927).
2. See *Business Week*, 27 May 1985, 3 June 1985, 1 July 1985.
3. See *Forbes*, 2 December 1985.
4. See *The Economist*, 25 December 1976, 17 April 1982.
5. See *Fortune*, June 1965.
6. Quoted in Frank H. Knight, *Intelligence and Democratic Action* (Cambridge, Mass.: Harvard University Press, 1960), p. 57.
7. Adam Smith, *The Wealth of Nations*, Book V.

1. POWER AND PUBLIC POLICY

1. Jack Kemp, *An American Renaissance* (New York: Harper & Row, 1979), p. 11.
2. William Graham Sumner, *The Challenge of Facts and Other Essays* (New Haven: Yale University Press, 1914). In these essays, Sumner articulates an ideology that bears an uncanny resemblance to the contemporary neo-Darwinist literature. Compare Robert H. Bork, *The Antitrust Paradox* (New York: Basic Books, 1978), and George Gilder, *Wealth and Poverty* (New York: Basic Books, 1981).
3. *Business Week*, 4 July 1983, pp. 55–56. For a more detailed exposition of these views, see chapter 25 *infra*.
4. Quoted in *National Journal*, 1 December 1984, p. 2298.
5. Kevin P. Phillips, *Staying on Top* (New York: Random House, 1984), pp. 158–59.
6. Address by Lewis Engman to the Financial Analysts Federation, Detroit, 7 October 1974.
7. Alfred D. Chandler, Jr., *The Visible Hand* (Cambridge, Mass.: Harvard University Press, 1977), p. 1.
8. American Column & Lumber Co. v. United States, 257 U.S. 377 (1921).

382 ■ NOTES

2. ECONOMISTS AND POWER

1. John Maynard Keynes, *Essays in Biography* (New York: Harcourt, Brace & Co., 1933), p. 250.
2. Theodore Roszak, ed., *The Dissenting Academy* (New York: Pantheon Books, 1968). For recent, penetrating critiques of the economics profession, see Robert Lekachman, *Economists at Bay* (New York: McGraw-Hill, 1976), and Alfred S. Eichner, *Why Economics Is Not Yet a Science* (Armonk, N.Y.: M.E. Sharpe, 1983).
3. Joan Robinson, *Economic Philosophy* (Garden City, N.Y.: Anchor Books, 1964), p. 81.
4. Leo Rogin, *The Meaning and Validity of Economic Theory* (New York: Harper & Bros., 1956), p. 4.
5. George J. Stigler, "Monopoly and Oligopoly by Merger," *American Economic Review Proceedings* 40 (May 1950):30–31.
6. Robert L. Heilbroner, *The Worldly Philosophers*, rev. ed. (New York: Simon and Schuster, 1961), pp. 214, 217, and 218.
7. Rogin, *Meaning and Validity*, pp. 11–12.
8. Kenneth Boulding, "The Economics of Knowledge and the Knowledge of Economics," *American Economic Review Proceedings* 56 (May 1966):9.
9. This view, although it may be shared by only a minority of economists, is hardly iconoclastic. One notable exception is Professor Wassily Leontief (Nobel Laureate, past president of the American Economics Association, and father of input-output analysis), who writes, "Year after year economic theorists continue to produce scores of mathematical models and to explore in great detail their formal properties; and the econometricians fit algebraic functions of all possible shapes to essentially the same sets of data without being able to advance, in any perceptible way, a systematic understanding of the structure and operations of a real economic system." ("Academic Economics," *Science* [9 July 1982]:107.) To this assessment, Professor Paul A. Samuelson (Nobel Laureate, past president of the American Economic Association, and mathematical economist extraordinaire) adds this admonition: "The first duty of an economist is to describe what is out there: a valid description without a deeper explanation is worth a thousand times more than a clever explanation of nonexistent facts." ("A Brief Post-Keynesian Survey" in *Keynes' General Theory: Reports of Three Decades*, ed. Robert Lekachman [New York: St. Martin's Press, 1964], p. 339.)
10. Kurt Rothschild, *Power in Economics* (London: Penguin Books, 1971), p. 7.
11. Samuelson, "A Brief Post-Keynesian Survey," p. 339.
12. Paul A. Samuelson and Robert M. Solow, "Analytical Aspects of Anti-Inflation Policy," *American Economic Review Proceedings* 50 (May 1960):192.
13. Gottfried Haberler, *The Challenge to the Free Market Economy* (Washington: American Enterprise Institute, 1976), p. 4. See also Haberler, *Stagflation* (Washington: American Enterprise Institute, 1985).
14. Haberler, *The Challenge*, p. 5.
15. Ibid., pp. 17–18.
16. Robert Eisner, "Sacrifices to Fight Inflation," *New York Times*, 8 November 1979. See also Hendrik Houthakker, "A Positive Way to Fight Inflation," *Wall Street Journal*, 30 July 1974.
17. *New York Times*, 17 February 1980.
18. Paul A. Samuelson, "A Brief Post-Keynesian Survey," p. 339.
19. John Kenneth Galbraith, *The New Industrial State* (Boston: Houghton-Mifflin, 1967).
20. Joseph A. Schumpeter, *Capitalism, Socialism and Democracy* (New York: Harper & Bros., 1943), pp. 82–106.

PART II: THE APOLOGETICS OF POWER

1. John Bates Clark, *The Control of Trusts* (New York: Macmillan, 1901), p. 17.
2. Richard L. Nelson, *Merger Movements in American Industry* (New York: National Bureau of Economic Research, 1959), pp. 161–62; F. M. Scherer, *Industrial Market Structure and Economic Performance*, 2nd ed. (Chicago: Rand McNally, 1980), p. 121.
3. George J. Stigler, "Monopoly and Oligopoly by Merger," *American Economic Review* 40 (May 1950):30.
4. John Blair, *Economic Concentration* (New York: Harcourt Brace Jovanovich, 1972), p. 262; Robert L. Heilbroner, *The Economic Transformation of America* (New York: Harcourt Brace Jovanovich, 1977), p. 110; Henry R. Seager and Charles A. Gulick, *Trust and Corporation Problems* (New York: Harper & Bros., 1929), p. 224.
5. Nelson, *Merger Movements*, pp. 5, 34, 53, 102.
6. Quoted in Gabriel Kolko, *The Triumph of Conservatism* (New York: Free Press, 1963), pp. 69–70.
7. Quoted in George E. Mowry, *The Era of Theodore Roosevelt* (New York: Harper & Row, 1958), p. 132.
8. Woodrow Wilson, *The New Freedom* (New York: Doubleday, 1913), p. 165.
9. Ibid., pp. 166–67.
10. Charles J. Bullock, "Trust Literature: A Survey and A Criticism," *Quarterly Journal of Economics* 15 (February 1901):191.
11. Wilson quoted in John Milton Cooper, *The Warrior and the Priest* (Cambridge, Mass.: Harvard University Press, 1983), pp. 194–95.
12. Quoted in Richard Hofstadter, *Social Darwinism in American Thought*, rev. ed. (Boston: Beacon Press, 1955), p. 45.
13. Sidney Sherwood, "Influence of the Trust in the Development of Undertaking Genius," *Yale Review* 8 (February 1900):363–64.
14. Robert H. Bork, *The Antitrust Paradox* (New York: Basic Books, 1978), pp. 118, 164.
15. House Subcommittee on Monopolies and Commercial Law, *Mergers and Acquisitions Hearings*, 97th Cong., 1st sess., 1983, p. 176.
16. Louis D. Brandeis, *The Curse of Bigness* (New York: Viking Press, 1935), p. 116.
17. E.A.G. Robinson, *The Structure of Competitive Industry* (Cambridge, England: The University Press, 1947), p. 45.
18. *Wall Street Journal*, 21 February 1985.
19. A.R. Burns, "Antitrust Symposium," *American Economic Review* 39 (June 1949): 603.

3. OPERATING EFFICIENCY

1. *Business Week*, 22 October 1984, p. 152.
2. Ibid.
3. Ibid., 27 May 1985, p. 88.
4. Ibid., 3 June 1985, p. 88.
5. Ibid., 1 July 1985, p. 53.
6. Yale Brozen, *Concentration, Mergers, and Public Policy* (New York: Macmillan, 1982), pp. 56–57.
7. Robert H. Bork, "Antitrust and the Theory of Concentrated Markets," in *Industrial Concentration and the Market System*, ed. Eleanor M. Fox and James T. Halverson (Chicago: American Bar Association, 1979), p. 86.
8. House Select Committee on Small Business, *Steel—Acquisitions, Mergers, and Expansion of 12 Major Companies, 1900–1950, Hearings*, 81st Cong., 2nd sess., 1950.
9. See Justice Day's dissenting opinion in United States v. United States Steel Corp., 251 U.S. 417 (1920).

384 ■   NOTES

10. House Subcommittee on the Study of Monopoly Power, *Study of Monopoly Power Hearings*, part 4A, 81st Cong., 2nd sess., 1950, p. 967.
11. *Business Week*, 25 February 1985, pp. 50–51.
12. Experts are agreed that an annual capacity of 4 million tons constitutes the minimum efficient scale for a modern, integrated steel plant with a narrow product range. Yet, as late as 1980, some 75 percent of the integrated steel plants operating in the United States had an annual capacity of less than 4 million tons, i.e., less than the minimum efficient scale. (The average capacity of the U.S. Steel Corporation's plants was 2.9 million tons.) This contrasts sharply with the size distribution of integrated plants in Japan. For further details, see Walter Adams and Hans Mueller, "The Steel Industry," in *The Structure of American Industry*, 7th ed., ed. Walter Adams (New York: Macmillan, 1986).
13. *Wall Street Journal*, 12 January 1981.
14. *New York Times*, 24 February 1984, 7 August 1983, sec. 3.
15. Congressional Budget Office, *The Effects of Import Quotas on the Steel Industry* (Washington, D.C.: July 1984), p. 23.
16. *New York Times*, 16 July 1982; *Wall Street Journal*, 12 January 1981.
17. Donald F. Barnett and Louis Schorsch, *Steel: Upheaval in a Basic Industry* (Cambridge, Mass.: Ballinger, 1983), pp. 92–93.
18. Ibid., p. 191.
19. *Wall Street Journal*, 12 January 1981.
20. U.S. International Trade Commission, *Carbon and Certain Alloy Steel Products*, vol. 1 (Washington, D.C.: July 1984), pp. 97, 110.
21. *Fortune*, 29 April 1985, p. 266.
22. Walter Adams and James W. Brock, "The Automobile Industry," in *Structure of American Industry*.
23. Senate Subcommittee on Antitrust and Monopoly, *The Industrial Reorganization Act Hearings*, part 4, 93rd Cong., 2nd sess., 1974, pp. 2468, 2655.
24. Eric J. Toder, *Trade Policy and the U.S. Automobile Industry* (New York: Praeger, 1978), p. 133.
25. Lawrence J. White, "The Automobile Industry," in *The Structure of American Industry*, 6th ed., ed. Walter Adams (New York: Macmillan, 1982), p. 150.
26. Adams and Brock, "The Automobile Industry."
27. The average plant operated by the four largest Japanese firms produces an average annual output of approximately 460,000 cars; the comparable average plant size for GM and Ford (considered together) is on the order of 182,000 cars per year.
28. Quoted in U.S. Congress, Temporary National Economic Committee, *Investigation of Concentration of Economic Power*, monograph no. 13, 76th Cong., 3rd sess., 1941, pp. 130–31.
29. J. Patrick Wright, *On A Clear Day You Can See General Motors* (Grosse Point, Mich.: Wright Enterprises, 1979), pp. 100, 114–115.
30. *Wall Street Journal*, 19 December 1983.
31. House Subcommittee on Commerce, Transportation, and Tourism, *Future of the Automobile Industry Hearing*, 98th Cong., 2nd sess., 1984, p. 237.
32. *Wall Street Journal*, 9 January 1985.
33. *Business Week*, 4 March 1985, p. 94.
34. Peter F. Drucker, *Concept of the Corporation*, rev. ed. (New York: John Day Co., 1972), p. 56.
35. Senate Subcommittee on Antitrust and Monopoly, *Economic Concentration Hearings*, part 8-A, 91st Cong., 1st sess., 1969, p. 260.
36. Ibid., part 8, p. 4737.
37. House Antitrust Subcommittee, *Investigation of Conglomerate Corporations*, part 7, 91st Cong., 2nd sess., 1970, p. 327.

38. Robert H. Hayes and William J. Abernathy, "Managing Our Way to Economic Decline," *Harvard Business Review* 58 (July–August 1980):74.
39. Joel Dean, "Causes and Consequences of Growth by Conglomerate Merger: An Introduction," *St. John's Law Review* 44 (Spring 1970):29.
40. Cited in Senate Subcommittee on Antitrust and Monopoly, *Mergers and Industrial Concentration, Hearings*, 95th Cong., 2nd sess., 1978, p. 183.
41. *Business Week*, 30 June 1980, p. 81.
42. House Subcommittee on Monopolies and Commercial Law, *Mergers and Acquisitions Hearings*, 97th Cong., 1st sess., 1983, p. 255.
43. *Business Week*, 16 August 1982, p. 103; *New York Times*, 15 November 1981, sec. 3.
44. *Business Week*, 23 May 1983, p. 130.
45. *Fortune*, 11 January 1982, p. 34.
46. Dennis C. Mueller, "The Effects of Conglomerate Mergers," *Journal of Banking and Finance* 1 (1977):344.
47. *New York Times*, 27 January 1985.
48. F.M. Scherer, "Mergers, Sell-Offs, and Managerial Behavior" (Berlin paper, 1984), p. 22.
49. Joe S. Bain, *Barriers to New Competition* (Cambridge, Mass.: Harvard University Press, 1956), pp. 73, 85–88.
50. F.M. Scherer, *Industrial Market Structure and Economic Performance*, 2nd ed. (Chicago: Rand McNally, 1980), p. 94.
51. F.M. Scherer, et al., *The Economics of Multi-Plant Operation* (Cambridge, Mass.: Harvard University Press, 1975), p. 339.
52. F.M. Scherer, *Industrial Market Structure*, 118.
53. F.M. Scherer, *Economics*, 393.
54. House Subcommittee on the Study of Monopoly Power, *Hearings*, p. 996.
55. *Business Week*, 22 October 1984, p. 152. For additional evidence on the burdensome inefficiencies of corporate bureaucracy, see Mark Green and John F. Berry, *The Challenge of Hidden Profits* (New York: William Morrow, 1985).
56. Congressional Budget Office, *Effects of Import Quotas*, p. 6.
57. Quoted in *Business Week*, 22 October 1984, p. 153.

4. INNOVATION EFFICIENCY

1. John Kenneth Galbraith, *American Capitalism* (New York: Houghton-Mifflin, 1952), p. 86.
2. Joseph A. Schumpeter, *Capitalism, Socialism and Democracy*, 3rd ed. (New York: Harper & Row, 1950), pp. 81–106.
3. John Jewkes, David Sawers, and Richard Stillerman, *The Sources of Invention*, 2nd ed. (New York: W.W. Norton, 1969).
4. Senate Subcommittee on Antitrust and Monopoly, *Economic Concentration Hearings*, part 3, 89th Cong., 1st sess., 1965, pp. 1078, 1103–06.
5. Daniel Hamberg, *R&D* (New York: Random House, 1966), p. 16.
6. Senate Subcommittee on Antitrust and Monopoly, *Economic Concentration Hearings*, p. 1081.
7. Jewkes, Sawers, and Stillerman, *Sources*, p. 144.
8. Ibid., pp. 144–45.
9. Senate Subcommittee on Antitrust and Monopoly, *Economic Concentration Hearings*, p. 1086; *New York Times*, 18 April 1976.
10. Edwin Mansfield et al., *The Production and Application of New Technology* (New York: W.W. Norton, 1977), p. 45 (emphasis added).
11. Ibid., pp. 204–05.
12. Senate Subcommittee on Antitrust and Monopoly, *Economic Concentration Hearings*, p. 1478.

13. National Science Board, *Science Indicators* (Washington, D.C.: 1976), p. 118.

14. F.M. Scherer, *Industrial Market Structure and Economic Performance,* 2nd ed., (Chicago: Rand McNally, 1980), p. 422.

15. Edwin Mansfield, "Composition of R and D Expenditures: Relationship to Size of Firm, Concentration, and Innovative Output," *Review of Economics and Statistics* 63 (November 1981):612 (emphasis added).

16. Senate Subcommittee on Antitrust and Monopoly, *Economic Concentration Hearings,* p. 1259.

17. Edwin Mansfield, "Industrial Research and Development Expenditures: Determinants, Prospects, and Relation to Size of Firm and Inventive Output," *Journal of Political Economy* 72 (August 1964):336.

18. Senate Subcommittee on Antitrust and Monopoly, *Economic Concentration Hearings,* pp. 1296–99.

19. Hamberg, *R&D,* pp. 100–01.

20. *Business Week,* 18 April 1983, p. 80.

21. *Wall Street Journal,* 10 September 1984.

22. *Business Week,* 18 April 1983, p. 80.

23. Senate Subcommittee on Antitrust and Monopoly, *Economic Concentration Hearings,* p. 1115.

24. Jewkes, Sawers, and Stillerman, *Sources,* pp. 170–83.

25. Senate Subcommittee on Antitrust and Monopoly, *Economic Concentration Hearings,* p. 1304.

26. Ibid., pp. 1302–03.

27. For a more detailed analysis, see Walter Adams and Hans Mueller, "The Steel Industry," in *The Structure of American Industry,* 7th ed., ed. Walter Adams (New York: Macmillan, 1986).

28. Walter Adams and Joel B. Dirlam, "Big Steel, Invention, and Innovation," *Quarterly Journal of Economics* 80 (May 1966).

29. *Fortune,* October 1966, p. 135.

30. Quoted in R. Easton and J. Donaldson, "Continuous Casting," *Iron and Steel Engineer* 43 (October 1966):80.

31. U.S. Office of Technology Assessment, *Technology and Steel Industry Competitiveness* (Washington, D.C.: 1980), p. 290.

32. *Wall Street Journal,* 3 August 1983.

33. Senate Subcommittee on Antitrust and Monopoly, *Economic Concentration Hearings,* p. 1123; Donald A. Moore, "The Automobile Industry," in *The Structure of American Industry,* rev. ed., ed. Walter Adams (New York: Macmillan, 1950), p. 303.

34. Quoted in Senate Subcommittee on Executive Reorganization, *Federal Role in Traffic Safety Hearings,* part 3, 89th Cong., 2nd sess., 1966, p. 1266.

35. Senate Subcommittee on Antitrust and Monopoly, *The Industrial Reorganization Act Hearings,* part 3, 93rd Cong., 2nd sess., 1974, p. 1954.

36. *New York Times,* 26 April 1981, sec. 3.

37. Senate Committee on Commerce, *Automotive Research and Development and Fuel Economy Hearings,* 93rd Cong., 1st sess., 1973, p. 369.

38. Lawrence J. White, "The Automobile Industry," in *The Structure of American Industry,* 5th ed., ed. Walter Adams (New York: Macmillan, 1977), p. 195.

39. House Subcommittee on Transportation, Aviation, and Materials, *Automobile Research Competition Act Hearing,* 97th Cong., 2nd sess., 1982, p. 38.

40. House Subcommittee on Economic Stabilization, *To Determine the Impact of Foreign Sourcing on Industry and Communities Hearing,* 97th Cong., 1st sess., 1981, p. 54.

41. J. Patrick Wright, *On A Clear Day You Can See General Motors* (Grosse Point, Mich.: Wright Enterprises, 1979), p. 4.

42. The following is drawn from McDonald v. Johnson & Johnson, 537 F. Supp. 1282 (D. Minn. 1982).

NOTES

■ 387

43. Scherer, *Industrial Market Structure*, p. 438. See also John Blair, *Economic Concentration* (New York: Harcourt Brace Jovanovich, 1972), pp. 199–254.
44. Mansfield, "Composition of R and D Expenditures," p. 612.
45. *Detroit Free Press*, 19 March 1985.
46. *Business Week*, 18 April 1983, pp. 84–89.

5. SOCIAL EFFICIENCY

1. Alfred D. Chandler, Jr., *The Visible Hand* (Cambridge, Mass.: Harvard University Press, 1977), p. 1.
2. Willard F. Mueller, *The Celler-Kefauver Act: The First 27 Years*, Study Prepared for the House Subcommittee on Monopolies and Commercial Law, 96th Cong., 1st sess., 1979, p. 75.
3. Quoted in Anthony Sampson, *The Sovereign State of ITT* (New York: Stein & Day, 1973), p. 125.
4. Carl Gerstacker, "The Structure of the Corporation" (Address prepared for the White House Conference on the Industrial World Ahead, Washington, D.C., 7–9 February 1972), quoted in Richard J. Barnet and Ronald E. Muller, *Global Reach* (New York: Simon and Schuster, 1974), p. 37.
5. Randall Meyer, "The Role of Big Business in Achieving National Goals," reprinted in *Economics: Mainstream Readings and Radical Critiques*, 3rd ed., ed. David Mermelstein (New York: Random House, 1976), p. 81.
6. Allyn A. Young, "The Sherman Act and the New Antitrust Legislation," *Journal of Political Economy* 23 (1915):214.
7. Joseph Kraft, "Annals of Industry," *The New Yorker*, 5 May 1980, p. 140.
8. John Kenneth Galbraith, *The New Industrial State*, 2nd ed. (Boston: Houghton Mifflin, 1971), p. 76.
9. Wilfred Owen, *The Accessible City* (Washington, D.C.: Brookings Institution, 1972), p. 1.
10. United States v. National City Lines, 186 F. 2d 562 (1951).
11. Senate Subcommittee on Antitrust and Monopoly, *Industrial Reorganization Act, Hearings*, part 3, 93rd Cong., 2nd sess., 1974, p. 1810.
12. Ibid., part 4A, pp. A-2–A-3.
13. George M. Smerk, *Urban Transportation* (Bloomington, Indiana: Indiana University Press, 1965), p. 50.
14. See Seymour Melman, *Profits Without Production* (New York: Alfred A. Knopf, 1983), p. 41.
15. Quoted in John Keats, *The Insolent Chariots* (New York: Lippincott, 1958), p. 14.
16. Senate Committee on Commerce, *Automotive Research and Development and Fuel Economy Hearings*, 93rd Cong., 1st sess., 1973, p. 564; Ed Cray, *Chrome Colossus* (New York: McGraw-Hill, 1980), p. 524.
17. Senate Committee on Commerce, *Automotive Research and Development Hearings*, p. 70.
18. Ibid., p. 424.
19. Franklin M. Fisher, Zvi Griliches, and Carl Kaysen, "The Costs of Automobile Model Changes Since 1949," *Journal of Political Economy* 70 (October 1962):348.
20. *Fortune*, 22 October 1979, p. 48.
21. Paul Blumberg, "Snarling Cars," *The New Republic*, 23 January 1983, p. 12.
22. National Academy of Engineering, *The Competitive Status of the U.S. Auto Industry* (Washington, D.C.: National Academy Press, 1982), pp. 20, 70.
23. A small, light-weight car developed by General Motors was marketed in Australia in 1948 by a GM subsidiary; Ford's light car appeared the same year as the French Ford Vedette. Lawrence J. White, "The American Automobile Industry and the Small Car, 1945–1970," *Journal of Industrial Economics* 20 (April 1972):181.

24. National Academy of Engineering, *Competitive Status*, p. 70.
25. *Fortune*, August 1957, p. 105.
26. White, "American Automobile Industry and the Small Car," p. 191.
27. Ibid., p. 180.
28. Lawrence J. White, *The Automobile Industry Since 1945* (Cambridge, Mass.: Harvard University Press, 1971), pp. 228–29.
29. Senate Committee on Commerce, *Automotive Research and Development Hearings*, p. 619. Internal company memoranda suggest that General Motors became sufficiently concerned about automotive air pollution as to begin researching the problem as early as 1938. See "Smog Control Antitrust Case," *Congressional Record*, 18 May 1971 (House edition) pp. 15626–27.
30. Senate Subcommittee on Air and Water Pollution, *Air Pollution—1967 (Automotive Air Pollution) Hearings*, part 1, 90th Cong., 1st sess., 1967, p. 158.
31. "Smog Control Antitrust Case," pp. 15627, 15633.
32. National Academy of Sciences, *Report by the Committee on Motor Vehicle Emissions*, 12 February 1973, reprinted in *Congressional Record*, 28 February 1973 (Senate edition) p. 5832.
33. The auto industry's record of social efficiency is equally deplorable on the safety front. For the classic exposé, see Ralph Nader, *Unsafe At Any Speed* (New York: Grossman, 1965). An updated auto safety analysis is provided in Walter Adams and James W. Brock, "Bigness and Social Efficiency: A Case Study of the U.S. Auto Industry," in *Corporations and Society*, ed. Arthur Selwyn Miller and Warren Samuels (Greenwich, Conn.: Greenwood Press, 1986).
34. Kraft, "Annals of Industry," pp. 155–56.
35. *Fortune*, 30 April 1984, p. 276; 22 August 1983, p. 170.
36. Stephen Martin and Walter Measday, "The Petroleum Industry," in *The Structure of American Industry*, 7th ed., ed. Walter Adams (New York: Macmillan, 1986).
37. See John Blair, *The Control of Oil* (New York: Vintage Books, 1976). Also, see Senate Committee on the Judiciary, *Petroleum Industry Competition Act of 1976 Report*, part 1, 94th Cong., 2nd sess., 1976.
38. Senate Special Subcommittee on Integrated Oil Operations, *Market Performance and Competition in the Petroleum Industry Hearings*, part 5, 93rd Cong., 2nd sess., 1974, p. 1597.
39. Quoted in Senate Subcommittee on Antitrust and Monopoly, *Governmental Intervention in the Market Mechanism Hearings*, part 2, 91st Cong., 1st sess., 1969, p. 725.
40. See Robert Engler, *The Brotherhood of Oil* (New York: New American Library, 1978).
41. Senate Special Subcommittee on Integrated Oil Operations, *Market Performance*, part 3, pp. 1021–22.
42. Ibid., part 1, p. 325.
43. Ibid., p. 320.
44. Senate Subcommittee on Antitrust and Monopoly, *Governmental Intervention*, p. 308.
45. Joint Economic Committee, *Horizontal Integration of the Energy Industry Hearings*, 94th Cong., 1st sess., 1976, p. 50; Senate Subcommittee on Antitrust and Monopoly, *Interfuel Competition Hearings*, 94th Cong., 1st sess., 1976, p. 13.
46. The following is documented in George W. Stocking and Myron W. Watkins, *Cartels in Action* (New York: Twentieth Century Fund, 1946), pp. 91–93, 491–95.
47. *Washington Post*, 11 August 1981.
48. For additional evidence, as well as documentation supporting the thesis that the energy crises of recent years have to an important degree been orchestrated by the oil giants, see Fred J. Cook, *The Great Energy Scam* (New York: Macmillan, 1982), and Robert Sherrill, *The Oil Follies of 1970–1980* (Garden City, N.Y.: Anchor Books, 1983). For a classic treatment, see Robert Engler, *The Politics of Oil* (Chicago: University of Chicago Press, 1961).

49. Oliver E. Williamson, *Markets and Hierarchies* (New York: Free Press, 1975), pp. 158–59.
50. *Business Week,* 6 December 1982, p. 14.
51. *Fortune,* 4 April 1983, pp. 141–42; *Wall Street Journal,* 15 August 1983. Detailed analyses of conglomerate acquisition sprees by Gulf & Western and other firms during the 1960s are contained in Federal Trade Commission, Staff Report, *Economic Report on Corporate Mergers,* 28 August 1969, reprinted in Senate Subcommittee on Antitrust and Monopoly, *Economic Concentration Hearings,* part 8A, 91st Cong., 1st sess., 1969.
52. *Fortune,* 11 January 1982, pp. 34–39.
53. *New York Times,* 17 March 1985, sec. 3.
54. Senate Subcommittee on Antitrust and Monopoly, *Economic Concentration,* part 8A, p. 20.
55. Richard Posner, *Economic Analysis of Law* (Boston: Little, Brown, 1977), p. 11.

PART III: THE POLITICAL ECONOMY OF POWER: A HISTORICAL PERSPECTIVE

1. Henry C. Simons, *Economic Policy for a Free Society* (Chicago: University of Chicago Press, 1948), pp. 87–88.

6. THE REVOLUTION OF 1776: AMERICAN GOVERNMENT

1. Walter Lippmann, *The Good Society* (New York: Grosset & Dunlap, 1937), pp. 45–46.
2. Adam Smith, *The Wealth of Nations* (Modern Library ed. 1937), pp. 547–48.
3. Ibid., p. 550.
4. *The Federalist* (Middletown, Conn.: Wesleyan University Press, 1961). Our citations of Madison's views are taken from *Federalist No. 10* (dated 22 November 1787) and *Federalist No. 51* (dated 6 February 1788).
5. Lippmann, *Good Society,* p. 254.
6. Thomas Jefferson, *Writings,* vol. 3 (New York: G.P. Putnam's Sons, 1894), pp. 225–26.
7. Richard A. Posner, *Economic Analysis of Law* (Boston: Little, Brown, 1972), p. 492.
8. Myers v. United States, 272 U.S. 52 (1926), pp. 240ff.
9. Hans J. Morgenthau, *The Purpose of American Politics* (New York: Alfred A. Knopf, 1962), p. 286.
10. Ibid., pp. 277–78.
11. Ibid., pp. 282–84.

7. THE REVOLUTION OF 1776: BRITISH ECONOMIC POLICY

1. William Cunningham, *The Growth of English Industry and Commerce* (Cambridge, England: The University Press, 1890), pp. 425–26, 424.
2. Eli F. Heckscher, *Mercantilism,* rev. ed., vol. 1 (New York: Macmillan, 1955), p. 161.
3. Walter Lippmann, *The Good Society* (New York: Grosset & Dunlap, 1937), p. 10.
4. Heckscher, *Mercantilism,* p. 173.
5. Thomas Mun, *England's Treasure by Foreign Trade* (New York: Macmillan, 1895), pp. 7–8.
6. Adam Smith, *The Wealth of Nations* (Modern Library ed., 1937), p. 418.
7. Ibid., pp. 418–19.
8. Ibid., p. 612.
9. Ibid., pp. 612–13.
10. Ibid., p. 129.
11. Ibid., p. 122.

12. Ibid., p. 124.
13. Ibid., p. 691.
14. Ibid., p. 700.
15. Ibid., p. 712.
16. Arthur M. Schlesinger, Jr., *The Age of Jackson* (Boston: Little, Brown, 1945), p. 317.

8. THE ROLE OF ANTITRUST

1. Corwin D. Edwards, *Maintaining Competition* (New York: McGraw-Hill, 1949), p. 3.
2. Ayn Rand, *Capitalism: The Unknown Ideal* (New York: New American Library, 1966), pp. 46, 48 (emphasis added).
3. Adam Smith, *The Wealth of Nations* (Modern Library ed., 1937), p. 423.
4. Lionel Robbins, *The Theory of Economic Policy in English Classical Political Economy* (London: Macmillan, 1952), p. 56.
5. *The Works of Jeremy Bentham*, vol. 3, ed. J. Bowring (1962), p. 185.
6. Frank H. Knight, *Freedom and Reform* (New York: Harper Bros., 1947), p. 205.
7. Robert H. Bork, *The Antitrust Paradox* (New York: Basic Books, 1978).
8. United States v. Columbia Steel Corp., 334 U.S. 495 (1948).
9. Walton Hamilton and Irene Till, *Antitrust in Action*, monograph no. 16 (Washington, D.C.: Temporary National Economic Committee, 1940), pp. 59–60.
10. Ibid., pp. 23–24.
11. Benjamin N. Cardozo, *The Nature of the Judicial Process* (New Haven, Conn.: Yale University Press, 1921), p. 168.
12. Oliver Wendell Holmes, Jr., "The Path of the Law" *Harvard Law Review* 10 (1897): 465–66.

9. CONSPIRACY

1. For a lively discussion of these antitrust violations, see John Herling, *The Great Price Conspiracy* (Washington, D.C.: Robert B. Luce, Inc., 1962).
2. United States v. Westinghouse Electric Corporation et al., (E.D., Pa.), Criminal No. 20399, filed 1960.
3. Perhaps they were familiar with Cicero's First Oration against Cataline: "Do you not realize that your plans are fully revealed, do you not see that your conspiracy is now identified and fully understood by all? Do you suppose that any of us is not aware of what you did last night and the night before, where you were, whom you summoned, what plan you adopted? O Tempora! O Mores! The Senate knows the circumstances, the Consul sees them. . . ." Quoted in Herling, *Price Conspiracy*, epigraph.
4. Almarin Phillips, *Market Structure, Organization and Performance* (Cambridge, Mass.: Harvard University Press, 1962), p. 230.
5. United States v. Addyston Pipe & Steel Co., 85 F. 271 (6th Cir. 1898).
6. United States v. Trans-Missouri Freight Association, 166 U.S. 290 (1897).
7. United States v. Joint Traffic Association, 171 U.S. 505 (1898).
8. United States v. Trenton Potteries Co. et. al., 273 U.S. 392 (1927).
9. United States v. Socony-Vacuum Oil Co., 310 U.S. 150 (1940).
10. For a comprehensive classification of Section 1 offenses, see Corwin D. Edwards, *Maintaining Competition* (New York: McGraw-Hill, 1949), pp. 41–42.
11. Appalachian Coals v. United States, 288 U.S. 344 (1933).
12. On the other hand, it is noteworthy that neither the courts nor Congress have been willing to accord special treatment under the antitrust laws to such diverse groups as doctors, dentists, lawyers, architects, accountants, and real-estate agents.

13. American Tobacco Co. v. United States, 328 U.S. 781 (1946). For an excellent analysis of this case, see William H. Nicholls, *Price Policies in the Cigarette Industry* (Nashville: Vanderbilt University Press, 1951).
14. Quoted in Nicholls, *Price Policies*, pp. 401ff.

10. MONOPOLY

1. Douglas F. Greer, *Industrial Organization and Public Policy*, 2nd ed. (New York: Macmillan, 1984), p. 121; F. M. Scherer, *Industrial Market Structure and Economic Performance*, 2nd ed. (Chicago: Rand McNally, 1980), p. 121.
2. See George J. Stigler, "Monopoly and Oligopoly By Merger," *American Economic Review* 40 (May 1950): 23.
3. William G. Shepherd, "Causes of Increased Competition in the U.S. Economy, 1939–1980," *Review of Economics and Statistics* 64 (November 1982):613. For an examination of the decline of some major American monopolies in the periods 1910–1935 and 1948–1973, see William G. Shepherd, *The Treatment of Market Power* (New York: Columbia University Press, 1975), appendix B, tables B.1 and B.2.
4. Shepherd, "Causes of Increased Competition," 618. For a detailed analysis of the computer industry, see Gerald Brock, "The Computer Industry," in *The Structure of American Industry*, 7th ed., ed. Walter Adams (New York: Macmillan, 1986). On monopoly in photography, see James W. Brock, "Industry Structure and Market Power: The Relevance of the 'Relevant Market,'" *Antitrust Bulletin* 29 (Fall 1984): 535.
5. Joseph A. Schumpeter, *Capitalism, Socialism and Democracy*, 3rd ed. (New York: Harper & Row, 1950), pp. 82–106.
6. George Gilder, *Wealth and Poverty* (New York: Basic Books, 1981), pp. 37–38.
7. Northern Pacific Rail Road Co. v. United States, 356 U.S. 1, 4 (1957). For an articulate contemporary statement, see John J. Flynn, "Monopolization Under the Sherman Act: The Third Wave and Beyond," *Antitrust Bulletin* 26 (Spring 1981):26.
8. Standard Oil Co. v. United States, 221 U.S. 1 (1911). The court decided a companion case against the American Tobacco trust two weeks following its ruling in Standard Oil, on essentially the same grounds. See United States v. American Tobacco Co., 221 U.S. 106 (1911).
9. Quoted in Henry R. Seager and Charles A. Gulick, Jr., *Trust and Corporation Problems* (New York: Harper & Bros., 1929), p. 120.
10. Ibid., p. 230.
11. Ida M. Tarbell, *The Life of Elbert H. Gary* (New York: Appleton, 1930), p. 205.
12. United States v. United States Steel Corp., 251 U.S. 417 (1920).
13. *Fortune*, March 1936, p. 157.
14. Milton Handler, *A Study of the Construction and Enforcement of the Antitrust Laws*, monograph no. 38 (Washington, D.C.: Temporary National Economic Committee, 1941), pp. 78–79.
15. United Shoe Machinery Corp. v. United States, 258 U.S. 451 (1922).
16. United States v. United Shoe Machinery Corp., 110 F. Supp. 295, *affirmed per curiam*, 347 U.S. 521 (1954).
17. For a study of the failures of structural monopoly policy in the photographic industry, see James W. Brock, "Persistent Monopoly and the Charade of Antitrust: The Durability of Kodak's Market Power," *University of Toledo Law Review* 14 (Spring 1983):653.
18. Dissenting opinion in United States v. American Column & Lumber Co., 257 U.S. 337 (1921). Economist Thomas Nixon Carver articulated this crucial aspect of the monopoly problem in 1915, when he wrote:
"The larger the corporation, the greater is its power, either for good or for evil, and that makes it especially important that its power be under control. If I may use a

homely illustration, I will take the common house cat, whose diminutive size makes her a safe inmate of our household in spite of her playful disposition and her liking for animal food. If, without the slightest change of character or disposition, she were suddenly enlarged to the dimensions of a tiger, we should at least want her to be muzzled and to have her claws trimmed, whereas if she were to assume the dimensions of a mastodon, I doubt if any of us would want to live in the same house with her. And it would be useless to argue that her nature had not changed, that she was just as amiable as ever, and no more carnivorous than she always had been. Nor would it convince us to be told that her productivity had increased and that she could now catch more mice in a minute than she formerly could in a week. We should be afraid lest, in a playful mood, she might set a paw upon us, to the detriment of our epidermis, or that in her large-scale mouse-catching she might not always discriminate between us and the mice." Thomas N. Carver, *Essays in Social Justice* (Cambridge, Mass.: Harvard University Press, 1925), p. 332.

19. United States v. Aluminum Co. of America, 148 F. 2d 416 (1945).
20. Eugene Rostow, *A National Policy for the Oil Industry* (New Haven: Yale University Press, 1948), pp. 126–27.
21. American Tobacco Co. v. United States, 328 U.S. 781 (1946).
22. United States v. E.I. Du Pont de Nemours and Co., 351 U.S. 377 (1956).
23. At the conclusion of the trial, the jury upheld the bulk of Berkey's charges. See Berkey Photo, Inc. v. Eastman Kodak Co., 457 F. Supp. 404 (1978).
24. Berkey Photo, Inc. v. Eastman Kodak Co., 603 F. 2d 263 (1979).
25. See James W. Brock, "Structural Monopoly, Technological Performance, and Predatory Innovation: Relevant Standards Under Section 2 of the Sherman Act," *American Business Law Journal* 21 (Fall 1983):291.
26. On this issue, see Brock, "Industry Structure."

11. THE MERGER PROBLEM

1. *Fortune*, May 1952, p. 162.
2. Public Law No. 212, 38 U.S. Stat. 730–40 (1914).
3. U.S. Congress, Temporary National Economic Committee, *Investigation of Concentration of Economic Power Hearings*, 76th Cong., 1st sess. (1939), part 5-A, p. 2379.
4. F. M. Scherer, *Industrial Market Structure and Economic Performance*, 2d ed. (Chicago: Rand McNally, 1980), p. 548.
5. House Committee on the Judiciary, *Report No. 1191*, 81st Cong., 1st sess. (1949), p. 8.
6. Brown Shoe Co. v. United States, 370 U.S. 294 (1962).
7. United States v. Aluminum Co. of America, 148 F. 2d 416 (2d Cir. 1945), p. 428.
8. Robert Bork, *The Antitrust Paradox* (New York: Basic Books, 1978), pp. 205–6.
9. Ibid., p. 221.
10. Ibid., pp. 226–27, 248.
11. *Annual Report* of the Council of Economic Advisers (1985), pp. 188–89.
12. Joe S. Bain, *Industrial Organization*, 2d ed. (New York: John Wiley & Sons, 1968), p. 658.
13. Oliver E. Williamson, "Economies as an Antitrust Defense Revisited," *University of Pennsylvania Law Review* (April 1977):704.
14. U.S. Department of Justice, *Revised Merger Guidelines* (Washington, 14 June 1984), pp. 35–36.

12. HORIZONTAL MERGERS AND JOINT VENTURES

1. Simon N. Whitney, *Antitrust Policies: American Experience in Twenty Industries,* vol. 2 (New York: Twentieth Century Fund, 1958), p. 7.
2. United States v. Bethlehem Steel Corp., 168 F. Supp. 576 (1958).
3. For additional evidence on merger-induced giantism in steel, see Federal Trade Commission, *Report on the Merger Movement* (Washington, 1948), pp. 70–134; and House Select Committee on Small Business, *Steel—Acquisitions, Mergers, and Expansion of 12 Major Companies, 1900–1950 Hearings,* 81st Cong., 2nd sess., 1950.
4. F.M. Scherer, *Industrial Market Structure and Economic Performance,* 2nd ed. (Chicago: Rand McNally, 1980), p. 546.
5. United States v. Von's Grocery Co., 384 U.S. 270 (1966).
6. Federal Trade Commission, *Economic Report on the Structure and Competitive Behavior of Food Retailing* (Washington, 1966), pp. 325, 366–72. Evidence regarding the inflationary effect of concentration on food prices is provided in Senate Subcommittee on Antitrust, Monopoly and Business Rights, *Impact of Market Concentration on Rising Food Prices Hearings,* 96th Cong., 1st sess., 1979, pp. 68–69.
7. A detailed analysis of the government's horizontal merger policy in the grocery retailing field is contained in Willard F. Mueller, *The Celler-Kefauver Act: The First 27 Years,* prepared for the House Subcommittee on Monopolies and Commercial Law, 96th Cong., 1st sess., 1980, pp. 38–50.
8. United States v. Penn-Olin Chemical Co., 378 U.S. 158 (1964).
9. Ibid., p. 177.
10. An alternative and stricter policy approach was suggested by Justice William O. Douglas in his dissent. As he viewed it, the joint venture was tantamount to a division of the market among competitors—a division that would be held per se illegal under the Sherman Act. To rule otherwise, Justice Douglas contended, would permit the antitrust laws to "be avoided by sophisticated devices."
11. Memorandum by John E. Kwoka, Jr., regarding GM-Toyota joint venture, Federal Trade Commission, 3 October 1983, p. 22.
12. Ibid., pp. 25, 36.
13. See House Subcommittee on Commerce, Transportation, and Tourism, *Future of the Automobile Industry Hearing,* 98th Cong., 2nd sess., 1984, pp. 497–506.
14. Ibid., pp. 522–23.
15. Ibid., p. 541.
16. See generally House Subcommittees of the Committee on Energy and Commerce, *Oil Industry Mergers Hearings,* 98th Cong., 2nd sess., 1984, especially statements by Walter Adams and Edwin Rothschild.
17. *Petroleum Intelligence Weekly,* 12 March 1984. In its year-end review of the industry, *Forbes* points out that exploration for new crude reserves was discouraged by "the huge debt loads some companies incurred, either through buying other companies or through buying in their own stock. Money that might have gone for exploration went for debt service." *Forbes,* 13 January 1986, p. 187.
18. Indeed, economist John E. Kwoka contends that the domestic auto oligopoly has raised small-car prices sharply and deliberately conceded this segment of the market to foreign producers. See John E. Kwoka, Jr., "Market Power and Market Change in the U.S. Automobile Industry," *Journal of Industrial Economics* 32 (June 1984):509.

13. VERTICAL MERGERS

1. Marathon Oil Co. v. Mobil Corp., *Trade Regulation Reporter,* par. 64,739, p. 74,803 (30 November 1981); Marathon Oil Co. v. Mobil Corp., 669 F. 2d 378, p. 382 (1981).
2. Corwin D. Edwards, *Maintaining Competition* (New York: McGraw-Hill, 1949), p. 98.

Also see John Blair, *Economic Concentration* (New York: Harcourt Brace Jovanovich, 1972), pp. 25–40.

3. Corwin D. Edwards, "Vertical Integration and the Monopoly Problem," *Journal of Marketing* 17 (April 1953):404.

4. Willard F. Mueller, "Public Policy Toward Vertical Mergers," in *Public Policy Toward Mergers*, ed. J. Fred Weston and Sam Peltzman (Pacific Palisades, Calif.: Goodyear Publishing Co., 1969), p. 152.

5. For detailed analyses of vertical integration, vertical power, and their economic consequences in the steel, petroleum, and amateur photography industries, see the following: Walter Adams and Joel Dirlam, "Steel Imports and Vertical Oligopoly Power," *American Economic Review* 54 (September 1964):626; Walter Adams and James W. Brock, "Deregulation or Divestiture: The Case of Petroleum Pipelines," *Wake Forest Law Review* 19 (October 1983):705; James W. Brock, "Industry Structure and Market Power: The Relevance of the 'Relevant Market,' " *Antitrust Bulletin* 29 (Fall 1984): 535. A masterful survey of vertical power in the telephone industry is presented by Judge Harold Green in United States v. American Telephone & Telephone Co., 524 F. Supp. 1336 (1981).

6. Brown Shoe Co. v. United States, 370 U.S. 294 (1962).

7. The merger was also horizontal in part, because Kinney manufactured a small amount of shoes, while Brown had previously acquired a number of other shoe retailers.

8. United States Steel Corp. v. Federal Trade Commission, 426 F. 2d 592 (1970).

9. See Federal Trade Commission, *Economic Report on Mergers and Vertical Integration in the Cement Industry* (Washington, 1966), pp. 1, 96–98.

10. Ibid., 14–15.

11. In all, the Federal Trade Commission challenged 24 vertical acquisitions of cement users by cement producers between 1960 and 1970. See Willard F. Mueller, *The Celler-Kefauver Act: The First 27 Years*, prepared for the House Subcommittee on Monopolies and Commercial Law, 96th Cong., 1st sess., 1980, p. 29.

12. Ibid., p. 30.

13. United States Steel Corp. v. Federal Trade Commission, p. 603.

14. Mueller, *Celler-Kefauver Act*, p. 32.

15. Robert H. Bork, *The Antitrust Paradox* (New York: Basic Books, 1978), pp. 226–27, 245.

16. F. M. Scherer, "The Posnerian Harvest: Separating Wheat From Chaff," *Yale Law Journal* 86 (April 1977):986.

17. Federal Trade Commission, *Economic Report on Cement Mergers*, p. 101.

18. *Wall Street Journal*, 5 April 1985.

19. See Robert H. Hayes and William J. Abernathy, "Managing Our Way to Economic Decline," *Harvard Business Review* 58 (July–August 1980):73. For example, one cost handicap suffered by General Motors is that the firm "is highly vertically integrated. It buys 70 percent of its parts in-house. By contrast, Chrysler buys only 30 percent, allowing it to shop around." *The Economist*, 12 October 1985, p. 38.

20. Senate Subcommittee on Antitrust and Monopoly, *The Petroleum Industry Hearings*, part 2, 94th Cong., 1st sess., 1976, pp. 1229–30.

14. CONGLOMERATE MERGERS

1. Senate Subcommittee on Antitrust and Monopoly, *Economic Concentration Hearings*, part 8A, 91st Cong., 1st sess., 1969, pp. 260, 501–510.

2. Federal Trade Commission, *Statistical Report on Mergers and Acquisitions* (Washington, 1981), pp. 110, 113.

3. Willard F. Mueller, *The Celler-Kefauver Act: The First 27 Years*, prepared for the House Subcommittee on Monopolies and Commercial Law, 96th Cong., 1st sess., 1980, pp. 82, 84.

4. Robert H. Bork, *The Antitrust Paradox* (New York: Basic Books, 1978), p. 248.
5. *Dun's Review,* August 1981, p. 38.
6. Bork, *Antitrust,* p. 248.
7. Corwin D. Edwards, "Conglomerate Bigness as a Source of Power," *Business Concentration and Price Policy* (Princeton, N.J.: National Bureau of Economic Research, 1955), p. 332.
8. Senate Subcommittee on Antitrust and Monopoly, *Economic Concentration Hearings,* p. 321.
9. Edwards, "Conglomerate Bigness," pp. 334–35.
10. Senate Subcommittee on Antitrust and Monopoly, *Economic Concentration Hearings,* p. 401.
11. Federal Trade Commission v. Procter & Gamble Co., 386 U.S. 568 (1967).
12. Edwards, "Conglomerate Bigness," p. 342.
13. Senate Subcommittee on Antitrust and Monopoly, *Economic Concentration Hearings,* pp. 329–31.
14. United States v. General Dynamics Corp., 258 F. Supp. 36 (1966).
15. United States v. Ingersoll-Rand Co., 218 F. Supp. 530, p. 552 (1966).
16. Edwards, "Conglomerate Bigness," p. 335.
17. Senate Subcommittee on Antitrust and Monopoly, *Economic Concentration Hearings,* part 8, p. 5125.
18. Ibid., part 8A, pp. 461–62.
19. Corwin D. Edwards, *Economic and Political Aspects of International Cartels,* study for the Senate Subcommittee on War Mobilization, 78th Cong., 2d sess., 1946, p. 27.
20. Ibid., p. 19.
21. Additional evidence on the anticompetitive impact of large conglomerate mergers can be found in the following: Senate Subcommittee on Antitrust and Monopoly, *Mergers and Industrial Concentration Hearings,* 95th Cong., 2nd sess., 1978; John M. Connor, et al., *The Food Manufacturing Industries* (Lexington, Mass.: Lexington Books, 1985), pp. 241–72; Stephen A. Rhoades, *Power, Empire Building, and Mergers* (Lexington, Mass.: Lexington Books, 1983); and Samuel Richardson Reid, *The New Industrial Order* (New York: McGraw-Hill, 1976).
22. *Fortune,* June 1965, p. 194.

15. THE LIMITATIONS OF ANTITRUST

1. Walton Hamilton and Irene Till, *Antitrust in Action,* Temporary National Economic Committee, monograph no. 16 (Washington, D.C.: 1940), p. 4.
2. *New York Times,* 19 May 1985, sec. 3; Senate Subcommittee on Antitrust and Monopoly, *The Antitrust Improvements Act of 1975 Hearings,* 94th Cong., 1st sess., 1975, p. 377; Richard A. Posner, "A Statistical Study of Antitrust Enforcement," *Journal of Law and Economics* 13 (1970):395.
3. Ibid., p. 389.
4. Mark J. Green, *The Closed Enterprise System* (New York: Grossman, 1972), pp. 168–69.
5. Senate Subcommittee on Antitrust and Monopoly, *Antitrust Improvements,* p. 378.
6. Edward A. Ross, *Sin and Society* (Boston: Houghton Mifflin, 1907), pp. 29–30.
7. Quoted in John Herling, *The Great Price Conspiracy* (Washington, D.C.: Robert B. Luce, Inc., 1962), p. 195. For an interesting study of antitrust penalties, see Kenneth G. Elzinga and William Breit, *The Antitrust Penalties: A Study in Law and Economics* (New Haven: Yale University Press, 1976). As for public policy, *The Economist's* posture is appropriate:

> The burglars of Brixton, the Bronx or other such "disadvantaged" areas do not theorise about their way of life and its consequences. If they get caught, they risk imprisonment. Common criminals expect to "do time." White-collar criminals, by

contrast, do not. Stealing millions by computer transfer of bank balances or an insider manipulation, rarely, even when detected, leads to jail. . . . Reject the temptation to be lenient. It has more validity when applied to the burglar than to the businessman. . . . If more intelligent, educated and socially privileged criminals were to rub shoulders with the lags from Brixton and the Bronx, white-collar crime would diminish—in Lloyd's of London and elsewhere. (25 May 1985, p. 17.)

8. Posner, "A Statistical Study," p. 405.

9. See James W. Brock, "Persistent Monopoly and the Charade of Antitrust: The Durability of Kodak's Market Power," *University of Toledo Law Review* 14 (Spring 1983):653, and sources cited therein.

10. See United States v. American Tobacco Co., 221 U.S. 106 (1911), and American Tobacco Co. v. United States, 328 U.S. 781 (1946).

11. Clair Wilcox, *Public Policies Toward Business*, 4th ed. (Homewood, Ill.: Richard D. Irwin, 1971), p. 263.

12. See Walter Adams, "Dissolution, Divorcement, Divestiture: The Pyrrhic Victories of Antitrust," *Indiana Law Journal* 27 (Fall 1951):1; Green, *Closed Enterprise*, pp. 178–212; Kevin J. O'Connor, "The Divestiture Remedy in Sherman Act Section 2 Cases," *Harvard Journal on Legislation* 13 (1976):687. The recent, massive reorganization of AT&T stands as a rare exception that proves the rule. It demonstrates that restructuring under the antitrust laws is indeed feasible.

13. William G. Shepherd, *The Treatment of Market Power* (New York: Columbia University Press, 1975), p. 189.

14. *Congressional Record*, 78th Cong., 2nd sess. 13 May 1976, vol. 122, p. 13872.

15. National Commission for the Review of Antitrust Laws and Procedures, *Report to the President and Attorney General* (Washington, 1979). For additional discussion of the "no-fault" proposal, as well as an excellent bibliography, see John J. Flynn, "Statement Before the Commission," reprinted in *Antitrust Law Journal* 48 (1979):845. Others have proposed an absolute ceiling on firm size as an alternative means for controlling monopoly. See Henry C. Simons, *Economic Policy for a Free Society* (Chicago: University of Chicago Press, 1948), p. 52, and Walter Adams, "Is Bigness a Crime?" *Land Economics* 27 (1951):287.

16. House Subcommittee on Monopolies and Commercial Law, *Corporate Initiative Hearing*, 97th Cong., 1st sess., 1982, p. 39.

17. Walter Measday, "The Petroleum Industry," in *The Structure of American Industry*, 6th ed., ed. Walter Adams (New York: Macmillan, 1982), p. 66.

18. Both of these proposals are reprinted in Harvey J. Goldschmid, H. Michael Mann, and J. Fred Weston, eds., *Industrial Concentration: The New Learning* (Boston: Little, Brown, 1974), pp. 441–56.

19. In substance, Senator Hart's proposal was quite similar. It would have established an Industrial Reorganization Commission and an Industrial Reorganization Court to implement the restructuring of major oligopoly industries.

20. Willard F. Mueller, *The Celler-Kefauver Act: The First 27 Years*, prepared for the House Subcommittee on Monopolies and Commercial Law, 96th Cong., 1st sess., 1980, p. 18.

21. W.T. Grimm & Company, *Mergerstat Review* (Chicago, 1985), p. 6; *New York Times*, 13 March 1986.

22. Federal Trade Commission, *Concentration Levels and Trends in the Energy Sector of the U.S. Economy* (Washington, 1974), p. 140.

23. Ibid., pp. 45–51.

24. Green, "Closed Enterprise," p. 281.

25. House Subcommittee on Oversight and Investigations, *Mergers and Acquisitions of the Top 20 Oil Companies, 1978–81, Staff Report*, 97th Cong., 2nd sess., 1982, p. 23; Council of Economic Advisers, *Annual Report* (Washington, 1985), p. 194.

26. *New York Times*, 19 May 1985, sec. 3.

27. Michael Pertschuk, "Love That Market," *The New Republic*, 14 May 1984, p. 11.

28. For trenchant criticisms of recent merger enforcement policy, see Joseph P. Bauer, "Government Enforcement Policy of Section 7 of the Clayton Act: Carte Blanche for Conglomerate Mergers?" and Louis B. Schwartz, "The New Merger Guidelines: Guide to Governmental Discretion and Private Counseling or Propaganda for Revision of the Antitrust Laws?" both in *California Law Review* 71 (March 1983).

29. ITT, *Annual Report*, 1968, p. 7.

30. Anthony Sampson, *The Sovereign State of ITT* (New York: Stein and Day, 1973), p. 234.

31. Senate Committee on Foreign Relations, *The International Telephone and Telegraph Company and Chile Report*, 93rd Cong., 1st sess., 1973, pp. 4–5.

32. Sampson, *Sovereign State*, p. 254. Also see Harlan M. Blake, "Beyond the ITT Case," *Harper's*, June 1972, pp. 74–78.

33. See "Do Mergers Really Work?" *Business Week*, 3 June 1985, pp. 88–100. The article carries the poignant subtitle: "Not very often—which raises questions about merger mania."

34. Cited in Sampson, *Sovereign State*, p. 223.

35. Hamilton and Till, *Antitrust*, p. 119.

16. THE REGULATION OF POWER

1. Lincoln Steffens, *The Shame of Our Cities* (New York: Hill and Wang, 1960), pp. 3, 22, 74, and 107.

2. Paul H. Douglas, *Ethics in Government* (Cambridge: Harvard University Press, 1954), pp. 33–34.

3. Horace M. Gray, "The Passing of the Public Utility Concept," *Journal of Land & Public Utility Economics* 16 (1940):8. For a comprehensive, two-volume treatise on public utility regulation, see Alfred E. Kahn, *The Economics of Regulation* (New York: John Wiley & Sons, 1970–71).

4. Letter from Richard Olney to Charles E. Perkins, quoted in Matthew Josephson, *The Politicos* (New York: Harcourt, Brace & World, 1936), p. 526.

5. House Committee on the Investigation of the U.S. Steel Corporation, *Hearings*, vol. 3, 63d Cong., 1st sess. (1911), p. 79.

6. The late Professor Clair Wilcox, for example, wrote some 20 years ago:

> Regulation, at best, is a pallid substitute for competition. It cannot prescribe quality, force efficiency, or require innovation, because such action would invade the sphere of management. . . . Regulation fails to encourage performance in the public interest by offering rewards and penalties. Competition offers both.
>
> Regulation is static, backward-looking, preoccupied with the problems of the past. It does nothing to stimulate change, seeking to maintain order on the basis of the old technology. It is slow to adapt to change; new problems appear, but regulatory thinking lags. Competition, by contrast, is dynamic. (Wilcox, *Public Policies Toward Business* [Homewood, Ill.: Richard D. Irwin, 1966], pp. 476–77.)

7. Donald Baker, "The Antitrust Division, Department of Justice: The Role of Competition in the Regulated Industries," *Boston College Industrial and Commercial Law Review* 11 (1970):571.

17. AIRLINE REGULATION

1. Quoted in Senate Subcommittee on Administrative Practice and Procedure, *Civil Aeronautics Board: Practices and Procedures Report*, 94th Cong., 1st sess., 1975, p. 213.

2. Senate Subcommittee on Administrative Practice and Procedure, *Oversight of Civil*

Aeronautics Board Practices and Procedures Hearings, vol. 1, 94th Cong., 1st sess., 1975, p. 50.

3. Senate Subcommittee on Aviation, *Regulatory Reform in Air Transportation Hearings on S. 2551, S. 3364 and S. 3536,* 94th Cong., 2nd sess., 1976, p. 335.

4. Senate Select Committee on Small Business, *Future of Irregular Airlines Report,* 83rd Cong., 1st sess., 1953, p. 18.

5. Richard E. Caves, *Air Transport and Its Regulators* (Cambridge, Mass.: Harvard University Press, 1962), p. 169.

6. Senate Subcommittee on Administrative Practice and Procedure, *Civil Aeronautics Board Report,* pp. 78–79.

7. Senate Select Committee on Small Business, *Role of Irregular Airlines in United States Air Transportation Industry Report,* 82nd Cong., 1st sess., 1951, pp. 8, 16.

8. House Antitrust Subcommittee, *Airlines, Report Pursuant to H. Res. 107,* 85th Cong., 1st sess., 1957, p. 81; Horace M. Gray, "The Airlines Industry," in *The Structure of American Industry,* 3rd ed., ed. Walter Adams (New York: Macmillan, 1961), pp. 477, 498–99; Senate Subcommittee on Administrative Practice and Procedure, *Civil Aeronautics Board Report,* pp. 244–45; idem, *Oversight of Civil Aeronautics Board Hearings,* p. 32.

9. Senate Subcommittee on Administrative Practice and Procedure, *Civil Aeronautics Board Report,* p. 79.

10. See ibid., p. 85. See also Hardy K. Maclay and William C. Burt, "Entry of New Carriers into Domestic Trunkline Air Transportation," *Journal of Air Law & Commerce* 22 (1955):147.

11. George W. Douglas and James C. Miller, *Economic Regulation of Domestic Air Transport* (Washington, D.C.: Brookings Institution, 1974), p. 152; Caves, *Air Transport,* pp. 146–48; Lucile Sheppard Keyes, "Passenger Fare Policies of the Civil Aeronautics Board," *Journal of Air Law & Commerce* 18 (1951):48–49.

12. Paul Cherington, *Airline Price Policy* (Boston: Graduate School of Business Administration, Harvard University, 1958), pp. 85–86; Caves, *Air Transport,* p. 362; Senate Subcommittee on Administrative Practice and Procedures, *Civil Aeronautics Board Report,* p. 108.

13. Moss v. Civil Aeronautics Board, 430 F. 2d 891, pp. 900–901 (1970).

14. Caves, *Air Transport,* pp. 146–48.

15. Ibid., pp. 144–45, 154–55, 159.

16. Senate Subcommittee on Administrative Practice, *Oversight of Civil Aeronautics Board Hearings,* vol. 2, p. 1206.

17. Senate Subcommittee on Aviation, *Hearings on S. 2551,* p. 327. For example, by insisting that carriers charge equal fares for equal distances, the CAB forestalled selective price competition along particular routes; a carrier was required to reduce its fares on *all* routes in order to lower its fare for any single route. Also, by evaluating the permissibility of proposed fare reductions in terms of their impact on carriers in all affected markets, the CAB frustrated system-wide fare reductions. And perhaps most important, "reasonable" fares were determined on the basis of average *industry-wide* costs, rather than on the basis of an individual carrier's costs, thereby preventing lower-cost carriers from reducing their fares. See Senate Subcommittee on Administrative Practice and Procedure, *Civil Aeronautics Board Report,* pp. 109, 118–120.

18. Lucile Sheppard Keyes, "Notes on the History of Federal Regulation of Airline Mergers," *Journal of Air Law & Commerce* 37 (1971):367–68, 371.

19. Ibid., p. 362.

20. Richard J. Barber, "Airline Mergers, Monopoly, and the CAB," *Journal of Air Law & Commerce* 28 (1971):199.

21. Senate Subcommittee on Aviation, *Hearings on S. 2551,* p. 330. Capacity agreements collectively arrived at between carriers in major transport corridors during the early

1970s provide an apt case in point. See Senate Subcommittee on Administrative Practice and Procedure, *Civil Aeronautics Board Report*, pp. 143–44.
22. Senate Subcommittee on Administrative Practice, *Oversight of Civil Aeronautics Board Hearings*, vol. 1, p. 55.
23. Senate Subcommittee on Aviation, *Hearings on S. 2551*, p. 325. Along particular routes, concentration also remained extremely high. According to the Justice Department, over 70 percent of the revenue passenger miles flown by the trunk carriers in 1972 was flown in markets in which only one or two carriers were certificated.
24. William A. Jordan, *Airline Regulation in America* (Baltimore: Johns Hopkins Press, 1970), pp. 27–28.
25. Senate Subcommittee on Administrative Practice, *Oversight of Civil Aeronautics Board Hearings*, vol. 1, p. 686.
26. Ibid., p. 55.
27. "Airline Regulatory Reform: Will It Get Permission to Take Off?" Remarks by John H. Shenefield, Acting Assistant Attorney General, Antitrust Division of the Department of Justice, before the Ad Hoc Committee for Airline Regulatory Reform, Senate Caucus Room, Washington, D.C., 28 June 1977.
28. Senate Subcommittee on Administrative Practice and Procedure, *Civil Aeronautics Board Report*, p. 41.
29. Ibid., p. 3.
30. Senate Subcommittee on Administrative Practice, *Oversight of Civil Aeronautics Board Hearings*, vol. 1, p. 52.
31. Ibid., vol. 2, p. 1208.
32. Senate Subcommittee on Aviation, *Regulatory Reform in Air Transportation Hearings on S. 292 and S. 689*, part 3, 95th Cong., 1st sess., 1977, p. 1381.
33. Senate Subcommittee on Aviation, *Hearings on S. 2551*, p. 329.
34. For a fascinating analysis of the deregulation of the airline and trucking industries, see Martha Derthick and Paul J. Quirk, *The Politics of Deregulation* (Washington, D.C.: Brookings Institution, 1985).
35. House Subcommittee on Aviation, *Review of Airline Deregulation and Sunset of the Civil Aeronautics Board Hearings*, 98th Cong., 1st sess., 1983, pp. 4–6, 40, 487; *Wall Street Journal*, 22 November 1983; House Subcommittee on Aviation, *Effects of Airline Deregulation and Legislation to Advance the Date for Sunset of the Civil Aeronautics Board Hearings*, 97th Cong., 1st sess., 1981, pp. 48, 61; Douglas W. Caves, Laurits R. Christensen, and Michael W. Tretheway, "Airline Productivity under Deregulation," *Regulation* 6 (November/December 1982):26.
36. Said *Business Week* editorially: "Most businessmen would interpret Crandall's remarks as an illegal invitation to fix prices. So did the Justice Dept. . . . In February, 1983, Justice filed a complaint in federal court charging American and Crandall with trying to fix prices and asking the court to bar Crandall for two years from any airline job with authority over prices. Then followed two years' negotiations with American and Crandall. On July 14, 1985, Justice allowed American and Crandall to sign a consent decree without admitting any guilt in the Braniff affair. Deterrence, anyone?" (15 August 1985, p. 92.)
37. It is important to emphasize that *economic* deregulation (i.e., deregulation of fares, routes, entry, etc.) does *not* conflict with *safety* regulation and safe air travel. Former CAB Chairman Alfred E. Kahn provides the following comparisons of the U.S. domestic aviation safety record, calculated on the basis of yearly averages over the five-year period preceding deregulation of the industry versus the five-year period since deregulation: Accidents involving fatalities—before deregulation, 15, after deregulation, 10 1/2; fatalities—before deregulation, 206, after deregulation, 138; fatalities per 100,000 flights—before deregulation, 3.21, after deregulation, 1.85. (*New York Times*, 24 September 1985.)

18. TRUCKING REGULATION

1. Senate Committee on the Judiciary, *Federal Restraints on Competition in the Trucking Industry: Antitrust Immunity and Economic Regulation Report*, 96th Cong., 2nd sess., 1980, pp. 9–10.
2. *Motor Carrier Act, 1935*, Senate Rept. no. 482, 74th Cong., 1st sess., 1935, p. 3.
3. Fritz Machlup, *The Political Economy of Monopoly* (Baltimore: Johns Hopkins Press, 1952), pp. 298–99.
4. James Nelson, "The Effects of Entry Control in Surface Transportation," in *Transportation Economics* (Princeton, New Jersey: National Bureau of Economic Research, 1965), p. 387.
5. Senate Committee on the Judiciary, *Federal Restraints on Competition Report*, p. 30.
6. Senate Select Committee on Small Business, *Competition, Regulation, and the Public Interest in the Motor Carrier Industry Report*, 84th Cong., 2nd sess., 1956, p. 10.
7. Cited in Alfred E. Kahn, *The Economics of Regulation*, vol. 2 (New York: John Wiley & Sons, 1971), pp. 16, 18.
8. Senate Select Committee on Small Business, *Competition and the Public Interest Report*, p. 6.
9. Senate Subcommittee on Antitrust and Monopoly, *Oversight of Freight Rate Competition in the Motor Carrier Industry Hearings*, vol. 2, 95th Cong., 2nd sess., 1978, p. 851.
10. Senate Committee on the Judiciary, *Federal Restraints on Competition Report*, pp. 34, 39.
11. Thomas Gale Moore, "Deregulating Surface Freight Transportation," in *Promoting Competition in Regulated Markets*, ed. Almarin Phillips (Washington, D.C.: Brookings Institution, 1975), pp. 57–58.
12. Walter Adams, "The Role of Competition in the Regulated Industries," *American Economic Review* 48 (May 1958):535–37.
13. "Unregulated" private carriers, too, were tightly reined in by the ICC. See House Subcommittee on Surface Transportation, *Regulation of Carriers Subject to the Interstate Commerce Act Hearings*, 94th Cong., 2nd sess., 1976, p. 52.
14. Nelson, "Effects of Entry Control," p. 387.
15. Senate Subcommittee on Antitrust and Monopoly, *Oversight of Freight Rate Hearings*, vol. 1, p. 57.
16. Senate Committee on the Judiciary, *Federal Restraints on Competition Report*, p. 73.
17. Nelson, "Effects of Entry Control," p. 406.
18. Senate Subcommittee on Antitrust and Monopoly, *Oversight of Freight Rate Hearings*, vol. 1, p. 21.
19. Senate Select Committee on Small Business, *Trucking Mergers and Concentration Hearings*, 85th Cong., 1st sess., 1957, p. 111.
20. Senate Committee on the Judiciary, *Federal Restraints on Competition Report*, p. 29.
21. Senate Select Committee on Small Business, *Trucking Mergers Hearings*.
22. Senate Subcommittee on Antitrust and Monopoly, *Oversight of Freight Rate Hearings*, vol. 2, p. 897.
23. Senate Committee on the Judiciary, *Federal Restraints on Competition Report*, pp. 45, 57, 63–64.
24. Senate Subcommittee on Antitrust and Monopoly, *Oversight of Freight Rate Hearings*, vol. 3, pp. 1328–29.
25. Ibid., p. 1328.
26. Senate Committee on the Judiciary, *Federal Restraints on Competition Report*, pp. 45, 80–81, 84.

27. Ibid., pp. 84–86.
28. Senate Subcommittee on Antitrust and Monopoly, *Oversight of Freight Rate Hearings*, vol. 2, p. 864.
29. Senate Committee on the Judiciary, *Federal Restraints on Competition Report*, p. 65.
30. Ibid., p. 92.
31. House Subcommittee on Surface Transportation, *Regulation of Carriers Hearings*, p. 3.
32. Senate Committee on the Judiciary, *Federal Restraints on Competition Report*, p. 91.
33. House Subcommittee on Surface Transportation, *Regulation of Carriers Hearings*, p. 51.
34. Senate Committee on the Judiciary, *Federal Restraints on Competition Report*, p. 38.
35. Senate Subcommittee on Antitrust and Monopoly, *Oversight of Freight Rate Hearings*, vol. 1, p. 24.
36. Senate Committee on the Judiciary, *Federal Restraints on Competition*, p. 17.
37. Nelson, "Effects of Entry Control," p. 402.
38. Senate Committee on the Judiciary, *Federal Restraints on Competition Report*, p. 103.
39. James R. Snitzler and Robert J. Byrne, *Interstate Trucking and Fresh and Frozen Poultry under Agricultural Exemption*, Marketing Research Report No. 224 (Washington, D.C.: Department of Agriculture, 1958); idem, *Interstate Trucking of Frozen Fruits and Vegetables under Agricultural Exemption*, Marketing Research Report No. 316 (Washington, D.C.: Department of Agriculture, 1959).
40. House Subcommittee on Transportation, *Transportation Act of 1972 Hearings*, 92nd Cong., 2nd sess., 1972.
41. Senate Committee on the Judiciary, *Federal Restraints on Competition Report*, pp. 126–27.
42. Ibid., p. 97.
43. Ibid., p. 118.
44. House Subcommittee on Surface Transportation, *Regulation of Carriers Hearings*, pp. 44–45.
45. Senate Committee on the Judiciary, *Federal Restraints on Competition Report*, pp. 41, 43, 140.
46. Ibid., p. 137.
47. *Wall Street Journal*, 8 March 1982; Thomas Gale Moore, "Rail and Truck Reform— The Record So Far," *Regulation* 7 (November/December 1983):33–41; House Subcommittee on Surface Transportation, *Implementation of the Motor Carrier Act of 1980 Hearings*, 98th Cong., 1st sess., 1984, pp. 23–36, 237–45.
48. Ibid., p. 242.

19. THE LIMITS OF DEREGULATION

1. Charles F. Phillips, *The Economics of Regulation*, rev. ed. (Homewood, Illinois: Richard D. Irwin, 1969), p. 23.
2. For a more detailed discussion, see Walter Adams and James W. Brock, "Deregulation or Divestiture: The Case of Petroleum Pipelines," *Wake Forest Law Review* 19 (October 1983):705.
3. General Accounting Office, *Petroleum Pipeline Rates and Competition: Issues Long Neglected by Federal Regulators and in Need of Attention* (Washington, 1979), p. 3.

4. *New York Times,* 27 October 1981.
5. Senate Subcommittee on Antitrust and Monopoly, *Administered Prices: Drugs Report,* 87th Cong., 1st sess., 1961, pp. 210, 220.
6. Ibid., p. 212.
7. Ibid., pp. 212, 216.
8. Ibid., pp. 217–219, 220. For similar examples, see Joan Claybrook, *Retreat from Safety* (New York: Pantheon Books, 1984), pp. 47–51.
9. Morton Mintz, *At Any Cost* (New York: Pantheon Books, 1985).
10. Quoted in Sheldon Engelmayer and Robert Wagman, *Lord's Justice* (New York: Anchor Press, 1985), pp. 256–59. For the asbestos story, see Paul Brodeur, *Outrageous Misconduct* (New York: Pantheon Books, 1985).
11. Robert E. Litan and William D. Nordhaus, *Reforming Federal Regulation* (New Haven: Yale University Press, 1983), p. 36.
12. Mark Green and Ralph Nader, "Economic Regulation v. Competition: Uncle Sam the Monopoly Man," *Yale Law Journal* 82 (April 1973):885.
13. Senate Subcommittee on Surface Transportation, *Motor Vehicle Safety and the Marketplace Hearings,* 99th Cong., 1st sess., 1983, pp. 71–76.
14. Allyn D. Strickland, *Government Regulation and Business* (Boston: Houghton-Mifflin, 1980), p. 30.
15. Senate Committee on Environment and Public Works, *Environmental Emergency Response Act Report,* 96th Cong., 2nd sess., 1980, pp. 8–10.
16. Ibid., p. 3.
17. *New York Times,* 1 May 1985.
18. Senate Committee on Environment and Public Works, *Environmental Emergency Report,* p. 3.
19. Claybrook, *Retreat from Safety,* p. 167. Other safety features forced on the automobile industry by law include directional signals, bumpers, and headlights. Green and Nader, "Economic Regulation v. Competition," p. 885.
20. Douglas F. Greer, *Business, Government, and Society* (New York: Macmillan, 1983), p. 466.
21. Ibid., p. 480.
22. Ibid., p. 443.
23. Mark Green and Beverly Moore, Jr., "Winter's Discontent: Market Failure and Consumer Welfare," *Yale Law Journal* 82 (April 1973), p. 910.

20. THE PROTECTION OF POWER

1. Quotas had not been established for specific products, nor for individual exporting countries (other than Japan). Moreover, both the Japanese and the Europeans claimed that fabricated structural steel and cold-finished bars were not included in the VRA limitations.
2. International Trade Commission, *Certain Carbon Steel Products from Belgium, the Federal Republic of Germany, France, Italy, Luxembourg, The Netherlands, and the United Kingdom,* 731-TA-18-24, oral decision, 15 October 1982. The opinion by Commissioner Paula Stern was printed in *Federal Register,* 26 November 1982, pp. 53520–34.
3. Ibid., p. 53524.
4. According to estimates prepared by the Congressional Budget Office, this legislation, if enacted, would have raised domestic steel prices 3 to 7 percent, raised prices of imported steel 24 to 34 percent, and cost U.S. consumers $4.3 to $5.9 billion per year in income transfers and efficiency losses. Congressional Budget Office, *The Effects of Import Quotas on the Steel Industry* (Washington, July 1984).
5. International Trade Commission, *Carbon and Other Alloy Steel Products,* Rept. 1553, vol. 1 (Washington, July 1984), pp. 87–119, 123.

6. In addition to quotas limiting the Common Market's share of steel imports to 5.4 percent of the market, the restraints set the following shares, by country: Japan (5.8 percent), South Korea (1.9 percent), Brazil (0.8 percent), Spain (0.67 percent), South Africa (0.42 percent), Mexico (0.36 percent), and Australia (0.18 percent). *Wall Street Journal*, 20 December 1984.

7. Ibid., 15 March 1985, 29 November 1985. The scenario in stainless steel was almost identical. Successive stainless steel proceedings, like their carbon steel counterparts, seemed to validate the proposition that temporary relief is typically transmuted into permanent protection.

8. These estimates are based on the trigger prices of January 1978 and thus do not take account of subsequent 10.63 percent price increases. Generally, see Walter Adams and Hans Mueller, "The Steel Industry," in *The Structure of American Industry*, 7th ed., ed. Walter Adams (New York: Macmillan, 1986), and sources cited therein. For a penetrating analysis, see Craig R. MacPhee, *Restrictions on International Trade in Steel* (Lexington, Mass.: D.C. Heath, 1974).

9. *Wall Street Journal*, 7 January 1985; Federal Trade Commission, *Aggregate Costs to the United States of Tariffs and Quotas on Imports: General Tariff Cuts and Removal of Quotas on Automobiles, Steel, Sugar, and Textiles* (Washington, December 1984), p. VI–20.

10. U. S. Council on Wage and Price Stability, *A Study of Steel Prices* (Washington, July 1975).

11. "Worldwide Steel Pact Held 'Must,' " *The New York Journal of Commerce* (9 July 1976):1, 6. For a discussion of steel cartels operating between World Wars I and II, see Federal Trade Commission, *Report on International Steel Cartels* (Washington, 1948), and Ervin Hexner, *The International Steel Cartels* (Chapel Hill: University of North Carolina Press, 1943).

12. The "Fair Trade in Steel Act," introduced in Congress in 1984, contained a novel provision requiring the steel industry to reinvest in steel operations "substantially all of the cash flow from the steel sector." See Congressional Budget Office, *Effects of Import Quotas*, p. 37.

13. See *Business Week*, 13 May 1985, p. 102; 2 December 1985, p. 132.

14. *Wall Street Journal*, 11 November 1984, 3 April 1985, and 20 May 1985.

15. *Wall Street Journal*, 7 January 1985.

16. See International Trade Commission, *A Review of Recent Developments in the U.S. Automobile Industry, Including an Assessment of the Japanese Voluntary Restraint Agreements*, USITC Pub. 1648 (Washington, February 1985); Robert W. Crandall, "Import Quotas and the Automobile Industry: The Costs of Protectionism," *Brookings Review* 2 (Summer 1984); *Wall Street Journal*, 3 December 1984, and 14 February 1983; *New York Times*, 8 April 1984, sec. 3. The extensive arrangements made by the Big Three firms for foreign sourcing of parts and entire automobiles are collected and tabulated in Senate Subcommittee on International Economic Policy, *Free Trade—Myth or Reality: The Auto Industry, A Case Study*, 98th Cong., 2nd sess., 1984, pp. 23–24.

Joint ventures in the United States between American and Japanese auto producers scarcely bode well for the domestic industry's future; a General Motors official concedes, for example, that 70 percent of the value of the components in the Chevrolet Nova model, which is made by the General Motors–Toyota joint venture in California, comes from Japan. *New York Times*, 13 June 1985.

17. *Wall Street Journal*, 7 January 1985. Reports the Organization for Economic Cooperation and Development (OECD): "U.S. transactions prices for cold-rolled sheet steel in January 1984 were around 20 percent higher than prices in the European market and nearly 40 percent higher than prices on third markets." *(Costs and Benefits of Protection* [Paris, 1985], p. 48.)

18. This is especially the case as regards the bogeyman of "Japan Inc." and its alleged

capacity for "targeting" selected American industries for annihilation. For evidence that this supposed state-industry goliath, which in recent years is ceaselessly trotted out in support of protectionism, is largely a mythical construct concocted by special interests, see Gary R. Saxonhouse, "What Is All This About 'Industrial Targeting' in Japan?" *The World Economy* 6 (September 1983):253.

It is also important to note that import penetration and competition in the United States are less than that experienced by other industrialized nations. See C. Fred Bergsten and William R. Cline, *The United States–Japan Economic Problem* (Washington, D.C.: Institute for International Economics, 1985), p. 73.

19. Certainly merger-induced giantism provides no magical answer to the competitive failures of American companies on world markets. For example, LTV's acquisition of Republic Steel in 1984 represented a combination of the nation's third and fifth largest steel concerns and was touted by LTV at the time as "a landmark in the annals of America's basic industries as they strive to compete in the modern world marketplace." Two years later, however, the *Wall Street Journal* characterizes the LTV-Republic combination an "ill-fated merger," and concludes that the inefficiences and losses suffered by the combined firms "call into question the premise behind some large mergers —that the combined resources of two ailing companies can create more strength than either could muster alone." *Wall Street Journal,* 30 November 1984, 6 January 1986.

20. The Japanese automobile industry is an excellent case in point, particularly as regards the important role of competitive industry structure. "A generation ago," the *Wall Street Journal* recently editorialized, "Mr. Honda wanted to expand his motorcycle company by making cars. But the planners at Japan's Ministry of International Trade and Industry (MITI) didn't like the idea. They wanted only two companies—Toyota and Nissan. . . . But Japan is a free country, so Mr. Honda went ahead. Today Honda Motor is universally respected for making excellent cars—and selling an extraordinarily large number of them. What's more, other upstarts followed Mr. Honda and Japan now has nine successful and hotly competitive automakers." *Wall Street Journal,* 11 December 1984.

21. THE PROMOTION OF POWER

1. The following account is drawn from Hugh B. Anderson, *Midland Power Plant Project: A Case History in Legal and Regulatory Incentives to Economic Waste* (Lansing, Mich.: Michigan Department of Attorney General, October 1984).

2. Department of Energy, Energy Information Administration, *Survey of Nuclear Power Plant Construction Costs* (Washington, D.C.: 1983), p. 9.

3. *New York Times,* 3 September 1984, 20 January 1985, sec. 3. Gurwitz and Chall provide a sobering study of the impact on electricity rates of nuclear power plants currently under construction. Aaron S. Gurwitz and Daniel E. Chall, "Nuclear Power Plant Construction: Paying the Bill," Federal Reserve Bank of New York, *Quarterly Review,* (Summer 1984).

4. See industry and utility testimony in Joint Committee on Atomic Energy, *Atomic Power Development and Private Enterprise Hearings,* 83rd Cong., 1st sess., 1953.

5. Joint Committee on Atomic Energy, *Amending the Atomic Energy Act of 1946, as Amended, and for Other Purposes Report,* 83rd Cong., 2nd sess., 1954, p. 9.

6. Joint Committee on Atomic Energy, *Atomic Power Development Hearings,* p. 283.

7. House Committee on Interior and Insular Affairs, *Nuclear Fuel Cycle Policy and the Future of Nuclear Power Hearing,* 97th Cong., 1st sess., 1982, pp. 278, 569–85.

8. Ibid., pp. 592–96, 601.

9. Joint Committee on Atomic Energy, *Development, Growth, and State of the Atomic Energy Industry Hearings,* part 2, 85th Cong., 1st sess., 1957, p. 712.

10. House Committee on Interior and Insular Affairs, *Nuclear Fuel Cycle Hearing,* pp. 602–12.

11. Ibid., p. 618.
12. Ibid., pp. 615–616, 622; Donald L. Barlett and James B. Steele, *Forevermore: Nuclear Waste in America* (New York: W. W. Norton, 1985), pp. 140–41.
13. House Committee on Interior and Insular Affairs, *Nuclear Fuel Cycle Hearing*, pp. 620, 622–23. The decommissioning experience as the nation's earliest nuclear power plants are now being retired is not reassuring. Pacific Gas & Electric Company's Humboldt Bay plant, near Eureka, California, is "costing a lot more to get rid of than it did to build." *Wall Street Journal*, 16 July 1985.
14. House Committee on Interior and Insular Affairs, *Nuclear Fuel Cycle Hearing*, p. 619.
15. Joint Committee on Atomic Energy, *Development, Growth Hearings*, pp. 446–47.
16. Joint Committee on Atomic Energy, *Governmental Indemnity and Reactor Safety Hearings*, 85th Cong., 1st sess., 1957, p. 156.
17. See Barry P. Brownstein, *The Price-Anderson Act: Is It Consistent with a Sound Energy Policy?* Policy Analysis No. 36 (Washington, D.C.: Cato Institute, 17 April 1984), p. 6:
    Some advocates of Price-Anderson argue that because the government indemnity has never been used . . . Price-Anderson is not a subsidy. However . . . Price-Anderson allows utilities to commit less capital to insuring nuclear plants, so the act results in a reallocation of resources away from more highly valued uses—and thus it is indeed a subsidy.
18. Quoted in Daniel Ford, *The Cult of the Atom* (New York: Simon and Schuster, 1982), p. 236.
19. Ibid., pp. 55–56.
20. Mark Hertsgaard, *Nuclear Inc.* (New York: Pantheon, 1983), p. 54; Ralph Nader and John Abbotts, *The Menace of Atomic Energy*, rev. ed. (New York: W. W. Norton, 1979), pp. 142, 188; John G. Fuller, *We Almost Lost Detroit* (New York: Berkeley Books, 1984).
21. See Ford, *Cult*, p. 98.
22. Ibid., pp. 67–69, 80, 94–95, 107–9, 195.
23. Ibid., pp. 105–7, 140–47, 150, 198–99, 201.
24. Ibid., pp. 76, 115, 188.
25. *New York Times*, 10 November 1974.
26. Stephen Hilgartner, Richard C. Bell, and Rory O'Connor, *Nukespeak* (New York: Penguin, 1982), pp. 59–60, 101–08, 121; Ford, *Cult*, pp. 117–120, 128–29; Hertsgaard, *Nuclear*, p. 73.
27. House Committee on Government Operations, *Energy Reorganization Act of 1973 Report*, 93rd Cong., 1st sess., 1973, p. 4; Senate Committee on Government Operations, *Energy Reorganization Act of 1974 Report*, 93rd Cong., 2nd sess., 1974, p. 20.
28. Ford, *Cult*, pp. 213–14; *New York Times*, 16 October 1983.
29. House Committee on Government Operations, *Licensing Speedup, Safety Delay: NRC Oversight Report*, 97th Cong., 1st sess., 1981, p. 43. For a comprehensive overview, see Union of Concerned Scientists, *Safety Second: A Critical Evaluation of the NRC's First Decade* (Cambridge, Mass.: Union of Concerned Scientists, 1985).
30. House Committee on Government Operations, *Nuclear Power Costs Report*, 95th Cong., 2nd sess., 1978, pp. 3–4, 10.
31. Ibid., pp. 13–14, 20, 74.
32. House Committee on Interior and Insular Affairs, *Nuclear Fuel Cycle Hearing*, pp. 270–71.
33. Barlett and Steele, *Forevermore*, pp. 74–120.
34. General Accounting Office, *Cleaning Up the Remains of Nuclear Facilities—A Multibillion Dollar Problem* (Washington, 16 June 1977), p. ii.
35. General Accounting Office, *Cleaning Up Nuclear Facilities—An Aggressive and Unified Federal Program Is Needed* (Washington, 25 May 1982), p. i.

36. Cited in House Committee on Government Operations, *Nuclear Costs Report,* p. 12.
37. House Committee on Interior and Insular Affairs, *Nuclear Fuel Cycle Hearing,* pp. 625–28; *New York Times,* 3 September 1984.
38. Richard Hellman and Caroline Hellman, *The Competitive Economics of Nuclear and Coal Power* (Lexington, Mass.: Lexington, 1983), p. 157.
39. House Committee on Government Operations, *Nuclear Costs Report,* p. 31; idem, *Nuclear Power Costs Hearings,* part 2, 95th Cong., 1st sess., 1977, p. 1182; Irvin C. Bupp et al., "The Economics of Nuclear Power," *Technology Review* 77 (February 1975):21.
40. Joint Committee on Atomic Energy, *Development, Growth Hearings,* p. 158.
41. Hellman and Hellman, *Competitive Economics,* pp. 81–82.
42. House Committee on Government Operations, *Nuclear Costs Report,* p. 27.
43. Ibid., pp. 42–43; *New York Times,* 28 February 1984.
44. *Forbes,* 11 February 1985, p. 92.
45. Anderson, *Midland Power Plant Project,* pp. 17–18.
46. Ibid., pp. 14–15.
47. Ibid., p. 11.
48. *Wall Street Journal,* 15 December 1980.
49. *Wall Street Journal,* 1 September 1983, 28 June 1983.
50. House Committee on Interior and Insular Affairs, *Nuclear Fuel Cycle Hearing,* p. 40.
51. Department of Energy, Energy Information Administration, *Nuclear Plant Cancellations: Causes, Costs, and Consequences* (Washington, 1983), pp. x, xxii, 69.
52. House Committee on Government Operations, *Nuclear Costs Report,* p. 75.
53. These estimates, made by expert Charles Komanoff, are cited in *New York Times,* 24 June 1984, sec. 3.
54. Amory B. Lovins, *Soft Energy Paths* (Cambridge, Mass.: Ballinger, 1977), p. 55.
55. Hertsgaard, *Nuclear,* p. 250.

22. THE BAILOUT OF POWER

1. Senate Committee on Banking, Housing and Urban Affairs, *Emergency Loan Guarantee Legislation Hearings,* part 2, 92nd Cong., 1st sess., 1971, pp. 718, 1173.
2. House Subcommittee on Economic Stabilization, *The Chrysler Corporation Financial Situation Hearings,* part 1B, 96th Cong., 1st sess., 1979, p. 1309.
3. *Newsweek,* 10 September 1979, p. 66.
4. *Saturday Review,* 19 January 1980, p. 31.
5. *Newsweek,* 14 November 1983, p. 96.
6. House Subcommittee on Financial Institutions Supervision, Regulation and Insurance, *Inquiry into Continental Illinois Corp. and Continental Illinois National Bank Hearings,* 98th Cong., 2nd sess., 1984, p. 458.
7. *Wall Street Journal,* 26 July 1984.
8. House Subcommittee on Financial Institutions Supervision, Regulation and Insurance, *Inquiry into Continental Illinois Corp.,* pp. 299–300.
9. Generally, see Senate Committee on Banking, Housing and Urban Affairs, *Emergency Loan Hearings; New York Times Sunday Magazine,* 9 May 1971; and General Accounting Office, *C-5A Wing Modification: A Case Study Illustrating Problems in the Defense Weapons Acquisition Process* (Washington, 1982).
10. In the late 1950s, and gambling that airlines were not ready to convert their fleets to jet aircraft, Lockheed produced the turboprop Electra commercial airplane. The firm guessed incorrectly, however, and failed to earn a profit on the craft.
11. Senate Committee on Banking, Housing and Urban Affairs, *Emergency Loan Guarantee Hearings,* p. 236.
12. Ibid., pp. 6, 221, 633.
13. Ibid., pp. 33, 134.

14. Ibid., pp. 77–78, 633, 684.
15. Ibid., p. 80.
16. Ibid., p. 241.
17. Ibid., pp. 6, 22.
18. See House Committee on Banking and Currency, *Emergency Loan Guarantee Act of 1971 Report*, 92nd Cong., 1st sess., 1971, pp. 12–20; Senate Committee on Banking, Housing and Urban Affairs, *Emergency Loan Guarantees to Major Business Enterprises Report*, 92nd Cong., 1st sess., 1971, pp. 17–29. For the company's admission that it gambled on Rolls-Royce, see idem, *Emergency Loan Hearings*, pp. 305–306.
19. Senate Committee on Banking, Housing and Urban Affairs, *Emergency Guarantees to Major Enterprises Report*, p. 3.
20. General Accounting Office, *Guidelines for Rescuing Large Failing Firms and Municipalities* (Washington, 1984), pp. 10–12.
21. For a detailed rebuttal to Chrysler's claim that it suffered disproportionately under government automotive regulations, see House Subcommittee on Economic Stabilization, *Chrysler Corporation Hearings*, pp. 447–565.
22. Senate Committee on Banking, Housing and Urban Affairs, *Chrysler Corporation Loan Guarantee Act of 1979, Hearings*, parts 1 and 2, 96th Cong., 1st sess., 1979, p. 179.
23. Ibid., pp. 179–81.
24. *Saturday Review*, 19 January 1980, p. 30.
25. Senate Committee on Banking, Housing and Urban Affairs, *Chrysler Loan Guarantee Hearings*, pp. 818–819.
26. Ibid., pp. 1041–42.
27. Ibid., pp. 1039–40.
28. Ibid., p. 1054.
29. House Subcommittee on Economic Stabilization, *Chrysler Corporation Hearings*, p. 586.
30. Senate Committee on Banking, Housing and Urban Affairs, *Chrysler Loan Guarantee Hearings*, p. 948.
31. Ibid., p. 155.
32. *Wall Street Journal*, 3 December 1979.
33. General Accounting Office, *Guidelines for Rescuing Large Failing Firms*, p. 17.
34. Lee Iacocca, *Iacocca* (New York: Bantam Books, 1984), p. 221. For an in-depth exposition of the Chrysler bailout, see Robert B. Reich and John D. Donahue, *New Deals: The Chrysler Revival and the American System* (New York: Times Books, 1985).
35. Senate Committee on Banking, Housing and Urban Affairs, *Chrysler Corporation Financial Situation and the Implications for Public Policy Hearings*, 96th Cong., 1st sess., 1979, p. 25.
36. Senate Committee on Banking, Housing and Urban Affairs, *Emergency Loan Hearings*, pp. 83, 225.
37. House Committee on Banking and Currency, *Emergency Loan Act Report*, p. 15.
38. *Business Week*, 15 May 1971, p. 160.
39. Senate Committee on Banking, Housing and Urban Affairs, *Emergency Loan Hearings*, p. 796.
40. *Washington Post*, 9 September 1979.
41. Senate Committee on Banking, Housing and Urban Affairs, *Emergency Loan Hearings*, pp. 126, 285.
42. Ibid., p. 794.
43. Ibid., p. 21.

23. THE LABOR-INDUSTRIAL COMPLEX

1. John Kenneth Galbraith, *American Capitalism: The Concept of Countervailing Power* (Boston: Houghton-Mifflin, 1952), pp. 110, 118, 122. In fairness to Galbraith, it must be noted that he recognizes inflationary periods as special situations in which countervailing power tends to be eroded.
2. Heinrich von Stackelberg, *Marktform und Gleichgewicht* (Vienna: Julius Springer, 1934), p. 100.
3. Robert Liefmann, *Cartels, Concerns and Trusts* (New York: E. P. Dutton, 1927), p. 80.
4. A. C. Pigou, ed., *Memorials of Alfred Marshall* (New York: Kelley and Millman, 1956), pp. 288–89.
5. A complete exposition of all of the major arguments jointly asserted by management and labor, together with full documentation, may be found in Walter Adams and James W. Brock, "Tacit Vertical Collusion and the Labor-Industrial Complex," *Nebraska Law Review* 62 (1983):621.
6. Of course, we have seen in chapters 17 and 18 that experience following in the wake of a substantial loosening of governmental regulatory control refutes the dire predictions and arguments of management-labor coalitions against deregulation of airlines and trucking—both in regard to specific contentions that small communities would suffer and that efficiency would be undermined, as well as with respect to the other arguments that comprised their case against competition. Rather, the evidence strongly suggests that the public and the economy generally have greatly benefitted from competition in each field. But, coalescing power is driven by *private*—not public —gains and, as we shall shortly see, the private gains to these coalitions from eliminating competition have not (as their early proponents recognized) been insubstantial.
7. Again, full treatment and documentation may be found in Adams and Brock, "Tacit Vertical Collusion."
8. Ibid., p. 697.
9. Thomas Gale Moore, "The Beneficiaries of Trucking Regulation," *Journal of Law and Economics* 21 (1978):333.
10. Ibid., pp. 337, 339, 342.
11. For the empirical record of pricing in the automobile industry, see Walter Adams and James W. Brock, "The Automobile Industry," in Walter Adams, ed., *The Structure of American Industry* (New York: Macmillan, 1986).
12. Adams and Brock, "Tacit Vertical Collusion," p. 702.
13. *Wall Street Journal*, 20 March 1981.
14. Ibid. The virulence of coalescing power in the automotive labor-industrial complex merits mention. According to Paul A. London, for example, the latest settlement reached between Chrysler and the UAW, in the fall of 1985, demonstrates that "the American public can't continue to pretend that there is a way to deal with the trade deficit and the inflation problem without attacking monopolistic price and wage setting in the industries where price and wage problems start." Paul A. London, "Car Bomb," *The New Republic*, 25 November 1985, pp. 14–15.
15. Adams and Brock, "Tacit Vertical Collusion," p. 705.
16. This does not mean that divisive issues never arise within labor-management complexes. For example, domestic "content" legislation proposed in the early 1980s, which if enacted would mandate specified proportions of automotive components to be manufactured in the United States, divided the UAW (which supports such legislation in the interest of job creation) and management (which opposes this proposed constraint on its efforts to increasingly obtain automobiles and parts from abroad).

Nevertheless, even here the coalescing nexus between management and labor bred a remarkable degree of solicitude. Thus rather than outrightly declaring their opposition to domestic content, management followed a more diplomatic tack and characterized such legislation as a second-best option. "The proposed legislation should be viewed as an instrument of last resort," Ford Motor Company politely suggested, "to be considered when other measures to correct trade inequities and imbalances have been tried and have failed. . . ." As an example of what a "more effective" policy might entail, Ford's Phillip Caldwell intimated that "voluntary" import restraints could be extended. House Subcommittee on Trade, *Fair Practices in Automotive Practices Act Hearings*, 97th Cong., 2nd sess., 1982, pp. 306, 341.

17. Henry C. Simons, *Economic Policy for a Free Society* (Chicago: University of Chicago Press, 1948), p. 115.

18. Ibid., p. 120. For a similar conclusion see Mancur Olson, *The Rise and Decline of Nations* (New Haven: Yale University Press, 1982), p. 233.

24. THE MILITARY-INDUSTRIAL COMPLEX

1. The following account is drawn from Senate Committee on Banking, Housing and Urban Affairs, *Emergency Loan Guarantee Legislation Hearings*, part 1, 92nd Cong., 1st sess., 1971; Joint Economic Committee, *The Acquisition of Weapons Systems Hearings*, part 5, 92nd Cong., 1st and 2nd sess., 1972; *New York Times Sunday Magazine*, 9 May 1971; Morton Mintz and Jerry S. Cohen, *Power, Inc.* (New York: Viking Press, 1976); General Accounting Office, *C-5A Wing Modification: A Case Study Illustrating the Problems in the Defense Weapons Acquisition Process* (Washington, 1982); *Wall Street Journal*, 12 May 1983; *New York Times*, 20 December 1983, sec. 3, p. 24. Generally, see Berkeley Rice, *The C-5A Scandal* (Boston: Houghton-Mifflin, 1971).

2. Executive Office of the President, *Budget of the United States Government* (Washington, Fiscal Year 1986), p. 5-5.

3. See Robert W. DeGrasse, Jr., *Military Expansion, Economic Decline* (Armonk, N.Y.: M. E. Sharpe, 1983), p. 8.

4. House Committee on Appropriations, *Department of Defense Appropriations for 1983 Hearings*, part 8, 97th Cong., 2nd sess., 1982, p. 11.

5. General Accounting Office, *DOD Loses Many Competitive Procurement Opportunities* (Washington, 1981).

6. House Committee on Armed Services, *Weapons Acquisition Policy and Procedures: Curbing Cost Growth Report*, 97th Cong., 1st sess., 1982, p. 30. For a comprehensive treatment, see Jacques S. Gansler, *The Defense Industry* (Cambridge, Mass.: MIT Press, 1982).

7. House Committee on Appropriations, *Defense Appropriations Hearings*, pp. 342–44; *New York Times*, 5 January 1984; *Wall Street Journal*, 19 February 1983.

8. Joint Committee on Defense Production, *Defense Industrial Base: DOD Procurement Practices Hearings*, part IV, 95th Cong., 1st sess., 1977, pp. 76–78.

9. For additional evidence, see Christian Marfels, "The Structure of the Military-Industrial Complex in the United States and Its Impact on Industrial Concentration," *Kyklos* 31 (1978):409.

10. House Committee on Appropriations, *Defense Appropriations Hearings*, pp. 65–66.

11. *New York Times*, 22 May 1984.

12. House Committee on Appropriations, *Defense Appropriations Hearings*, pp. 66–67.

13. *Time*, 7 March 1983, p. 16.

14. Senate Committee on Governmental Affairs, *Management of the Department of Defense Hearing*, part 9, 98th Cong., 2nd sess., 1985, pp. 48–49; *New York Times*, 28 August 1985.

15. Senate Committee on Governmental Affairs, *Management of Defense Hearing*, pp. 59, 90. Congress attempted to counteract these failings in 1983 by enacting legislation calling for the establishment within the Pentagon of an independent Office of Operational Testing and Development. Yet the Pentagon's political leadership opposed this

step, and the Office's effectiveness has been severely circumscribed. See *National Journal* (13 October 1984):1914–17.

16. Senate Committee on Governmental Affairs, *Management of Defense Hearing*, part 7, p. 4.

17. Generally, see ibid., especially pp. 142–205, 240–45, 464–68, and 524–49.

18. Ibid., pp. 4–5, 17–18; *Wall Street Journal*, 22 August 1985. For an account of efforts by "whistleblowers" inside the Pentagon to call attention to fraud and corruption, and the obstacles they confront, see Dina Rasor, *The Pentagon Underground* (New York: Times Books, 1985).

19. House Committee on Appropriations, *Defense Appropriations Hearings*, pp. 145, 153, 239, 241.

20. *New York Times*, 30 April 1985.

21. *Cincinnati Enquirer*, 14 August 1983.

22. House Committee on the Budget, *Review of Defense Acquisition and Management Hearings*, 98th Cong., 1st sess., 1984, p. 241.

23. This account is drawn from Joint Committee on Defense Production, *Conflict of Interest and the Condor Missile Program Report*, 94th Cong., 2nd sess., 1976.

24. General Accounting Office, *Report Prepared for Senator William Proxmire* (Washington, 29 September 1982), pp. 10, 17.

25. Senate Subcommittee on Reports, Accounting and Management, *To Amend the Federal Advisory Committee Act Hearings*, 94th Cong., 2nd sess., 1976, pp. 310–311.

26. Gordon Adams, *The Politics of Defense Contracting* (New Brunswick, N.J.: Transaction Books, 1982), pp. 86, 91.

27. *New York Times*, 16 March 1983.

28. *Common Cause*, June 1982, p. 20.

29. Quoted in Peter Navarro, *The Policy Game* (New York: John Wiley & Sons, 1984), p. 257.

30. House Committee on Appropriations, *Defense Appropriations Hearings*, pp. 70, 793.

31. Senate Committee on Governmental Affairs, *Management of Defense Hearings*, part 6, p. 6.

32. Ibid., p. 19.

33. *New York Times*, 15 December 1981. For classic expositions of cost maximization imperatives in the supply of weaponry, see Seymour Melman, *The Permanent War Economy* (New York: Simon and Schuster, 1974), and A. E. Fitzgerald, *High Priests of Waste* (New York: W. W. Norton, 1972).

34. House Committee on Appropriations, *Defense Appropriations Hearings*, pp. 206–207.

35. General Accounting Office, *Navy's F/A-18 Program Faces Budget Concerns and Performance Limitations as Aircraft Enter the Fleet* (Washington, 1983), p. 16.

36. House Committee on Appropriations, *Defense Appropriations Hearings*, p. 294; *Time*, 7 March 1983, pp. 26, 29; *New York Times*, 19 September 1984.

37. *New York Times*, 29 February 1984, and 15 March 1984; *Wall Street Journal*, 26 December 1984.

38. *New York Times*, 6 February 1983.

39. Navarro, *The Policy Game*, p. 267;

40. *National Journal* (15 September 1984):1727.

41. *Wall Street Journal*, 15 August 1983.

42. *Cincinnati Enquirer*, 14 August 1983.

43. Navarro, *The Policy Game*, p. 270.

44. *Cincinnati Enquirer*, 14 August 1983.

45. House Committee on Appropriations, *Defense Appropriations Hearings*, p. 153.

46. *Wall Street Journal*, 6 March 1984. Generally, see James Coates and Michael Kilian, *Heavy Losses* (New York: Viking Press, 1985), especially pp. 247–74.

47. *Business Week*, 3 June 1985; *New York Times*, 2 May 1985.

48. For a recent argument in favor of the nationalization option, see Tom Riddell, "Concen-

tration and Inefficiency in the Defense Sector: Policy Options," *Journal of Economic Issues* 19 (June 1985):451.
49. A survey of these studies is tabulated in Senate Committee on Armed Services, *Competition in Contracting Act of 1983 Hearings*, 98th Cong., 1st sess., 1983, pp. 264–65.
50. Senate Subcommittee on Antitrust and Monopoly, *Competition in Defense Procurement Hearings*, 90th Cong., 2nd sess., 1969, pp. 22–23.

25. INDUSTRIAL POLICY: THE NEOLIBERAL VISION

1. One such grouping, LICIT (Labor-Industry Coalition for International Trade), for example, includes among its member organizations both major industrial firms (Bethlehem Steel, Corning Glass Works, B. F. Goodrich Company, Ingersoll Rand Company, St. Joe Minerals Corporation, W. R. Grace & Co., Westinghouse Electric Corporation, Weyerheuser Company) and major trade unions (Amalgamated Clothing & Textile Workers Union; Communications Workers of America; International Union of Electrical, Radio and Machine Workers; International Brotherhood of Electrical Workers; American Flint Glass Workers Union; Industrial Union Department, AFL-CIO; International Ladies Garment Workers Union; International Association of Machinists and Aerospace Workers; United Paperworkers International Union; United Rubberworkers of America; United Steelworkers of America). LICIT spokesmen presented their version of industrial policy to the House Subcommittee on Economic Stabilization, *Industrial Policy*, part 1, 94th Cong., 1st sess., 1983, pp. 121–134, pp. 666ff.
2. See Ira C. Magaziner and Robert B. Reich, *Minding America's Business* (New York: Harcourt Brace Jovanovich, 1982) and Robert B. Reich, *The Next American Frontier* (New York: Times Books, 1983). For the views of an illustrious financier, see Felix G. Rohatyn, *The Twenty-Year Century* (New York: Random House, 1983). For the views of a leading journalist, see Kevin P. Phillips, *Post-Conservative America* (New York: Random House, 1982) and *Staying on Top* (New York: Random House, 1984). Among the many symposia on the subject, two may be of particular interest: Michael L. Wachter and Susan M. Wachter, eds., *Toward a New U.S. Industrial Policy?* (Philadelphia: University of Pennsylvania Press, 1981), particularly the contributions of Frederic M. Scherer, Almarin Phillips, Lawrence R. Klein, George C. Eads, and William H. Branson; and William J. Adams and Christian Stoffaes, eds., *French Industrial Policy* (Washington, D.C.: Brookings Institution, 1986), particularly the contributions of Robert Zysman, Henri Aujac, Robert Boyer, and William J. Adams.
3. Robert S. Ozaki, "How Japanese Industrial Policy Works," in *The Industrial Policy Debate*, ed. Chalmers Johnson (San Francisco: ICS Press, 1984), p. 54.
4. Gary R. Saxonhouse, "Tampering with Comparative Advantage in Japan?" (Statement given before the U.S. International Trade Commission, Washington, D.C., 15 June 1983, mimeograph), pp. 4–5.
5. Ibid.
6. Ibid., pp. 6–8. See also Gary R. Saxonhouse, "What is All This about 'Industrial Targeting' in Japan?" *The World Economy* 6 (September 1983):253–73.
7. *New York Times*, 19 October 1980. For a contrary view see Willard F. Mueller, "The Anti-Antitrust Movement," *Congressional Record*, 97th Cong., 1st sess., 20 July 1981, vol. 127, pp. S7947–S7952.
8. United States v. Bethlehem Steel, 168 F. Supp. 576 (S.D.N.Y. 1958).
9. *Wall Street Journal*, 26 January 1981.
10. House Subcommittee on Economic Stabilization, *Industrial Competitiveness Act Hearings*, part A, 98th Cong., 1st and 2d sess., 1984, pp. 62, 63.
11. Ibid., p. 65. See also the statements by Sol C. Chaikin, president of the International Ladies Garment Workers Union, and Lee A. Iacocca, chairman of the board, Chrysler Corporation, in ibid., pp. 129–63, 167–203.

12. Charles L. Schultze, "Industrial Policy: A Dissent," *Brookings Review* 2 (Fall 1983):11.

13. Theodore J. Lowi, *The End of Liberalism* (New York: W. W. Norton, 1979).

14. Ibid., p. 64.

15. For an excellent discussion of the origins of the NRA, see Ellis W. Hawley, *The New Deal and the Problem of Monopoly* (Princeton, N.J.: Princeton University Press, 1966). See also David Lynch, *The Concentration of Economic Power* (New York: Columbia University Press, 1946), pp. 150–58.

16. Hugh S. Johnson, *The Blue Eagle from Egg to Earth* (New York: Doubleday, 1935), pp. 177, 178.

17. Quoted in Arthur M. Schlesinger, Jr., *The Coming of the New Deal* (Boston: Houghton-Mifflin, 1959), p. 110.

18. Clair Wilcox, *Public Policies Toward Business* (Homewood, Ill.: Richard D. Irwin, 1971), p. 680.

19. Ibid., p. 681.

20. Lionel Robbins, *The Great Depression* (London: Macmillan, 1934), p. 147.

26. THE OPPORTUNITY SOCIETY: THE NEO-DARWINIST VISION

1. *Wall Street Journal*, 1 July 1985. See also George W. Stocking, "Saving Free Enterprise from Its Friends," *Southern Economic Journal* 19 (April 1953):431–44.

27. A PUBLIC PHILOSOPHY

1. Henry C. Simons, *Economic Policy for a Free Society* (Chicago: University of Chicago Press, 1948), p. 241.

2. Ben W. Lewis, "Economics by Admonition," *American Economic Review* 49 (May 1959):390.

3. *Forbes*, 18 November 1985; *Business Week*, 27 May 1985, 22 October 1985, 3 June 1985, and 1 July 1985.

4. The same considerations apply to the "privatization" of formerly government-operated industries and firms. Like deregulation, "privatisation is not the philosopher's stone." As *The Economist* points out,

   The reasons governments give for selling off state assets are far less important than how they do it. Mrs. Thatcher has found a dubious doctrine (that reduction of state power always increases the individual's freedom, wealth and happiness) where other privatisers seek pragmatism (state treasuries want to raise money without printing it). But privatisation will be judged a success only if the privately owned British Telecoms or Montedisons or NTTs are more efficient. And, *pace* new zealots, privatised monopolies are not necessarily more efficient than nationalised ones. Ask Con Edison's blacked-and-browned out customers in New York." *(The Economist, 23 February 1985, p. 11.)*

5. Quoted in *Business Week*, 1 July 1985, p. 24.

6. Dina Rasor, *The Pentagon Underground* (New York: Times Books, 1985), p. 289.

7. When utilized in acquiring "tank-busting" projectiles, this procurement method led to a drop in the cost of shells from $80 to $13 per round. See James Coates and Michael Kilian, *Heavy Losses* (New York: Viking Press, 1985), pp. 154–55.

8. Ibid., pp. 172–73; *New York Times*, 3 October 1984.

9. Coates and Kilian, *Heavy Losses*, pp. 241–43.

10. Josephus Daniels, *The Wilson Era* (Chapel Hill, N.C.: University of North Carolina Press, 1944), p. 345.

11. Simons, *Economic Policy*, pp. 43–44.

12. Quoted in *New York Times,* 10 November 1985, sec. 3.
13. Malcolm Baldrige, "Rx for Export Woes: Antitrust Relief," *Wall Street Journal,* 15 October 1985.
14. House Subcommittee on Economic Stabilization, *Report of the President's Commission on Industrial Competitiveness Hearings,* 99th Cong., 1st sess., 1985, p. 109.
15. *New York Times,* 10 November 1985, sec. 3 (emphasis added).

NAME INDEX

SUBJECT INDEX

WALTER ADAMS is former President of Michigan State University, where he is now Distinguished University Professor of Economics. He has taught at the Universities of Paris and Grenoble, the Salzburg and Falkenstein Seminars, and the Industrial College of the Armed Forces. He has served on presidential commissions during the Eisenhower, Kennedy, and Johnson administrations, and has frequently appeared as an expert witness before congressional committees. His previous books include *Monopoly in America* (1955), *Is the World Our Campus?* (1960), *The Brain Drain* (1968), and *The Structure of American Industry* (7th ed., 1986).

JAMES W. BROCK is Associate Professor of Economics at Miami University in Ohio. A popular teacher and a prolific writer, he has contributed articles to diverse professional journals, including the *Quarterly Journal of Economics and Business*, *Journal of Post-Keynesian Economics*, *Challenge*, *California Law Review*, *Nebraska Law Review*, *Wake Forest Law Review*, *Antitrust Bulletin*, and *American Business Law Journal*.